MJBQC: A LIFE WITHIN AND WITHOUT THE LAW

Michael Beloff QC, once described as 'the Bar's Renaissance Man', has had a distinguished career as advocate, arbitrator, and judge. An outsider of mixed Russian Jewish heritage with four immigrant grandparents and immigrant mother, he had an insider's education as a scholar at Eton and Oxford, with a professional life culminating in his offices as President of Trinity, one of the most famous of the historic Oxford Colleges and Treasurer of Gray's, one of the four mediaeval Inns of Court.

In this candid story he reflects on the development of his vocation through its various staging posts from his childhood to his swan song as barrister after fifty years in practice, highlighting his most important cases, in particular those with a political dimension as well as a quintet of high-profile libels.

He uses his personal experience to illuminate the arts of both advocacy and judging to evaluate how the Bar and the law has reformed during his professional lifetime and to predict and assess the likelihood of future changes.

Familiarly called 'the Godfather of Sports Law', he has had, both as Counsel and Panellist, involvement in some of the major sporting scandals of the age, and gives special insights into the areas where sport and law intersect – doping, corruption, match fixing and transgender participation. On these issues as well as on those born of his university experience such as the Oxford admissions system and freedom of speech on campus, he expresses views which, if sometimes unfashionable, are always honest.

His portfolio roles have led to his encounters with many interesting people, from Blair to Bolt, from a two term-President of the USA to the heir apparent to the throne of the UK, tales of which provide the icing on the cake of this intriguing memoir.

MJBQC: A Life Within and Without the Law

Michael Beloff

·HART·

OXFORD · LONDON · NEW YORK · NEW DELHI · SYDNEY

HART PUBLISHING

Bloomsbury Publishing Plc

Kemp House, Chawley Park, Cumnor Hill, Oxford, OX2 9PH, UK

1385 Broadway, New York, NY 10018, USA

29 Earlsfort Terrace, Dublin 2, Ireland

HART PUBLISHING, the Hart/Stag logo, BLOOMSBURY and the Diana logo are
trademarks of Bloomsbury Publishing Plc

First published in Great Britain 2022

Copyright © Michael Beloff, 2022

Michael Beloff has asserted his right under the Copyright, Designs and
Patents Act 1988 to be identified as Author of this work.

A catalogue record for this book is available from the British Library.

A catalogue record for this book is available from the Library of Congress.

ISBN:	HB:	978-1-84946-666-0
	ePDF:	978-1-50996-140-5
	ePub:	978-1-50996-141-2

Typeset by Compuscript Ltd, Shannon

To find out more about our authors and books visit www.hartpublishing.co.uk.
Here you will find extracts, author information, details of forthcoming events
and the option to sign up for our newsletters.

To Judith and the memory of Helen

sine quibus non

FOREWORD

I believe that I am the only person who has played a triple professional role with Michael Beloff, namely (i) as a junior barrister led by him in court in the 1980s and 1990s (on more than one occasion), (ii) as a first instance and appellate judge who heard him (on occasions too numerous to specify) as an advocate in the next two decades, and (iii) most recently in the present decade, as a fellow arbitrator. I am therefore well familiar with his life, as the title to this memoir has it, 'within the law'.

As a leader, Michael was solicitous, appreciative and demanding towards his juniors – and it was such fun being led by him: far from being a distraction, his sense of humour encouraged an esprit de corps in the legal team. As an advocate, he was unusually clear and concise in his submissions, as well as being exceptionally fluent (and very hard to interrupt), and his good humour and wit reinforced his persuasiveness. As a fellow arbitrator, he was unsurprisingly efficient and decisive, while also being highly collegiate – and, of course, good company.

I am less familiar with Michael's life 'without the law' (although, as a guest at high table at Trinity College, Oxford, I gained a brief insight into his role as President there). However, apart from conveying a characteristically clever ambiguity, those three words are apt even for someone like me whose knowledge of Michael Beloff is very largely professional. His friendly and engaging character meant that those working with him had the pleasure and privilege of getting to know him personally as well as professionally.

The unparalleled breadth of Michael's practice 'within' the Bar and his many roles 'without' the Bar means that this book is not simply an informative and engaging description of the legal world between 1965 and 2022, but it also throws a fascinating light on many other aspects of life in the United Kingdom in that period. As anyone who reads this book will quickly appreciate, the qualities which have always been apparent in Michael the social animal and M Beloff QC, the barrister, do not desert him when he turns his hand to be MJBQC, the memoirist. In this book, Michael correctly states that a 'split personality [is] not unique but not uncommon at the Bar'. However, that is simply not true in Michael's case: he is the same intelligent, friendly, quick, humane, witty, fluent person professionally, personally, and, now, as an author.

Lord Neuberger of Abbotsbury,
sometime President of the Supreme Court and Master of the Rolls

CONTENTS

ABOUT THE AUTHOR

Michael Beloff was educated at the Dragon School in Oxford, Eton, where he was a King's Scholar and became Captain of the School and Editor of the *Chronicle*, and at Magdalen College, Oxford, where he was a Demy, took a first in history and became President of the Union. After taking another degree in Law, he was called to the Bar by Gray's Inn in 1967 and took silk in 1981. He became head of the Bar Associations in both Administrative and Sports Law. He was President of Trinity College, Oxford between 1996 and 2006 and Treasurer of Gray's Inn in 2008.

Among his various judicial roles, between 1996 and 2014 he was a Judge of the Courts of Appeal of Jersey and Guernsey, becoming Senior Ordinary Appeal Judge in both. Among his various arbitral roles, as a member of the Court of Arbitration for Sport from 1996 he arbitrated at five summer Olympics, and he chaired the ethics and disciplinary bodies in two major international sports: cricket and athletics.

In a citation for an honorary degree by the Open University he was described as 'one of the leading lawyers of the twentieth and twenty first centuries'. He adopted the sobriquet MJBQC in the interests of brevity and before the birth of email.

Prologue

The first question that I would pose to myself in cross-examination would be 'Why on earth did you think anyone would be interested in your story?'[1] I could pray in aid Eric Morecambe's favourite riposte 'There's no answer to that', but I'll try to provide a more convincing reply. I aim not just to record the turns and twists of my life, but to paint on a wider canvas, using my own career to illuminate changes in the profession, the Bar of England and Wales, of which I have been a member for over half a century. The Bar is often, like Oxford University, my secondary professional location, depicted as a repository of conservatism, but it has been a place of significant evolution, if not quite revolution.

I do not pretend that I have been a typical barrister. Had I been, I doubt that any potential reader (family and polite friends apart) would want to follow me down memory lane. The number of cases which I have argued and have found their way into the law reports – the indication that, at any rate from a lawyer's perspective, they are of some significance – number more than 475 (only a bare handful of which appear in journals I edited); and many others, without any such significance, hit the headlines of broadsheets or tabloids because of the identity of my (or my opposing counsels') clients.

I have appeared in the highest courts in London – the House of Lords, the Supreme Court and the Privy Council more than 70 times; and in the Courts of many Commonwealth jurisdictions, as well as in the European Court of Justice (ECJ, now CJEU) at Luxembourg and the European Court of Human Rights (ECtHR) at Strasbourg, distinct bodies, too often pre- and even post-Brexit confused in the media.

Because I eschewed full-time judicial appointment, my time as an advocate significantly exceeded that of my contemporaries who exercised no such self-denial of the fruits of public office, for some sweet, for others bitter. So, as the 1960s sitcom put it, 'Never Mind the Quality, Feel the Width' (or length).

I have appeared twice in novels by Jeffrey Archer (hereinafter 'Jeffrey'),[2] once as a QC,[3] once, inaccurately, elevated to the now obsolete post of Senior

---

[1] Though 15 years ago someone expressed an eccentric desire to write what he termed an authorised biography titled 'GENTLEMAN OF THE BAR; A LIFE OF MICHAEL BELOFF QC'. I declined the proposal in case my acceptance unmasked it as a leg pull or one prompted by the putative author's revelation that he was applying to become a member of the Reform Club and so might be taking a roundabout route to solicit a supporting vote.

[2] A familiar pleading device.

[3] *The Fourth Estate* (Archer, 1996) p 431.

Law Lord.[4] I am the only barrister who has been discussed in various organs of the press as both a potential Lord Chancellor and a potential Vice-Chancellor (of Oxford) without being a realistic candidate for either post. I have been profiled with headlines ranging from 'Is this the most influential man in Britain?'[5] to 'Is this the most stupid clever man in Britain?' – neither being remotely true (or at any rate, in the case of the second, I trust not) but descriptions which, when one surveys the field, are not always inconsistent.

My criminal work was essentially confined to my early days at the Bar. I was not, unlike Sir Ivan Lawrence QC, present, according to his entertaining yarns, at the genesis of every event which mutated into a whiskery anecdote beloved of the after-dinner speaker at a circuit Bar Mess. I can tell no titillating tales of murder or mayhem – still less of clients saved from the gallows (a penal option removed by legislation in the year of my call) – or even of scabrous porn. The only allegedly indecent video I had to watch for professional purposes – about lesbian antics in a women's prison – was so unerotic that it would have prompted a Casanova or a Sappho to take a vow of chastity.

Yet another criminal silk – for any lay reader I note that such adjective conventionally describes the barrister's profession, not propensities – Bill Clegg QC, inscribed his own memoir to me with the words 'Now you can read what a real barrister does'. To which I would reply 'But in the Bar's house there are many mansions'. I was a jack of many trades, if a master, if at all, of only a few. The breadth of my civil practice once earned me the soubriquet 'the Bar's Own Renaissance Man',[6] which I declined to interpret as meaning no more than that I had passed my middle age.

Of the sexier subjects in the reminiscences of my barrister contemporaries, I can at least score on the libel front. I was also there at the birth of modern judicial review and at the conception of human rights litigation, with cases that often touched on high profile political issues. I have been familiarly described as the Godfather of Sports Law,[7] if only by virtue of being all but first in the then barely tilled field.

This book differs from some of my peer group's memoirs in that it is not a covert exercise in premature autobiography like 'The Justice Game', written by Geoffrey Robertson, a prominent member of the dingo diaspora from down under and iconoclastic advocate. What is actually his volume two, 'Rather his Own Man', puts him less circumspectly – but no less readably – centre stage.

I never for my part contemplated that kind of self-marked mid-term report. For me the curtain has finally fallen on the Courts' stage; *e finita la commedia* (or whatever name would be appropriate to my performance). Peter Taylor,

---

[4] *A Prisoner of Birth* (Archer, 2008) pp 432–33.

[5] Boris Johnson, then a *Spectator* scribe and editor, accepted an invitation to dine at Trinity noting, tongue in cheek, that I had been 'officially' so recognised.

[6] JP Flintoff, 'A Man for all Sessions' 90 *Legal Business*, May 1991.

[7] eg, Jonathan Taylor QC, 'Lawyer of the Week' *The Times* (9 May 2019).

a Lord Chief Justice whose tenure of that high office was cruelly cut short by illness, once advised me to stay at the Bar for no more than 25 years, generously anticipating my promotion to the High Court Bench – a step that, when push came to shove, I declined to take.

The fiftieth anniversary of my call to the Bar, which I reached in 2017, seemed as good a time as any other to plot my retirement from arguing cases. Like General Patton's old soldiers, most old barristers never die, they merely fade away. As long as they pay their annual subscription to the Bar Council and keep up their tally of continuing professional development (CPD) points, where there's life, there's hope, if diminishing, of yet another brief.

In any event, though the Law Courts were my primary workplace, where, in addition to my speaking part, I had a variety of part-time judicial appointments culminating in my role as Senior Ordinary Appeal Judge in the Courts of Appeal of Jersey and Guernsey (I will explain the significance of the apparently dismissive epithet 'ordinary' later), they were not exclusively so. I sat in an adjudicative capacity in other fora, most notably as an international sports arbitrator. And while I resolutely (and wisely) demur from being called an academic, despite two visiting professorships, I did serve for 10 years as President of Trinity College, Oxford – hence my earlier reference to the University – as well as being a somewhat promiscuous writer and frequent lecturer by preference (all expenses paid) abroad.

As a consequence of this quasi-portmanteau life my paths have crossed with those of a range of interesting persons, politicians and perjurers (categories which juries found to overlap in the case of two of my closest friends), scholars and sportspersons, authors and actors – in discrete people pods which rarely intersected. Their very variety added spice to my life.

One of my all too rare hobbies is to collect books autographed by those I have entertained, or simply, like Margaret Thatcher or Jacques Delors, persons with whom I have had encounters, brief or not. What might otherwise risk being monochrome pages may gain colour as they troop through. I am conscious that I shall name drop serially, but not gratuitously. Isaiah Berlin, when challenged with a similar offence, responded 'That is just what the Queen Mother was saying to me the other day'. It so happens that I can work both these legendary figures into my own narrative. I have – to pursue this detour to the end of the yellow brick road – met the Queen and all her children,[8] the Duke of York apart (his loss or mine?).

Though I have been on first-name terms with three Prime Ministers – or, stretching a point four, I have no recollection of any of them discussing sex, and, even if they had, I would not be tempted like Sasha Swire to inflate my sales figures by revelation of intimate conversations. I am a devout believer in freedom of expression but no less in privacy too. If I do not display charity to all, I manifest a modicum of malice towards only a few. The political diarists Alans

---

[8] Though my acquaintance with Prince Edward at Calgary barely exceeded a nod since, being more interested in athletics than actual royalty, I was anxious to engage in conversation with Steve Moneghetti, the Aussie marathon star who was standing nearby.

Clark and Duncan used insults of the almost great if rarely good to generate headlines. I have resisted such temptations too. I rejected the idea of writing F next to those mentioned whom I would claim as friends. After all, they might disagree. I have put DNB next to a select handful indicating that I wrote their obituary essay in the Dictionary of National Biography. For them it's too late to complain.

Barristers, when referring to judgments of judges who have since been promoted to a higher rank, deploy the formula ('as he then was'). When writing about my contemporaries of the same or younger generation, whether at school, college or the Bar, I would have to look forward, not back, and write, for the avoidance of doubt – another favourite legalism – 'later …' or 'the future …'. To avoid invidious discrimination between those too famous to demand detail and those not quite at that level I have left the majority of descriptions of the *dramatis personae* to the footnotes, indicating somewhat arbitrarily, and without any superfluous chronological qualification, the positions, whenever achieved, by which they are best known.

I have not assiduously organised my life around any particular set of principles, but four eclectic guides have resonated with me. First Marmee's reflection in *Little Women* (a book which I must, in my pre-teen years, have read a dozen times), 'I am angry nearly every day of my life, … but I have learned not to show it, and I still hope to learn not to feel it, though it may take me another forty years to do so'. Second, George Orwell's' commandments in his essay 'Politics and the English Language' on how to purify one's prose. Third the advice of a university pal, David Ambrose,[9] always to send a note of congratulations to my friends on their achievements and a note of thanks to anyone who has hosted or helped me.

The first I have aspired to with no success, the second with only limited success (*si monumentum requiris circumspice*, ie just read on) and the third with all but total success. It is a trivial price to pay for an accretion of goodwill, as well as prompting several folios of handwritten or, at any rate, signed replies in which the respondents usually felt obliged to reciprocate my own compliments. While a loyal Old Etonian I find wisdom in the Wykehamist motto 'Manners makyth man' (woman too). Gore Vidal wrote 'Every time a friend succeeds, I die a little'. My reaction never went so deep. A mild and temporary bout of envy sufficed.

The fourth – and by far the most important signpost–was the Delphic maxim, plagiarised by Socrates, in translation 'Know thyself'. So, in this memoir I've tried, as well as expounding, where desirable, a little light law or setting my own activities in context, to record disasters as well as triumphs, so as to resist what my aunt Nora once described as the lure of repeating, Toad of Toad Hall like, 'oh the cleverness of me'. In many a scramble for the glittering prizes in life's decathlon in which I've competed, I've sometimes been there, but I've also sometimes been only thereabouts (ie, not quite there) and sometimes not even near a podium place. I tick or click on all the boxes of the seven deadly sins, apart possibly from sloth.

---

[9] Playwright.

Which, if any, of the seven virtues I possess, I shall not say for fear of further referencing the box marked pride.

Nor have I simply constructed an *apologia pro vita mea*. It is not that, as Edith Piaf sang, 'Moi, je ne regrette rien'. As virtuoso vocalists go I'm more in the Frank Sinatra camp, 'Regrets I've had a few'. But I certainly don't regret everything. If I've decided from time to time that too much honesty is not the best policy, I am at least conscious of my failures. But while my modesty is not false, my immodesty (more accurately vanity) is not false either.

Malcolm Rifkind,[10] in setting out flattering press comments on one of his Parliamentary speeches, wrote 'Far be it for me to say whether these bouquets were deserved. The reader will understand why I found it irresistible to quote them'. My similar, and no less irresistible, predilection for quoting favourable references in whatever context may be a sign of a lack of total confidence that they were in fact merited, but not necessarily of total confidence that they were not. Most have been squirrelled away until exposed in my epilogue (non-spoiler trigger warning). I have an insatiable appetite for press cuttings with my name in them. Far from believing that photographs steal one's soul, I am – another design fault – more prone to reject as non-proven anything about me which is unrecorded in visual or written form.

I cannot help the fact that my most frequently used vowel will be not 'e' but 'I'. That's what all memoirs dictate. At least I avoid the apparent hypocrisy inherent in the declarations of interest made by barristers writing about their own cases which are actually an ingenious, if somewhat transparent, method of publicising their involvement. I did think of deploying the device of writing my story as a biography until I realised that this would be itself a kind of hypocrisy. As a lawyer, I naturally consider direct evidence to be superior to hearsay.

The Master in College at Eton writing a reference for me as someone suitable to be admitted as a student of Gray's Inn included the comment 'He is a fundamentally honest person quite capable of laughing on occasion at his own ridiculous antics'. What those antics were I cannot for the life of me recall. I doubt that they went so far as running through cornfields as Theresa May claimed to be her example of teenage mischief; I'm more of a tiptoe through the tulips person. But be that as it might, I'll take the rough with the smooth and feign pleasure that I was not always delineated as a buttoned-up goody two shoes. And I was after all admitted to the Inn.

Because I am an inveterate hoarder I have retained, as well as such public prints as law reports and press cuttings, the vast majority of letters I've received as well as copies of those which I sent in typescript. Apart from nostalgic pleasure that re-reading actual letters, sometimes handwritten but all with actual signatures, gives – how sterile in comparison seem e-mails, more apt for deletion than

---

[10] Foreign Secretary and short-lived candidate for the Tory leadership in 2006.

retention – they do at least fill the gaps in the memory. Shakespeare's Henry V hit the button when he said 'Old Men Forget'.

Sometimes the cache of correspondence has prompted unanswered, maybe unanswerable, questions. Why on earth was I writing to Jeremy Paxman[11] to apologise for being unable to host a drinks reception for him and Matthew Parris[12] (where and for what?) on the excuse, which I assured him was not a joke, that I had to advise an International Lap Dancing Company (which?) on their constitutional rights (ditto?)? As you will see later[13] – if later is a point you reach at all – I finally solved at least part of the riddle.

One primary source was mother's diary, kept, war years apart, from the 1930s through to the 2000s. The regular letters I wrote from Trinity to Jeffrey during his sojourn at Her Majesty's Pleasure are as close as I ever came to compiling a chronicle of my own daily doings. Jeffrey never replied (because, I console myself, of some regulatory restraint in the Prison rules) but he did parlay a version of his equivalent into three volumes of well-remunerated *Prison Diaries*.[14] That I should be so lucky. I also seem to have kept every menu from every formal lunch or dinner I ever attended. Were there nothing else by way of record it would seem that my life during adulthood was just a sequence of special meals.[15]

By way of postscript to this already lengthy introduction (cue rude cry from the replicas of Bertie Wooster's tough eggs at the back of the hall 'do get on with it'), I note only this. Throughout when I write 'he', 'unless the context otherwise requires' to use one legal cliché, 'he' embraces 'she' to use another one and an even hoarier joke too. That at least will cut a few words out.

---

[11] Acerbic broadcaster and author.

[12] MP, broadcaster and columnist.

[13] Chapter 13, 'Life at the Bar'.

[14] In which I get a single mention (Archer, 2002) Vol 1, p 71, but not for my epistolary efforts.

[15] I was also furnished with documents by the archivists at the Dragon, Eton, Magdalen, Trinity and Gray's Inn for which I ought to, and do, thank them. Likewise my editor Sinead Moloney, my PA Yvonne Cavanagh and my barrister son Rupert for saving me from sundry errors of syntax, style and subject.

1

Roots and Branches

Three of my grandparents were gold medallists at the University of St Petersburg; the fourth was a chemist born in the Russian shtetl of Tzczuzin. It was he, Simeon, my father's father, the unacademic one of that quartet, who made such fortune as the family had. Shrewdness is a far better guarantee of riches than scholarship.

I start with that generation of my forebears as I had assumed that the records of any earlier ancestors were inaccessible behind the old Iron Curtain making me, for that if no other reason, more than a rank outsider candidate for the popular television programme *Who Do You Think You Are?* The wife of my paternal great-aunt's brother did compile a family tree penetrating a little further back into the mists of time but it identified none even of my great-grandparents, who were, from the compiler's point of view, genealogically just off-piste.

Professor Bryan Sykes, author of *The Seven Daughters of Eve*, with the aid of a swab of my DNA,[1] established that of these original Ur-women I was a direct descendant, through my mother, of Xenia. She, according to Oxford Ancestors, lived 25,000 years ago on the southern margins of the Great Plains, stretching from the low-lying British Isles in the West to Kazakhstan in the East. This intriguing scientific exercise still left millennia of my ancestry untilled, let alone providing a precise answer to the question of my geographic origins.

Another piece of the jigsaw was filled in when my daughter Natasha on some random Google search found that the Beloff family's lineage could be traced to the House of David (no less) as descendants of Rabbi Meir Katzenellenbogen, the Maharam of Padua.[2] The discovery that the family on my father's side (along with millions of others) might (but only might) be descended from the biblical King David, would also not have wholly filled the intervening gap of some centuries. So back to my grandparents I must go …

On his sixtieth birthday Simeon gave to the gathered family a vignette of his early life, typed up by his secretary on fragile now (and maybe even then) yellowing paper. He was one of seven children, five boys and two girls, reared in what became the Wilno district in Poland. His father died when he was only five. His mother, aided by his elder sister, combined a domestic role with management

---

[1] A guest at Trinity who volunteered the research.

[2] Neil Rosenstein, *The Unbroken Chain: Biographical Sketches and Genealogy of Illustrious Jewish Families from the 15th–20th Century*, Volumes 1 and 2, Revised Edition (Rosenstein, 1990).

of a small shop. An orthodox Jew, Simeon studied the Bible and the Talmud. It was only in his mid-teens, after a move to Grodno, that he broadened his learning to include Russian, history and maths.

Next, he persuaded a university student to give him chemistry in exchange for Hebrew lessons – a form of intellectual barter. His peripatetic journey continued via Lida to Warsaw where he qualified as an apprentice chemist. He then turned to trade, first in turpentine, next in other chemicals and pills procured from Archangel. With his elder brother Isaac he developed his business in Petrograd and, with his younger brother Arkady, opened a branch in Moscow. Starting from financial scratch he had to rely on counterparty credit and bank loans.

He married Mary, my graduate grandmother, in 1911 and opened an office in London. There the couple came to live in 1912. He changed the family name from Rabinowitch to Beloff, retaining a Russian flavour but easier for the English to pronounce (Arkady more simply shortened it to Rubin). He acquired homes in fashionable Hampstead; a chauffeur who drove him in a Daimler to his City office at Cooksons Produce, of which he was managing director, located in Mincing Lane, while he read the *Financial Times* ('*Ze Financial*' as he called it with his heavy accent); a maid (who duly married the chauffeur); and two farms in Bedfordshire, Redhills (cows) and Dyers Hall (pigs). For my paternal grandparents the scenes in the first staging of the musical *Fiddler on the Roof* were as vivid as yesterday.

Simeon and Mary had five children, all of whom made some mark in their different ways. Max, the eldest and my father, became a historian. He was Professor of Government and Public Administration at All Souls, Oxford, the founding father of the University of Buckingham and a Thatcherite life peer – a less than entirely predictable end of a political pilgrimage for someone who, as an undergraduate, had been to the left of his then Liberal contemporary Michael Foot[3] and had been a teller for the victorious ayes in the famous Oxford Union debate in 1933 on the motion that 'This House will under no circumstances fight for its King and country'. An intellectual who regarded, with monocular vision, an Oxford First as the gold standard of a person's worth, he used to read Proust in an exquisitely bound volume with wafer thin paper on the beach in Cannes, oblivious to the ambient noise.[4] He was always a dedicated patron of the gifted young, a commitment which I inherited.

When Max died, he was commemorated not only in the conventional obituary in *The Times* but in an editorial entitled 'Lord of Liberty'.[5] He was a controversialist, never knowingly understating his case – not always, indeed if ever, the most effective form of advocacy. In the 1960s he excoriated the campaign for nuclear

---

[3] At a party hosted by Lord Paul at the children's zoo dedicated to the memory of his daughter Ambika, I introduced my six-year-old grandson, also called Max, to Michael Foot. 'He's better looking' was the great orator's only comment.

[4] When we switched family summer vacations to Italy there was a memorable outing to Portofino where we had a *dejeuner sur la plage* in the company of Hugh Gaitskell, Maurice Bowra, Stuart Hampshire, Isaiah Berlin and Mary McCarthy – the social democratic elite at playtime.

[5] His own memoir is entitled *An Historian in the Twentieth Century* (Beloff, 1992).

disarmament (CND) as indulging in Aldermasturbation; in the 1990s he drew a comparison between the rise of Tony Blair and the rise of Adolf Hitler. At his memorial service in Oxford, David Butler[6] said, 'No cause in Oxford was considered completely lost until Max Beloff supported it' – quip excised from the printed text. At its counterpart in Buckingham, Margaret Thatcher curiously contented herself with a reading of Kipling's 'If'.

Renee Soskin, the second in line, herself a mother of six, was an (unsuccessful) Liberal Parliamentary candidate for Hampstead, an aspirant (though only marginally more successful) theatrical producer, a headmistress of a designedly inexpensive private school and a JP. In 1968 she sat on a panel that I had cobbled together in a church hall in Islington for a session on human rights. The event ended with a desperate call to the police when the debate became hotter than I had anticipated. Human rights are not always the fount of sweetness and light, not least because they have an inherent tendency to collide with each other.

Renee achieved a measure of unexpected posthumous recognition, when in the overture (sic) to Richard Davenport-Hines' book on the Profumo scandal *An English Affair*, he describes her peroration in a speech at his own school prize giving thus – 'she thundered' with 'sumptuous indignation' (the verb, adjective and noun are all his) 'Private schools are more indispensable than ever at this time of Deplorable Breakdown of Public Morals'. A distant relative of her husband was said to be for a brief time a paramour of Princess Margaret, but the dates show that she could not have had that affair in mind.

Nora, the third, a graduate of Bletchley Park and Lady Margaret Hall, spent most of her professional life as a journalist with the *Observer*, serving as a foreign correspondent (Washington, Paris, Moscow) and becoming the first female lobby correspondent[7] and Harold Wilson's *bête noire*.[8] She was sacked just when she had by letter accepted a new post of European correspondent from the then editor Donald Trelford. Writing at the same time to the new owners that Trelford himself should be dismissed, she had carelessly put each letter in the wrong envelope.[9] She contracted a surprising marriage in the autumn of her life to Clifford Makins, the *Observer*'s sports editor, described by his first female football correspondent with a painful accuracy, as a man with trousers 'held up by string or old pyjama cords and which hung in swags around his toecaps, while his underpants rose over the waist like a greyish-white cummerbund'.[10] No less surprisingly in her last years she became a devotee of the Serbian cause in the Balkan wars.[11] Like her elder two siblings she moved over the decades from Europhilia to Euroscepticism.

---

[6] Knighted for his work as a psephologist. As a teenager I played tennis with him on my parents' hard court.

[7] These various posts animated her book *Transit of Britain* (Beloff, 1973).

[8] Philip Ziegler, *Harold Wilson* (Ziegler, 1993) p 267.

[9] Donald Trelford, *Shouting in the Street* (Trelford, 2017) p 372.

[10] Julie Welch, *The Fleet Street Girls* (Welch, 2020) p 90.

[11] She was also an early patron of a predecessor version of Deliveroo. Libby Purves, 'What's Bad for the Waiter Is Bad for Us All' *The Times* (28 September 2020).

While I have a vivid recollection of my father waking me from my ten-year-old slumbers to listen to Adlai Stevenson's US Presidential concession speech in 1952, it was Nora who was chiefly responsible for my continuing interest in politics as well as for my awareness that I was not by nature suited to sally into that ruthless arena.[12]

John, the fourth, who trained as an architect, switched to psychology in which subject he held a number of university posts, but became diverted into less orthodox, indeed ambiguous realms of study. He served as President of the Society for Psychical Research and established the first UK chair of parapsychology at Edinburgh, named after Arthur Koestler. This unusual activity earned from his impertinent Beloff nephews the soubriquet 'ectoplasmic John'.[13]

Anne, the youngest, a scientist and professor of biochemistry, married Ernst Chain, winner of a Nobel prize for his work on Penicillin.

This eclectic bunch supplied me with an interesting family hinterland. In particular I was, like Wodehouse's Bertie Wooster, well supplied with formidable aunts. Indeed, I had a formidable great-aunt too in Arkady's wife Essia. During one 1960s summer she acquired an ad hoc nanny to look after their two American granddaughters. She had difficulty with the pronunciation of the young Asian woman's name, referring to her for convenience simply as 'the Burmese'. This anonymised employee was in fact Aung San Suu Kyi, then a student at St Hugh's, but later the first lady of Myanmar, whose initial reputation as a liberal icon was destroyed by her refusal to condemn the government's treatment of the Rohingya.

No-one of that side of the family, parents, aunts or other, harboured a gene which could propel me to a career at the Bar. That responsibility must be laid at my mother, Helen's, door. Her father, Samuel Dobrin, was a member of the Imperial Russian bar and practised as a lawyer in Soviet Russia until 1925. Disenchanted with communism, he then as part of some official delegation quit the country of his birth determined to make a life in England. In contemporary parlance he might be called an asylum seeker.

Qualifying as a barrister, Samuel joined the Middle Temple and Chambers at 2 Garden Court but, in the closed enclave of the English Bar in the 1920s and 1930s, had to content himself with scholarly writings about the Soviet constitution and allied subjects, advising Soviet institutions and appearing as an occasional expert witness.[14] He also founded the Department of Russian Studies at the University of Manchester.

Once when on my feet in the Privy Council[15] against Robert Walker[16] and at the receiving end of some hostile questioning from Lord Bridge in the Chair,

---

[12] Before my call to the Bar I was offered the chance to become a political columnist for the *Spectator*, a blandishment I rejected with a modicum of wistful regret.

[13] My cousin Molly, Arkady's daughter, who was born precisely seven years before me, gives further evidence of my irreverence in a privately published memoir 'My bumpy ride' describing me as an 11-year-old as 'brilliant and totally shameless'. She had the distinction when a member of the Oxford University Dramatic Society (OUDS) of acting alongside the young Maggie Smith, a professional, brought in as was then usual to give leadership to the student amateurs.

[14] See eg *Lazard Bros v Midland Bank* [1933] AC 289 where he and his evidence are referred to in the speech of Lord Wright.

[15] [1988] 1 WLR 1039.

[16] Law Lord and Supreme Court Justice (JSC) as Lord Walker of Gestingthorpe.

I sought to divert him, as one might a savage dog with a bone, by pointing out that the Professor Dobrin, referred to in the law report under discussion, was my relation. This earned me an only temporary respite before Lord Bridge returned to the attack.

My mother, Helen, accompanied her parents out of Russia – a country and whose people commanded her allegiance throughout her life. Her brother Misha chose to stay. Of that pair the leaver was wiser than the remainer. I only met Misha once when the family went on an Intourist tour, newly available to foreign visitors, to Moscow and Leningrad in 1967, a fascinating trip but one which instilled in me forever a strong emotional dedication to the superiority of democracy over dictatorship. Later visits to Russia have not changed my mind.

Helen graduated in law from King's College London, but in the habit of those times forswore the chance of a professional career in favour of motherhood to my obvious benefit. I have often been asked about the impact on my career of having a (relatively) famous father; I was already in my forties when Lord Justice Sebag Shaw, meeting him in his familiar London haunts of the Reform Club, said 'You must be Michael Beloff's father'. Previously it was I who was habitually asked 'Are you any relation to Max?', or sometimes to Nora. Yet it was my mother who channelled all her inherent energy and drive into ensuring the best for me and my younger brother, Jeremy. Reared in St Petersburg, she lived through its incarnations as Petrograd and Leningrad to see it, before she died, reacquiring its original name. If one lives long enough, life sometimes comes full circle.

This diverse ancestry enabled me when I was Treasurer of Gray's Inn in 2008 to point out in my speech to the newly called that though I was indisputably a private school educated Oxbridge pale male (if not yet stale) all four of my grandparents and my mother were immigrants.

Three out of that four were Jewish but my mother's mother Olga was not. In consequence a Jew to others, to a Jew I am not a Jew. Whatever the classification I have never been an observant one.[17] While my paternal grandparents were alive, I attended Seder at their house. With the aid of some tuition in Hebrew I was barmitsvahed, encouraged by the promise (fulfilled) of a trip to Italy as my reward, where I acquired, though resistant at the time, my love of art. I was defined in terms of faith more by the fact that I did not attend Chapel at Eton, though, somewhat inconsistently, I did attend house prayers (and later had no qualms about attending chapel in right of office at both Trinity and Gray's Inn and saying any appropriate orisons or grace). I have always, for better or for worse, travelled light in terms of belief whether spiritual or political. One of Simeon's favourite sayings was 'The world is mad' – an observation which resonates as well today as it did in his lifetime.

Simeon used anxiously to ask me 'Are there any Jewish boys at Eton?' There were in fact during my time there a mere handful, including Rufus Isaacs, descendant

---

[17] Once being temporarily bewildered when in mid-September two more devout colleagues wished me a happy new year.

of one of the leaders of the Bar of the early part of the last century. On a communal bus journey transporting our school generation to an anniversary dinner, I puzzled with my neighbour over the name 'Reading' in the list of attendees. I appreciated, only belatedly, that it was not some misplaced reference to a subject taught to the less intellectual boys but a recognition of Rufus Isaacs' inheritance of the Marquisate. In College, the scholars' house, there was also Michael Yudkin, the son of the celebrated dietary expert, inevitably nicknamed in those unreconstructed days 'Yidkin', and at the end of my time Michael Burton[18] whose surname was immune to any similar corruption.

I was not myself, one occasion apart, the victim of even verbal anti-Semitism[19] – not for me to cry 'Me Too' – though I was subject to what are now but not then called classic micro-aggressions – mispronunciation of my surname, questions as to where I came from, odd references occasionally and casually dropped into conversations to which I was privy (but not directed at me) to 'the yellow Yid' and 'Jewboy'. These remarks always made me think less of the speaker. I deplore racist vocabulary, but I was brought up on the old saying 'Sticks and stones may break my bones but words will never hurt me' (something perforce I had to ignore when advising clients on defamation). That words, wise or foolish, may sometimes cause offence is not, in my view, a sufficient basis for their suppression, still less for severe sanctions on those who utter them without hostile intent and on a single occasion many moons ago especially when vocabulary is so volatile[20] and a lexicon becomes a labyrinth.

My paternal grandparents were dedicated to Jewish charity work, Simeon privately providing assistance to those fleeing from the Nazis. Both were particularly disturbed by the conviction of the Jewish businessman John Bloom for the Rolls Razor fraud, for fear that it would revive the trope about money-grabbing Jews. They felt that a minority immigrant body owed a responsibility to the host community to be on its best behaviour rather than expecting the host community to adjust its own culture where at odds with that of the immigrant body. Such a view might today be regarded as old fashioned, even obsolete. Not only some, but all their best friends were Jewish.

The advent of anti-discrimination laws and the concept of racially aggravated offences post-dated their deaths and my youth. In my father's time there were quotas for the number of Jews at some famous London private schools because it was feared that admission based on academic merit would hand them too many places, not too few.

I cannot imagine that, though proud of being Jews, my father's parents would have wished to parade in the streets under a banner inscribed 'Jew Pride'. Neither

---

[18] High Court Judge GBE. Treasurer of Gray's Inn.

[19] I have it on good authority that one of my students at Trinity wrote in an essay 'Hitler thought that the Jews were disgusting. Perhaps they were'. I had no recollection of this eccentric, if qualified, observation written, I would surmise, in haste and probably repented at leisure.

[20] With words veering between the acceptable and the unacceptable depending on who says them, to whom and when eg, queer, black, women etc.

do I believe that they would have called for the removal of a statue of Simon de Montfort because of his expulsion of the Jews from Leicester in 1231. History after all is history; it is about the then not the now.

If anything, I was guilty – the appropriate adjective in this context – of a sense of superiority in being a Jew. In his valedictory address in 2015 in the Lord Chief Justice's Court to an assembled throng of the legal great and good, Lord Justice Rix had a moving passage about his own family origins as a descendant of immigrants. As I looked around it struck me how many of the leading judges and barristers among the living gathered together there (as well as absent friends) could tell a similar story. To name but a handful from the bench, six out of the last seven Masters of the Rolls have been Jewish (five to date being Peers too) and from the bar QCs Lords Grabiner[21] and Goldsmith[22] (there may even be a few commoners too) not to speak of Sir Francis Jacobs QC, who enhanced the legally amphibious office of Advocate-General at the ECJ. They made their own diversity.

I admire the Jews' record of achievement in the United Kingdom, not only in the law but in so many other areas of professional, cultural and political life, disproportionate to their small numbers. In the wider world Jews too have flourished in activities ranging from pugilism to piano playing. I take particular delight in the fact that the greatest woman athlete of the last century, Irena Szewinska,[23] was Jewish. I met her at the Beijing Olympics and still treasure the badge of the Polish team which she gave me. The endurance and revival of anti-Semitism, whatever its various sources, can hardly be ascribed to Jews' failure to pull their weight.

When I was a lad the (relatively) newly founded state of Israel was popular among the left of centre intelligentsia. To it the open-air industrious egalitarianism of the Kibbutz was hugely attractive. In 1965 the Oxford Union held a debate on the motion proposed by George Young[24] that 'The creation of the state of Israel was one of the mistakes of the twentieth century'. The President trustingly appointed me and Jeffrey Jowell, another Jewish ex-President,[25] as tellers. The motion was defeated. It is by no means clear that there would be a similar result in a debate on the same motion in 2022.

I only visited Israel once in the company of Leon Brittan[26] and Anthony Lester[27] just after the Six Day War, a conflict which showed the world that the Israelis were as successful as warriors as they were as farmers. If – an unlikely speculation – Israel were to play cricket against England I am confident that I would pass the Tebbitt test. But, even if I have led an ostensibly insider's life, I have never

---

[21] New Labour peer who migrated to the cross benches, Master of Clare College.

[22] A Blairite Attorney-General and Trinity parent. He later joined a prestigious US law firm.

[23] Sprinter, long jumper and medallist at three Olympic Games, nee Kirzentstein.

[24] Baronet, Cabinet Minister during the Major and Cameron administrations, Tory life peer and Companion of Honour (CH). I was an usher at his wedding and am godfather to one of his daughters.

[25] Public Law scholar, QC and knight (Kt), with whom, when a non-resident member, I shared a room in Blackstone chambers.

[26] Home Secretary, Conservative Peer and European Commissioner.

[27] Liberal Democrat Peer and human rights expert.

rid, or ever wished to rid, a sense of myself, because of my un-English ancestry, as something of an outsider.

By happenstance I was counsel in the first reported case brought by a Jew for racial discrimination[28] under the Race Relations Act 1976. The issue whether Jews were an ethnic group or a religious group only was not raised by the defendant company. Under the updated equality legislation the distinction has become irrelevant.

Neither genes nor Jewishness steered me inevitably to the Bar. That was rather lack of other talents.

Although my mother was a pianist of near concert standard, my efforts stopped at two-fingered playing of 'Mary had a little lamb', or more precisely, 'Mary had a little …'. I had no artistic bent; at Eton the Master in charge of art, Willie Blunt,[29] failed to teach me to write in a readable script, let alone to draw a recognisable person or scene. I may have hoped to author best-selling fiction; but hope was not father to the deed. There is not even the conventional extract of a tormented adolescent novel hidden among my attic lumber – only a single (what I thought arresting) opening line of an unfinished first chapter of a running romance refer-ring to Pheidippides as he sped from Marathon to Athens with news of the Greek triumph – 'He knew that he was going to die'. If I could reason, rhyme I could not – so a line was drawn through poetry as well as prose.

Michael Rudman,[30] another Oxford contemporary, watching me speak at the Oxford Union, claimed to have detected some thespian glimmering. In fact, my theatrical career terminated at the Dragon School with a double role in Macbeth as second witch (understudy) and the unfortunate page, pudgy in hose, at whom the Scottish king let loose the vituperative volley 'The devil damn thee black, thou cream faced loon'.

I had no entrepreneurial spirit. Despite a mark of 394 out of 400 in my maths O levels, I had hit a glass ceiling: later I could barely add with the aid of a calcula-tor. If, according to David Baddiel, Jews don't count, this Jew can't count either. To excuse that innumeracy I have to rely on Sherlock (or was it Mycroft?) Holmes's explanation that the brain can only hold so much information at any one time. Quantification of fees was for my clerks, of damages for my juniors.

In my case, of CP Snow's *Two Cultures*, never the twain would meet. I did not believe my brother, always far more science- and techno-savvy, when he advised me that inserting one's fingers into an electric socket was not recommended on health and safety grounds. The phrase short sharp shock aptly describes what happened next. Maybe I'm lucky to have stayed alive past my sixth birthday.

Many jobs for which I would have been no less unsuited did not even exist in my youth – IT consultant, intimacy co-ordinator, sensitivity reader, wellness guru – I would have been unsuited for those too as I would have been for such non-, but profitable, activities as are attendant upon the role of celebrity or influencer.

---

[28] [1980] IRLR 427.
[29] Brother of the Master of the Queen's Pictures and traitor, Anthony Blunt.
[30] Theatre Director and intermittent husband of Felicity Kendall, the actress of *The Good Life* fame.

When a child, for long-forgotten reasons, I thought I might become a dress designer. I would never have been a rival to Giorgio Armani; although as an adult I did try to pose a threat to George Carman, nicknamed Giorgio Carmani, the greatest jury advocate of the epoch.[31]

I did not indeed even consciously choose the Bar. It was my parents who considered the Bar to be a likely option recognising that I appeared to enjoy speaking to a wider audience than one (although devoid of any semblance of gifts of song or dance I was nonetheless the show turn, in the absence of competition, at family parties). My mother would have preferred me to be a doctor – another role to which I would have been comprehensively unsuited. When as President of Trinity I toured schools, nominally giving careers advice to future potential barristers but in fact touting for high-quality applicants to the College, I counselled the sixth formers 'your parents are not always wrong'.

I was born in Adlington on 18 April 1942. I was told by my mother – but have never checked – that there is a plaque commemorating the event in the local hospital because I was the first baby born there during the Second World War – presumably, if true, because of the absence of so many men on wartime duty rather than of any regional continence or chastity. My father too was away – a member of the Royal Corps of Signal Men (*Pte) stationed on the north Wales coast – a prophylactic measure against a surprise German attack which never came. (To avoid misunderstanding of the last two sentences he was present at my conception, if not at my birth.) Our house was in Alderley Edge, now, but not then, the favoured area in which stars from the Manchester football superclubs build palatial residences with pool, pool room, cinema and gymnasium.

Once during the Commonwealth Games in 2002 when I had a car and driver at my disposal as a member of the ad hoc panel of the Court of Arbitration for Sport (CAS) I decided to pay a pious visit to seek out my first family home, only to discover that it had been demolished and replaced with a stumpy block of flats. I left with no photograph but a belated appreciation of what an effort it must have been for my mother to push a pram with two small sons and all her shopping up the hillside in the midst of a war whose eventual outcome no sentient adult could predict with any certainty.

Here endeth the first chapter.

---

[31] Dominic Carman, *No Ordinary Man* (Carman, 2002).

2

Early Days to Eton

When my father was appointed to a readership at Nuffield College, Oxford, the family moved with him. I was sent to Greycotes, a girls' school with only a few boys. Baroness Hale,[1] in a speech, once called me 'a male feminist'. That status, if merited, may have stemmed from that early experience. It certainly inoculated me against the male chauvinism to which my later education might otherwise have exposed me.

In 2004 in the wake of a broadcast interview, I received out of the blue a letter from a Mary (surname not supplied). She wrote that, more than 55 years before, she had been what *she* called 'a mother's help' and used to escort me and my brother to school. I was, according to her, 'a clever little boy always chatting away about prehistoric animals'. Her successor, what *I* called a 'nanny', was a spiritualist. I am not conscious that this extracurricular exposure to either a Jurassic or a spirit world left any permanent mark on me. The Greycotes' Headmistress[2] wrote to my father when I left that I had been 'wonderfully keen about everything'. A little more selectivity on my part might have been advisable.

I was then replanted at the Dragon School, a boy's school with only a few girls, known as hags whether pretty or plain (if any); the few female teachers were then, as now, more courteously known as Mas. In my Butterworths commentary on the Sex Discrimination Act 1976 I gave the school as an example of a body which, by opening up its doors to a mere handful of girls, might have inadvertently triggered a legal duty to achieve total equality. I received from one of the senior masters an indignant letter complaining that my speculation was damaging to the school. With an exquisite sense of timing, a junior clerk handed me the letter to read at just the moment that my case was about to be called on in the High Court. This imprudent, if well-intentioned, interruption did nothing to diminish my usual sense of apprehension – au contraire.[3]

---

[1] The first female Law Lord (sic) and President of the Supreme Court reciprocally referenced in my 2009 Barnard's Inn reading for Gray's Inn, 'Sisters in Law-the irresistible rise of Women in Wigs'; see Barnard and Shuttleworth *An Illustrated History of Gray's Inn* pp124, 134 fn 10. Linda McDougall in *Cherie, the Perfect Life of Mrs Blair* (McDougall, 2001) writes 'Beloff has always enjoyed women and their company' p 158. This sentence is open to misconstruction but it is certainly true that I find misogyny inexplicable.

[2] Mrs Cunliffe immortalised in the name of the Close where the school has been superseded by a residential estate.

[3] Four members of my Dragon generation (more or less) have compiled private accounts of their time there; one Alan Macfarlane, a Professorial Fellow of Kings, Cambridge as part of an ambitious socio-anthropological account of his own life; a second, Peter Jay, UK Ambassador to the USA; a third, Tom Stanier, a broadcaster – the latter pair writing expressly for the pleasure – or at any rate

If not the best of times, it was a better time for us born during the war, the pre-boomer generation. Rationing slowly disappeared if, to our collective disappointment, of sweets last of all. It was the age of the *Dandy* and the *Beano*, comics on which my parents frowned. They were more tolerant of the *Eagle* which had a modicum of serious content. I myself read it for the exploits of Dan Dare and Harris Tweed. Clad in compulsory schoolboy corduroy, it was only later that I understood the source of the latter's name. We bought dinkies with our pocket money and played conkers, marbles and Lurky, a mutation of hide and seek, whose climax involved kicking a tin can out of a chalked circle in the playground.

Days started with physical exercise (PT) in the same location led by Colonel Pernell, a decorated veteran of the Boer War. He was also assigned to teach me to box; my mother believing that a capacity for self-defence was a necessary accomplishment for a boy. On one occasion the ex-soldier was diverted by some summons and left me and my opponent swinging minute by minute ever less forcefully at each other until his much-delayed return. I was never destined to become a Muhammad Ali, whose exploits in the ring later so excited me that I could barely sleep on the night of his global championship fights, awaiting the result which was always the first item on the BBC morning news.[4]

In summer we Dragons learned to swim, held up on a canvas belt in the less than pristine waters of river Cherwell, graduating finally with a full clothes test. In winter we could sometimes skate on the frozen school lawn: global warming was yet to come.

It was not all play and no work. Academic success was expected and achieved partly as a result of the high proportion of dons' sons (and occasional daughter) in its student constituency. But to nature the school added nurture with a host of gifted, if sometimes eccentric, teachers. LA Wilding ('Law') was the head of classics, author of standard textbooks on teaching Latin as well as an inspiring instructor. C Jacques ('Jacko') gave history some space and spice and a sense of our island and empire story; our syllabus reflected a world still substantially painted red which would then have seemed to us part of the natural order of things. WAC Wilkinson ('Wilkie') was head of maths aided and abetted by the irascible AD Haigh ('Tubby'). CCF Dodd taught French often in French. He would stride into class instructing us 'Repetez les voyelles a … e … i … o … u', each perfectly articulated by him, if not by us. The defaulters earned the rebuke 'Ah mon pauvre idiot' with the occasional light slap on the cheek (probably grounds for dismissal nowadays).

---

interest – of their families; a fourth, David Lewis, a solicitor and Lord Mayor of London, 'Aim as High as the Sun' – a translation of the school's Latin motto *Arduus ad Solem*; a fifth, Ian Senior, an economist, gave an evocative speech at an Old Dragons' reunion of the senior generation in September 2018. Without access to that trove of reminiscence I would have remembered less about Dragon days I should.

[4] When the pugilist was still called Cassius Clay, Jeffrey came to watch the rematch between him and Sonny Liston on television at my parents' house. Jeffrey fell asleep on the sofa and I was unable to wake him before the suspect bout came to a premature conclusion. Mind you I can only just talk. Attending with my eldest grandson Max the world cup final between England and New Zealand at Lord's in 2019, as guests of the International Cricket Council (ICC), I almost missed the historic final over, my anxiety to ensure a swift passage out of the ground.

One contemporary, later a highly distinguished historian, provoked the comment 'Dieu soit loué M ... est absent'. I enhanced my francophonic learning with a week spent at the Lycée Janson Sailly in Paris, the school of my French pen friend, among whose alumni was Valery Giscard d'Estaing. Gerd Somerhoff, German-born great-grandson of Robert Schumann and a Second World War internee, taught science (not my forte) and JB Brown ('Bruno') masterminded annual productions of Shakespeare and Gilbert and Sullivan in which I never starred, still less sang. Carpentry was known as Barsonry after its instructor Mr Barson; I once made an almost usable wooden pencil case. The full-time teachers were assisted by temporary teaching assistants, called stooges, usually from the (then) empire.

I did, however, start my career in debating – part of the Dragon extra-curricular cultural scene. I would stand awkwardly on a schoolroom radiator while other boys, astute to catcall any verbal infelicity, perched on the windowsill behind me and dug their shoes into my back. I have never since spoken in a more physically demanding environment. I also learned to declaim. A report in *The Draconian*, the school magazine, in Summer 1954, noted 'Upper 1 finished the morning's proceedings with great distinction with Stanier, Beloff and Jeffery to cap last year's Virgilian success with a beautiful passage from Alcestis in which Beloff was outstanding with his moving and musical speaking of Greek'. If possibly Greek to me then, it is certainly Greek to me now.

The Dragon was unusually large for a preparatory school; about 400 odd pupils enjoying an informal atmosphere created by its founder 'Skipper' Lynam who passed the reins of headship to his brother Hum and then to his son Joc, headmaster in my time. Hum still had the role of delivering fortnight reports by hand in which the subject teachers would scribble comments no longer than three words, sometimes glossed equally succinctly by Hum himself.

While Peter Jay's vignette makes the school in the early 1950s seem at times and in places almost Hobbesian I cannot improve on his analysis, worthy of a prominent former diplomat. 'It inculcated serious respect for scholastic achievement, profound admiration for athletic prowess, great enthusiasm for the stage and above all a deep attachment to the special air of anarchic laissez faire and reflex disregard for authority' quite unlike, so we Dragons thought, our nearest, more upper- than middle-class, neighbour Summerfields, a feeder school for Eton.

In those unsentimental days, innocent of data protection, the *Draconian* not only listed the pupils form by form recording their sets and places in Classics (the benchmark) but also in English, Maths and French and, equally unconscious of any need for privacy, the pupil's home address. I myself scribbled in the margins of my copy additional information about who had done what academically – a revelation of an early inherent and somewhat unlovable competitiveness. I was still, it appears, extremely keen.

At the end of my time at the Dragon I received a form prize in Upper 1, the top set, for an amalgam of high places in several subjects, but being first in none (just as decades later I was awarded a Lifetime Achievement Award at the annual

Chambers Bar Directory gala, not being thought by then sufficiently outstanding in any single area of practice).[5]

The major prize was my Eton scholarship, for which I was only eligible to sit through the fortuity of having an English-born father; the school statutes still excluded the sons of immigrants from the competition.[6] I was seventh in the roll, at the tender age of 12 years 1 month – though I was comprehensively overshadowed by one Richard Jeffery, top scholar of the year (and first in every subject in Upper 1) and could claim no more than a fraction of the credit for the day's holiday celebration that the Dragon traditionally granted. My mother's diaries show a degree of anxiety about the prospect, only equalled by her joy at the actual outcome (she caringly took me for a brief holiday to Bournemouth before I went to sit the exams at Eton itself). I shared the former emotion, since the results of my contemporaries, scholars elect at other public schools, came before Eton's. I certainly shared the latter. When Law telephoned the result to our home, though in shock I initially confused his voice with that of a cheerful but uninvolved family friend Garogy, so delaying my appreciation of the message's full import.

The 11 scholarship papers were testing; and biased firmly towards the classics. Latin verse and prose composition; Latin and Greek grammar; and Latin and Greek translation, complemented by an English essay; a (truly) general paper; French; and two Maths papers. One of my former teachers at Greycotes wrote a note of congratulation only slightly tempered by her comment that she had expected me to do a little better.

A perennial feature of the Dragon experience is that prizes are awarded for summer holiday diaries, in which the immature authors unselfconsciously indulge in candid apercus about their family, friends and even school staff, in a manner, if not a style, resembling the unvarnished reports of retiring ambassadors. My four volumes record, in handwriting which improved year on year without ever attaining anything more than bare legibility, the unremarkable pursuits of a schoolboy in the holiday (did I really collect the numbers of railway locomotives – train spotting as it was called?) coupled with a daily diet of reading and some additional tuition in maths in my last summer vacation. On one occasion the tutor, Wilkie, gave me sixpence to fetch him some tobacco from a nearby shop – a mission which, I suspect, would be frowned upon today.

Two clues only from the diaries heralded my later interest in the law and athletics. In 1953 I referred to an idea I had for a book with characters based on Dragon contemporaries, whom, I wrote, I was not prepared to identify (even in the diary itself) in case I were sued for libel. In 1954 I recorded that, while on holiday

---

[5] I passed the 11 plus by a sufficient margin to be offered a place at Magdalen College School, then, but no longer, a grammar school, but I had already been identified as a likely scholarship candidate for Eton or Winchester.

[6] The discriminatory nationality clause was only abandoned while I was at the school. Tim Card, *Eton Renewed* (Card, 1994) p 241.

in France, I was so impatient to find out what was happening in the Vancouver Games (the occasion of the famous Bannister/Landy clash) that I was prepared to read the sports reports in *Le Monde* and *Figaro* rather than wait for the later arriving English newspapers.

Because I left the Dragon at such a young age, my academic achievements apart,[7] I achieved nothing of note in any extra-curricular activity, chess apart, being neither, in the school patois, particularly beef (ie strong) or fleb (ie weak). (I never worked out why the latter epithet, a corruption of flesh, was thought to be the opposite rather than a subset of the former.) Though featured in the school profiles of Eminent Dragons,[8] as a young Dragon eminent I was certainly not. Being a dayboy ('daybug') I was not fully integrated in the in-house social activity of the boarders. When I made the after-lunch speech at the fiftieth anniversary of my generation's arrival at the school and recited all the things I had not done, one quick-witted contemporary, the later Lord Mayor of London, started an ever more doleful chorus of 'aaaahs' at the end of each sentence. By then I was too far down the pre-prepared forensic track to beat a sensible retreat. In Court I was readier to cut my losses.

With the benefit of hindsight I appreciated how much the Dragon had done for me,[9] even if I passed largely beneath the radar and had to wait for my secondary schooling before caterpillar started slowly to turn into some form of butterfly. I had certainly enjoyed my time there, surviving the endless colds of the dank winters and the full hand of ailments, mumps, measles (both German and standard variety) and chicken pox, now largely eradicated by vaccination.

My son Rupert and daughter Natasha and all three grandsons Max, Luke and Jack became Dragons (in a school now completely co-ed). The trio, the third generation of my Dragon family, can enjoy a heated indoor swimming pool, a computer centre, newbuild classrooms in place of prefabs, and school trips to continents east, west and south rather than, as in my time, merely to places such as Coopers Marmalade Factory in nearby Wolvercote. The facilities had certainly improved since my time, if had the fees commensurately, leading to a perceptible change in the demographic.[10] But its unusual size for a private preparatory school is not the only aspect which makes it special. In between the schooldays of the two Dragon

---

[7] In the school's Moberly essay in 1954 on King John, prize not awarded because no entry was of sufficient standard, I was singled out as the example justifying the examiner's general comment 'A catalogue of facts does not constitute an essay' and his particular comment that I 'should learn to select' – wise words which are equally applicable to a barrister's submission and which I wish I could honestly claim that I stored for such future use.

[8] But certainly outranked by the likes of John Betjeman, Leonard Cheshire VC, Sir John Kendrew, Tim Henman, Antonia Fraser and Cressida Dick.

[9] In a Walk Down Dragon Lane with the Beloff Family *Dragon Community News* Summer 2021 I described my time there as 'Breathless, Blossoming, Brilliant', high marks for alliteration, if not imagination.

[10] Jack once went on a playdate with a Russian school friend to whose house he was taken by two security guards.

generations of my descendants I became a Governor[11] and gained some insight into, if not making any significant contribution to, why that was.

Next to Eton. My parents being away in Princeton where my father was teaching on sabbatical, I was escorted to College by his mother to whom the school was as novel an environment as it was to me. The first-year scholars, awkward in the school dress of black jacket and stiff collar, were still housed in Long Chamber, a series of curtained off cubicles – a compromise between a dormitory and individual rooms – with a bed and desk (Burrys). We had to learn and were tested on such arcane school-specific matters as Eton's geography and slang. The 70 scholars were Tugs (the *gens togata* in our scholars' gowns) distinguished from the Oppidans who were accommodated in individual houses of M'Tutors with lower populations scattered about the campus (not a word we ever used). But both Colleger and Oppidan alike endured early school at 7.30am before breakfast which subsequent experiments have suggested is out of sync with teenage biorhythms.

We were fags liable to be summoned by a sixth former with a stentorian shout of 'boy … y … y …' to perform some menial task usually as a messenger – the last to arrive would be selected. Once I was sent by Colin Shepherd[12] to go to kick someone's arse. Mission not accomplished.

Members of the Eton Society (Pop), the self-selecting body of school prefects, endowed with such privileges as the right to wear spongebag trousers and gaudy waistcoats, had a school-wide jurisdiction. Off to watch some match in a distant pitch on a cold afternoon I was hailed, like a human taxi, by the Captain of the Oppidans and sent to his far-away house simply to fetch his scarf. About turn. In the spirit of Mufasa encouraging young Simba in *The Lion King*, I told myself that one day Pop's privileges might all be mine. They were, but I was circumspect in their exercise: I did once administer an all but intangible siphoning (beating) to a friend for some trivial misdemeanour just to establish the continued existence of the supreme penal power in the same way as its proprietor will exercise an annual right of way. The practice was all but obsolete school-wide and later was rightly and formally abolished.

Because I was the youngest Colleger, the matron in college (M'dame) Miss Iredale-Smith ('the Airedale'), whose obituary in *The Times* was written by Foreign Secretary Douglas Hurd, entertained me to supper in her own home. Despite her attention the most notable achievement of my first half was to lose about a stone in weight;[13] I had been a plump little lad. Maybe the Eton should supplant

---

[11] I appear in a photograph of the Governors in David Lewis's memoir, *Aim As High As The Sun* (privately published, 2020) at p189 but am not singled out at p195 as one of those who served in that capacity during his three decades of membership for whom he had particular respect – an absence which is a tribute to his powers of discrimination between the team leaders and the footsoldiers. Given that the book is illuminated with photographs culled from his Mayoral year from the Queen of England to the President of France I am fortunate to have a toehold in it at all.

[12] Managing Director of the Savoy.

[13] If I had, as some teenage snobs claimed with scant evidence, an 'oiky accent', it soon mutated into an Eton drawl.

the Cambridge diet? The Airedale was succeeded in her post by the younger and more formidable Naomi Johnstone from naval stock of whom it was written she 'could have run an empire'.[14] The Master in College was Stevie McWatters.[15] He was something of a sportsman. His successor Raef Payne was more aesthete than athlete. My tutor whom I was 'up to' in the proper patois was RMA Bourne, a legendary oarsman who, in private business (p/ hole) – a weekly face to face hour devoted to subjects other than the curriculum – introduced me to PG Wodehouse and Agatha Christie.

In academic terms my early years at Eton were characterised more by displays of potential than of attainment. It was not until my third half (term) that I achieved a distinction in trials (examinations). The curriculum was heavily biased towards Latin and Greek. Assigned to the top stream I was taught by RC Martineau ('Mange' – so-called because of a discoloured patch on the top of his skull), DP Simpson (inevitably 'Dippy') and Charles Willink ('Chunky' – I assume a comment on his physique), all scholars who would have fitted happily into an Oxbridge senior common room.

For Collegers, once 'O' levels were surmounted the choice was binary. If one did not have exceptional mathematical or scientific talents one was expected to continue with classics. My father wanted me to pursue history. Given my youth, a compromise was feasible. It was agreed that if I studied Latin and Greek to A level, I could then switch to the paternal choice (Eton had just joined the mainstream of national exams, sacrificing its own internal test – the evocatively named 'Grand July'). That switch brought me into contact with the two most influential of my Eton Tutors.

The first was Alan Barker, later successively headmaster of the Leys and of University College School – in that era many Eton teachers (beaks) graduated to headships at other schools – and the husband of Jean[16] who plied us with tea during tutorials. Mr Barker, suave in suit and manner, foresaw for me a career in law and politics. 'You should aim to be QC MP'. The second was Ray Parry, a volatile Welshman, as passionate as Mr Barker had been polished, who once played cricket for Glamorgan and also had a high achieving wife, Margaret, headmistress of St Mary's, Calne. My move to history for my advanced studies had set a precedent for others;[17] and Mr Parry, a Balliol man, had the pleasure of having taught three Brackenbury scholars (winners of Balliol's top history award) from my sub-junior election: Derek Parfit, who became, according to his *Times* obituary, the most influential British philosopher since Wittgenstein but at the time was aficionado of his own secular Trinity, Bird (Miles Davis), Bard and Bardot, Anthony Cheetham[18] and

---

[14] Adam Nicholson and Eric Anderson *About Eton* (Anderson and Nicholson, 2010) p 157.
[15] As I learned later, a Trinity Oxford graduate.
[16] Baroness Trumpington and a Tory minister in the Thatcher administrations.
[17] Tim Card, in *Eton Renewed* (Card, 1994) wrote: 'The history department attracted very clever boys', p 242.
[18] A highly successful publisher of Orion books etc.

Edward Mortimer.[19] Derek inevitably outscored me in the Roseberry Scholarship – Eton's premier award for history – leaving me with another proxime, the Andrew Duncan prize.

Anthony Cheetham's father was then the UK Ambassador to Hungary and I was invited to stay in the Budapest Embassy. It was there I first became acquainted at a party with vodka martinis in more than ample quantities. Whether they were stirred or not I was certainly shaken with the inevitable consequences. On the next day, when the guests were off on a duck shoot – not an outing which anyway attracted me – I did not survive beyond halfway down the embassy drive before making my still slurred excuses and walking gingerly back to the residence. I have never been drunk since. Once was more than enough.

Eton imported real Frenchmen to teach French; M'sieur Cottereau impressed me by opening the door in his house when I came to read an essay to him at 11.30 am still clad in blue silk pyjamas. His successor M'sieur Ferrieux was a less flamboyant figure. Both immeasurably enhanced my accent. I became a member of Le Cercle Français along with fellow francophones Jonathan Steele[20] and George Young. Russian I was taught by a series of masters who had opted to study the language as part of their stint of national service. If national service still existed, the option would surely now be Mandarin. That I needed to be taught it at all was my own fault. Realising very early on that it was not the language of my toddler playmates I resisted taking advantage of the presence of my Russian speaking mother's mother Olga, becoming a foolish victim of my own precocity.

My headmaster was Robert Birley, without doubt in the top three of those who had held that post in the twentieth century. His post-war work in Germany and his later endeavours in South Africa marked him out as someone as humane as he was wise; and he added greatly to my intellectual *savoir faire* when I became a member of his Essay society which met regularly in his drawing-room to dissect each other's contributions.

But I would attribute most of my intellectual upward mobility to the stimulus of my contemporaries in College. I once thought that our generation (looking backwards and forwards I spanned more than 10 years) achieved less than it might have in later life, as if the effort of winning an Eton scholarship, the blue riband for an ambitious prep school boy, had exhausted its members for good. With a more sensible perspective I can see that I was wrong. College bred judges and editors of national newspapers, fellows of Oxbridge colleges, QCs and MPs (though not in a combination described by Mr Barker). All (at any rate most) scholars were clever, if some were more clever than others. College was an academic hot house in which a few wilted but which also enabled some exotic plants to bloom.

In a colour supplement many years later, I was classified (wrongly) as a genius. I did point out to the journalist that in College I was one of a quartet of friends who messed (had tea) together and that I was without question the least intellectually gifted of the four – Derek and Edward became Prize Fellows of All Souls, and the fourth, Francis Cripps, grandson of Sir Stafford, took the best Cambridge first in economics since the war but (I choose the conjunction with care) later became an adviser to Tony Benn.

College was not only segregated by intellect but also physically cut off from Oppidan houses. Involvement in school-wide activities became the major mechanism for wider social contact. Eton had its own hierarchies distinct from those in the outside world. My contemporaries included Prince William of Gloucester (prematurely deceased in a flying accident) and Prince Michael of Kent, whom I later encountered when he was Patron of the Royal Automobile Club (RAC) and I was a Steward. No deference on account of their rank was paid to them inside the school nor indeed to Prince Birendra of Nepal, esteemed as a God in his own small nation but later the victim of assassination in a battle of thrones. Offspring of peers, all hereditary then, were, if not two a penny, hardly more expensive. David Sainsbury[21] was to me Keeper (Captain) of Athletics not an heir to the wealth of the grocery business.[22] I gave no thought to the liquid provenance of a Courage, a Whitbread or a Tollemache among my Oppidan counterparts.

One of those domestic hierarchies, indeed the foremost, was sporting. As editor of *Narcissus*, published for the annual fourth of June celebrations, I decided that in defiance of that self-admiring name, it would take a more objective look at the school 'warts and all'. I argued that 'Games are played not for enjoyment but for prestige. The School is controlled by a race of athletocrats, arrogant in their colours as ostentatious as those of Joseph's coat. They are followed by fawning and adoring sycophants'. I ended with a resonant cri de coeur 'Eton must realise that athletic snobbery is out of date'.

My view may have been influenced by my own lack of success at team games other than chess. I was first board for the Buckinghamshire postal chess team in which role I endured a seemingly endless match against one Peter Paskin, with in my corner a far superior player, Adrian Hollis.[23] I did win my cap for athletics and set a (temporary) school record in the breaststroke, although I failed in three years actually to win the school's competition in the discipline, defeated by a bespectacled college contemporary, whose sole sporting talent this was. (At least unlike a future socialite grandee, a familiar figure in gossip columns in later years, who must remain unnamed, I never sank to the bottom of the pool during a race, as he did, in what remain mysterious circumstances.)

Another hierarchy was cultural. In this I prospered more. Under the patronage of the Earl of Gowrie[24] (Grey) I became President of the Debating Society, where I am recorded as having spoken 31 times and was on the committee of both the

---

[21] An early member of the SDP but afterwards Minister of Science in a Blair administration ending up as Chancellor of Cambridge University.

[22] I suspect that at that stage of my life my mother would have done all the shopping.

[23] Son of Sir Roger Hollis, Head of MI6 and later a classics don at Keble.

[24] A Cabinet Minister in the first Thatcher administration and a poet both before and after.

Literary and Political Societies, all of which held their meetings in the elegant Election chamber decorated with the portraits of eminent old Etonians (OEs).

In the adjacent Election Hall I won the Loder declamation prize judged by Sir Harry Hylton-Foster, the Speaker of the House. I further honed my oratorical skills in (recitations (Speeches), part of the fourth of June celebrations), delivered in Upper School, ornamented with the busts of yet more eminent OEs (as well as with walls in which the names of sixth formers were inscribed). For that I wore the same courtly garb I next wore on the day of my admission as a QC just over two decades on. Rereading the reviews of these various performances in the Eton College Chronicle I note that the spirit of impartial criticism was alive and well. The mother of one of my closest friends wrote of my recitation from Richard II, 'in spite of beautiful diction his interpretation was too derivative and so lacked spontaneity and conviction'. Touché. She had spotted too large a helping of Gielgudian pastiche. At least no-one ever wrote that I was inaudible. To be heard is a necessary, if not a sufficient, quality for an advocate.

I exercised pen as well as tongue. I contributed to one journal, *Off Parade*, published on St Andrews Day 1956, and edited another, *Fresco*, published on the same day the next year, along with Hugh Cecil.[25] Through Hugh's solicitations – his lineage was grander than mine – we procured brief reminiscences under the rubric Eheu Fugaces from alumni including Harold Macmillan, Jo Grimond,[26] Anthony Powell[27] and Julian Slade.[28] These I innocently showed to Nora who then scooped them for *The Observer*, her journalistic instincts winning out over any auntly loyalty. Lesson learned. However, I kept the original contributions exercising – so I would plead in my defence – the *soi-disant* senior editor's literary *droit de seigneur*.

I appear, either through bravado or *faute de mieux*, to have supplied to these ephemera an excessive number of pieces and poems, the former showing an indifference to the boundary between satire and sarcasm, the latter, a display of unexplained but typical teenage angst. The last line of one verse read 'Scarlet the spear of pain and loneliness'. As Molesworth, the chief character in Ronald Searle's *Down with Skool*, would have put it 'Nuff said'.

The crowning point was my spell as College Editor of the *Chronicle*. My predecessor summarised the choice between me with 'Talent but no taste' and my rival with 'Taste but no talent'. Whether either comment was fair did not bother me once I occupied the chair, shared again with Hugh as my Oppidan opposite number. We flirted with change, loath to sacrifice one page out of four to charts of rowing competitions; and bridled at the mild censorship that the Master responsible, always conscious of Fleet Street's avidity for any news about Eton, sought to impose.[29]

---

[25] Son of Lord David Cecil and later a professional historian.
[26] Liberal party leader.
[27] Novelist CH.
[28] Composer and co-writer of the musical *Salad Days*.
[29] In my first year I wrote a letter to the *Daily Express* setting out my preferred selection for the England football team, printed only because of the Eton address. I received only a mild reprimand for my juvenile naiveté.

My editorials were replete with in-jokes, with the life span of a mayfly, some verging on the indecent only apparent to a small group of cognoscenti.

There were a number of Oppidans with literary and cultural tastes who became part of that circle including the amply proportioned Christopher Lennox Boyd, a generous Maecenas,[30] ie he took us out regularly to high teas at excellent local hotels, along with Hugh, Oliver Walston,[31] who would invariably greet me with the phrase 'Wotcha Cockeez' (or was it 'Coquilles'?) borrowed from a Peter Sellers film which I reciprocated verbatim, and David Tweedie who abandoned youthful drollery for a sober career as a city solicitor.

My great ambition, despite my censorious words, was to get into Pop, elected twice a term by the current membership. In my penultimate half I failed first time round by a single vote – a disappointment made more bitter because the cohort who came round in the traditional way to congratulate the winner veered both towards and then away from my room in Upper Tower[32] – so near and yet so far – en route to elect the then Captain of the school who was ex officio a member. I was destined to hold that position in my next half and was desperate to be elected by choice not compulsion. It came good for me in the second election of the half so that come summer I could be adorned in peacock plumage on the first day back, and not just a few days later. These things meant much to those who were chosen and maybe more to those who were not. When Pop celebrated its 150th anniversary dinner in 2005 Boris Johnson, one of the two speakers alongside Douglas Hurd, made much of the fact that he had been a member, whereas David Cameron, then leader of the Opposition, had not. Posh was one thing, Pop quite another. History may briefly have altered the order of precedence between these two Conservative political rivals, but to plagiarise Chinese premier Zhou Enlai's remark in 1972 when asked about the impact of the French Revolution, it may be 'too early to say'.

As a by-product of my mixing with the Etonian *upper gratin*, I became a D list debs' delight, invited, according to the custom, to dinner parties by persons with whom I was previously wholly unfamiliar. On one occasion I dined in the wrong place – I should have been with another group two floors up – but my hostess was too polite to point this out, and I joined unwittingly in the chorus of praise for Cathy's zabaglione.

In the same penultimate half I fell firmly between two stools. I wanted to test my speed in an away match at Winchester on their famous track which was less than the conventional 440 yards circuit – a trap for the unwary visiting team – against their star Mike Hogan.[33] But I also wanted to win the Rosebery[34] for which I was, in the absence of Derek Parfitt, the ante-post favourite. In the end I pulled

---

[30] The collector of the greatest British cache of mezzotints.

[31] Whose mother had a famous affair with Graham Greene and who himself became a cutting-edge farmer of the family estate.

[32] One of the three prime locations in College.

[33] An Olympian in the 400m hurdles at Tokyo 1964 (not 2020).

[34] The set book was a volume from Winston Churchill's 'History of English Speaking People'. No objection was taken to the fact that the author was an old Harrovian. Now a different kind of objection might be made.

out of the match (for which I had trained) and came one place lower than the year before in the Rosebery (for which I hadn't) to Hugh and Edward. The half was otherwise memorable as the only time, when invited to lunch, I encountered the Provost, Claude Elliot. He announced to the assembled company that it was a day of rejoicing and we should raise our glasses, since Princess Margaret had just become engaged to Anthony Armstrong-Jones. Given the final outcome of that official liaison we may have rejoiced too soon.

But if my penultimate half left much to be desired, the same could not be said of my final half. My Magdalen demyship firmly in my pocket, I became briefly a language specialist, adding French to my S levels in Latin, and History and Russian to my A level in Ancient History, winning the Headmaster's French prize, and, as the sole candidate (like a previous winner, the controversial Tory cabinet Minister, Duncan Sandys), the Duke of Newcastle's Russian prize (the late Duke must have turned in his grave). As Captain of the School and Editor of the *Chronicle* – a post I selfishly retained for a second tour of duty – I spent much of my time on foot carrying messages for the Headmaster or on a bicycle taking copy to the *Chronicle's* printers in Slough. On the fourth of June in the procession of boats I rowed in Monarch, peopled by school grandees, and narrowly avoided immersion when the VIII had to rise and present their oars. In between I took full advantage of a glorious summer to lounge by the open-air swimming pool, then only two years old.

The high-water mark was a visit of the Queen which in the 1950s was something she made every few years since Eton was conveniently close to Windsor. In those deferential days the media regarded it as a photo opportunity rather than an occasion for class conscious criticism. As Captain of the School I was presented to her and then had to ask the entire school gathered in school yard to say three cheers for Her Majesty the Queen and Prince Philip. I managed to perform that task without mangling my words. Jonathan Aitken[35] (hereinafter Jonathan A) told me that it was then that he realised I was destined for something – quite what he did not specify.

In the last school concert of that half four senior leavers sang the Vale. It says something about the tone deafness of the other three that I was mandated to sing the third verse, musically more demanding than the others. The chorus to all four verses ends with the line 'Never forgotten shalt thou be' which I could silently pretend referred to the singer, not the school. The concert ended with the school song (not the Eton Boating song – that occupied the pre-penultimate slot in the programme) with its emotional crescendo

Donec oras Angliae

alma lux fovebit

Floreat Etona

Floreat Florebit

sung by the entire school *multissimo cum gusto*. Small wonder that old Etonians are more prone to vanity than to victimhood.

---

[35] Cabinet Minister, convict and clergyman in that order.

Finally the half came to an end. I received the usual quota of photographs, backed onto elegant cream cardboard, from other leaving contemporaries, usually in stick ups, if they were in sixth form – if I learned anything at Eton it was how to tie a bow tie – and additionally with carnations if they were in Pop. Self-indulgently and disappointingly for the recipients I had mine taken in a heavy sweater over a vest in what I thought was as close as I could get (which was not very) to a James Dean look.

My last night I never went to bed. When my mother came to collect me the next morning I left, tired and tearful, the place in which I had spent what were certainly up till then my happiest days, but conscious as I wrote in the Chronicle that I was leaving 'the security of communal life'.

Over the years my attitude to Eton has varied; like a chameleon it has adapted to its environment. At Oxford I played my connection down, even on occasion apologising for it. In my middle age I was neutral about it but would exploit it if and when the occasion presented itself. One of the Queen's Bench Masters (holders of judicial posts at the lowest rung of the High Court), Master Bickford Smith, was an old Etonian and often wore its tie. I would, appearing before him, do the same, hoping that he would say a silent snap, and favour me over my non-Old Etonian opponent. Whether this device worked I could not tell. In the 1970s the Masters were a famously eccentric bunch. Another of them travelled to the far shores of political correctness in diverging from the case in hand by references to his 'coon grandson'. *Autre temps autres moeurs* indeed.

In my last decades I came to be properly, even improperly, proud of Eton; and would seize on any excuse to revisit; I spoke at the Law Society, formed since my school days, and Wootton (philosophical) Society, already then flourishing, and once to assembled beaks at the invitation of Eric Anderson, Provost after his successful headmastership and brief sojourn as Rector of Lincoln. In a question and answer session the questions were not, Paxman-like, endlessly repeated, but rather piled one on top of the other so that I had to keep them in my head all at once before responding, an experience which served as a refresher training for being belaboured by a sequence of all but simultaneous questions from a quintet of Law Lords.

Still more recently it was decided to invite speakers to address the sixth form on the topic of the speaker's choice. I was the guinea pig for this exercise and spoke about an advocate's duties. Just as I arrived I bumped into Simon Henderson, the new headmaster and son of my old friend Giles Henderson,[36] who had shared Roman law tutorials with me at the feet of Lennie Hoffmann.[37] He told me that he was on his way to greet John Kerry[38] who was to address the whole school.

---

[36] Two-time senior partner of Slaughter and May and Master of Pembroke College, Oxford.
[37] Versatile Law Lord, whose non-disclosure of his links with Amnesty International caused a re-run of the case of General Pinochet.
[38] US Senator, Democrat candidate for the Presidency Secretary of State.

The fact that my audience reached double figures was accordingly an achievement in itself. I joined John Kerry for dessert in the Provost's lodgings, where I was staying, and enjoyed a quarter of an hour's chat with him, still apparently contemplating a possible run against Donald Trump in 2020.[39]

When I was invited (or simply decided) to put my two pennyworth in when some position in or connected with the law fell vacant, between candidates of otherwise equal merit (but are they ever?) I would regard a candidate's Etonian background as a plus rather than a minus, not least when the very status became a lazy term of abuse not only in the mouths of class warriors but even in those of the *bien pensants*. (I have learned, however, over the years, that in these kinds of selection exercises a vote against has five times the weight of a vote in favour.) I am, I readily confess, inordinately proud of my membership of Pop and have bought endless pairs of Pop socks and a couple of Pop ties, the wearing of which as charms gives me some minor psychological boost.

I was disappointed not to be asked to speak at the dinner to celebrate the half-century of those who left in 1960 – that honour went to Magnus Linklater,[40] the journalist, but was reinstated in that role when a dinner was held to celebrate the half-century of those who had come up in 1954. Even Eton recognises the benefits of keeping connection with its alumni as often as is seemly so as to tempt them into a nostalgic benefaction.

I would have loved to become a Fellow of Eton, a member of its governing body, and rejected an offer to become a governor of St Paul's in order to avoid a possible conflict of interest. One of the Fellows is chosen by the beaks. David Hirst, a Lord Justice, fulfilled that role for a substantial period and suggested my name as a candidate to succeed him. The electorate may have thought it had had a surfeit of old Colleger lawyers, and duly plumped for the Vice Chancellor of Liverpool's John Moores University, leaving me in runner-up position. My only consolation was that in third place was Oliver Letwin,[41] for a few weeks during the peak of parliamentary Brexit hysteria, the de facto leader of the country.

Another fellow is, again by tradition, the nominee of the Lord Chief Justice. When Harry Woolf became Chief I let him know of my continued ambition. But this was second time unlucky. Harry wrote to me saying that the fellowship wanted someone who was at least a High Court judge. Robert Carnwath,[42] with his usual insouciant attitude, turned down the proposal and Michael Burton was appointed. That was the only time when I had any serious regrets about not becoming a senior judge.[43]

---

[39] But now President Biden's climate change envoy.

[40] Editor of *The Scotsman*.

[41] MP, Cabinet Minister, Kt.

[42] JSC. Another delightful old sparring partner and the epitome of a laid back lawyer.

[43] A term of art to be distinguished from a top judge which is tabloid speak for any holder of judicial office, however lowly, who has committed some indiscretion, however minor.

In my all but seventh age of man I have no qualms at all about being an old Etonian and none about admitting it. A Guttenberg bible in the College library, extensive and beautiful playing fields (whether the battle of Waterloo was won there or not), an unrivalled contribution to British political history, of what could one ever have been ashamed other than to have enjoyed so many benefits shared by so few?

3

Oxford Blueless

Kings College, Cambridge, was the default destination of Eton scholars, especially classicists; and my parents thought that an Oxford home should be complemented by a Cambridge education. I was offered a place at Kings on the initiative of Noel Annan, the Provost, when I was 16, sight unseen, on the basis of my first tranche of A level results. In those days in many colleges the Heads of Houses still had the first and sometimes the only word on admissions; nowadays it would be unusual for them to have any word at all. But, somewhat riskily, I declined the offer.

My choice caused Noel Annan to write a letter to my father inquiring why I had made what was to him an inexplicable choice. But I had even then set my sights on a Union career. I had noted that the Oxford version was older, larger and better than its Cambridge equivalent (the same being true of the University). I decided to try my luck at Magdalen, Oxford, one of the six colleges where my father, once a senior Demy (scholar), eventually enjoyed dining rights and whither I duly went. Harry Mount, the journalist,[1] claimed in an article in the *Daily Telegraph* that this was an example of some form of alumni preference at play, to which I responded in a letter that, as an open Demy, I owed my admission to heredity, not nepotism (I probably meant genetics but I have an intermittent tendency to the slapdash).

Had I opted for Cambridge I would have been part of that Union generation which included so many future members of the Conservative cabinets of the Thatcher-Major era, including Leon Brittan, Norman Fowler, Ken Clarke, Michael Howard and Norman Lamont, with some of whom I debated as part of an Oxbridge touring circus in other universities in our student days and all of whom became friends, whom I entertained at Trinity.

My Demyship at Magdalen was in Modern Subjects, a curious title for an examination which consisted of papers in Latin and Mediaeval History. At the time of the mandatory interview I had bronchitis. The Fellows kept their distance for fear of infection. It is possible that they gave a charitable interpretation to those of my croaked answers that they could actually hear. The family was on a skiing holiday in Switzerland when the news of my award arrived by telegram, prompting my father, a lover of both puns and Proust, to say that I was now a demi-madeleine.

The Oxford of the early 1960s was still a predominantly undergraduate university. There was a divide between those who had two years' national service behind

[1] The editor of *The Oldie*.

them – involuntary gap years – and those, like I, fresh out of school. The 'working class boy at Oxford' was a species anatomised both internally and externally. With grammar schools still at their nationwide peak, ex public schoolboys had to contest on equal terms for the prizes in Oxford's cornucopia. The onlooker could not always distinguish between the provenance of those who wore cavalry twill or tweed or of those who, like I, wore suedette jackets and jeans. Jonathan A told me after a meeting with the Queen that she asked him whether the University was now mixed. He took this to refer to a melange of classes rather than races since Oxford's constituency was still overwhelmingly white of hue.

Women were a minority part of the student population located in the five women's colleges. How exceptional in terms of intellect that group must have been! Though Philip Larkin said that sex was only discovered in 1963, there was a certain amount of it around earlier than that, even in face of restrictive rules underpinning a college quasi-curfew. When a St Hilda's student or Hildebeast was sent down for being found with a man in her bedroom after hours, the campaign for her reinstatement was led by Tyrone Fernando.[2]

It was a generation to whom political debate was important. Since Oxford students anticipated little difficulty in finding gainful employment after graduation (BBC traineeships and advertising being favoured flavours) there was more scope for other than self-centred activity. Then, as now, the two major parties were split; the leftish Tories in the Oxford University Conservative Association (OUCA) joined the Blue Ribbon club – a spin-off of the Bow group founded by Cantab Geoffrey Howe; left-wing Labourites aligned themselves with the New Left and the Campaign for Nuclear Disarmament (CND)[3] in opposition to the mainstream Gaitskellites. The standard-bearer for the latter was Brian Walden,[4] whose crown was inherited by Bob Skidelsky,[5] and for the former Dennis Potter,[6] whose crown was inherited by Paul Foot.[7] No platforming was a future phenomenon but I deplored, in a memorandum, its predecessor, a tendency which I described a little loosely as 'left wing McCarthyism'[8] to shout down rather than to challenge speakers of opposite views to the shouter.[9]

Those who wished to speak others' lines rather than their own found a traditional home in OUDS (the Oxford University Dramatic Society). The most

---

[2] Foreign Secretary of Sri Lanka, the foreword to whose autobiography *Winds for Fire* I wrote at his request.

[3] Rip Bulkeley, a contemporary of that persuasion, in 2017 wrote a pamphlet 'Wrong-Righting Years: Memoirs of the 1960s Oxford Left', many of whom appeared from its pages to have lost none of their radical zeal over the years. Not all youthful socialists become hedge fund managers in the fulness of time – or even QCs.

[4] MP and television inquisitor.

[5] Biographer of Mosley and Keynes and a Peer via the SDP, a Tory and later a cross-bencher.

[6] TV dramatist.

[7] Campaigning journalist.

[8] Christopher Hollis *The Oxford Union* (Hollis, 1965) p.26.

[9] I remain unrepentantly of that opinion.

memorable production in my time was *Twelfth Night* directed by Michael Rudman, whose cast included, amongst future professional thespians, Michael York (then Johnson) famously clothed in many Hollywood films and Annabel Leventon, famously unclothed on the stage in Kenneth Tynan's *Hair*, as well as Paul Collins who became a circuit judge and waxed lyrical about fighting soups. Those who wished to write rather than speak could choose between Isis and Cherwell. Of my generation Simon Jenkins became editor of the *Times* and Nick Lloyd editor of the *Daily Express*, both of whom were knighted for their services to journalism, and Peter Grimsditch editor of the *Daily Star*, who was not. At a time when, unlike the present, sport as well as scholarship could be a passport to admission, the University boasted internationals such as Stuart Wilson (rugby for Scotland) and the Nawab of Pataudi (cricket for India).

When I came up to Magdalen in 1960, I had exaggerated ambitions for a triple crown blue – then awarded to all members of University teams in major sports, a first then awarded to a small fraction of examinees in final examinations, as well as the Presidency of the Union, then – as now – elected by its members. I was swiftly reminded that my athletic aspirations exceeded my abilities. On my second night I met the Captain of the college team in company with another fresher (previously unknown to me) who reeled off times of a quite different order to mine. He was Adrian Metcalfe, in 1963 the best 400 metre runner in the world and a relay silver medallist at the first Tokyo Olympics. As a result of this meeting the focus of my attention quickly moved from Iffley Road to the Union Bar.

The President of Magdalen was Tom Boase, aptly described by one memorialist as 'the very picture of a English mandarin – tall, silver haired, charming, cultured and witty',[10] a bachelor art historian, rumoured to be the lover of the celebrated actress and beauty Peggy Ashcroft which seemed implausible for at least two reasons. He was the antithesis of a hands-on Head of House which I later tried to become, and I have no recollection of him but the visual with a very little audio thrown in.

Magdalen had its own environmental charms. As a scholar I had the luxury of all three years in a suite of rooms in Longwall quad with the deer park visible from the rear window. On the same floor was Pete Bocock, a brilliant Carthusian,[11] who, an owl, used to retire at approximately the time as I, a lark, rose, enabling us to share the bathroom situated between our rooms without border skirmishes. Given my Union ambitions my social life was mainly spent outside Magdalen, though I happened to be in the College buttery when Richard Burton strolled in with Elizabeth Taylor – they were performing *Faust* at the Playhouse in which the latter's role needed no words to attract wide eyed attention. News of that celebrity couple's visit spread around by word of mouth with a speed which Marconi would have admired.

---

[10] RW Johnson *Look Back in Laughter: Oxford's Postwar Golden Age* (Johnson, 2015) p 8.
[11] Who after his PPE first worked for the World Bank. He nicknamed me Jowls for no very obvious reason.

At Magdalen I overlapped with some future-to-be notables particularly from the USA: Les Aspin in charge of the Pentagon in the first Clinton administration, David Souter and Stephen Breyer, Supreme Court justices. Stephen took time out to woo and wed Joanna Hare the strikingly beautiful and clever daughter of Viscount Blakenham[12] to the chagrin of her many English admirers. Many years later they entertained me to dinner in their fashionable Georgetown residence. One of the historians in the year above me was Adam Roberts, then a spokesman for unilateral nuclear disarmament, later knighted as President of the British Academy; from CND to KBE.

I became a member of the Gridiron Club (the Grid). My ancestry fell far short of that which would have made me eligible for the Bullingdon. To expand Alan Clark's famous put down of Michael Heseltine, not only would I be the sort of person who bought his own furniture, but I would have had to do so on HP. I also became through Jeffrey's good offices, a member of Vincents, the Blues club though not myself a Blue, which gave me inordinate pleasure precisely because of my lack of perceptible entitlement.[13] Over the succeeding years I wore out a series of its elegant ties – silver crowns on a dark blue background.

I was told, when elected, that if ever when in some far-away country I found myself short of the currency equivalent of a bob or two, I could successfully tap anyone with similar neckwear for the necessary. I never needed to find out if this was true, but once when litigating in Hong Kong, I was taken aback to be asked by a stranger, who had spotted the tie, for the 'match result'. I had forgotten, if I ever knew, that it was the day after the rugby blues encounter at Twickenham. I had my final comeuppance when I was the guest speaker at the club's annual dinner in 2015. This was the only time on which, in a life of serial speechifying, I have ever had to cut short my remarks because of barracking by a heckler so drunk as to be immune to my increasingly agitated repartee.[14]

I was taught history by Karl Leyser, Bruce MacFarlane and AJP Taylor, an illustrious trio – Karl was a magnetic lecturer on matters mediaeval. He was at the time courting Henrietta, herself later an history fellow of quality. Occasionally en route to St Hilda's for purely platonic purposes I would pass Karl under a lamppost whispering sweet nothings into her ear with my eyes self-consciously averted. Bruce, another medievalist, was a bachelor constantly accompanied by a Siamese cat, and unknown to me at the time, a Marxist.[15] He, like Lord Acton, knew much and published little so that his tutorials gave his tutees privileged access to his learning. AJP was a modernist, a celebrity and the ultimate teledon who lectured in one of the larger rooms in Examination Schools at what for undergraduates was the challenging hour of 9am without ever imperilling his chances of a full house.

---

[12] Tory politician and Chairman of the Party.

[13] This excited envy from no lesser a legal figure than my old sparring partner when he was at the bar, JSC Lord Simon Brown, *Second Helpings* (Brown, 2021) p.17.

[14] In speaking at the end of the 1960s at the Nottingham University Law Society at a graveyard slot between dinner and dance I simply shouted back to the aspirant Fred Astaires and Ginger Rogerses.

[15] Johnson (Johnson, 2015) p 89.

At the end of my first year, I won the university HWC Davis prize for history, recycling yet again a version of my unoriginal thoughts on the decline of the Carolingian empire, a staple which served me from O levels to Finals. I took tea with Davis's widow and robustly resisted the blandishments of Hugh Trevor-Roper[16] to yield up part of my monetary award which, because of the vagaries of investment, was in excess of the standard annual sum. This unexpected success coupled with my plotting of an upward trajectory in the Union led to a limit – how can I put this delicately? – on the hours I devoted to my studies. I was only galvanised into action when AJP at the end of my second year, at Presidential Collections (which then involved marching up the length of hall to a high table populated by almost the entire fellowship), delivered himself of a verdict Tacitean in its brevity and irony – 'Mr Beloff would doubtless have done a good term's work – PAUSE – had he done any work at all'. Indeed, in a letter of congratulations on my result in Finals he wrote perspicaciously 'I can claim some credit for it, not by teaching you anything but by giving you a fright'.

In Finals, where I placed second or third in the University (the chairman of the examiners, Professor Southern, having marginally changed his assessment in two letters to Macfarlane) my marks described a straight linear decline from first to last paper. This reflected not any decrease in interest in or knowledge of the topics examined, but rather a growing weariness in dealing with two papers a day. Many of my scripts were illegible. While others of my peer group enjoyed their post-finals frolics, I had the miserable experience of having to read aloud large chunks of what I had written to be typed up under the controlled supervision of some modestly remunerated junior don. Finals adventitiously coincided with the destruction of the political career of John Profumo.[17] I consoled myself with the thought that at least someone was under worse pressure than I.

I've never regretted my history degree,[18] but I resisted the momentary lure of embarking on further research. I was no true scholar, merely a good examinee. Knowledge of the past may not be necessary to an understanding of the law – though as the likes of Tom Bingham and Jonathan Sumption[19] (hereinafter Jonathan S) proving useful in that sphere too – but is necessary to an understanding of the present. In purely professional terms it led to three early sets of instructions through the good offices of Humphrey Waldock, an All Souls' colleague of my father,[20] which required the skills of an historian rather than of a lawyer.

The first concerned the boundary dispute between Venezuela and Guyana, over a piece of land that makes up two-thirds of Guyana's territory – the Esequibo region – owned by the Spanish since colonisation, but to which both Venezuela and Great Britain – who ruled Guyana at the time – laid claim. In 1897, the two

---

[16] Lord Dacre, Regius Professor, Master of Peterhouse and the dupe of Hitler's faked diaries.
[17] Secretary of State for War. Lover of Christine Keeler.
[18] It also explains my fondness for footnotes both in this book and in my legal opinions.
[19] JSC, author of the multi-volume *100 Years War* and the Reith lecturer in 2019.
[20] Chichele Professor of International Law, and President of the ECtHR Kt.

countries agreed to an arbitration committee, which defined the border between the two countries, attributing the majority of the region to Guyana. One of Venezuela's lawyers, in a memorandum published only posthumously, suggested the agreement was the result of a political deal between Great Britain and Russia, a theory with some support in material in the public domain.

I was instructed by Charles Russell & Co on behalf of the Government of Guyana together with Waldock and Sir Francis Vallatt.[21] My task was to ascertain what, if any, further evidence from any surviving public or private records of the major players there was to suggest dirty work at the crossroads. Over drinks in the Reform Club,[22] AJP gave me a steer. One potentially relevant cache of documents was located in Christ Church library. In signing the book in which temporary users' names had to be inscribed I found that I was following in the footsteps of another researcher, acting on behalf of the Venezuelan government into the very same issue.

The two knights paid a site visit to the disputed boundary accompanied by our senior clerk but not, alas, by their junior. I did, however, make the acquaintance of Sonny Ramphal, then Guyana's Attorney General who later became Secretary-General of the Commonwealth. When Treasurer of Gray's Inn, of which he was an honorary bencher, I made a speech at Marlborough House to celebrate the publication of a book in honour of his eightieth birthday. Just after my speech a member of the audience collapsed. As I yielded the podium to the next speaker, David Steel,[23] I whispered a sincere good luck.

I was next instructed by the FCO to investigate the extent of the territory of Gibraltar ceded by Spain to Great Britain in the Treaty of Utrecht in 1713. For this I had to delve not only into the Foreign Office documents, but also the French archives in the Quai d'Orsay in Paris.

Both of these long-standing disputes remains unresolved to this day and will doubtless provide much work for lawyers – though not, I suspect, for historians – in the future.

The third brief owed more to the fact that I was an anglophone rather than just a graduate in history and law. I was asked to check for accuracy the English submissions of Eduardo Jiménez de Aréchaga,[24] an advocate in the Barcelona Traction case at the International Court of Justice (ICJ) at the Hague, which concerned abuse of rights in a complex commercial context and pitted Belgium against Spain. de Aréchaga, an Uruguayan, thought it better to address the Court in English but was uncertain of his command of English legal idiom. Billeted in an agreeable hotel in Scheveningen, I worked with him in the morning and used the

---

[21] Former legal adviser to the Foreign Office.
[22] Of which my father had put me up for student membership. Later I attended a unique lunch for those who had scored a half-century of membership. I also became a member of its Political Committee.
[23] Leader of the Liberal Party.
[24] Later a Judge himself of the ICJ.

afternoons to explore the various historic cities with stations on the Amsterdam-Rotterdam railway.

Attending the Court to observe the implementation of my labours, I encountered on its steps Dr Francis Mann,[25] who had occasionally instructed my pupil master and who greeted me as if I were an old friend. The pleasure I felt from recognition by this legendary solicitor reminded me to display a similar, if less memorable, courtesy to young lawyers when I myself graduated to senior ranks.

During my time as a history student, I steadily climbed the Union ladder. I was not by any stretch of the imagination the most glamorous of my year group. That palm would be indubitably awarded to Wynford Hicks, a striking figure with auburn locks whose looks enabled Jeremy Thorpe[26] in a debate to refer to him as 'the Honourable member from Oberammergau'. His reputation was such that one could gain a passport to almost any party of the 'bring a bird and a bottle' variety by uttering the magic mantra 'I am part of Wynford Hicks' entourage'. He proclaimed grandly that he came to Oxford to make history, not to read it, giving proof of the second part of that statement by being temporarily rusticated for failing his prelims. Had his rhetorical skills matched his physical presence he would undoubtedly have preceded me in the President's chair. Years later, when Charlotte Fawcett/Wahl, artist and Boris Johnson's mother, was interviewed in Tatler she recalled that she had been one of his girlfriends, adding the fatal post-script 'He was extremely handsome but ... rather boring ...'. Wynford next floated into my consciousness as a writer on the *Radio Times* with a piece entitled 'Why the Indian cricketers are welcome', a somewhat low-key enterprise for a sometime charismatic anarchist. *Sic transit gloria universitatis.*

After my first paper speech the veteran *Oxford Mail* reporter John Owen wrote that I might emulate my father, himself an ex-Librarian of the Society. I duly became Secretary. With the assistance of three young dons, Uwe Kitzinger,[27] David Butler and David Shapiro,[28] a brains trust produced by Max, I successfully fended off a speculative challenge by my defeated rival Noel Picarda,[29] advanced on the peculiar ground that I had broken the rules against canvassing by showing his, not my, photograph to some of my friends. Next, I became Librarian. (In the Union the Librarian is senior to Treasurer, books taking precedence over banknotes.) So, I seemed destined to take the final step without difficulty.

However, before submitting myself to the electorate a choice had to be made of the motion for the Presidential debate by the contenders. My opponent

[25] Partner in Herbert Smith; author of the *The Legal Aspect of Money* (Mann, 1938).
[26] Another (ill fated) Leader of the Liberal Party.
[27] First President of Templeton College Oxford.
[28] A political scientist.
[29] Mimic (especially of a Pyrrenian bus driver) and Liberal party candidate, quite unlike his scholarly brother Hubert, expert on the law of charities, whom I was one day to lead in the House of Lords in a case about the Visitatorial Jurisdiction [1993] AC 682.

John McDonnell[30] was a Roman Catholic. I had associated myself in my previous speeches with three then-fashionable liberal causes, the abolition of capital punishment, the decriminalisation of male homosexual acts and abortion law reform (though I had been refused permission to address the all-female Somerville students on the last of those topics). It seemed appropriate as well as politically shrewd for me to attack the Catholic church's opposition to the latter two, despite the advice of Lord Longford,[31] to whom my father had introduced me in the hope that he would dissuade me from entering into the dangerous territory of a religious debate. John swept me aside with a passionate speech in which he uttered the unforgettable line 'I could say – to hell with the Pope'. This salutary experience taught me the need, if not necessarily to believe in what one said, at least to seem as if one did.

But next term against less formidable opposition, including Wynford, I had a relatively easy victory[32] of which I learned at a Canning Club dinner in the Elizabeth, then Oxford's best restaurant, long since closed down. I inherited the coveted office at the top of the Union building, use of its telephone, a budget for filling the term's card and since my Presidency fell in the Michaelmas term, a long vacation in which to woo prospective speakers.[33] My list, when pricked, was given cautious approval by Simon Jenkins, then editor of *Cherwell*.[34] It was only in later years that the Union's guests were offered the easier option of making prepared speeches rather than actually debating.

For the debate which took place once a week on a Thursday, I gratuitously altered the traditional layout of the term card – a variation which did not survive me. The usual formula for speeches was two undergraduates followed by only two guest speakers before the motion was thrown open to the floor. The first debate of a Michaelmas term, as always on the motion 'This House has no confidence in Her Majesty's Government',[35] pitted Dick Crossman[36] against Bill Deedes.[37] In my farewell debate the main speakers were Jo Grimond, my father and Brian Pollitt, my Cambridge opposite number, son of the Communist party leader Harry Pollitt,

---

[30] A QC.

[31] Labour Cabinet Minister, prison reformer. Caricatured as 'Lord Porn'.

[32] In Brockliss's *Magdalen College, a History* (Brockliss, 2008) my election was implausibly referenced as, inter alia, an example of the College's transformation from a sporting to a serious institution, p 661.

[33] Today those elected President take a year's sabbatical because of the increase in the Presidential workload.

[34] My Isis profile, which demotically called me Mike and was illustrated by a photograph which showed that I was still trying unavailingly to look like James Dean, stated 'Nobody can deny that he fits the part perfectly; there is certainly nobody in sight more eligible for his chair'. Invited to a debate in 2021 by the Union's first Chinese President I told him that it was 60 years since my own Presidency. This he announced to the House to warm applause. To my embarrassment I realized afterwards that it was only 59 years but decided not to rectify the mistake — an option not available to the honest advocate who must never mislead a Court.

[35] In the 1960s it was always mano a mano between two front benchers. In 1997 it proved impossible to procure a Cabinet Minister to defend the new elected Blair administration. Why spoil a national electoral victory by risking a defeat in the Oxford Union? Control was the other side of the coin of spin.

[36] Labour Cabinet Minister and diarist.

[37] Tory Cabinet Minister and journalist.

an exotic red bloom in an otherwise wholly blue Cambridge garden. (Osbert Lancaster, cartoonist, the fourth of the planned quartet was cut off by fog, still a meteorological hazard on the roads from London to Oxford.).

I was followed as President by Girish Karnad,[38] a Rhodes scholar contemporary at Magdalen. His popularity was such that he was unopposed. During his term I successfully moved the admission of women to full membership of the Union,[39] despite the opposition of traditionalists, a combination of old-fashioned Tories and equally old-fashioned Labour chauvinists[40] (the lead speaker for their cause had a later career in one of the larger Trades Unions). Fifty years on I was the only man allowed to speak in a debate to celebrate that breakthrough alongside the likes of Tessa Jowell,[41] Rachel Johnston[42] and Edwina Currie[43] – a recording of which found its way into the video entertainment provided in BA business class.

One by-product of Union office was a series of invitations to speak at other unions. I spoke at a debate in Cambridge to mark the fortieth anniversary of Rab Butler's Presidency.[44] The honorand was by then Master of Trinity whose partially withered hand I had shyly to shake. It was at the Cambridge Union that, during a debate on contraception, a student interrupted my speech on a point of information, that male contraceptives had a failure rate of 1 in 10,000. My impromptu retort was 'We are indeed fortunate to have the honourable member with us in the house tonight'. Oh well, it sounded good at the time.

At a dinner at King's College, London, the Queen Mother, Chancellor, was the guest of honour. I opened my speech by saying that this was obviously a significant occasion and, when my observation was greeted with loud and loyal applause, added 'I'm glad to see that you all regard my visit as being as important as I do myself'. This act of impudent *lèse majesté* did not result – as it might have in earlier times – in my incarceration in the Tower.

I was increasingly typecast as a humorous not a serious speaker, noted most for my juvenile cracks at the expense of my Union contemporaries.

Sir George Young is well known for his chevalierie – a French word meaning horseplay.

One of Jonathan Aitken's girlfriends said to another; 'Doesn't he dress well' – to which the other replied 'yes and quickly too'.

Tariq Ali has just cut his first disc – thirty-three revolutions per minute.

I became in the late 1960s a regular performer at the annual eights week debate – a summer frivolity which brought on the clowns – in the company of such new

---

[38] India's most renowned modern playwright, and an extremely handsome man who starred in Bollywood movies in order to finance his writing career, and whom I met again when he took up a post as Director of the Nehru centre in London.

[39] A cause espoused a generation earlier by my father. (Hollis, 1965) p 198.

[40] Tariq Ali in his memoir *Street Fighting Years: An Autobiography of the Sixties* (Ali, 2005) refers to it as 'a long and often bitter struggle', p 34.

[41] Popular Blairite Cabinet Minister who died early of cancer.

[42] Writer and Boris's sister.

[43] Minister, author and John Major's mistress.

[44] Rab, a serial Tory Minister, was twice passed over as Leader of the Party.

breed satirists as Richard Ingrams, John Wells and Willie Rushton of the *TWTW*, *Private Eye* generation, until succeeded as court jester in (or out of) residence by Gyles Brandreth.[45] I passed the mantle to Gyles with what he decided was his second favourite well-wishing note 'Congratulations on your election to the Presidency – a revaluation of the currency – if anyone can turn the Union's dance macabre into a frug, you can'.[46] Whether he achieved such terpsichorean transformation I do not know, but Gyles himself became a man of many parts from wit (permanent) to Whip (temporary).

When my brother became President in 1966 he invited Diana Rigg,[47] famous for her role as the stunningly attractive Emma Peel in TV's *The Avengers*, to speak in eights week debate. She agreed on condition that someone explained to her the format. I was willingly cast as the messenger and visited her in her cottage near Stratford-on-Avon where she was in Shakespearean repertory at the theatre. She took little, if any, note of my advice and was a *succès fou* on the night in question, her appearance being greeted by a shout from a member of the audience 'don't say anything just stand there'. The Union's own it-girls Edwina and Ann Widdecombe,[48] then a fey and slender figure, were temporarily relegated to the shadows.

Appointed on my return to Trinity[49] in 1996 to the Oxford Literary and Debating Union Trust (OLDUT), a supervisory body for the Union required by Charity law,[50] I helped the then President organise the 175th anniversary debate in 1997, while masquerading as the Senior Trustee. I spoke with my father, Patrick Mayhew,[51] Peter Jay, Kenneth Baker,[52] Ann Widdecombe, Boris Johnson and Sir Robin Day,[53] placing Jeffrey last on the order paper in the anticipation, fully vindicated in the event, that he was the one person in that *galere* to ensure that only those with an unendurable thirst or overwhelming essay crisis would be prompted to leave before he performed.

Boris was captured in the team photograph taken before we entered the hall characteristically scribbling notes for his speech at the last moment on a student's shoulder. Immediately after we left it he dictated a piece for the *Daily Telegraph* in which he referred to my 'rapturously received gags' which may have been better

---

[45] In his diary *Something Sensational to Read in the Train: The Diary of a Lifetime* (Brandreth, 2009) p 164 he describes one 'Funny (sic) debate in which we appeared with, among others, James Robertson Justice before a sticky (sic) house'.

[46] Ibid, p 198.

[47] Actress in many media and a Dame.

[48] MP, Shadow Home Secretary and nicknamed Doris Karloff for her views on crime and punishment.

[49] The noun 'return' will be explained in chapter 6 'Transition to Trinity'.

[50] On which I served for 25 years representing at the end not only the older but the obsolete generation. I declined in 2020 a bipartisan invitation to chair an inquiry into how to reform the Union to bring it into line with diversity best practice in the wake of an incident in which a blind black student was controversially removed from the debating chamber. I had no desire to be caught unnecessarily in the crossfire of the contemporary culture wars.

[51] Attorney-General, Secretary of State for Northern Ireland.

[52] Home Secretary, Chairman of the Conservative Party.

[53] In his memoir *Speaking for Myself* (Day, 1999) he describes the debate and quotes his entire speech for good measure, ch 40.

for his improved misquotation.[54] (I had described Jeffrey as the sprinter's error, not terror, though maybe he was both.) Boris also wrote a letter thanking me 'for inveigling (me) into much more distinguished company for the debate'. Not so fast Boris. The company may have been more distinguished then, but in the fulness of time as PM you overtook them all.

The Union was a laboratory in which I could test my forensic skills. I have always valued my connection with it, though I never indulged in the habit of addressing even outside the chamber someone by reference to an office held within it, for example 'The Honourable ex-treasurer from Lincoln and St Anthony's' in a remote simulation of the way MPs refer to each other in the Commons. (This affectionate affectation was often deployed by those such as Robin Day, Peter Jay or Tony Howard who never achieved that status.[55])

Between my first act as a historian and my second as a lawyer I represented the Union on the biennial debating tour in the USA sponsored by the English-Speaking Union.[56] My co-debater was Jonathan A.[57] We started our adventures at McGill in Montreal (no dear reader, I do know that Montreal is not in the USA) visiting in all 38 campuses, east of the Mississippi, and one prison, where one of our opponents – we were not told which – was serving a life sentence for the murder of his girlfriend. Another said jokingly that we might win the debate, but we would not win the fight afterwards (at least we thought he was joking).

We endured early mornings, late nights and endless hedge-hopping in small propeller-powered aircraft, trying to give our hosts their money's worth in the debates and to keep a fixed smile on our faces at the associated social occasions.

The format of campus debating, which allowed for cross-examination and rebuttals as well as opening statements, was closer to courtroom than to Commons advocacy. The last few months of 1964 were a period impregnated with politics. Harold Wilson had just been elected Prime Minister for the first time. Lyndon Johnson was battling to secure the Presidency in his own right. We attended rallies by Barry Goldwater seeking to depose him, and Bobby Kennedy running for Senate in New York hoping to succeed him. I shook hands in Manhattan with John Lindsay, a New York mayoral candidate, who mistook me for a resident voter. But the topics for debate were themselves prudently designed to avoid domestic political controversy.

As reflected in the high-level electoral contests, the USA was experiencing the first tremors of a decade of troubles. The civil rights movement was gathering steam. We faced one significant dilemma. Our programme included a visit to Mississippi State, which was still, though we had not been told in advance, a segregated university. What to do to square courtesy with conscience? We fashioned

---

[54] Issue of 27 June 1998.

[55] Editor of the *New Statesman*.

[56] It was some consolation for having to pull out of a televised debate in New York through an inconvenient bout of tonsillitis to be replaced by George Young.

[57] Which prompted an understandable comment in the student press and *Private Eye* that two old Etonians were not appropriate ambassadors for Oxford.

a compromise. We participated in the scheduled debate but made an opening statement that 'our visit did not, in any way, express approval of the policies of segregation'. We also debated at Hampton University Virginia, a private historically black research institution founded in 1868 after the American Civil War to provide education to freedmen.

Seeing our role as being to entertain[58] we skated carefully above the surface of events which we sought nonetheless to absorb. Despite the exhaustion, the whistle-stop tour was one of my formative experiences. We were encouraged by literary agent Graham Watson, of Curtis Brown, to turn those experiences into a book, entitled *A Short Walk on the Campus*, of which we sold the serial rights to the *Sunday Telegraph*. Much of the drafting was done at Playford Hall, Jonathan's moated family home where I spent several entrancing holidays, sometimes accompanied by girlfriends, not all of whom were immune to his charms. He was indeed the playboy of Playford as well as already a rising figure in Tory party.

The book had mixed reviews both sides of the Atlantic. The *New York Times* wrote 'We would have liked them more had they perhaps liked themselves less' (hmmm), but Jonathan's contacts in the high Tory establishment procured an endorsement in the *Daily Mail* that we were 'consistently funny and frighteningly able' from Ian MacLeod, the future Chancellor, whose premature death severely wounded the Heath government. It was Jonathan who embarked on a successful career as author and journalist (as well as other things of which more later, though there is no need, on reflection, to anticipate his later doings, if I chose to do so, with the cautionary spoiler alert). Nonetheless at that stage we agreed a role-reversing last sentence of the preface. 'There is always a difficulty in writing a book with two authors and Michael would like to take this opportunity of thanking Jonathan for his help with the punctuation'.

I had indeed some pretensions of my own as a scribbler. I had presented myself in my first term to the office of *Isis*, the weekly magazine whose horizons stretched beyond the University (*Cherwell* was a newspaper more focussed on University affairs). *Isis* was edited by Paul Foot, another member of the famous Foot tribe, already a radical,[59] and after him by the Earl of Gowrie, my old Eton patron, who employed me as a theatre critic and even art reviewer.

In my last year of my first degree the editor was Michael Wilding.[60] He accorded me the luxury of a weekly column under the soubriquet Diogenes[61] in which I gave currency to some worthy sentiments, a little, but not excessively, left of centre, on the good brave causes of the day. For *Cherwell* I briefly wrote on matters athletic with Jeffrey, something we reprised in the *Observer* for the Olympics of

---

[58] David Walter, *The Oxford Union* (Walter, 1984) 'Michael Beloff cracked insults in the mainstream tradition of Unionites. He and Aitken developed an elaborate routine of exchanging slurs', p 182.

[59] A prize-winning journalist and polemical author.

[60] Novelist and Professor of English at the University of Sydney.

[61] Which I later recycled when I wrote a column on matters legal for the journal *New Society* edited by Paul Barker.

1968 where our contributions dwindled to a trickle before totally evaporating. Much influenced by my Aunt Nora, I once toyed with the idea of a career in Fleet Street – but I did not have the thick skin and sturdy liver, which appeared to be the essential qualifications of a successful journalist.

More superficially plausible was a political career. Answering questions put to me by the author of my *Isis* profile I said 'At Eton I was a meritocratic conservative; now I suppose you could describe me as a non-aligned radical. I shall probably go into politics; I don't know which party I shall join, Labour or Liberal', adding, somewhat embarrassingly, 'it will depend upon the image they offer'. Motto – always insist on checking the proofs! I did not formally align myself at university with any political faction, preferring to float between party lines, although temporarily beguiled by Wynford's advocacy into seeing the charms of anarchy, if in a purely theoretical sense.[62] My only formal commitment was service on the committee of the Liberal Club along with Paul Tyler.[63] As a member of the (Conservative) Canning Club, in 2019 I attended a resurrected reunion dinner in Lincoln's Inn addressed by Dominic Grieve[64] who was himself introduced by Michael Gove[65] – a piquant combination given that each was on opposite sides of Brexit – the great issue of that year.

Compared to me the Vicar of Bray was a model of consistency. I called myself as a socialist on the back cover of *A Short Walk on the Campus* and was indeed for a brief time a member of the Labour party (lapsed by the turn of the decade). I spent a couple of weeks, which I hugely enjoyed, canvassing for Brian Walden, then MP for Birmingham All Saints in the general election of 1966. In an eve of poll speech, at the Bullring, George Brown, then the party's deputy leader, alluded in terms which were hardly circumspect – it was not his style – to Ted Heath's assumed sexual proclivities, exciting wild applause from the packed auditorium. Brian explained to me that there were only two forces which motivated the electorate, which he articulated in his rasping Midlands accent as 'greed and fear'.

It was not, however, that somewhat disillusioning sentiment which decided me against embarking on such a perilous route. It was rather that, of the essential qualities for a successful political career, I lacked two – courage and conviction. The three political slogans I most admire are Cicero's 'Salus reipublicae suprema lex', Lyndon Johnson's, 'I'm in favour of a great many things and against mighty few' and General de Gaulle's enigmatic observation to opponents of his Algerian policy 'Je vous ai compris', but the second and third may in practice be incompatible.

In switching to read for a second degree in law I cannot pretend that I was enraptured by romantic tales of the great advocates or even by legal soaps. But

---

[62] Only Rip Van Winkles can retain the passionate radicalism of their student days. The saying that the only two certainties are death and taxes ignores the third which is that the young will, tragedy aside, grow old.

[63] Liberal MP and peer.

[64] Attorney-General Kt.

[65] Holder of various Cabinet posts.

the funds were available, the state scholarship extended, and I was happy to enjoy the prospect of a further five terms, amid the dreaming spires, now with home comforts. As for the soaps, I did at least share the postprandial stage with Michael Dennison (Boyd QC) at a law society dinner at Keble which had the unique distinction of having as its law fellows Peter North,[66] who later became Vice Chancellor of Oxford University, and David Williams,[67] who became the equivalent at Cambridge.

My law tutors were, were that possible, a still more distinguished trio than my History ones: John Morris, a towering great red-faced mountain of a man of conservative views and a fierce manner,[68] master of two of the most complex of legal subjects, conflict of laws and the rule against perpetuities; the blind Rupert Cross, whose vigorous realism betrayed no sign of his disability; and Gunter Treitel. The last two became holders of the Vinerian Chair, the most prestigious law chair in Oxford. The first, even more impressively, had turned the chair down. At a fund-raising dinner for another Magdalen Law fellowship I likened them to the Manchester United *force de frappe* of the late 1960s, Law, Best, Charlton. I was farmed out to Lenny Hoffmann for Roman law together with Giles Henderson. By happenstance Lennie became a law lord at the same time as I was elected as President of Trinity and Giles became senior partner of Slaughter and May, so I hosted a dinner for the trio ensuring that it was mentioned in *The Times* legal gossip column. Why let the opportunity for gratuitous publicity go to waste?

I was glad that I did spend a little time in the academic study of law with its opportunity to learn about the principles and pedigree of modern legal rules. It was a bonus if not a bedrock for a barrister-to-be and gave me at any rate in theory a head start over others, who had come straight into the law from other disciplines. However, once in practice I appreciated why such essential and necessarily front-loaded elements of the law of contract, offer and acceptance, consideration, infants (sic), virtually never featured in actual litigation, which was more often concerned with subjects which just missed the cut of an eight-week term such as remedies. Clients are interested chiefly in who gets what rather than why.

At the same time as I was dipping my toe in the waters of tort law I was travelling on a bus whose automatic doors closed on a passenger trying to leave. As a result he was dragged a few feet along the pavement. He suffered no injury but the driver was charged with careless driving. I had no more than five minutes after the accident written a note of what I thought I had seen and was duly called as a witness for the prosecution. There were uncertainties in the details in my note, though not enough for the driver to avoid conviction.[69] An appreciation, born of

---

[66] A specialist in Private International Law, Principal of Jesus, at whose seventieth birthday party in the Inner Temple I spoke.

[67] A constitutional lawyer, President of Wolfson (Cambridge) and to whose festschrift I contributed a chapter.

[68] (Johnson, 2015) p 66. Oddly we took silk on the same day!

[69] I later wrote a column in *New Society* about the incident that featured in the first edition of Michael Zander's *Cases and Materials on the English Legal System* but was culled from later editions.

this experience of how fragile is human memory about sudden events is something I carried forward with me to both bar and bench.

I was vivaed for a first in law but was disconsolate, although not surprised, by my failure to get over the line.[70] My plea in mitigation had two strands, one honourable, one not. I had done a nine-term course in five terms (honourable). But suffering from more than my usual bout of insomnia, aggravated by exam stress, I took an amphetamine pill, prescribed for my mother's aged mother. This gave me the illusion, but without the substance, of writing a brilliant paper in Jurisprudence (dishonourable). I grinned, like the poster of Jack Nicholson in *The Shining*, at Giles Henderson sitting a few rows back. Jurisprudence was my worst paper – though it should in theory have been my best.

In anticipation of Magdalen's 550th anniversary in 1998, I proposed to David Clary, the then President, that, as part of its fundraising, the College should exploit the presence amongst its alumni of two US Supreme Court Justices and the Senior Law Lord, Nicolas Browne-Wilkinson, to form an incomparable Tribunal to judge a moot. Jonathan S and I, both also alumni, could lead two Magdalen students. The cast list was duly assembled. The moot took place in Magdalen's newest auditorium. Gunter Treitel, the only survivor of my three law tutors, was an honoured guest.

Scrolling back in time and sideways to the other college which bulks large in my career, my first contact with Trinity was as accidental as it was in the long run fortunate.[71] Rupert Cross had persuaded Trinity to engage me as a temporary tutor; which Michael Maclagan, history fellow and Richmond Herald, told me could be 'dignified by the title Lecturer in Law'. (The vacancy occurred because the College's appointee to a vacant law fellowship, Alan Milner,[72] was unable to take up his post in succession to the departing John Kelly[73] for another year.) If my failure to achieve a first somewhat impaired its dignity, no effort was made to gazump me by a better appointment, so, with a bare five terms of a law degree under my belt, away I went – sometimes just ahead of my pupils, sometimes just behind.

I spent an enjoyable year in a cramped pair of rooms at the top of a staircase in Dolphin Yard, teaching six or so undergraduates. (Two became QCs, two Professors of Law and did not suffer overmuch from my tuition. One of them, Robert Engelhart,[74] later joined me in Blackstone chambers.).

---

[70] I wrongly suggested in a brief addition to *The Times* obituary of Neil McCormick, widely predicted to become the First Prime Minister of an independent Scotland, that he had shared this fate provoking a correction from his Balliol tutor Dom Harris, which *The Times* unfairly failed to publish.

[71] Justin Cartwright in *This Secret Garden: Oxford Revisited* (Cartwright, 2008) wrote 'Michael Beloff was a young law don at Trinity when I came up in 1965. Thirty-five years later, a hugely successful barrister, he became President of the College', p 82.

[72] Then (by repute) teaching the law of witchcraft in Nigeria. Editor of a series of law reports of small Commonwealth Jurisdictions.

[73] Attorney-General of Ireland.

[74] QC prominent in media law. I wrote a reference for him to study at Harvard Law School. He modestly suggested that he was admitted because the selectors confused me with my father. Surely not …

During that decade Trinity's accomplishment lay more on the field of play than in examination schools. I regarded the small number of those of that vintage who bucked the socio-athletic trend and achieved firsts, the likes of John Fleming,[75] Peter Birks[76] and Fergus Millar,[77] as being the equivalent of those monastic scholars who kept the flame of civilisation flickering during the Dark Ages.

The then President was Arthur Norrington of Norrington Table fame – it ranked colleges in terms of their overall places in Finals, a mechanism that seemed designed to shame his own college into achieving better things. Giving my termly reports to Governing Body, which he chaired, I said of one student 'He epitomises the Balliol image of the Trinity man' – an observation which provoked the frostiest of silences.

Although I was at the very bottom end of the academic food chain I organised a series of talks called 'A degree in what?' in which various young dons, including the likes of Anthony Kenny,[78] Vernon Bogdanor,[79] Derek Parfit and Stephen Lukes,[80] led discussions about the purpose rather than the content of their subjects. The object of the exercise was to divert a generation of incipient campus rebels into concentration on their academic studies. Why I ever imagined that this would dissuade them from more exotic pursuits such as occupying the Vice Chancellor's offices or plotting a takeover of the university by a coalition of students and workers, I cannot in retrospect, comprehend.

1966 saw the opening of the Cumberbatch building, Trinity's contribution to the brutalist architecture so fashionable in that decade. It was opened by Tony Crosland,[81] the charismatic Labour politician, who had both studied and taught at Trinity. Among the honorary fellows at the celebratory dinner was Lord Goddard – the best known (if not most admired) Lord Chief Justice of the twentieth century. As the only law tutor in situ I had the doubtful privilege of sitting next to him. I used later to quip in after-dinner speeches at sundry law societies that he was a judge 'of few words but very long sentences'. Of his conversational contribution as my neighbour on that occasion I, overawed, can recall nothing.

I twice sought to cross one more Oxford bridge first as an historian next as a lawyer. My father, never a Prize Fellow of All Souls himself, would dearly have wished me to surpass him in that particular contest. By way of preparation we used to spend walks discussing a single word – a feature of the All Souls essay paper. I fared no better than he. On my first effort, the successful candidate was another historian Christopher Makins, Wykehamist son of Lord Sherfield, himself a Prize Fellow. Christopher had successfully concealed his intellectual distinction behind

---

[75] Deputy Governor of the Bank of England and Warden of Wadham.
[76] Regius Professor of Civil Law.
[77] Camden Professor of Ancient History.
[78] Master of Balliol, Warden of Rhodes House.
[79] Constitutional Scholar, Fellow of Brasenose, Professor at Kings College London.
[80] Fellow of Balliol and radical political philosopher.
[81] Foreign Secretary.

an upper-class Oxford social life and went on to a successful diplomatic career but an early death.

Warden Sparrow himself[82] walked up the drive of our home at 352A Woodstock Road to convey the news to my father; and left me a letter in which he wrote 'I had been privately hoping you'd become a Fellow from the day when you first came round to see me (I was ill in bed you may remember)' – If I remembered then, I don't remember now. He added 'whether it makes it better or worse a case that you didn't just miss it I don't know but there it is'. My own clear view is that it makes it worse. Isaiah Berlin wrote charitably that 'a better future is forecast for you here and everywhere', adding that my Russian translation 'made sense'. СПАСИБО.

On my second effort I was proxime to Edward Mortimer, who started, he told me, one of his essays in the history paper with the words 'Like Lyndon Johnson Henry I …'. How far this seemingly striking analogy was pursued, he did not reveal. Whereas the convention is to elect two Prize Fellows annually, on this occasion unusually, the choice was limited to Edward. Close but no cigar. Warden Sparrow took up his pen again to say how 'terribly sorry he was'. Another Fellow, a lawyer, wrote that my non-election was 'an example of its corporate death wish'. Suffice it to say that All Souls has survived and prospered, providing me with two of my most illustrious Bar pupils, David (Lord) Pannick QC and Launcelot (Lord Justice) Henderson. I did contemplate a third effort a year later (after all had not Lord Wilberforce, future senior law lord, required three shots before he hit the target?); and David Daube[83] told my mother – or so she said – that in his view I would succeed as a lawyer next time. But when I went to see the Warden my nerve failed me and I concealed my original purpose by feebly canvassing his opinion on whether I should choose a chancery over a common law practice.

My failure cast a long shadow over me, not mitigated by the occasional reference to me in various publications as being a Fellow, which I did not trouble to correct (just as in later years I was inaccurately, but less flatteringly, referred to as a member of the Social Democrats). I was not minded to console myself that the *salon des refusés* contained many persons whose achievements in later life sometimes surpassed those of the elected. Nor would I paraphrase the proposed epitaph of Alexis Piron, the French satirical poet, who was not elected to the Académie Française, 'il ne fut rien, pas même académicien'.

---

[82] Warden of All Souls, a conservative controversialist who is remembered for his scholarly analysis of the precise forms of sexual congress indulged in by Mellors and Lady Chatterley. Nowadays the chameleon adjective gay would describe him.

[83] The outstanding Roman law scholar of his generation and holder of the Regius chair in the subject.

4

An Utter Barrister

I joined Gray's Inn because John Morris was a Gray's man and did not recognise even the existence of alternatives. In that as in sundry other things, he was clearly right. A fellow student was Tariq Ali, with whom I travelled down from Oxford to eat our compulsory 36 dinners.[1] Tariq contrived a scheme by which his wealthy father would pay me to give Tariq tuition in law – his degree was in Politics, Philosophy and Economics (PPE) – and we would split the sum. This less than wholly honourable scheme, though arguably consistent with Tariq's ambition to transfer wealth on a worldwide basis from the rich to the poor, was never implemented. Tariq foreswore the law in favour of a career as a protest leader (notably in Grosvenor Square against the Vietnam war), writer and broadcaster. Years later when Treasurer of Gray's I invited him to speak to the students. He gave a riveting address about the heady days of 1968 so repaying any debt he might have owed the Inn.

Academic education completed and Inn selected, the next step was to obtain a pupillage. Conscious of the onward roll of time's winged chariot, I rejected the possibilities of a US law school or a year with a city law firm.[2] My father arranged for me to speak to Harry Fisher QC, himself a prize Fellow of All Souls, head of 1 Hare Court, a small but highly prestigious set which included not only Roger Parker[3] and Pat Neill,[4] who like Pooh Bah in the Mikado, became, in addition to his best-known posts, Lord High Everything else, but also Gordon Slynn,[5] all of whose paths I crossed later on several diverse occasions. I remember nothing about the interview other than that Harry Fisher almost immediately said that his chambers would not be in a position to offer me a place.

I eventually found such a place in a set of chambers in a way unusual even in those days when nepotism flourished, and unacceptable in modern times. Rupert Cross managed to persuade the head of Fountain Court, a former pupil of his, to offer me not only a pupillage, but also a tenancy, sight unseen. The Chambers, Fountain Court, were certainly in the Premier League, harbouring such nascent

---

[1] Tariq Ali (Ali, 2005) p 74 described it as 'a bizarre process'.
[2] Nowadays a single degree is by itself an insufficient passport to a place in a magic circle chambers and I would, if starting anew, be prudent to avail myself of any such opportunity on the table.
[3] Lord Justice.
[4] Life Peer, Warden of All Souls, Chairman of the Press Council.
[5] Judge at the ECJ where he was known as a juriste de grand Vitesse and Law Lord, DNB.

talents as Tom Bingham[6] and Mark Potter,[7] but I did not venture down this golden path. I was persuaded by another friend of my father and Fellow of All Souls, Philip Lewis,[8] to try my luck at what was then 2 Hare Court – a less renowned set.

By pure chance, but my misfortune, its most prominent member, Sir John Foster QC, yet another member of the All Souls mafia, was, like Dame Nellie Melba, the operatic diva, retiring for the nth time, taking advantage of the rules that then allowed barristers to claim all outstanding fees tax-free. His contemporaries thought that Sir John might, on the basis of talent alone, have become either Prime Minister or Lord Chancellor. Because of his preference for the good life or, rather, the good things of life, he became neither. I once went to hear Sir John, again a revenant to practice, address the appellate committee of the House of Lords. Bent over the lectern with a voice so husky it was barely audible (think Jack Hawkins in his later years) he was continually prompted by Lord Wilberforce in the chair, displaying due deference to a senior figure along the lines of 'What you are saying Sir John is etc etc'. You have to be very grand indeed to be coddled in that way.

Sir John was accompanied out of the Chamber exit door by the scarcely less successful Mark Littmann QC, appointed as Deputy Chairman of British Steel, and Paul Sieghart, then the doyen of human rights jurists. Their simultaneous departure coincided with my arrival but was not – as far as I am aware – caused by it.

In the thus denuded 2 Hare Court, there were no silks and only 12 members. Now relocated and rechristened Blackstone Chambers, it has 100 plus members, half of whom are in silk, and would rank itself at least on a par with Fountain Court whose fortunes have remained unimpaired over the intervening period.

My path into chambers was not a smooth one. In the 1960s there were Bar Exams, but no compulsory lectures, or separate professional training. I studied for mine exclusively from a second-hand set of Gibson and Weldon notes. I failed my paper on company law first time round, having been put further off my stroke by my adjacent African examinee who expostulated under her breath but audibly about 'that damned Hogg and Cramphorn', an apparently important case with which she had the advantage over me of at least some familiarity.

Nor did my initial attempt to win a scholarship from Gray's Inn fare better. Equity regards that as done which ought to be done. My paper on the subject did not provide proof of the truth of the maxim. It ought to have been done, but done it was not. I wrote not a single word other than my name, rather like Winston Churchill in one of his entry papers for Harrow, but, lacking his courage, I simply walked out of the room after five minutes. Second time round I fared better in both these tests, and won the Atkin Scholarship, the good news being

---

[6] Holder of the triple crown of Master of the Rolls, Lord Chief Justice and Senior Law Lord.
[7] President of the Family Division even though never previously a family lawyer.
[8] Editor of *Gatley*, the libel practitioners' bible.

communicated by Dingle Foot QC, the then Treasurer, via my Aunt Nora. If at first you don't succeed ...

I was not a very conscientious pupil, albeit I tried to look the part by wearing self-consciously the traditional colourless garb. I was in my mid-twenties and acutely aware that my college contemporaries were already out there earning in the market, while I was in some kind of mediaeval servitude, actually paying the sum of £100 for the privilege of trotting round at my pupil master's heels learning from his trials and his errors, the former happily outnumbering the latter.

I was apprenticed to Anthony (Tony) Lincoln, a small dapper man, who wrote elegantly about law for the *Spectator* under the moniker RA Cline and always kept a half-empty bottle of Vichy water on his desk. Tony had a mixed commercial and defamation practice, neither premier cru. The latter enabled me to gaze open-eyed at various minor celebrities who came to him for advice, including one broadcaster with an unusual complaint; in an article ranking the leading names in his profession he had not been the subject of some libellous comment, worse still, he had not been mentioned at all. No writ was in the event issued.

Tony was a gifted pleader at a time when pleadings (formal statements of a party's case) were regarded as something of a literary exercise. I lacked his facility and tended to be distracted by cliched phraseology such as 'and/or', once meaninglessly deploying the latter in a case of alleged duress by the defendant to compel the plaintiff's entry into a contract by describing him as 'a man of giant size and/or menacing appearance', when the alternative undermined rather than enhanced the addition. Another favourite was 'without prejudice to the foregoing'. These verbal badges failed to add verisimilitude to what was otherwise my bald and unconvincing narrative.

Pupillage to a senior junior also gave me the chance to see some of the great men of the Bar in action. A celebrated libel action, *Littler v London Artistes*, about the dimensions of the defence of fair comment, pitted the two impresario brothers Littler against each other. As brothers they made the Milibands look like best mates; indeed, they could have given Cain and Abel a run for their money. I had to leave the courtroom during the cross-examination of one of them by Desmond Ackner[9] to look up some case or other, and returned just on time to hear the formidable QC asking the by then helpless witness 'Do you actually like your brother?'.

Ackner also represented the Thalidomide victims in their action against Distillers. During one consultation he developed a severe nose bleed; I was able to lend him a grubby handkerchief into which he haemorrhaged copiously. I lacked the nerve to ask him to pay for the laundry. Or was this a matter of foresight about a later patron?

Sometimes I was farmed out to other juniors for a day. I accompanied Anthony Steen, later a long-serving Tory MP, whose robust comment in defence of his

---

[9] A Law Lord, DNB.

claims for expenses for his Devon country house, accusing his critics of jealousy, was an unfortunate postscript to his public service. Appearing in the Slough Court he asked the Judge, the notoriously peppery Claude Duveen, for 'the usual order', only for the Judge to retort 'What is the usual order Mr Steen?'. Silence in Court best described what followed. It taught me (or should have done) never to seek an order without knowing its basis in the rules of court. Many years later Mr Justice Brightman,[10] the most courteous of men (and Mrs Thatcher's pupil master) obliged me to spend my lunchtime with the Supreme Court Practice (alias the White Book) to be able to tell him that which he certainly knew, but I had omitted to check, on what legal provision my application was founded. Twice bitten once vicariously, once directly, I did not make the same mistake again.

At the end of my pupillage I was, despite my indifferent performance, offered a tenancy. I was in fact the only pupil that year so the competition was not strong. My predecessor, the left-wing hereditary peer Lord Gifford, was shortly to depart chambers as a result of writing a letter to *The Times* in which he inadvertently gave the impression that 2 Hare Court was the headquarters of Frelimo, the Mozambique liberation movement.[11]

In my first case I was instructed to apply for bail at the Bow Street Magistrates' Court for The Love Affair, one of those ephemeral pop groups which flourished for a scintilla of time in the late 1960s. Its members were charged with causing a public nuisance by posing next to the statue of Eros, god of love, then the centrepiece of Piccadilly Circus, in order to advertise their hit single. This forced traffic to come to a standstill as they were besieged by adoring fans. So naive was I that I walked straight into the dock and had to be directed to my proper place at the advocate's bench by a friendly policeman.

In my early years I passed well under the radar. I had to defend sundry persons charged with minor offences before often unsympathetic JPs. On one occasion, having heard my client give evidence, the Bench decided that criminal penalties were inappropriate and ordered him to be detained under mental health legislation for the purposes of treatment. When I went to say goodbye to him in the cells he asked me pitiably 'Does this mean I'm mad?', to which I responded, with a cautious measure of diplomacy 'Only in the eyes of the Thames Magistrates'.

I delivered pleas in mitigation for driving offences in further-flung magistrates courts. Once, making the false assumption that the name of the Court would coincide with the name of the town, I found myself at 10am in Surrey when I should have been in Kent. I finally arrived at my due destination after a difficult cross-country journey by train, involving several changes, at 2pm. This was the first but also the last time I have ever been late for court – although I continue to have recurrent nightmares about the possibility even after my retirement.

---

[10] Lord Brightman.

[11] He later set up his own set in Lambeth, as well as practising in the Caribbean. His own memoir is aptly entitled *A Radical Lawyer*.

I became very, even over, familiar with the Willesden Magistrates' Court, whither I was regularly sent by the one-man firm Goudie & Co, of whom the proprietor became a senior QC and whose articled clerk became his wife and a Labour life peeress.

My instructions in that far-flung palace of justice usually consisted of a single sheet with the name of the case and client on the outside, and the simple but compelling words 'counsel is instructed to do his best' on the inside. The firm's clientele was drawn mainly from the recent immigrant community. Once, going into the lobby of the Court in search of my client, I asked, 'Is anyone here called Patel', only to have about half a dozen young men rise to their feet and say 'I am Patel', rather as the army of gladiators called out 'I am Spartacus' in the penultimate reel of the eponymous film starring Kirk Douglas. The firm's upmarket work at the Quarter Sessions or even the Old Bailey was sent to a young Alexander (Derry) Irvine, later Lord Chancellor.

Briefs would sometimes be marked 5 and 2. I have divided intelligence as to what those mesmeric figures meant. One colleague said the 2 was what the solicitor paid the clerk; the 5 was for the barrister, another that the 2 was for the notional conference with the client even if the hurried interchange with the client, seen for the first time just before going into court, could be dignified with the name of conference at all. In the habit of those by gone days, I trotted too around County Courts, gradually learning that leading questions were not allowed in examination in chief, except, as the antique joke has it, 'by leading counsel', what use ought to be made of an agreed bundle and that litigation was a game in which the price of not quitting was double. The habitual cry of my Nigerian-born solicitor from the Midland firm of Currie & Co when we lost some hopeless case, as we usually did and paid the usual price, was 'Oh no not costs'. But the other party's costs, on top of our client's, it necessarily was.

To the client all cases are important; but to Counsel some cases are more important than others. In an anthology Stephen Sedley[12] describes an early encounter between us in the Bow County Court[13] where his client claimed damages for being, as he puts it, 'hit by a shower of shit from the bilges of a moored freighter' whose owners I represented. I put to the Plaintiff in cross-examination 'Where there's muck, there's brass'. My argument that this was a fiction designed merely to make ill-gotten gains failed. He won all of £13.

I did undefended divorces in the High Court – bread and butter to the fledgling barrister – but long since off the forensic table, and was naively amazed by some of the seriously aesthetically challenged persons, no longer in the first flush of youth, who admitted serial adulteries as the price for obtaining the release from marriage. Once a Judge, known to be a devout Catholic, refused my client the order I sought on some technicality and not – I hasten to add – because he believed (as he may

---

[12] Lord Justice Sedley.

[13] Stephen Sedley, *Law and the Whirligig of Time* (Sedley, 2018) where he refers to me as 'another young and eager barrister named Beloff, newly emerged from the chrysalis of the Presidency of the Oxford Union', p 269.

in his heart have done) that those whom God has joined together let no man, even in the Divorce Registry, put asunder. I had to renew my application before a more amenable Court. I also, as a family lawyer, achieved a *Daily Express* headline for one of my losses in the Abertillery magistrates' court – 'Kiss in car not grounds for separation'.

Occasionally I ascended to quarter sessions where, especially at Newington Causeway, some of the toughest eggs on the unreconstructed bench then sat. I once had to make a plea on behalf of some scion of a wealthy father who had hired the services of an expensive psychiatrist to proffer some Freudian or Jungian explanation of my client's petty crime. I was so unnerved by the terrifying reputation of the Judge presiding that I asked my client 'Are your full names A B Smith' only to have the Judge roar at me 'Those are not his *full* names Mr Beloff'.[14] The Newington Causeway first team would have been outscored in any competition for rudeness only by those who operated out of the Middlesex Guildhall, now home of our spanking new Supreme Court, which I never entered without an involuntary shudder at the remembrance of things past and judges long since dead.

I appeared regularly on minor procedural matters before the Queen's Bench Masters, and before the Judge in Chambers in Room 98 – a less terrifying environment than Room 101, the torture chamber in George Orwell's 1984, but still bearing for good and sufficient reason its Victorian nickname of the Bear Garden.

I travelled not infrequently to the north-east (paying a small sum then exacted for the privilege of appearing in a circuit other than my own) where I had to try to explain why a request for further and better particulars of some critical element in a personal injury pleading had been met by Stanley Brodie,[15] a senior junior in my chambers, with the bald and wholly unjustified reply 'Not entitled' which seemed to be a synonym for 'Cannot be bothered'. I travelled with no less frequency to the north-west to accompany a Liverpool silk, Andrew Rankin, who – in another archaic tradition of those days – had had to join a London set on his elevation to the front row. Playing at home, he held court in a room in the bowels of St George's Hall, very much king of all he surveyed. He weighed more than 20 stone in his socks, and negotiating a settlement in a personal injury dispute, he would sometimes imprison his less amply proportioned opposite number with his arms planted on the wall of the robing room until agreement (in the broadest sense of the word) could be reached. He introduced me to the phrase to describe a set of instructions with a high fee potential; 'It's a dripping roast'.

Andrew brought me into a number of planning appeals in which – with a ferocious fluency – he overwhelmed the tyro local authority solicitor seeking to uphold a decision to refuse permission for some unaesthetic development. He once persuaded the inspector to sit until 9pm so that he could do another case the next day – and to overturn a ban on building a set of stables over Lloyd George's grave. The train fare for these provincial adventures, east or west, usually exceeded my brief fee.

---

[14] Smith was not his surname; his was more refined.
[15] QC and Treasurer of the Inner Temple.

Both lark and owl, Andrew was wont to rise early and retire to bed late. He was also a hearty trencherman. At a late dinner on the eve of a case he chastised the waiter with the words 'T' fish in Newcastle are very small tonight'. He would usually review his papers with me after the meal. He was an exhausting, if generous, taskmaster.

On another occasion, the prosecution appealed the decision of a lay bench that there was no case to answer in a charge against his client of breach of the recent breathalyser laws. Andrew responded to the question from the High Court judge as to whether the Justices had taken that unusual course of their own initiative, with one of his stock phrases 'That was the reality of the situation'. The Judge perspicaciously found that proposition hard to credit given Andrew's track record in overwhelming not only his opponents but the tribunal before which he was appearing.

I did less work with Tony Lincoln. Once, because of a double booking, he abandoned me in my first case in the Court of Appeal.[16] I started my timid submissions by asking how I could best assist the Court. After all I had to start somewhere. I was let down lightly by Lord Justice Roskill[17] who said of one of our points 'It was argued in reply, if I may say so, with particular skill by Mr Beloff in Mr Lincoln's absence in an argument which lost none of its merit by its lack of success'. Say so he might indeed. His words, owing more to his charity than to his critical faculties, helped to soothe the wound. It took me some time in practice before I realised not to be too upset by losing. It is the best advocates who are often given the toughest cases.

Tony and Andrew could hardly be more distinct in terms of physique (Little and Large? Ronnie Corbett and Ronnie Barker?), character and forensic style but working with (or under) each accelerated my learning curve, both as to what and what not to do in court.

My early years at the Bar were hard pounding but producing few pounds. 'Cheque with brief' was a revealing formula, a Delphic synonym for a small fee. I acquired the habit of never turning down any set of instructions which were then few and far between; but which later, when there was a surfeit rather than a shortfall, left me ill-equipped to maintain the life-work balance rightly preferred by the newest generations at Blackstone Chambers. They find themselves regularly and promptly instructed in major cases in the Supreme Court and elsewhere as juniors to Chambers' large contingent of stellar silks. Such lucrative patronage was all but never available to me. I would hold myself out as open for hire during the long vacation which, as a matter of fact as well as of form, occupied the entirety of the months of July and August, hoping, in the absence of others, to feed off the scraps of any briefs which still were tendered to Chambers in these *mois blancs*. I once appeared in the Companies Court, not my natural milieu, with a heavy

---

[16] [1969] 2 LLR 129.
[17] Law Lord.

summer cold against Donald Nicholls,[18] whose happy hunting ground it was. Game, set and match, if such it could be called, to Nicholls.

I still continued to 'devil' for more senior barristers, especially where the case involved issues of administrative law in which my interest was burgeoning. One was the case of *Congreve v Home Office*[19] where Lord Denning, accepting the content of the argument I had drafted while expressing it in far more memorable lines, excoriated the department for cancelling the TV licences of holders who had, to avoid a sharp increase in their licence fee, presciently taken out a new licence during the currency of their existing ones.[20] Bernard Levin,[21] instinctively misgovernment averse, described in *The Times* the barrister who appeared triumphantly in the case as if he were a combination of Demosthenes and Clarence Darrow, so prompting him to make an ill-advised premature application for silk, a rank he sadly never then or later attained. For that at least I could not be blamed, but it did teach me to wait for my own application some years hence when the time was indubitably ripe. I introduced Anthony Lester to *Entick v Carrington*, the celebrated case involving John Wilkes, which I had learned about in history at Oxford, whereas it had passed him by in law at Cambridge. When the fat years finally came, they were all the more appreciated because of the lean years which had preceded them.

Meanwhile I had to supplement my meagre Bar earnings in various extracurricular ways. I continued to teach at Trinity as a weekender at very unsocial hours, Friday before dinner, Saturday morning after breakfast. I did not dare to emulate Lenny Hoffmann who, combining a tutorial fellowship at University College with a flourishing practice at the Chancery Bar, used to give tutorials on the train between Paddington and Oxford, until the college's governing body suggested that the time had come to choose. My timetabling nonetheless also sometimes went awry and I had to give a tutorial on the afternoon of my wedding with, as Tom Cloete,[22] one of my tutees, recalls, my new wife sitting on my knee. Weekenders, usually young barristers, are all but obsolete beasts in the academic legal menagerie.

I also continued to write. Graham Watson was keen for Jonathan A and me to build on *Campus's* modest success. If two and a half months in the USA had been a fragile foundation for *Campus*, my two weeks in Russia on a highly regulated tour would barely support a chapter. We contemplated a joint book on various aspects of Public Speaking – The Origin of Speeches – which shrunk to a frivolous essay in *Harper's Bazaar*. In his next book *The Young Meteors* in which Jonathan charted the trailblazers in various walks of life at the end of the swinging sixties, he disappointingly failed to include me in his brief reference to lawyers.

I explored another phenomenon of the same period, chronicling the infancy of the seven new universities opened in the era of the Robbins report (but

---

[18] Second senior Law Lord.

[19] 1976 QB 629.

[20] I had also suggested that Congreve would be a more euphonious plaintiff than the other candidate, the prosaically named Hart.

[21] Acerbic journalist and author.

[22] Judge in South Africa.

not its product): Sussex, Essex, Lancaster, East Anglia, York, Warwick, Kent (at Canterbury), a septet to which I gave the adhesive name 'The Plateglass Universities'. This book was also serialised in the *Sunday Telegraph*. I only wish it had been as well, as it was widely, reviewed. It did, however, lead to my becoming a commentator for *Encounter* on various aspects of the student revolution of that time, innocent as I was of the journal's funding by the CIA.

I received an invitation from the Melbourne Students Union to participate in a symposium on the same subject. The invitation was delayed because of a postal strike. I did wonder whether it had in fact been intended for my father but I decided to take it at face value, not least because my expenses were paid and I was able to visit for the first time, Hong Kong, Sydney and San Francisco, as well as New York for the second time. It provided the raw material for another *Encounter* essay. More useful may have been my contributions to Mrs Beeton's classic handbook on *Householder Management* and to another do-it-yourself manual on the *Law of Pruning*. They would certainly have had a wider potential readership.

I libel read for the *Observer*, in what had become a 2 Hare Court dedicated franchise, passing from Tony Lincoln through to me, fourth in line, and in due course, onwards and downwards.[23]

I was engaged by a Liveryman as a speech writer, making efforts (vain) to insert some humour into his oratory. He was tone-deaf where jokes were concerned and no more capable of delivering a funny punch line than Margaret Thatcher. For the record he was also unable to emulate her more admired rhetorical talents.

More financially fruitful was my short-lived role as a legal adviser to a long running legal soap *Justice* starring Margaret Lockwood as a trail-blazing female barrister. She was still a star of such luminosity and influence (she had ensured that her current boyfriend had a major part in the productions) that I barely dared to say hello to her in the Leeds studio where the scenes were shot. I did become friends with Anthony Valentine,[24] a young actor brought in in later episodes to freshen up the plot.

The role of legal adviser was essentially redundant. I quickly came to appreciate that leading questions, prohibited in evidence in chief in a real court of law, are essential to the drama in a fictional one; and that the slow rhythm of litigation has to be unnaturally accelerated like in the 1950s television programme *London to Brighton by Rail in Five Minutes*. Nonetheless when the 50 or so episodes were aggregated in 2019 into a boxed set of DVDs I purchased it for the pleasure of seeing my name in the credits somewhere below Ms Lockwood's hair stylist and the Gaffer. I duly located it in episodes 47 and 49.

I did other unremunerated non-Bar work giving talks on law to branches of the Workers Educational Association, the legacy of a relationship with a socialist university girlfriend, and talks on many things (as the Walrus advised the

---

[23] I discuss this episode further in chapter 9, 'Good Names and Bad'.
[24] His other roles included Raffles and the Commandant of Colditz.

Carpenter to do) on late-night chat shows at the behest of other friends, Andrew Phillips[25] and Jeffrey (and several decades later, Edwina Currie, who flirted with me over the airwaves at some hour just past midnight in her eponymous programme Red Hot Currie with an audience which must have consisted almost entirely of long-distance lorry drivers).

All this left me with no time to sample the delights of the political and sexual revolution of the late 1960s – the *soixante-huit* succeeded by the *soixante-neuf*. I can claim not only never have taken any drugs (Olga's therapeutic pill apart), but never to have been to a party where to the best of my knowledge and belief – the usual formula in an affidavit – drugs were being taken.

But the early struggle did not entirely naught avail. Moving into the 1970s I had the first of two lucky breaks. Anthony Lester (then a junior in my Chambers) had been instrumental in the drafting of the first Race Relations Act 1968. The Act had a paternalist, even colonialist philosophy. The alleged victims of discrimination had to complain to the Race Relations Board (RRB), a quango, which would assess the merits of the complaint, and then, if it passed the test, institute proceedings in its own name on the victim's behalf. Anthony arranged for the Board's solicitors, Bindman & Co, to instruct me on a regular basis.

I would travel to designated county courts, mainly in Birmingham, to advance claims, usually on behalf of Sikhs refused admission to Mecca Dance Halls. Mecca, who could well afford it, always instructed a senior silk to outgun me, but my main obstacle was more often the Judge. On one occasion I was asked 'Mr Beloff are you telling me that there is a law against this kind of thing?'. On another occasion the alleged victim and my first and key witness was not present in court at the then usual sitting time of 10.30am. I made some hasty apologies to the judge and sent my solicitor to inquire what had happened, only to discover that the witness had been detained on entering the Court for being in possession of an offensive weapon, that is to say the Sikh's ceremonial sword. Not the most auspicious start to a race relations claim.

I was briefed by the RRB against Robert Relf, who advertised his house for sale on a board inscribed 'only to an Englishman'. Refusing to comply with the Judge's order to remove the offending sign, he was inevitably sentenced for contempt of Court. The application to commit him to prison was watched from the back of the Courtroom by a group of middle-aged men, tattooed, muscular and bald, the curdled crème de la crème of the local National Front. I had at least the privilege of a police escort back to Birmingham New Street. Mr Relf was only freed from custody, and the RRB from a public relations disaster, as the result of the benevolent intervention of the Official Solicitor. No credit to me.

These cases involving a novel piece of legislation (hotly contested factual issues, far senior opponents, and unsympathetic tribunals) gave me a grounding in the realities of adversarial litigation denied to my contemporaries in far smarter commercial sets. The experiences all taught me to think on my feet against stern

---

[25] Lord Phillips of Sudbury, Senior Partner of Bates Wells and Braithwaite solicitors.

odds, and to deploy and burnish my immature advocacy skills. Juniors who nowadays sit behind fashionable leaders in expensive arbitrations, or eye-catching cases in appellate courts, make far more money than I ever did as a junior junior but are in some ways less well trained for the long haul of the Bar.

I represented one of the parties in a long-running electoral dispute in the Indian Workers Association of Southall (Southall station on the Oxford-Paddington line exceptionally has its description in Hindi as well as in English). The arbitrator was Ralph Gibson QC.[26] I put to one of the other side's witnesses that he had been responsible for improper voter manipulation. His ready agreement to this proposition suggested that he had simply misunderstood my question rather than that I had scored a palpable hit. It mattered not. The hearing lasted so long that a fresh election had taken place with the winners and losers reversing roles before the award, which was therefore by then not even of academic interest, was handed down.

In the fourth Wilson administration, 1974–76, Anthony Lester was seconded *from* the Bar by Roy Jenkins, the then Home Secretary, to assist in the birth of modernised anti-discrimination legislation. Responsible for the spirit, and sometimes the letter, of the Sex Discrimination Act 1975 (SDA) and the Race Relations Act 1976, Anthony then promptly returned *to* the Bar to make a profitable practice out of interpreting the complexities of both of those statutes. But from my point of view, his career zig-zag was truly beneficial, since I acquired the residue of his race relations practice; and for several years represented not only the RRB, but as his second string, its successor the Equal Opportunities Commission (EOC).

Since my clerks tended to classify all matters involving ethnic minorities in an undifferentiated way I was marketed as an immigration lawyer, surfing on the tidal wave of the new appeals system established under the Immigration Appeals Act 1969. I became a regular at Thanet House just off Fleet Street and adjacent to the Wig and Pen, and more rarely at Harmondsworth detention centre in the vicinity of Heathrow as well as – temporarily – an expert in the extended family system of the Asian sub-continent. When I took silk in 1981 the Home Office presenters threw a small party for me. I prefer to think that this was a gesture of friendship and not a consequence of their relief at ridding themselves of a difficult opponent.

Once the avenues of the appeal system had been fully explored the only recourse was then to the Divisional Court, where leave applications were still heard orally by a three-man court – and man it necessarily was – usually presided over by the Lord Chief Justice Lord Widgery, whose russet features and military moustache complemented a barely concealed impatience and a judgment often erratic, and increasingly aggravated by ill health.[27]

---

[26] Lord Justice.

[27] In the Court of Appeal Lord Denning was more benign but no less decisive. I was pleading the cause of a person who wished to stay in the UK as a student. 'How old is your client?' he asked. When I said '65' he replied 'Isn't he rather old for a student?' As Gordon Slynn my opponent had said to me briskly before the case was called on 'There's nothing in this appeal is there?' There wasn't.

It was at the time usual for those seeking to wend their way through the immigration maze to seek the assistance of lawyers of their own ethnic or racial roots – not always to their advantage.[28] I wondered whether seeing a solitary white face among the ranks of black or Asian counsel, Lord Widgery might not have been tempted – unwisely – to say, when I rose to my feet, 'Dr Livingstone, I presume'.

My greatest – but short-lived triumph – was to persuade Lord Widgery that the word 'here' in the immigration rules should be construed as meaning 'there' – an ambitious submission – which met its proper fate before an appellate committee of the House of Lords. I had barely advanced to the podium in Committee Room 1 when Viscount Dilhorne,[29] presiding, said 'Mr Beloff, we've read your admirable petition. We do not think there could be any more to be said. Leave is refused'. So, the first words I ever uttered in our highest court were 'if your Lordship pleases'.

My second stroke of good fortune came via Adrian Metcalfe, whose opening up of my path as a sports lawyer I describe in chapter 10, 'My Sporting Life'.

I had also decided to become a part master of my own fate. To avoid becoming entirely dependent on the sponsorship of others, I took a time-honoured route of writing a book on a new legal subject, rather than simply updating and re-editing a classic, and solicited Butterworths to commission me to produce a commentary on the SDA which paid off in spades.

One of my first cases in this novel field involved Florence Nagle. She had been refused a trainer's licence by the Jockey Club, then omnipotent in the horse racing world, but had persuaded Lord Denning that such blatant sex discrimination might arguably offend against the common law. Rather than taking the matter to trial the Jockey Club backed down. In a sequel Mrs Nagle, the doyenne of trainers of Afghan hounds, set her sights on the Kennel Club, also an all-male enclave. I was led by James Fox-Andrews QC (I shun the obvious pun). Mrs Nagle, who attended the consultation in an expensive fur coat of a kind that can no longer be worn with safety in public, was in many ways the perfect client, wealthy enough not to have to concern herself about the price of principle. She lost the battle; but won the war. The Kennel Club also backed down.

Two other areas of law attracted my involvement, one old, one relatively new. The old was libel.[30] The new was employment. When I was called to the Bar employees' rights were by and large defined only by their contracts. Over the years legislation greatly enhanced those rights and gave fresh opportunity to self-employed barristers. It is an ill law that blows nobody any good.

One of our chambers' clients was Imperial Tobacco whose casebook gave me an insight into the parlous state of British industrial relations. The company adamantly refused to settle any case with an employee, however disproportionate were the costs incurred to the compensation potentially payable. The in-house

---

[28] A point I return to in chapter 14. 'The Art of Advocacy'.
[29] Former Lord Chancellor in the Macmillan administration.
[30] See further chapter 9, 'Good Names and Bad'.

lawyers enjoyed, not bonuses, certainly not success-related ones, but free cigarettes. I would travel to Bristol and Newcastle, where Imperial's factories were located, and stay in expensive hotels, schooling myself to remember that it was unwise to emulate my solicitors' alcoholic consumption if I had to be on my feet the next day, or even frankly the next week, and discussing my instructions through clouds of smoke.

I can best illustrate their take-no-prisoners attitude by one case where the sum claimed was £50. After lunch on the first day the clerk at the Industrial (now Employment) tribunal told Counsel that the Chairman had just died. My opponent uncharitably murmured that this was a somewhat extreme reaction to my advocacy! This reminder that there were more important things in life than a two-figure claim, for example life itself, went unnoticed. Imperial insisted that the case go ahead later.

My most vivid recollection of working for Imperial was when I was being led by Stanley Brodie. In those days there was a magic moment when briefs were deemed delivered. This meant that whether the case settled afterwards or not the client was in principle responsible for the full fee. For some reason briefs in the case in question were deemed delivered in the evening at 9pm; and I had to sit in Stanley's room until the clock metaphorically struck 9 at which point this not particularly athletic QC leapt to his feet and shouted 'we did it'. The case pitted Imperial against Bacardi, and Stanley against another leader of the old school, Charles Sparrow QC.[31] It revolved around Imperial's responsibility for the alleged practice of barmen at their outlets offering to customers who asked for Bacardi other sorts of rum as if Bacardi were simply a synonym for the latter, and not a protected brand name. My opposite number was Hugh Laddie.[32] While in the front row the two silks battled like rutting stags, Hugh and I, like naughty school-boys, passed surreptitious notes between us, not always laudatory of those whose efforts we were supposed to be supporting. Stanley also led me in a case[33] about the extent to which those whose affairs were to be inspected by Inspectors of the Department of Trade and Industry were entitled to be heard as to whether there was anything to investigate at all. We sought summary judgment on the basis that there was no viable defence and were struck out on the basis that there was no viable claim – the polar opposite of what we had hoped for.

Stanley was the epitome of an adherent to Rudyard Kipling's injunction to treat triumph and disaster just the same. If he sometimes provoked the less attractive of those two outcomes by some forensic overreach, he also achieved the more attractive by creative argument and advocacy. He was, in addition, a marvellous pleader. Once we were seeking to reopen up the possibility of a call to the Bar by an African

---

[31] An intellectual property specialist, expert in silverware and a (devout?) Roman Catholic who, when Treasurer of Gray's Inn, had a portrait of Thomas Cromwell removed (temporarily) from hall.

[32] A High Court Judge who quit the bench pleading boredom, became a professor at UCL and sadly died at a young age.

[33] [1978] Ch 201.

student who had fallen foul of the four times rule which in those days prevented the sitting of the Bar exams on more than a quartet of occasions. Stanley pleaded that the process breached the first rule of natural justice – hear the other side – and added, in words whose very opacity carried a concealed threat, 'and otherwise left much to be desired'. Stanley taught me, if nothing else, that in litigation there's no such thing as a certain loser, except, perhaps, when we made an application to commit Bill Park, then senior partner of Linklater and Paines, for contempt by – as we alleged – being responsible for the wrongful imprisonment of our client in a middle eastern state. Not only did we find difficulty in identifying any judge of the Commercial Court who had not been the beneficiary at the Bar of Bill Park's instructions, but the application itself could most charitably be described as adventurous, less charitably as foolhardy. Stanley was double-booked in another case and left Court while Bob Alexander[34] was setting out the case for the defence, only pausing in mid-sentence to say that Stanley brought to mind Frank Sinatra's lyric 'Pardon me while I disappear'. I am still uncertain as to what I would have done had my leader not reappeared to reply – fainted probably. The only bonus was that it was my first encounter with Bruce Buck of Skadden Arps, later best known as Chairman of Chelsea.

I appeared by coincidence in both the first and the last case in the National Industrial Relations Court, popularly called the NIRC, a specialist appellate body under the stewardship of Sir John Donaldson,[35] set up by the Heath Tory government as a gesture towards the Trade Unions. The best plans of politicians, as Robert Burns would have it, 'all gang agley'. The court became the focus of controversy, not conciliation, because of such cases as the jailing of the five Dockers for breach of a court order, and was replaced in the next Labour administration. Sir John was visibly keen to go out on a consensual note, but, despite all his heavy hints, neither my, nor my opponent's clients were disposed to settle.

Towards the end of my time as a junior I started to do work for the National Council of Civil Liberties, whose lawyers were Patricia Hewitt and Harriet Harman, the liberty belles, later stalwarts of the new Labour administrations.[36] This was another professional relationship which fructified when I advanced to the front row.

At a time when I was starting to dream seriously of such promotion I was summoned by the Attorney General, Sir Michael Havers.[37] He was reviewing candidates to appoint to Junior Counsel to the Inland Revenue, ranking second only to the post of Treasury Junior or Devil in terms of Government appointments, but one which was conventionally offered to a barrister with no previous knowledge of tax law. The Inland Revenue, like the Jesuits, believe that those they get

---

[34] Life Peer. Chairman of NatWest DNB.

[35] Master of the Rolls.

[36] Patricia as Secretary of State for Trade, Harriet ultimately as deputy leader of the Party.

[37] Briefly Lord Chancellor. His son Philip was later a QC whom I led in a case in the House of Lords which established that University Visitors were immune from judicial review, [1987] AC 795.

young, they have for life. Discounting the factors of prestige and possible promotion later to the High Court, I had no instinctive enthusiasm for so specialist a role, though I would have loved to have been Treasury Devil. Memory can sometimes play one false. I would be convinced that I had politely said 'No' to Sir Michael's blandishments had I not later unearthed a letter showing that I had in fact said yes. It was Robert Carnwath who took the honours.

My last major excursion as a junior was with Anthony Lester, an inquiry into how the Crown Agents, a little-known body, had lost millions of pounds in imprudent property speculation in Australia. We represented Mr Challis, the former finance director of the Crown Agents, Sancho Panza to the Don Quixote of the Chairman, Sir Claude Hayes, who became, as the months went by, a knight of increasingly woeful countenance.

The inquiry, with a projected estimate of six weeks duration, was protracted over several years; little in law takes less time than is predicted. In order to ensure that further funds for unjustified claims for fees were not lost to the Treasury, a head count, not unlike roll call at school, was each day taken of the multitude of barristers by an official, Mr Shepard, inevitably christened the Good Shepherd. The major section involving Mr Challis concluded, Anthony bowed out, leaving me with what for long periods became in effect a watching brief. When the former Prime Minister, Sir Alec Douglas Home, Foreign Secretary at the time of the financial disaster, appeared, I could think of no questions, pertinent or even impertinent to put to him. In any event, famously by his own admission, ignorant of matters economic, he appeared to suffer from an aristocratic amnesia. The publication of the Tribunal's report coincided with the invasion of the Falklands guaranteeing even less publicity, if any, than it might otherwise have gained. But for me the experience was largely beneficial. Not only did I obtain a client for the future, the Crown Agents itself under new and professional management, but I had a refresher course in advocacy by seeing and hearing the performance of the other counsel, so various in their styles and strengths (and weaknesses).

After a customary cooling-off period of seven years I had myself become entitled to take pupils with an entire freedom of choice. My first pupil, Richard Plender, was an academic from the University of Exeter Law School and the first of my three pupils to become a senior judge, the others being Lancelot Henderson and Andy Nicol. Lancelot, a prize fellow of All Souls, was steered my way by my father. He learned from me, a dedicated common lawyer, at least, maybe only, that he was more naturally suited to life at the Chancery Bar. Andy[38] was unwisely rejected by Tony Lincoln for a tenancy – when places were given to three other pupils – a decision which all but caused me to pack my bags in fury and leave Chambers.

Richard's influence was also responsible for three other Exeter alumni becoming my pupils. At a time when I was not yet rid of the fagmaster virus, and with an

---

[38] Mr Justice Nicol.

imminent dinner date, I asked one of the trio, John Kidd,[39] to purchase a pound of chocolates as a gift for my hostess. He returned with a pound's worth rather than weight of chocolates. When I expostulated at his expensive (to me) misunderstanding, he reminded me of the nineteenth-century case of *Raffles v Wichelhaus*, known to all students of contract law. This turned on the confusion between two ships, both named Peerless, leaving the port of Bombay in different months; the seller of bales of cotton believed that the shipment was due in December, the buyer believed it was due in October. I doubt whether there have been many, if indeed, any other cases in the intervening period which required consideration of that classic precedent.

Three other of my pupils would certainly have become High Court, indeed higher Court, judges, Charles Hollander[40] and Charles Flint,[41] both of whom imbibed my interest in sports law. The unrivalled star was David Pannick.[42] David became a Times Lawyer of the Week[43] as a result of his triumph in the first Brexit case. He responded to the conventional question 'who has inspired you in your career?' by responding 'Lord Lester of Herne Hill, QC, and Michael Beloff, QC. I acted as junior counsel to each of them on dozens of occasions. They taught me that advocacy is as much about listening as it is about speaking'. If that is indeed what I did teach David I did so unconsciously since I usually listened to other advocates with a measure of impatience in the fond belief that a case didn't truly start until I was on my feet. The benefit of having David as my pupil in my last junior year certainly contributed to my decision to apply for silk, and my success in obtaining it.

---

[39] John became an academic at the University of Queensland whence he pens letters on diverse subjects regularly printed in *The Times*.

[40] QC, a commercial lawyer, author of books on disclosure and conflict of interest and my successor as Chair of the IAAF Disciplinary Tribunal.

[41] QC, a commercial and public lawyer who became Chairman of the Sports Disputes Resolution Panel (SDRP) as well as having judicial roles on UEFA and other bodies.

[42] QC, Life Peer, one time *Times* columnist.

[43] 2 February 2017. In an interview with Counsel Magazine on 4 November 2021 he explained how my father's recommendation also saved him from Chancery, 'Michael Beloff was the go-to junior in the developing world of judicial review, discrimination and sports law and fun to work with'.

5

The Silk Road

A decision to apply for silk was, and still is, crucial to a barrister's career. Success in the application is no guarantee of success afterwards. New silks can swim – indeed surf the waves – but they can also sink. Timing is all. When the Lord Chief Justice Geoffrey Lane said that I had argued my (losing) case 'as always with great skill and persuasion and charm',[1] I optimistically took this hyperbole to be a covert invitation to apply rather than the soothing words so often uttered to the unsuccessful advocate. I also saw the possibility of promotion to the front row as compensation for my failure to become Revenue Junior the year before. Once locked into that post, I could not plausibly have sought to quit it so soon.

I needed two judicial referees. One was obvious, David Croom-Johnson[2] who presided over the Crown Agents inquiry had had an ample, if not excessive, exposure to my advocacy over the past year. Desmond Ackner had always seemed well disposed towards me; he regarded my previous year's income of something of the order of a mere sixty-odd thousand pounds as sufficient proof that I would not be inviting bankruptcy. Gordon Slynn offered his usual encouragement.

Before softer voices in the Lord Chancellor's department decided that the practice constituted cruel and unusual punishment, aspiring silks were informed of their success or failure on Maundy Thursday; and the letters were sent to one's chambers so that inquisitive colleagues, who rose early, could sift through the post and identify by the shape and size of the aspirant's envelope the outcome. I ensured that I was in chambers in good time to have the first reconnoitre. If one had been awarded silk, as I had, the envelope was small, and brown; it contained the glad tidings together with a peremptory request for payment of a fee for Letters Patent. If one had failed, as one of my senior colleagues had that year,[3] the letter was far larger, of the shape and colour which usually betokens an invitation to some glamorous party.

Slightly stunned by my success, which I celebrated that evening by watching *Chariots of Fire* to remind me that you can't always get what you want, I wandered out into the square and encountered Sam Stammler.[4] He told me that Tony

---

[1] [1980] 1 WLR 979.

[2] Lord Justice, Treasurer of Gray's Inn.

[3] In those days one was still expected as a courtesy to advise senior members of one's intention to apply.

[4] A leading commercial silk, head of Chambers at 1 Essex Court.

Grabiner in his chambers had got silk and inquired in a quite general way whether anyone had in 2 Hare Court. The form of his question suggested that he had not for a moment identified me as a potential applicant, so I answered in equally general terms and let him receive the news to this possibly lethal blow to the English legal system by other means.

I was due to appear before Lord Denning,[5] who sent his clerk down to the bowels of the Court to congratulate me. My opponent, a sardonic Midlands circuiteer, said to me outside that he supposed the Silk list was only full of slick Metropolitan juniors. For the second time that day I had to hold my peace. And then – to top it all – next day I met an Oxford neighbour in the street, David Yardley,[6] who hailed me with a 'well done' and then after a pause added 'I know someone once who got silk and never received a single brief'. Thank you David ... At least I have been able to avoid replication of the aborted career of that doleful and anonymous practitioner.

Still I was a first-time silk, aged 38 (admittedly barely two months short of 39) but only 13½ years from call. These things count, though they shouldn't. I was third from the foot of the list – the peculiar league table being ordered so that it is those at the bottom who can be seen to have made the swiftest ascent. Today it's published more blandly in alphabetical order. There was in those days no expectation that I would as a new silk, at a cost reflecting my proposed rather than my past income, host a lavish party in some exclusive environment not only for all the chambers members and staff but also, as would today be imperative (but in 1981 would have been improper) potential instructing solicitors. The convention at the time was for a more proportionate party and for a more selective guest list of mates rather than marketing prospects.[7]

Now all I needed was to get some work. Almost at once another Oxford neighbour, and solicitor, sent me a brief to represent a man accused of the murder of a local prostitute in a public lavatory in St Giles – so much, I thought, for my ambitions of a high-class commercial practice.

The *Actus Reus* was not in issue – the deed was done but I squeamishly left scrutiny of the photographs of the corpse to my experienced junior. The only defence was of diminished responsibility. My expert sported a hairstyle midway between that of Jimmy Hendrix and Keir Starmer in his unbarbered days and was

---

[5] A few years later Lord Weidenfeld discussed with me the possibility of writing Lord Denning's biography. The Judge replied 'I do not think my doings are worthy of such recognition' but not too long after started on a series of popular memoirs for which I may have given him the inspiration. He was a protean figure. When he was awarded an honorary degree at the University of Buckingham after a few of his usual soft spoken anecdotes, he drew himself up to his full height and at full volume enjoined his electrified audience about the need to support the police. I thought at that moment that had he pursued a different career he might have been a British de Gaulle. His affectionately autographed photograph sits on a shelf in my study.

[6] Later a client when local government ombudsman.

[7] One of my invitees was Peregrine Worsthorne, the ultra-conservative journalist (crazy name, crazy guy) who was never going to be a source of work but who repaid the hospitality by writing in his *Sunday Telegraph* notebook that my thank you speech showed how much more eloquent silks were than politicians. This may say more about the shortcomings of the latter than the merits of the former.

very much of the 'we are all guilty' school of uber-liberal psychiatry. The jury, unimpressed either by him or by me, convicted. I had a brief the next day in the more familiar milieu of Room 98 in the Royal Courts of Justice (RCJ) and went to ask my client, now back in the cells, whether he would have any objection if I left the formalities of the pre-ordained sentence to my junior. In relieving me of that duty he paid me the greatest compliment I have ever received: 'I suppose, Mr Beloff, you're off to your usual beat at the Bailey'. I thought then that if I can make someone with a list of convictions longer than both his arms believe that I was a real-deal criminal practitioner, I ought not to risk being unmasked in future. So that was both the first and the last criminal jury case I ever did, as a leader, with a misleading 100% average rather like those tail end county cricketers who knock up a quick century against a novice university team in late April in their only innings of the season. I did in fact visit the Old Bailey once more when I was giving character evidence on behalf of Jeffrey in his trial for perjury. But that's another story.[8]

It was an uneven start. There was the usual commercially unsavoury case in which the solicitor thought he could cut a few corners and knock a few noughts off the brief fee with a newly fledged silk. I could also feed on a diet of held over cases from my junior days, which one was allowed to do for another year, rather as a hibernating bear subsists on the food consumed and stored before the onset of winter.

My real and again quite unpredictable breakthrough came in the autumn of my novice silk year, when I was still living off the diminishing remains of my junior practice. I was on a bucket and spade holiday in Brighton with my two children, when my senior clerk telephoned and asked if I would like to do a case in Kuala Lumpur. I confess that I was not entirely sure of the whereabouts of Kuala Lumpur; to adapt what Neville Chamberlain said about Czechoslovakia, it was a faraway city of which I knew little. The case was about the wish of the Chinese – the minority ethnic community in Malaysia – to establish a university which would provide tuition in their mother tongue. Linguistic considerations apart, the positive discrimination policies of the Government in favour of the majority Malay Bumiputra made it more difficult for Chinese students to obtain college places. But the Government had refused them the necessary permission.

The applicants had originally briefed a Chancery silk who found himself entangled in an endless arbitration. Suspecting foul play at the crossroads, though there was none, but belatedly deprived of their leader of choice, a small group of Chinese-Malay lawyers flew to London. Their chef de mission, Soo Thien Ming, was a former student of Lincoln's Inn, who put himself through law school by washing dishes in the evening and had since become one of the most successful of Malaysian lawyers – he shrewdly chose ethnic Malays as his co-senior partner, including at one time the daughter of Dr Mahathir, the Prime Minister, who helped me shop for a present for my wife. The team wanted to find as a substitute

---

[8] See chapter 13, 'Life at the Bar'.

silk someone the wide open spaces of whose diary meant that there was *no* risk that he would be double-booked. I guess that they simply went through the bar list of administrative law specialists – in those days a rare breed – in alphabetical order until they found one who had a month to spare in three weeks' time. Had my paternal grandfather not changed the family surname I might never have been heard of again.

The case[9] dominated the national headlines in Malaysia since it exposed still lively racial tensions, which had burst into violence in the recently remembered past. It remains top of my own professional pops. I appeared with 11 Juniors – surely a record – against the Malaysian Attorney-General; had to cross-examine the deputy Prime Minister; was subject to an unsuccessful attempt to lure me into a honey trap; and during the appeal was threatened, equally unsuccessfully, by an anonymous telephone caller that if I didn't get out of town promptly my body would be found floating down the Klang River.

The Attorney-General, whom I apprised of the ominous message, and I met the Lord President in his chambers, to explain the situation. The Lord President for his part made a statement in open court in which he emphasised that I was doing my duty as an advocate rather than as an agitator. In case that did not do the trick, I was provided by my clients with two fearsome Sikh bodyguards, who accompanied me everywhere, as well as with official police protection organised by my opponent. At about 3am the next morning I heard a knock on the door of my hotel room, which I had declined to quit, more through sloth than through sangfroid; I feared that my security had been breached and my end was nigh. When I opened the door with extreme caution, and silent prayer, I encountered only the manager of the hotel who had come to enquire whether all was well. Sometimes service hospitality can be excessive.

I had for my argument the apparent benefit of an opinion authored by Professor Sir William Wade QC,[10] and Sir Peter Rawlinson QC,[11] to the effect that the Government's refusal was clearly motivated by unlawful racial discrimination – a proposition which may have been true but for which there was no admissible evidence. The opinion made no reference at all to the point ultimately decisive against my clients namely that, under the Malaysian constitution, any public body – which, it was held counterintuitively, included a *private* university – could only use the national language, Bahasa. The case was lost at first instance, and by a 4-1 majority in the Court of Appeal, the judges splitting on ethnic lines. Malaysia presciently withdrew the right of appeal in constitutional cases to the Privy Council which disabled my clients from taking the matter further – Tom Bingham told me informally that in that more detached forum they would probably have won.

---

[9] 1982 MLJ. There is a full description of the case in KK Soong's 'A Protean Saga: The Chinese Schools of Malaysia' 3rd ed, ch 9. I myself wrote about it briefly in 'Language and the Law Current Legal Problems' (1987) 139–40 based on an earlier lecture delivered by me at UCL.

[10] The doyen of academic administrative lawyers.

[11] A former law officer and Life Peer who features further at different junctures in this memoir.

This experience gave me many friends as well as a lasting affection for Malaysia, but, no less importantly from the professional standpoint, opened up new horizons of practice. Wordsworth wrote of Venice 'once did she hold the glorious east in fee', an example that my clerks strove mightily to emulate.

Next to Singapore, where Alan Taylor, an exuberant New Zealand solicitor friend, had obtained for his clients so extensive an injunction for freezing the assets of the other party, that it was all but bound to be overturned on appeal. I was duly instructed to argue the unarguable, the discomfort of a stopover at Colombo airport being mitigated by my first introduction to the Singapore sling in the swimming pool at the Raffles Hotel.

The local firm who had carriage of the unenviable action was Rodyks. The next year I reaped the harvest when I was briefed by the same firm on behalf of the Port of Singapore Authority (PSA) in an inquiry under the Singapore Tribunal of Inquiries Act. The subject matter of the inquiry was an accident which occurred when the mast of a converted drill ship, leaving its repair berth, snagged an overhead cable connecting mainland Singapore and the island of Sentosa, so causing the deaths of several hapless persons catapulted out of a cable car en route between the two locations.

It was another late return. The QC originally instructed, Michael Thomas, an admiralty or 'Wet Shipping' expert, had just been elevated to the position of Attorney General of Hong Kong. It was also not the easiest of briefs. First the inquiry had already been afoot for more than 12 days when I found myself flying eastwards, at the shortest of notice. Secondly the PSA were already receiving rough treatment at the hands of the presiding judge and, in consequence, of the local press; so there were all the makings of a major public relations disaster. Thirdly my knowledge of matters maritime (at that stage) was minimal. While I certainly knew my arse from my elbow, I was less confident that I knew my stern from my bow. I received a crash course directly from my instructing solicitor, Pathma Selvadurai of Rodyks and indirectly from Dick Stone QC,[12] representing the owners of the drill ship, Eniwetok.

Meeting the PSA's Chief Executive at dinner the first evening after landing, I was faced with the inevitable question – what was my experience in marine collision cases? The true answer was none. So, I said, with half-truth, that I was experienced in inquiries, as I was – not only Crown Agents, but the Brixton Riots in front of Lord Scarman.[13] But though many things were burnt in Brixton, boats were not among them.

---

[12] Treasurer of Gray's Inn and founder of an eponymous set of chambers.

[13] Cmnd 8427 1981/82. In that inquiry in which I had the smallest of roles I coined a couple of phrases which found their way both into the report (and in subsequent debates in Parliament) para 5.7.5 p.59 'If there be any persons – and there may be – who believe that crimes should go unpunished because they are committed by persons of a particular shade of skin, the Council are not of their number. If there are any who believe that the some of the violence to person and property which accompanied the Brixton disturbances were the legitimate self expression of an oppressed minority, the Council do not share that belief'.

During the course of the inquiry I was confronted with a real ethical problem. My client discovered in its archive a document in which a staff member had anticipated the possibility of the very kind of accident as had actually occurred. Naturally it was anxious to keep this potentially smoking gun in its holster. I had to say, with some trepidation, that I could not continue to act for it if it refused to disclose so obviously relevant a document. Disclosure was duly, if reluctantly, made.

The highlight in an otherwise humdrum proceeding was the unearthing and magnifying by my resourceful team of a photograph of the drill ship, which showed the master of the vessel being snapped in a studied pose at the exact moment when the mast hit the cable – a selfie with disastrous results. Unfortunately, we were bound by the rules of the game to disclose this to the Counsel to the Inquiry, a government advocate of great pertinacity, but whose cross-examination was of cardboard rather than cobalt quality. I sulked impatiently as he went tediously through a series of questions, which alerted the witness to his difficulty, without impaling him on the horns of it. When my moment came later in the day, I exploited it as best I could, which was by then not very much.

The inquiry lasted – as such inquiries always do – far beyond its estimated duration, and English counsel, anxious to return home for the holiday, persuaded the Judge that the derring-do of the Prime Minister Lee Kwan Yew's soldier son[14] – who had masterminded the rescue of the remaining occupants of the cable car – fell outside the terms of reference of the inquiry, concerned, as it was, with the causes of the accident, not its consequences.[15] The Judge, Lai Kew Chai, who indeed denied the son his moment of glory, was never promoted to the Court of Appeal. Was there a connection between these two matters? You decide.

After that I went back to Singapore on several occasions. Once I appeared for one of Lee Kwan Yew's detainees. This alleged subversive came into the conference room in the detention centre in his blue boiler suit, and promptly offered me a few Smarties. He had the look of a man who would find it difficult to raise his voice to a gander, let alone plot the overthrow of the city state.

The trial took place before the same Judge who had presided over the Sentosa Inquiry.[16] Bob Alexander and Anthony Lester had earlier represented other detainees; and Anthony had, incautiously, made some critical comments about the Singapore Government at a conference in London. To avoid any similar reproach I made it clear in my opening observations that I had come to Singapore to fight the case as a lawyer but would hold my tongue outside court. I lost the case, which had

[14] He later became Prime Minister himself.
[15] In the introduction to the report the judge wrote 'It has been a particular pleasure to have had the assistance of two Queen's counsel, Richard Stone QC and the Honourable Michael Beloff QC who brought to the Inquiry a professionalism consistent with the highest standards of the English Bar'. Without Richard's educational example I might myself have sunk like a stone.
[16] On a later occasion I wandered into his Court, and he embarrassed me by promptly adjourning the proceedings saying he had spied an old friend at the back of the room.

only even a veneer of plausibility because of the Government's refusal to provide any evidence at all of what my client was alleged to have done. Not long after, honour satisfied, it let my client out.

During the hearing itself my local solicitors were convinced that my hotel room was both bugged and videoed. So, we had conferences in the corridors but, though far from beach fit, I persisted in strolling naked round my bedroom. Maybe the tapes survive in the vaults of the Singapore Police HQ – although I doubt they would be of much interest to what used to be called top shelf magazines.

A Singapore case that never was involved a potential prosecution of the *Straits Times* for breaching the local official secrets legislation by disclosing that the latest estimate for the annual growth of Singapore's economy was only 8 per cent. I was instructed to represent the newspaper. To increase my chances of admission I procured statements testifying to my competence and integrity from Peter Taylor and Desmond Ackner, who had to be politely reminded to sign his in order to forestall any accusations of forgery. To my regret the newspaper decided that their continued relationship with the powers that be (or more accurately, during Lee Kwan Yew's premiership, the power that be) would be better served by acknowledging the breach. In the United Kingdom the revelation of an annual growth rate of 8 per cent would be a cause for national celebration rather than for criminal proceedings.

In Brunei I was on the other side of the national security argument – representing the Government in an unlawful imprisonment claim by a detainee who had been confined for almost six years without trial. The case wended its slow way through the various Court levels, initially before a strikingly attractive female registrar who crocheted throughout my submissions. Later when I was Vice Treasurer of Gray's Inn one of the Sultan's daughters was called to the Bar. At the reception, attended by the Sultan, his consort and a cohort of camouflaged security men, I asked the newly called daughter what kind of work she intended to specialise in on her return to Brunei. She replied 'Government work'. I commented that this was probably a wise choice on her part.

The Sentosa inquiry had led me into the field of shipping – though I still had to remind myself which was port and which starboard. I was briefed in two scuttling cases – effectively crime at sea cases where it is alleged that the ship owners wished to cast away their ships to lay hands on the insurance monies. The forensic exercise included scrutiny of the accounts of near insolvent concerns; and cross-examination of helmsmen who appear to have been blind to obvious dangers. I made acquaintance of a rare breed of specialist juniors, who were never happier than when, like Toad of Toad Hall, they were mucking around in boats and were all too glad to take the technical inquisition of some expert witnesses off my inexperienced shoulders.

The first case,[17] the *Zinovia*, went a little off course when my own accountancy expert, in answer to the first question posed to him in cross-examination about

[17] [1984] 2 LLR 264.

his previous career, confessed that he had been a professional bridge player – and not a very successful one at that. It was my instructing solicitor who had taken a risky gamble! There was, however, another reason for our loss. Tom Bingham, the trial judge, rejected the testimony of a seaman who claimed that the First Officer had told him in a casual airport conversation that he proposed to run the ship aground so that he could earn extra overtime. Tom explained in a public lecture that the improbability in all the circumstances of such a proposal being made influenced him more strongly that the demeanour of the witness.[18] The second case proceeded in calmer waters.

Scuttling cases are only rarely contested in modern times, and my appearance raised my profile among firms who specialised in shipping, both wet and dry – adjectives which reminded me of my Eton schooldays when oarsmen were called wet bobs and cricketers dry bobs. Shipping led Messrs Ince and Company (who had been on the opposite side of that same case, and who had apparently admired me in defeat – mine not theirs) to instruct me in the fields of insurance and reinsurance. I was even briefed to replace Tony Clarke on his appointment as Admiralty Judge[19] where the issue was whether the vessel had been sunk, not as part of a criminal conspiracy but by a so-called killer wave.

I found myself instructed by the same firm in the major post-war insurance case in the House of Lords, *Pine Top v Pan Atlantic*,[20] which revised the previous law as to material non-disclosure. I took part too over a period of some two years in an arbitration presided over by Lord Justice Kerr,[21] Lord Griffiths[22] and Judge Schwebel[23] – on behalf of the insurers of a number of major car dealers in Kuwait whose showrooms had been looted by locals during the first Gulf War. I was instructed to advance the unpromising argument that the looting was not a consequence of war, and that accordingly the insurers were not entitled to rely upon the war risks exclusion clause in their policy.

Our legal team's visit to Kuwait took place during the month of Ramadan. When we were offered coffee in the offices of one of our clients, the young lady receptionist, bearing all the hallmarks of a very orthodox Muslim, looked at us with such hostility that I was convinced that she would call the police to charge us with the offence of drinking between the hours of dawn and dusk. I declined the proffered cup and distanced myself in the forecourt from the rest of the lawyers, whose thirst appeared more potent than their fear. That visit to a Gulf state, by no means recovered from the ravages of the invasion, convinced me that one of the hardest jobs in the world at the time would have been to be Chief Executive of the Kuwaiti Tourist Board. No doubt the country has many charms, but they did not repose in vandalised retail outlets for automobiles.

---

[18] 'The Judge as Juror' *Current Legal Problems* vol 38, pp 14–15.
[19] Master of the Rolls, Law Lord and JSC.
[20] [1995] 1 AC 501.
[21] A commercial law specialist and father of Tim, of whom more later in chapter 13, 'Life at the Bar'.
[22] Law Lord, as well as, uniquely, President both of the MCC and of the Royal and Ancient. DNB.
[23] President of the ICJ.

At the hearing itself our expert was General Sir Peter de la Billière,[24] a small wiry man. The insurers' expert was John Simpson, the journalist, whose physique was of more ample proportions. I suspect that an alien visitor to planet Earth would have guessed wrongly which was the soldier and which the scribbler. Still the legal storm in the sand had a snowball effect. I was afterwards briefed in several cases involving war risks exclusion clauses as whether they applied or not to violent episodes in even further away places such as Trinidad and Mozambique.

The American author Horace Greely coined the phrase 'Go West Young Man'. I was well into middle age before I heeded that advice. In Bermuda I was instructed in Mentor, the name given to the largest ever reinsurance liquidation. Half a dozen senior silks attended a preliminary hearing. The Court building in Hamilton, the capital, has only one entrance, and in another court, the trial was taking place at the same time as ours of a man accused of murdering his wife with an axe. Counsel had an earnest debate about the protocol for what to do when, securely handcuffed, he passed by us. Did we smile, remembering that he enjoyed the presumption of innocence, give a neutral brief nod or simply turn away? An awkward grin coupled with an all but imperceptible inclination of the neck was the consensus. A lesser protocol issue arose as to whether I could wear Bermuda shorts in Court as did local counsel. I, lacking confidence in my knees, decided not to take the plunge.

The assigned judge, who hailed from Jamaica, appeared to have little pedigree in complex commercial litigation. Rather than expose our clients to the lottery of his judgment, not to speak of months away from family and chambers, all Counsel reached an agreement to settle.

One of those Counsel was John Thomas QC.[25] I left our hotel for the airport early – always anxious not to risk being late for the flight. Unfortunately, just afterwards it was announced in the hotel that the flight would be delayed. So, I spent several wasted hours in a lounge the size of a smallish beach hut. John, with a more relaxed attitude, was still in the hotel at the time of the announcement, took advantage of the delay to dine well in a local restaurant, The Lobster Pot, and, duly refreshed, enjoyed, unlike I, an excellent night's sleep on the return journey. The lesson? Only those who can hold their nerve can ever aspire to the highest judicial office.

Again, in Bermuda I once appeared against Sydney Kentridge QC.[26] He had flu; I developed a severe nosebleed. He coughed. I choked. The Judge either didn't notice or didn't care. On yet another occasion, taking a roundabout route to the same destination via Newark and Boston, I suffered the fate of separation, though

---

[24] Famed for his leadership exploits in the Gulf War.

[25] Lord Chief Justice.

[26] The celebrated South African silk, who in his home country represented Nelson Mandela and Steve Biko. In [1991] QB 212, in which I represented the former solicitor-general Sir Ian Percival who complained about the inadequacy of the sanction imposed by the Bar Council upon a fellow member of his chambers with whom he was in dispute, Tasker Watkins LJ stated that the case has been 'outstandingly well argued … by Mr Beloff and Mr Kentridge', p 222. I was greatly pleased by the adverb, the more so by being compared even once to so illustrious an advocate.

not divorce, from my luggage. So, I had only the clothes I had travelled in. It is a feature of Arbitration, unlike litigation, that it takes place behind closed doors, since commercial men do not like to expose their dirty washing in public and the Arbitrator was content to allow me to attend day one looking even more unkempt than usual before I was reunited with my only Brooks brothers lightweight suit.

On one visit to Bermuda I had coffee with David Waddington, a former client, who was rounding off his career in public service in the Governor's Mansion. He confessed to me that in that office he found it difficult to extend his working day past 11am. But I also acquired a new client in Julian Hall, the antithesis of an establishment figure and a thorn in the flesh of Bermuda's elected Government.[27]

For a decade or so I found myself treated as, or deemed to be,[28] a real commercial lawyer dealing not only with insurance but with bills of exchange, charter parties and banking practice. For a while I knew that which I have all but forgotten, the meaning of such technical words and phrases as demurrage, bunkers, retrocession and documentary credits, but was steered skilfully by a series of expert juniors who had imbibed these concepts with their mothers' milk. My commercial practice paid the bills that my public law practice would not.

Many senior members of the English bar have appeared in the House of Lords, the Supreme Court or the Privy Council. I must be the only one who has also appeared in the Coroners Court in Wan Chai, a red or, at any rate reddish, light district of Hong Kong.

So why me, why there, why then? The first inquest into a fatality at China Light and Power nuclear power station had resulted in a verdict of accidental death. The ex-pat English barrister had not lasted the course. There were two versions of what had happened; he claimed that he had been asked to suppress vital evidence inculpating the power company; the company claimed that he had simply failed to master his brief. When he went public, the inquest was reopened among a wave of media coverage. The company needed someone who was both wholly detached and seen to be so from the local scene. The coroner, a man not immune to the temptations of publicity, was, my solicitors surmised, predisposed to a hostile lack of care verdict. They were right and it took the Court of Appeal to overturn his ruling on the basis that such a verdict was not available in Hong Kong.[29]

There was an odd sequel to the case. The unhorsed barrister instructed a US law firm and issued proceedings out of Waco, Texas, claiming extravagant damages in the sum of 125 million US dollars for loss of reputation and loss of earnings arising

[27] Described by *The Times* on his premature death in 2009 as 'a flamboyant and controversial figure in Bermuda for three decades. Articulate, charming and charismatic, he was a man of great talent and ability, but these strengths were not always counterbalanced by coolness of judgment and political sagacity. He enjoyed a shooting-star career as a defence lawyer, before becoming mired in financial problems and bitter political infighting which almost, but never entirely, extinguished his flame'.

[28] Even appearing in lists in legal journals of the foremost commercial siks and as a commercial arbitrator along with the likes of Desmond Ackner, Sydney Kentridge, David Edward and Arthur Marriott.

[29] [1995] HKLR 67.

out of his dismissal.[30] The proceedings were then transferred to Florida and I was asked whether I would go to Miami and testify on the company's behalf. I was in Seville as a guest of the IAAF[31] (and as legal adviser to the British team) for the world track and field championships and had between then and the start of Oxford term a bare 48 hours to spare. So I agreed that if Exxon, the ultimate owners of the power station, paid premium travel from Seville to Miami and back to Oxford with accommodation thrown in I would oblige. I duly found myself as the sole passenger in the first class section of the Iberian airways plane from Madrid to Miami, lavishly looked after by three beautiful young stewardesses, touched down in Miami, was given a tour of the city and its Art Deco architecture by the Company's Floridian lawyer and arrived expectantly the next day at Court.

The claimant's attorney rose to his feet and addressed the Judge in sombre terms: 'Your honour I could not sleep last night'. The troubling thought flitted across my mind that he was going to ask for an adjournment on grounds of insomnia, so throwing into disarray my carefully scheduled but extremely tight travel plans. The attorney continued 'My opponent has been responsible for the worst form of professional misconduct I have ever encountered'. What could it be I wondered – bribing a witness, threatening a juror? All was swiftly revealed. His explanation for his disrupted slumbers was that in an affidavit his opponent had expressed a personal opinion rather than deposing only to facts. Hyperbole rarely helps. 'Taken under advisement' said the Judge, and I was called to the stand. Most of the questions I was asked about the details of the inquest I could not answer. As I repeatedly pointed out the events in question had occurred several years before, and I had not even been present when his client's brief was taken away. Months later I was astounded to read in a transcript of the same attorney's submissions that what he termed my 'non responsiveness' should be treated as a deliberate effort to mislead the Court. I was not, however, cited for contempt; but was never informed about the outcome of the case itself. Who knows? It may not have finished yet.

Trinidad, like Malaysia, is a country whose politics are dictated by ethnic considerations; but there is an almost even balance of those of African and of Indian ancestry. I have found myself, usually but not always, on the Indian side of the divide, in cases which either directly or indirectly reflected that split.

One visit acquired a peculiar cricketing triple tinge. The English squad, led by Mike Atherton, were staying, exhausted at the end of an arduous tour, in the same hotel as I. Brian Lara,[32] whose autograph I solicited on the steps of the hotel's entrance, seemed explicably in high spirits. One afternoon I was summoned to meet the President of the Republic in his official residence.[33] He offered me a glass

---

[30] A version of the story appears in *Private Eye* 22 April 2009 as 'An explosive tale' authored by Paul Foot who tracked me down but could not persuade me to take the debriefed lawyer's side.

[31] Now World Athletics.

[32] The West Indian batsman, the highest scorer of an innings in Test cricket.

[33] I met his successor in a dress rehearsal for the annual carnival held at the University of the West Indies.

of champagne. I was about politely to protest that this was hospitality and honour too far when he raised his own glass and invited me to toast Courtney Walsh, who had just taken his 500th test wicket. On the return flight I found myself sitting next to Henry Blofeld,[34] aka Blowers, a schoolboy hero as captain of the XI in my first year at Eton. Sleep became superfluous as the popular commentator, apprised of our common education, ran on auto pilot through his repertoire of entertaining cricketing anecdotes.

In a non-political case I had the task of representing reinsurers in a substantial civil claim. In 1990 Trinidad suffered an attempted coup d'état by the Muslimeen (a militant group of Muslims), resulting in the capture of the Parliament building 'the Red House', and the holding hostage of the Prime Minister and other senior Ministers, in a siege which was only ended after an amnesty (subsequently upheld as valid) offered to the insurrectionists. This unsurprisingly prompted some interesting constitutional motions; but my involvement arose out of the widespread looting which accompanied the coup. Many locals had taken advantage of the diversion of the civilian and military authorities, to seize everything and anything from the neighbourhood shops. My opponents' ambitious argument, rejected both at first instance before the unforgettably named Mr Justice Kangaloo and in the Court of Appeal, was that this looting was not even the indirect consequence of the insurrection and that the insurers were liable to indemnify the shop owners in full. We solemnly trooped around the Parliament examining the bullet holes and were reminded of the fragility of democracy as well as gaining sufficient insight into the cause and effect of burglary in less salubrious areas of Port of Spain. The claimants did not pursue an appeal to the Privy Council.

I also acted in Trinidad on behalf of John Uff QC,[35] who was chairing an enquiry into yet another claim of corruption in the local building industry. Judicial review was sought to prevent publication of his report. My opponent, another English silk, lost the case but acquired a new wife, who had a minor role in the proceedings. Swings and roundabouts!

International Arbitration is not only a means by which prematurely retiring judges can make up for lost fees. It offers more scope to advocates for overseas appearances. While there are strict rules governing rights of audience before national courts there are usually no such rules for private arbitration. In one arbitration held under the auspices of the Geneva chamber of commerce I acted for a freebooter who had sought to take advantage of the dissolution of the Soviet Union by negotiating inordinately profitable deals in one of the newly fledged 'Stans. Whenever my client was subjected to a particularly vigorous passage of cross-examination he took time out to lie down at the back of the room claiming that he was suffering from some kind of indisposition, a bit like Novak Djokovic at crucial moments in a key tennis match. The Prime Minister of the 'Stan, chief witness for

---

[34] The broadcaster and after dinner speaker.
[35] A construction law specialist, restorer of old violins and Treasurer of Gray's Inn.

the other side, was made of sterner stuff. However, at the end of the hearing he turned to the Arbitrators, pointed at me and said 'I have travelled thousands of miles to be here and that man has done nothing but insult me'. It is nonetheless always better to receive criticism than praise from the opposition.

The great Nigerian cement scandal took me initially to Bruges. Counsel for the other party was Tony Guest,[36] who regularly applied for time out not to lie down but to smoke. Not just because of the hours lost for him to indulge his addiction, the hearing had to be adjourned for a second session. When it was resumed it took place not in the beautiful medieval Belgian city, but in the bleak and functional surroundings of the Northgate Hall in the Temple. To satisfy the forum clause in the arbitration agreement the hall was deemed to be in Bruges. Always scrutinise the small print to avoid unexpected disappointment.

I used to appear before the Court of Arbitration for Sport (CAS) in Lausanne, of which I was also a member. On one occasion I had been nominated as an arbitrator by Celtic Football Club. UEFA the other party objected on the basis that I had, in another and wholly unconnected case, been party to a decision against them and I had to stand down. Celtic decided that if I could not be its nominated arbitrator, I could be its advocate, which I became without, on this occasion, any objection to this bizarre role reversal.[37]

Judicial review and Euro law combined took me to Gibraltar where I fended off the attack by the Moroccan Workers Association, and spent most evenings with Helen Mountfield, my English junior, walking round the entire colony. I also had an audience with the Prime Minister who handed me a private message for Tony Blair. What it said I do not know.

I was instructed by a Bangladeshi firm based in Dacca to challenge the denial of citizenship to the leader of the opposition, Professor Ghulam Azam, one of those who fought against the bifurcation of Pakistan. I had never heard of any English advocate being granted audience in the Courts in Dacca. Was there not, I enquired, some local law which defined it? The Ordinance was duly sent to me. Section 4 provided that no one could practise in the courts of Bangladesh, who was not a Bangladeshi citizen. That was it – but I, cautious as ever, read on. Section 40 provided that anyone who purported to appear in the Courts of Bangladesh, when not a Bangladeshi citizen, would be liable, upon conviction, to a prison sentence of up to 10 years. My role was sensibly reduced to the provision of written submissions. I was, however, made, as a result of Professor Azam's success, an overseas consultant to the Dacca firm 'The Law Counsel' and later authored for it an analysis of why the infliction of the death penalty upon those who had fought against the partition violated international legal norms.[38]

Reverting to the domestic side of my practice my first substantive appeal in the House of Lords, flying solo, was a VAT case pitting me for the first but not last

---

[36] The eminent academic lawyer and contract specialist.
[37] FN CAS 98/201.
[38] Published in documents and materials of the International War Crimes Tribunal of Bangladesh.

time against Simon Brown,[39] then the Treasury junior. The clerks had sold me to the solicitors, Herbert Smith, celebrated then as now for combative litigation, as someone familiar with administrative law. This was the truth in the sense that immigration law is indeed public, not private law – but scarcely the *whole* truth and certainly nothing but the truth. Immigration is at best a cousin of VAT law and then several times removed. Thank heaven for the audacity of the clerks' room! But the case itself was a harbinger of things to come. Public law was no longer to be perceived to concern itself primarily with the interests of disadvantaged groups – immigrants, prisoners or students – but was equally available in practice, as it had always been in principle, to commercial entities requiring new perspectives and expertise from both branches of the legal profession.

In 1983–84 – my early years in silk – I appeared in three of the most interesting public law cases of that decade, achieving what I called My Golden Treble[40] – *O'Reilly and Mackman;*[41] *ex parte Khawaja;*[42] and *ex parte Shah*[43] – all heard one after the other in the House of Lords. If I'd been asked at the time which of all the papers I then had cluttering up my shelves I would gladly give back, I would have nominated the first two. I'm glad that I never had the chance to make what would have been a serious mistake.

In one of my last junior cases I had successfully argued that judicial review could be brought against the decisions of prison boards of visitors.[44] My client was a Ronald St Germain whose surname as well as his Yale education suggested that he was no common or garden criminal. In the wake of the Hull prison riots in 1976 a succession of prisoners, apprised on the grapevine of this beneficial change in the law, brought motions in the Divisional Court to challenge, on procedural grounds, the loss of remission they had suffered for breach of the prison rules to the visible annoyance of Lord Widgery whose list was flooded with these claims.

O'Reilly, a prisoner in the same establishment, complained that he had been denied an opportunity to call alibi witnesses in his defence. He had lost 510 days remission. In one sense time was on his side; he was serving a 15-year sentence for armed robbery. In another sense it was not. There was a three-month time limit for judicial review, which had expired a long time before. David Pannick ingeniously advised him to seek instead a declaration, a remedy for which no such prescribed time limit existed. The prison governor argued that this bypass of the judicial review route was an abuse of process. The House of Lords, where I led

---

[39] Lord Brown of Eaton-under-Heywood. For the insatiably curious the case can be found in [1981] 1 WLR 1542.

[40] Verdict. 40th anniversary edition. Hilary term 2004 p12.

[41] [1983] 2 AC 237.

[42] [1984] AC 74.

[43] [1983] 1 AC 303.

[44] [1978] QB 678, [1979] QB 425. A delayed by-product was an invitation to give a lecture at a seminar on Prisons Law and Human Rights in Moscow in May 1996 whose proceedings were published in Russian under the title (translated) 'The gaoler and the just man'. Shouldn't that have been 'the unjust man'?

David, agreed with him. While neither statute nor procedural rules had made judicial review an exclusive remedy, Lord Diplock held that presumptively it should be.

In reaching this conclusion Lord Diplock exercised some judicial legerdemain. The House of Lords had listed another (housing) case *Cocks v Thanet* in which a similar point arose, but in which the claimant did not appear, so giving the respondent housing authority a free run. When on O'Reilly's behalf I sought to refer to the many earlier cases in which private law remedies had been granted for public law claims, Lord Diplock said that they had read and noted all the cases the week before. Conveniently he ignored the fact that they had heard only one side of the argument based on them. O'Reilly, designed to bring procedural health to public law, proved instead to be a virus which infected it since it gave rise to a series of cases as to whether and what exceptions there might be to Lord Diplock's rule, so postponing resolution of the substantive issue in those cases. It took two decades before the judiciary supplied an antidote.[45]

Khawaja simply seemed a common or garden – and on its face hopeless – immigration case. To succeed, Louis Blom Cooper[46] and I had to persuade the House of Lords to depart from a decision in *ex parte Zamir* heard only two years earlier. Our task was made no easier by the fact that Lord Wilberforce presided in both cases. The decision in our favour that whether someone was an illegal immigrant was a question of fact for the Court and not simply whether the immigration service reasonably thought that he was, spawned a classic statement of the modern law of habeas corpus from Lord Scarman. In this instance it was our team who exercised their own *legerdemain*, by way of leapfrog. In order to gain the right to open first, we ensured that our solicitors lodged the petition for leave to appeal earlier than the petition in another case, *Khera*, which raised the same issue but had actually been heard before *Khawaja* in the Court of Appeal. Judges sometimes said of Louis's submissions 'Not even Mr Blom-Cooper'. On this occasion there was no need for such an ambiguous encomium.[47]

The moral of that duo of cases is that the ripest forensic fruit can sometimes grow from the least promising of seedlings.

Ex parte Shah involved the question whether students, subject to immigration control, could nonetheless receive grants from local authorities for further education. The House was presided over by Lord Fraser, a kindly and tolerant Scots law lord, who allowed the proceedings – whose outcome turned upon the interpretation of just two words 'ordinarily resident' – to take nine days. That wouldn't be allowed to happen now in these clock watching days.

In due course I became the first chairman of the Administrative Law Bar Association (ALBA) – a late comer to the Bar's specialist bodies. I was proposed for the office by Robert Carnwath, after I had deftly suggested that the other candidate

---

[45] See Michael Beloff, 'The Fate of O'Reilly v Mackman: a Cautionary Tale' in *Constitutional Perspectives Essays in Honour of HM Servai* (Iyer, 2004) pp 227–41.

[46] QC, academic, author, campaigner Kt, DNB.

[47] [1984] 1 AC 74. See *Law and the Spirit of Inquiry. Essays in Sir Louis' Honour* (Blake and Drewry, 1999) pp 12–13.

discussed, Louis Blom Cooper, was 'perhaps a little too grand'. During my term of office I instituted a series of seminars in which judges and academics discussed the same legal issue from their different starting points as well as inviting membership from solicitors – a new departure which pragmatically ignored the body's name. Post, and maybe indeed proper hoc in 1991, under the auspices of the Judicial Studies Board (JSB), I gave a lecture on judicial review to an audience of conscript judges from Law Lords downwards. It was the afternoon of the Rugby World Cup final and Lord Justice Glidewell in charge of the event, in a spirit of transparency, closed the session by announcing the result to the dismay of some of the attendees who had hoped to watch it on television without such a well-intentioned spoiler.

The next year I gave ALBA's annual lecture entitled 'Judicial Review 2000, a Prophetic Odyssey'.[48] It was a journey with some false detours. I had assumed that the Courts would cut through the boundary between bodies with a public and a private source of power and focus on the extent of the power they exercised, whatever the source. More subtly the Courts continued to reserve judicial review for public bodies but applied its principles to monopolist private bodies. Different remedy, same result.

Turning closer to home, if not actually at home, I had various European ventures. The European Commission decided that in order to educate English practitioners in the dark art of advocacy at the ECJ and to indoctrinate them with an *ésprit Communautaire* they should be offered some work experience. This it did by instructing them as the Commission's representative in cases referred to the Court under the Article 177 procedure.

Since equal pay was then (indeed still is) a hot topic, and I had written a commentary on the Sex Discrimination Act, I was a fortunate guinea pig in this experiment. I was briefed at the Commission Headquarters in the Berlaymont in Brussels by a wily Italian tutor, Armando Toledano Laredo, who explained that the Commission's approach in these cases was as much informed by political – in the broad sense – as by legal – in the narrow sense – considerations. And so to Luxembourg with my carefully prepared script from which deviation was not an option.[49]

This mattered little. The oral part of the proceedings is indeed, in Bagehot's phrase, more dignified than efficient. Before the hearing started advocates were introduced to the Judges in their chambers and the President would ask each how much time he or she required for submissions. The maximum then was 30 minutes. The trick was to say 'I hope to be no more than twenty or so minutes' which gave the impression of intended brevity while, on close textual analysis, preserving one's right to the full half-hour. But whatever one said the President had a ready counter. 'Twenty minutes'. Pause. 'Perhaps fifteen? We have read it all already'.

I never in my several cases before that Court participated in one which lasted into the afternoon.[50] And, although the hearing is meant to give an opportunity to

---

[48] (1995) 58 MLR 143.

[49] [1980] ECR 1275, [1981] ECR 767.

[50] See Richards and Beloff, 'A View from the Bar' (ch 2), in *Practitioners' Handbook of EC Law* (Barling and Brearley, 1998).

the Judges to probe the submissions, the only time when I saw a light flicker on the bench and was poised to exploit my common law familiarity with forensic repartee, the Judge's actual question was 'Mr Beloff do you think you will finish your address before lunch?' Brevity never loses the advocates any points.

My top of the euro pops case – and silver medal on the podium of my forensic career – were my briefs on behalf of the redoubtable Helen Marshall – a play in two acts. Marshall One ruled that to compel a woman to retire at the age of 60 when a man could work until 65 constituted unlawful sex discrimination.[51] A man's complaint that it was discrimination in the leisure sphere to compel him to work on till 65 while a woman could retire at 60 was not seen to be within the scope of Community law.

It was a curious feature of this seminal case that the EOC had to be vigorously lobbied to grant support, since they had been advised by their favourite counsel Anthony Lester that Ms Marshall's claim was destined to fail.

I opened my submissions by observing that it was odd to be arguing whether a woman could be compelled to retire at 60 on the very day that Mrs Thatcher, the then Prime Minister, attained that age. Marshall One was the pebble which started the avalanche of domestic legislation on retirement ages and pensions and must have been, in terms of social and economic impact, one of the most influential judicial decisions of recent decades.

Marshall Two established that the cap on awards in the discrimination field itself offended against EU law.[52] As a result of this twin triumph Ms Marshall, and her lawyers, were jointly awarded the first but – as it proved – the only Women's Annual Defence League Award in 1991 conferred by Barbara Castle[53] in a splendid dinner at the Cafe Royal. My radical civil liberty lawyer friends had to watch in silence someone whom they regarded as a somewhat conservative figure being honoured for being at the cutting edge of women's lib.

I was less successful in the House of Lords when trying to defend the provisions of domestic law which prevented claims for unfair dismissal or redundancy payment being made until a part-time employee had been employed for a set period of time, which was held to be indirectly discriminatory against women.[54] That was a case which I had won comprehensively all the way up. It is little use having a majority of judges in your favour if the minority against you sit in the final appellate tribunal.

An Oxford academic in his book *The House of Lords in its Judicial Capacity* wrote that this was 'the worst case ever argued by the Government' in that elevated forum. When I wrote a mildly aggrieved letter to him, suggesting he had put the point a little strongly, he responded that what he *meant* to say was that it was the most difficult case the Government had ever had to argue. Lord Keith had indeed said of the Secretary of State's claim that qualifying periods increased the

---

[51] [1986] 1 QB 401.
[52] [1994] QB 126.
[53] Labour Cabinet Minister, sometimes called the Red Queen.
[54] [1995] 1 AC I.

availability of part-time work – and I quote again – 'did not contain *anything* capable of being regarded as factual evidence demonstrating the correctness of these views'. But lecturers no less than lawyers should be precise in their language.

I did, however, pursue my grievance with the publishers, encouraged by informal advice that I was given by Victoria Sharp, then a prominent libel junior[55] whom I had led on several media-related cases. She suggested that the offending passage carried a potential price tag for the Oxford University Press (OUP) of £10,000 but I should be prepared to settle for half the amount. In the end, averse to unarmed combat with this august dark blue institution, I settled for a private apology, corrections in any future edition, and a contribution of £500 to the scholarship I had set up at Trinity in my father's name.

My last appearance before the ECJ was in the Government's vain attack on the Working Time Directive.[56] For any member of the Bar the idea of a cap of 50 hours a week had a certain irony. Self-employment is not always beneficial to the employee. Alan Rodger[57] was the law officer in charge of the case. In consequence of our collaboration he invited me to the opening of the Scottish legal year. As we merrily retraced our steps to his New Town dwelling in high spirits after a most convivial evening in the Court complex, I wondered what the passers-by would think had they recognised this pillar of the north of the border legal establishment in out of school mode.

I first appeared in the European Commission for Human Rights (ECommHR) and the ECtHR at Strasbourg sitting behind Anthony Lester in the case of Reuben Silver,[58] which opened up the dark recesses of the prison censorship of inmates' correspondence.

Our client was a prisoner and serial letter writer. He objected to the fact that, under the prison rules then in force, his letters, including those to his lawyers and his rabbi, were read by the prison authorities and either censored or subject to lengthy delays in posting. By the time his application fell for consideration, he had died, but his family were entitled to continue the claim, though what benefit he could then have derived from it is less than obvious.

Mr Silver was found to have suffered a violation of his right to private life. I remember the case for two reasons; first that Anthony insisted that I work in the upper room in his house so that he could keep a weather eye on me – arguably a violation of my right to liberty – and secondly, that when the Court came to assess our costs, my bill survived intact whereas Anthony's was taxed down. Our solicitor[59] still refers to Silver, not as a case about prisoners' rights but as the case of counsels' fees.

Flying under my own flag I was instructed by Harriet Harman to argue that the inability of women settled in UK to bring in their husbands, while men could

---

[55] The first female President of the Queen's Bench Division.
[56] [1997] ICR 443.
[57] JSC.
[58] (1983) 5 EHRR 347.
[59] Stephen Grosz, an honorary QC.

bring in their wives, was discriminatory on grounds of sex and race.[60] Harriet already displayed the calmness of a successful politician by remaining unconcerned about the disappearance en route to Strasbourg of one of our clients.

My opponent was Lord Rawlinson, nicknamed on account of his hyper-plummy accent as Lord Raw-Haw. He introduced himself to the polyglot Court, comprised mainly of judges from civilian jurisdictions, as a common lawyer – *un avocat très ordinaire*. I sensibly resisted the temptation in my reply, to suggest impudently that this was the only true statement he had made in his entire submission. I won the case: but the victory was pyrrhic. The Government did not give wives the same rights as husbands: they took away the husbands' rights – equality of misery.

In Strasbourg I also acted for the Duke of Westminster – the only man to take on the Government who was almost as rich as they were – and Ernest Saunders, who claimed to be a good deal poorer.

The Duke challenged the compatibility of the leasehold enfranchisement legislation with Article 1 of the First Protocol of the ECHR which protects property rights.[61] My two juniors were Francis Jacobs and David Neuberger,[62] then best known as a landlord and tenant specialist. David used to accompany me on a morning walk from hotel to court and drafted a mean schedule or two, detailing the properties in the ducal Mayfair Estate to hand up to the judges. The case was heard together with a claim for compensation by the shareholders in the steel industry nationalised by a Labour Government which the new Conservative Government had somewhat uncomfortably to resist.

Grandees on both sides of the legal profession arrived at their destination only to find that their luggage, including their vital files, had been mislaid. It took Harry Kidd, the bursar of St John's, Oxford, part of the Duke's team, to track it down.[63] Sometimes an ounce of practical common sense is worth more than a ton of legal scholarship.

At the beginning of a five-day hearing Anthony, acting for the aggrieved shareholders, made a submission about the concept of indirect discrimination. He used the analogy (as he often did) of a door insufficiently wide for a fat man to get through. That evening I wrote a letter to Anthony (with the connivance of the other counsel) purporting to come from the President of the Commission, stating that the Icelandic Commissioner – a large man indeed, nicknamed Cyril Smithonsson because of his striking resemblance to the later discredited liberal MP – had taken offence at Anthony's submission and suggesting that Anthony might wish to apologise at the opening of the next day's proceedings. Anthony was prompted to consult all of his colleagues over the drafting and redrafting of the text of a heartfelt apology – until he was put out of his misery. Oh, wot larks!

---

[60] (1985) 7 ECHR 471.
[61] (1986) 8 ECHR 123.
[62] Master of the Rolls and President of the Supreme Court.
[63] Harry died before he could write his own history of the case.

Mr Saunders, head honcho of Guinness, had been convicted of various offences in connection with Guinness's attempted takeover of Distillers. I was instructed to challenge the finding of guilt on the basis that his privilege from self-incrimination had been violated when he was forced by law to answer questions to the DTI inspectors investigating the affair.[64] I was assisted, in the French rather than English sense of the word, by George Devlin, a private investigator, whose previous clients included the Kray twins and Lord Lucan, and to whom Mr Saunders had taken an unaccountable fancy. He was acting in the secondary English sense of the word as a lawyer. The Strasbourg Court held Mr Saunders had indeed been denied his right to a fair trial.

This was not the only miracle enjoyed by Mr Saunders. The Court of Appeal (Criminal Division) had ordered his early release from prison when he produced medical evidence that he was suffering from Alzheimer's. Lo and behold shortly afterwards he made a full recovery. The next time I saw Mr Saunders was in the first-class lounge at Gatwick airport whence he was flying to New York on some new business enterprise. When he and his fellow members of the Guinness 4 sought to have their convictions retrospectively quashed in the English Courts I led for Mr Saunders in the Court of Appeal (for my own casebook, but for no other conceivable purpose the reference is [2002] 2 Cr App R 15) but, displaying a keen sense of economy, he opted out of pursuing his case to the House of Lords, leaving the others to carry on the battle there, but without success.

Another unforgettable Strasbourg case came to me from Greece, against a backcloth of litigation arising out of the Colonels' short-lived coup d'état. Stran Industries, my client, had the benefit of an arbitral award against the Greek Government. Just before the hearing of a claim for its enforcement in the domestic courts, the Government changed the rules of the game by enacting legislation which deprived Stran of the fruits of victory. They claimed that this violated both their right to a fair trial and their property rights.[65] My Greek opponent, a government lawyer, suffered from air sickness and may have been in less than top form. In any event he spoke at such a rate that the interpreter was provoked to scream from behind her glass panel 'I can't keep up with this anymore'. The ECtHR gave Stran the largest award of compensation then ever made.

Because of that litigation background, I was asked by the Foreign and Commonwealth Office (FCO) to give a private talk to the visiting Mayor of Moscow on Human Rights. What, if any, impact it had on him I know not. Since my remarks had to be interpreted it may be that something was lost in translation. I was also asked by the FCO whether I might wish to become the UK representative on the UN Human Rights Committee or on the ECommHR. I genuinely felt that the posts required someone more unambiguously committed to a full frontal human rights agenda than I perceived myself to be and as both

---

[64] A not entirely impartial background is to be found in James Saunders' *Nightmare: Ernest Saunders And The Guinness Affair* (Saunders, 1990).

[65] (1995) 19 EHRR 293, Stran's was a coincidence of complaints made by another Strasbourg client the Russian business Yukos.

those subsequently appointed, most certainly were. I also was one of a small flock of specialists who gave talks to the judiciary in anticipation of the enactment of the Human Rights Act.

I acquired as a client the Church of Scientology in succession to an odd couple, Quintin Hailsham QC, later a Tory Lord Chancellor, and Peter Pain QC, later a High Court judge and an acknowledged man of the left.

My most interesting case for the Church was the application by L Ron Hubbard, the Church's founder, to enter the UK: the object being to test whether the one-time ban on Scientologists, lifted only in 1980, still applied to the Church's leader. The Home Office, astute to avoid reviving the public policy issue, disputed that Mr Hubbard was still alive: and therefore that he needed an entry permit. The response was, if he is dead, what objection can there be to giving him one? Impasse.[66] Having lost before Mr Justice Woolf the Church decided not to pursue the appeal. However, for explicable presentational reasons their representatives wished to withdraw it rather to have it dismissed. Through the usual (or maybe unusual) channels we informed the Master of the Rolls, Sir John Donaldson, of the terms on which the Court would not be troubled with a full hearing. We understood that he was agreeable to this proposal. Unfortunately, when the moment came he fluffed his lines, but since the media would probably not have appreciated the subtleties of the scripted phraseology, maybe it mattered little.

It was through the good offices of the Church that I took my only flight on Concorde. The experience was only slightly devalued by the fact that on the return journey from Dulles, the plane took off three hours late which somewhat defeated the object of the exercise for travellers whose schedules were tighter than mine.

The major and recurrent issue was the status of the Church. For it to be recognised as a religion conferred fiscal as well as reputational advantages. I co-authored an opinion with David Pannick to be transmitted to the Government, supporting the Church's claim which was later recognised in the immigration rules in 1996 and finally by the Supreme Court in 2013.

Similar issues arose with another client, the Plymouth Brethren, whom the Charity Commission refused initially to accept as a charity (the *Preston Down* case), a decision which we sought to challenge partly in reliance on Article 9 of the ECHR. In seeing the client's Australian representatives in consultation I was reminded, to respect their beliefs, neither to shake their hands nor to offer them coffee. Litigation, other than procedural, was avoided when upon review the Charity Commission changed its stance.

Did judicial review lie against a disciplinary decision taken in a religious context? Apparently not. I was instructed on behalf of the Chief Rabbi to defend a ruling by the Beth Din the rabbinical court of Judaism.[67] The case was listed for a

---

[66] The case is referred to in David Pannick's unpublished Francis Mann Lecture on Religion and the Law.

[67] [1992] 1 WLR 1036.

Friday hearing and his representatives, anxious to observe orthodox Jewish practice not to travel on the Sabbath, asked me to request the judge to rise before dusk.
I said that I did not think it necessarily wise to invite a secular court to adjust its
timetable for religious reasons but, I added, I had no doubt that with the weekend
imminent the judge would anyhow be anxious to rise as early as possible. And I
appeared to join the ranks of the very minor prophets as rise then he did.

No such temporal problems arose in the case where, on behalf of a Reverend
Williams, a priest taken in adultery, I sought to challenge his expulsion by the
Provincial Court of the Church of Wales. The Divisional Court again adhered to
the principle that there was a difference between what could be rendered unto
Caesar and what should be rendered under God. No split there in this aspect of
our Judaeo-Christian heritage.

Some regular clients produced a steady stream of work. For the Civil Aviation
Authority I would apply for a detention of aircraft whose owners had failed to
pay the landing fees. For the Department of Health I wrestled with the mysteries
of the Social Fund which prompted the thought that if I, with all the resources of
a Department of State behind me, found it so difficult to make my way through
the legal instruments in play, for those who depended upon the funds' benefits
for their very subsistence, the route must have been all but impenetrable. Despite
my Luddite-like aversion to technological development but with the assistance of
Ms Helen Mountfield,[68] aka (at any rate by me) thoroughly modern Hellie, my
junior *de choix* while I was at 4–5 Gray's Inn Square, I gave regular advice to the
Data Protection Registrar. Its legal adviser, Rosemary Jay, wrote to me when the
advices were belatedly filed in electronic form, 'They used to be like down and
outs in a large cardboard box, simply called "the Beloff Box"'. I advised Ofcom on
privacy issues and Ofgem on offshore transmission within the United Kingdom.[69]
With Rabinder Singh[70] I assisted in a fundamental restructuring of the Hong
Kong Stock Exchange, one of a hat trick of advices to Exchanges (the others being
London and Kuala Lumpur).

The most obvious switch in my practice as a silk was from being substantially
a plaintiff or claimant's lawyer to being substantially a defendant's or respondent's lawyer. though this was not always so. I appeared for Tamil refugees in the
case which gave rise to the concept of 'anxious scrutiny' to inform the executive
approach to cases where life and limb were at risk.[71] The case was paused for a
day while one member of the Appellate Committee went to a royal garden party.
I am convinced that the 24 hour hiatus gave those Law Lords not in receipt of a

---

[68] QC, Principal of Mansfield College.

[69] Once in 1993 on the issue of an interconnector with France having an audience in the Board
of Trade with its President Michael Heseltine. A summary of my advice was placed in the House of
Commons Library.

[70] Lord Justice. We were instructed by Geoffrey Lewis of Herbert Smith, biographer of Lord Hailsham
and Dr Francis Mann.

[71] [1987] AC 514.

similar invitation the chance themselves anxiously to scrutinise the Government case; certainly the fresh relish with which they besieged Treasury Counsel on the resumption of the hearing owed nothing to my submissions, by now concluded, which had not excited a sympathetic response at the time they were made.

But generally speaking such a switch is the way of the legal world. The letters QC and loss of and/or greying of hair is thought to impart weight. And my move from 2 Hare Court to 4/5 Gray's Inn Square,[72] later, brought with me clients from both local and central government with which my new set had substantial contacts. I surrendered one Christmas vacation to work on fending off a potential challenge to the approval of the Sizewell B nuclear reactor, storing the Layfield report in a special secure filing cabinet provided by the Government and housed next to my ageing Saab in the garage at the bottom of my Oxford garden. I was, along with Margaret Thatcher, one of only half a dozen people given advanced access to the report, though this was less than total consolation for the constraint on my indulgence in the seasonal festivities. Later, to discuss the inevitable judicial review,[73] I visited Paddy Mayhew in the Attorney General's Chambers, then in the Law Courts, with my junior Genevra Caws, one of the three best female barristers with whom I ever worked. Paddy said 'do bring your little lady with you'. I can easily imagine what Brenda Hale might have said about such an invitation.

Gordon Pollock and I were instructed to appear for Lonrho in a case arising out of Lonrho's long legal battle to publish a Government report on its unsuccessful bid in 1981 for House of Fraser, the owner of Harrods department store. The Trade and Industry Secretary had refused to publish the report until the police completed an inquiry into the purchase in 1985 of the same entity by the Egyptian-born Al Fayed brothers. Lonrho obtained a leaked copy of the report, and excerpts from it were published in a special edition of *The Observer*. It then sent copies of the newspaper to four of the Law Lords who were to decide on the issue of publication. As a result they charged Lonrho with contempt of the House of Lords.

Our first argument was that the Law Lords who had instituted the proceedings for contempt should recuse themselves from sitting; prosecutors should not become judges in their own cause. Gordon had carriage of this part of the case which was heard in the Moses Room. He displayed a degree of courage which I could not have matched in face of a resistant panel presided over by the senior Law Lord, Lord Keith, in his traditional combative bald-headed pose, resembling nothing so much as a wrestler waiting for the opening bell to sound. Gordon was not so much flash as ferocious. He irritated Lord Ackner by noting that his (Desmond's not Gordon's) father had been Tiny Rowland's dentist.[74] There were moments when, during the verbal crossfire, I would have preferred to be sitting behind

---

[72] See Chapter 13, 'Life at the Bar'. I sometimes call the chambers colloquially 4/5.

[73] [1988] JPL 749. Years on I had to wrestle with the legal problems caused by the disposal of nuclear waste. What comes up must go down …

[74] See my essay 'The End of the Twentieth Century' in Louis Blom-Cooper (ed), *The House of Lords 1876–2009* at p 235ff.

rather than beside him. By sheer force of personality he ground the committee down; and when a freshly constituted body were appointed to hear the case on its merits I had by far the easier task to have it dismissed.[75]

I also played a role as inquisitor in several inquiries set out below in reverse order.

In 1998 the independent television company, Carlton, was fined £2 million for a documentary *The Connection* in which actors pretended to be drug traffickers, after receiving a report from a three-man panel of experts of which I was one. The programme claimed to show evidence of a new heroin trafficking route from Colombia to the UK. It was feted with praise and awards but an investigation by the *Guardian* newspaper revealed it was a sham. Our strong sense was that the *Guardian* anticipated a whitewash and had rapidly to revise its coverage of our critical report which made several recommendations to avoid repetition. When our report was published Carlton's press release had a footnote 'For Further Information Please contact David Cameron'. For some reason in all 744 pages of his memoir *On the Record* Mr Cameron omits to mention this significant milepost in the making of the Prime Minister.

In 1991 a Channel 4 Despatches programme called *The Committee* made by Vox Productions alleged, with the support of a secret source, that members of the security forces, loyalist paramilitaries and local businessmen had formed a committee in Northern Ireland's protestant community to plan the killing of Catholics. The idea for this acutely sensitive project had passed up via Liz Forgan[76] to Michael Grade,[77] its Chief Executive and then to Channel 4's Board. Lawyers carefully vetted the transcript before Mr Grade gave approval for its transmission. The programme caused predictable outrage. An undertaking of secrecy had been given to the chief source, who claimed to be a member of the Committee and a refusal to reveal his name led to a substantial fine being levied on Channel 4. I was instructed to do a compliance audit of the programme checking every aspect of the production process and interviewing the key Channel 4 personnel involved. In the end I could identify no lack of care or breach of ITC's or Channel 4's rules and gave it 'a clean bill of health'.[78]

My role was confined to investigations in London, not Londonderry (for which I was for reasons which require no embellishment duly grateful). There was a yet further twist in the tale. Six months later the *Sunday Times* tracked down the secret source who claimed that his evidence was a hoax. Michael Grade stood by the programme and demanded a public inquiry which never took place.

---

[75] [1990] 2 AC 154. The case is described in 'Two Lives' by Edward du Cann, a Lonhro Director pp 248–50. In 2004, when visiting Cyprus to address the Oxford University Society, at the invitation of Tony Hart, an ex-president of the Union and Headmaster of Cranleigh, I encountered Edward as one of a group of expats in a clique who described themselves, a trifle sadly, as the 'A' team. Inevitably he gave me a signed copy of the book.

[76] Dame. The epitome of a multi portfolio-ed *Guardian* woman.

[77] Chairman of C5 and BBC. Life Peer.

[78] See Michael Grade, *It Seemed Like a Good Idea at the Time* (Grade, 2000) pp 345–49.

Some years later, together with Rabinder Singh, I advised the Independent Commission on Policing in Northern Ireland, chaired by Chris Patten,[79] on the human rights and discrimination aspects of the putative proposals.[80] The Commission looked forward to a bright future rather than backward to a mottled past.

I was appointed on the recommendation of Pat Neill, then Vice-Chancellor, by Oxford University's Hebdomadal Council and Congregation to chair a Tribunal along with two senior dons in what the BCC described as the first known case of plagiarism at Oxford in 800 years. The epithet 'known' was significant. The offender's doctorate on the topic of Rebus sic Stantibus in international law was substantially copied, sometimes all but verbatim for his thesis, from an earlier thesis published in three articles in learned journals. The offender's thesis was itself published in a monograph. An astute Cambridge student noticed the similarity between the two theses which had eluded not only the offender's Oxford supervisor but his two examiners, all of whom were leading specialists in the field. The offender's plea of 'mere coincidence' was on the evidence unsustainable. In consequence of our recommendation the offender, who had by then achieved a significant post in the Greek diplomatic service, was deprived of his degree.

Our report was published[81] but Pat Neill's successor decided that the postscript, which made recommendations to prevent recurrence of an action which we stigmatised as 'not only intrinsically deceptive, but inimical to proper academic inquiry and research' should not be circulated beyond the General Board,[82] then responsible for Oxford's academic administration, in case it encouraged other potential plagiarists. Three decades on in the era of the internet and world wide web I fear that such plagiarism will become both more prevalent and less detectable.

However not all my recommendations in other spheres fell on stony soil. I reviewed and only modestly revised the disciplinary rules for the Institute of Chartered Accountants but turned down an offer to chair its Disciplinary Tribunal which could have placed me in an invidious position of marking my own script. I did the same for the General Medical Council's code on confidentiality. Neither was controversial and, as I explained about the former, 'Change for change's sake is not a rational policy, nor is the grass on the other side always greener, indeed it may not be green at all'.[83] A maxim with some general merit?

---

[79] Last Governor of Hong Kong, European Commissioner, Chancellor of Oxford University. Life Peer.

[80] See Chris Patten, *First Confession: A Sort of Memoir* (Patten, 2017) p 179.

[81] See *Oxford University Gazette* 7 June 1990.

[82] By analogy with the 30 years rule I consider that the veil of secrecy should now be discreetly lifted.

[83] *Accountancy* January 1990 p24.

6

Transition to Trinity

In autumn 1994, I was arguing an insurance appeal in Bermuda Court of Appeal. It ended on a Friday. The only direct flight back to London was on Saturday. I wanted to spend, if possible, a full weekend with my family in Oxford before returning to London to make the opening speech on Monday in the libel trial which pitched Eastenders' star, Gillian Taylforth, against *The Sun*.[1] First, I tried, without success, to bribe a schoolboy, set to return for the start of a new school year, to give me his Bermuda–London air ticket. Next, I gambled on a switch of my flight to go back via New York on the Friday night. Bad call. New York became unseasonably blanketed under several feet of snow. Finally, I was able to negotiate a different flight via Toronto – not exactly as the crow flies – and got back with barely a day to spare.

Jet lag or no, I was on my feet in Court 14 at kick-off. The libel trial lasted a week. I was not able to stay for the jury verdict. I had to fly on to Hong Kong to represent China Light and Power in an inquest.[2] It was not until I was sitting in the lounge at Hong Kong Airport before my return that I first read of the drama of Gillian's collapse in Court after her 10–2 loss, one juror short of what she needed – front-page stuff in every national newspaper.

Such episodes caused me to wonder whether the continued excitement of a front-row lifestyle was outflanked by the concomitant exhaustion.[3] Always an insomniac, I started to experience physical – maybe psychosomatic – pain. In an alternative to the highway to the Bench, I explored a by-way, the possibility of headship of a house. It had to be Oxford: if there were blue blood in my veins it would be dark blue.

Being something of a romantic I ruled out of consideration any college founded less than four centuries ago. I dreamed of ancient buildings and portraits of historic figures in dimly lit halls. After four failed attempts including – whisper it not in Gath – at Balliol, Trinity's 'auld enemy', I succeeded at the fifth time of asking at Trinity, which was, in retrospect, always my most obvious destination.

Fortune, as ever, played its part. To fill up space in *Legal Business*, one of the new genre of legal magazines, which concentrated on professional gossip rather than case commentary, I was asked a series of questions, including who would be

---

[1] Chapter nine, 'Good Names and Bad'.
[2] Chapter five, 'The Silk Road'.
[3] One of my juniors later told me that she feared that I might kill myself by overwork.

my preferred dinner guest. My somewhat, but not wholly, frivolous answer – Steve Ovett[4] – clearly intrigued the editor more than the conventional choices of my peers such as Abraham Lincoln or Marilyn Monroe – or those of the truly syco-phantic, such as the Lord Chief Justice or Senior Law Lord. In a follow-up profile[5] in which I was asked what next lay in store for me, I said that I rather fancied being Head of an Oxford College. Shortly after I was contacted by Alan Milner, now the long-established Law fellow at Trinity, who asked whether my statement was just a throwaway line. When I confirmed that my interest was genuine, he told me that Trinity would be looking for a new President and offered to run my candidacy.

I duly submitted an application with a trio of eminent referees, Harry Woolf, Tom Bingham and David Williams, selected to paper over my own shortcomings. I travelled through the various stages of the long list via the long short list to the short list itself of the five or so candidates selected for interview. The day of the interview was the first time I had walked through the college gates in 30 years. I had hardly been, in the political sense, nursing the constituency. The engineer-ing fellow asked me about my attitude to modern technology (cautious answer, in principle supportive but in practice incompetent). The Chaplain inquired whether I would attend chapel (confident answer yes). I was able to say to my inquisitors that, if I had to chair a committee where dons dispute, guiding (*sed quaere*) discus-sion at a chambers meeting was no bad training. The best, if flustered answer I could give to the history fellow's question 'You have a perfectly good job, why on earth do you want to come here?' was a wish to seek new challenges exploiting my experience as a head of chambers.

On the day of the election itself I was at a Gray's Inn student away day at Cumberland Lodge in Windsor Great Park. As the hours passed I heard nothing; no news it seemed was to be bad news. And then, just before dinner, one of the staff told me that someone called Williams had been trying to reach me; it was Trevor, the Vice-President, one of a handful of fellows surviving from my time as a weekender. Optimistically assuming that his function was to inform the winner, not to console the losers, I rang him back, and promptly indicated my acceptance of the College's offer, to be formally confirmed at the next meeting of the Governing Body on the following Wednesday. At the end of my first year I found an enve-lope in my pigeonhole in the Porters' Lodge (no sender identified) which provided the detail of how the Governing Body had chosen me by a process of transferable votes. Two of my defeated rivals, one an eminent geneticist, another a senior offi-cial in the United Nations, themselves acquired headships shortly after. In these matters there's no accounting for taste.

Until election day, I, with some difficulty, all but kept silent, telling only my closest friends and allies in Chambers. The announcement had to be properly managed. Neither I nor they wished to suggest that I was quitting the Bar for good. I also told my referees. Harry, innocently assuming that I must at least have

---

[4] Multi-medalled middle distance athlete.
[5] 90 *Legal Business* May 1994.

informed my parents, congratulated my father. He, though taken by surprise, was pleased that I was fulfilling one of his own ambitions. However, when I belatedly spoke with my mother, her immediate, if disconcerting, response was 'But what about your career?' Some sons do 'ave 'em.

On the evening of the election day itself, just before I was leaving to speak at the Oxford Union with Peter Goldsmith, in defence of the profession against the rhetorical assault of Chris Mullin MP, I was telephoned for a comment by *The Times*. The editor, Peter Stothard, a Trinity graduate, had his spies standing under Trinity's Chapel Arch where the official announcement was posted. In haste I replied that I was very much looking forward to a *slower* pace of life – and the exact quotation duly appeared in next day's issue. Judith pointed out to me wisely that it would have been more sensible to say a *different* pace of life. No sooner had *The Times* hit the stands than I was telephoned by Jeffrey. He opened our conversation with the words 'I have just been speaking to the Prime Minister. Now I want to speak to the President' – one of his better lines.

The intervening year passed swiftly. On the eve of my departure to Atlanta for my baptism as a member of CAS I was a dinner guest of the President of the Law Society; adieu (or as it turned out au revoir) to full-time life as a barrister, hello to a different phase. I was still arbitrating at the Olympic Games when my term of office started in August 1996. On my first day back in England I bicycled into College only to be pulled up short by one of the vigilant lodge staff who shouted out 'Hey *you*; *you* are not allowed to bring your bicycle in here'. The lodge is the first port of call to the college. I was not going, on day one (or after), to drive a wedge between lodge and lodgings and duly dismounted. I learned only later of my unique privilege to be able to park my car in the front quad. Our new home was undergoing in Walter Annenberg's phrase 'elements of refurbishment' and we didn't actually claim our residence rights until Christmas, just in time for a suppliant group of Russians, misled by their tourist agency into a belief that the University never closed, to be allowed by me, in seasonal spirit, into the front quad for a five minute photographic session.

For me the college was and was to be treated as a community. At a governing body meeting I mentioned that the traditional transmural singing directed at, and reciprocated by, the adjacent Balliol (think Man Utd/Man City fans chanting, only slightly more decorously) was disturbing my slumbers. A senior Fellow commented that the President was expected to join in – a proposition I forbore to verify, in lieu raiding my burgeoning collection of airline bags for ear plugs.

As its 26th President it was something of a surprise to me to learn that in terms of age Trinity, founded in 1555, only ranks fourteenth among the Oxford colleges. It stands on the site of Durham College, established by the monks of the great Benedictine House at Durham as a prototype mediaeval summer school. When Henry VIII dissolved the monasteries in a fit of pique over papal interference in his marriage plans, Sir Thomas Pope, who had a principal role in distribution of the monastic assets, acquired the Durham site as a species of commission and founded Trinity. I would regularly say that I would be delighted if there was more than a physical link between Durham and Trinity colleges. Trinity would then have a claim to be the oldest college in the University as well as the best.

But there is one advantage of its late creation. It enjoys the luxury of space denied to older foundations within the walls of the city, not least the magnificent gardens. In the Guardian's *Good University Guide* these were once described as 'leased from Balliol'. After my rapid representations this heinous error was not repeated. Its central location, its intimacy, a function of its small size, as well as its cuisine were constantly described to me by the students as the College's most obviously attractive features.

Trinity's contribution to the nation's history was no less engaging. The college has nurtured three Prime Ministers – all in the eighteenth century – of somewhat uneven calibre (Chatham, North, Wilmington), two Archbishops of Canterbury, one Archbishop of York, a Lord Chancellor, a Lord Chief Justice, a Cardinal (Newman, since my time elevated to sainthood), a Foreign Secretary, Editors of *The Guardian* and *The Times*,[6] three Nobel Prize winners, an Olympic 400 metre gold medallist, a double VC, an Oscar nominee, and numerous other statesmen and scholars, Heads of House, and headmasters, Bishops and Judges, novelists and playwrights, actors and composers, poets and scientists. The most prestigious of these were commemorated in portraits in Hall, many of the others on the staircase behind the Old Bursary (site of Governing Body meetings and, no less importantly, of lunch) which I called the Rogues Gallery. Fictional characters had also populated the college, most notably the Great Gatsby, and Tiger Tanaka, James Bond's ally in *You Only Live Twice*.

There are lesser-known features of Trinity's history. William Hague told me that he started plotting his political career which culminated as Foreign Secretary, in Trinity's beer cellar. Bill Clinton's first-term special adviser on education during a pre-lunch walk around the front quad pointed out the very room where, he claimed, the future President famously didn't inhale. Trinity's twentieth-century graduates included Tony Crosland, Jeremy Thorpe, John Peyton, Jacob Rees-Mogg[7] (whose father Lord (William) of that name, a Balliol man, obviously appreciated the greater virtues of its neighbour for his son's education) and Jeremy Corbyn's economic adviser. I toyed with the idea of a modern political tour of the college. It remained only an idea.

No particular CV is specified for an Oxford head of house. The pool of potential appointees is of unplumbed depths. The job description was what public lawyers call 'open textured'. The College Statutes require from the President not only an oath of fidelity to the College's laws, but to the performance of the duties of office.

---

[6] At a Gaudy I told of a quartet of senior alumni taking the air in Broad Street late at night after a college feast and attracting a policeman's attention who suspiciously asked them to identify themselves: 'I am', said the first, 'the Leader of the House of Commons', 'I', said the second, 'am Editor of the Times', 'I', said the third, 'am Chairman of the BBC'. 'And you', said the policeman sarcastically to the fourth, 'I suppose are the Governor of the Bank of England'. 'Well', he replied, 'as a matter of fact I am'. The cast list was accurate if the scene was less so.

[7] MP, Leader of the House of Commons until moved to an ad hoc Ministry dealing with the benefits of Brexit and Government reform.

Prime among them is to be in residence at least six months of every year, at least six weeks of each must be in full term. There is an instant disparity between rule and reality. Even if, in the past, Heads of House would signify their presence in the College by walking once round the front quad before catching the 07.55 to London Paddington, their role in the new millennium could not properly be performed in absentia. Although not personally averse to doing a little bit of this and a little bit of that, I sought to avoid the reproach reflected in another of the more etiolated quips in the Oxford bumper fun book, 'what is the difference between the President and God? God is everywhere, but the President is everywhere except in Trinity'. Not the least of the charms of the Presidency was living above the office; commuting involved a descent of all of five steps.

The other obligations were a curious mixture of the particular and the general. The President has 'custody of the muniments and of the common seal of the College'; is superintendent of the property of the College; ensures that its laws are observed; has oversight of discipline and administration; and 'to take such part in the educational work of the College ... as the College shall, with his consent, from time to time determine' – the latter clause apparently carefully devised to invert George Bernard Shaw's famous saying so as to make it read 'those who can teach, and those who can't do'.

A little more elaboration was provided by the particulars of the job, which aspirants to the Presidency receive. In my case I was particularly struck by the requirement that the President dined in Hall as frequently as possible. In Trinity that was not a case of combining duty with pleasure, but rather of duty becoming the purest form of pleasure. I was excessively pleased by the tradition of Fellows and Students standing when the President enters Hall at dinner to be greeted by some conscript scholar intoning a brief grace. I was amused by the fact that when I sat down it was not at the head of the table but at one end because the then steward of common room thought it appropriate that my back (he may have put it more robustly) should be facing Balliol.

I was often asked: 'what does a Head of House actually do?'. I perfected a reply of no more than 30 seconds' length.

> Every day there are three time zones to inhabit and constituencies to face within them. The future (schools, parents, applicants), the present (students, academic and domestic staff, the university and, indeed, the world) and the past (alumni) – and I seek to suggest to them all, with some economy of truth, that their interests are identical.

When I chaired my own first governing body meeting I opened the proceedings by saying cautiously 'I must thank you for electing me; whether I should congratulate you too we must wait and see'. The difference between enjoyment and misery as a Head of House depends, if not exclusively, on whether there is a generally united governing body. I can truthfully say that there was no Fellow, had I found myself placed by him or her at dinner, who would have made me wish I'd opted for a takeaway in front of the telly – though this was a matter of minimal importance since I could organise the placings at dinner though not at dessert. There I was by convention not only *not* primus inter pares, but barely one of the pares, learning about the mysteries of the backhander of port to which the senior fellow present was entitled and, as in a game of pass the parcel, handing on the snuff box which contained a reddish powder which may well have dated back to the College's foundations. I certainly enjoyed the opportunity for continuing education by talking about subjects other than the law with so many fellows with different high-grade expertise.

There is a book to be written – were there to be a readership – on heads of Oxbridge colleges who lasted three years or less. Thereby hang several tales of how ostensibly intelligent people, selectors and selected, can so misjudge the future relationship. No wonder that more and more frequently head-hunters are employed; and probationary periods or limited renewable terms become the norm. Starting his term at Teddy Hall, the same time as I joined Trinity, was Sir Stephen Tumin, former chief inspector of prisons, who had in an earlier incarnation invited me to share a sandwich when I was sitting as an Assistant Recorder at the Willesden County Court, his previous fiefdom. He obviously found the Fellows more troublesome than those detained at Her Majesty's pleasure since the tom toms were beating audibly by the fourth week of his first term and he did not survive beyond the triennium.

One issue which confronted me was the explicable reluctance of Fellows to take on an additional role as a college officer, not because of any need to 'publish or perish' but because of a devotion to their subject expressed either in research or, if not universally, in teaching. My predecessor had left unfilled the key post of Estates Bursar in charge of the college's finances after the retirement of the economics fellow who had filled it for five decades. I was reading the business pages of *The Times* when I noticed an intriguing headline that a City high-flyer John Martyn, then finance director of Littlewoods, was retiring to Oxford to spend more time on charity work. I wrote to him out of the blue explaining that I too had come from a high-pressure London job and was already enjoying the different environment. John, who charmingly but wrongly assumed in accepting my offer that the post was unpaid, was enthusiastically appointed, *nem con.* The story of his capture featured not only in a substantial news story in *The Times* but in an editorial too, entitled 'The Joys of a Bursar'. It was a lucky strike.

A similar problem lay in the need to find someone to oversee the College's academic side. I decided that volunteers were a better bet than conscripts; and Trinity became only the second Oxford college to appoint a full-time senior tutor, Trudy Watt, who later became a benefactor too.

In both fields, while formally involved, I chose only rarely to interfere in the work of others better equipped than I.

In my last year a Chinese student at Tsinghua University, Beijing, the PRC's equivalent of MIT, applied to the college but, because of visa issues, was unable to be interviewed by Oxford's ambulant group of dons who annually toured the East for the purpose of assessing potential students. To admit him without such assessment would, it was argued by the Senior Tutor, open the door to a critical media who might misinterpret such departure from orthodoxy as a possible precedent for (or even sequel to) admission of, for example, founders' kin (were there still any such) or, more plausibly, of offspring of benefactors, past or promised, at the expense of a candidate who had passed through all the usual hoops.

I was unconvinced that the principle of equal treatment of applicants for places at Oxford, so greatly valued but in such short supply, then as it is now a hot button issue, would be violated in fact, even if in form in the case of the young man in question. He had won a youth Olympics prize for physics and was to be interviewed for a Jardine Scholarship by a panel, which I chaired, and which included a science professor from the University of Hong Kong. With some understandable reluctance, the Senior Tutor withdrew her objection. On my return to the College a year on, I inquired how the student had fared in his first public examinations and was told that he had come top in the whole university. Who dares (sometimes) wins.

My approach to admissions has always been a simple one: Oxford should solicit applications from every available constituency in the maintained as well as in the private sector, from home and abroad, so as to enable selection to be made from the best and brightest of their generation. But at the point of selection the only criterion should be the candidates' academic potential to pursue the desired degree course. For Oxford to admit (or even be compelled to admit) persons simply because they come from a particular social or ethnic group would be inconsistent with what I perceived to be its educational functions. Diversity should be the result of an outreach policy; it should not be its purpose. It was a position that I constantly reiterated in public as well as in private to sceptics convinced that there was deliberate bias against one or other segment of applicants.

Seeking to maximise the pool of able applicants was certainly virtuous. I enjoyed visiting schools, reprising my Chambers role as a recruiting officer, and using a talk about the Bar or, in the new century, human rights as my ticket for an invitation.[8] If I visited more schools in the private than the state sector (grammar schools apart) this was because the chances of attracting applicants from the former greatly outweighed the chances of attracting such applicants from the latter – a function of the fact that state schools so greatly outnumbered public schools. But I was a voluble fixture at open days for aspirant lawyers which the university law students themselves organised.

Colleges had agreed upon areas of the country on which access staff of each should focus. Trinity specialised in the northeast; I gave prizes at one of the Bradford grammar schools (male) and spoke at the other (female) and then over the hills to a comprehensive school in Halifax from whence hailed one of my outstanding undergraduates. But I found my talk to a group of comprehensive schoolteachers in the city itself discouraging because so many of them appeared

---

[8] Not all these talks were as discreet as they should have been. I suggested at one co-ed boarding school that a rule which said that a boy could only visit a girl's room or vice versa if the door was left open might be an infringement of privacy; likewise random drug tests at a co-ed day school. I am not aware that either rule was changed as a result of these incautious observations.

happy to inculcate in their pupils the depressing and unjustified view that Oxford was not for the likes of them.

The Dicey Trust, which brought sixth formers to Oxford for a weekend of civic talks, often used Trinity as a base. On one such occasion I was meeting the student participants at a reception with a view to selling the College as a potential destination and had to decide whether to move in a rightward or leftward direction for my next conversation. Making a random choice, I found myself speaking to a girl from a northern state school with no university connection at all among family or teachers, and I suggested that she might try for Oxford. The next time I met her was at the Freshers dinner on the first night of the new academic year. She greeted me with the words 'Hello Michael'. The Senior Tutor did suggest to her that 'President' was the more usual form of address; I was agnostic on the matter. I am as sure as I can be that had it not been for that chance dialogue she would not have conceived of making an Oxford, certainly a Trinity, application. She had a lively time at Trinity and is now a very successful barrister.

But the focus of attention is now increasingly about lack of opportunity for those from socially and educationally disadvantaged backgrounds, more specifically to those from racial minority backgrounds, so Oxford makes copious use of the buzz words of our age: equality, respect, and inclusivity. I, when President, enthusiastically addressed a group called 'Black Boys First' which visited Trinity, assuming, and hoping, that there was a female counterpart. But, while instinctively and intellectually opposed to any form of objectionable discrimination, I am uncertain as to what would be the 'right' proportion of the inaptly named BAME students in the annual University intake any more than I would be of the right proportion of white players in the racially diverse English football team. Gareth Southgate's team, whose loss in the Euro 2020 final happened only in the last minute and with the last kick of the game, was chosen from a squad of 26 of whom 10 were from non-wholly white backgrounds. The selection of both team and squad was made on the single and simple basis that they were the pick of the available footballing crop. Had it been made on the basis of the need proportionately to reflect the composition of the population at large it would have been far less successful than it was.

So I am uncomfortable with the note of somewhat defensive self-congratulation on the increase in the amount of those admitted from state schools (still lower than at my time as an undergraduate) or from sections of the BAME community (now far higher). For me the relevant issue remains are they, wherever they come from, the best candidates for their chosen course of study?[9]

In pursuit of ethnic diversity Oxford's first female Vice Chancellor in 2020 announced an agenda to decolonise the curriculum. For my part, while again instinctively enthusiastic to enlarge the map of learning, I am uncertain as to the virtue of such a starting point, and of the vocabulary employed. While British history

[9] I also firmly believe that those who wish to study at University should first decide what they want to study and only then decide, out of the universities which have the subject on their syllabus, where they would like to study it.

should certainly be shown warts and all, there is a risk that some, for unacademic reasons, simply wish to weaponise the warts. And how does one decolonise race-neutral science or maths? Only in Orwell's *1984* is its hero-victim Winston Smith forced to confess that the five fingers he can see are in fact only four.

In the actual selection process for undergraduates – when interviews took place after the end of Michaelmas term – I took no part; I was not indeed allowed even to sit inconspicuously at the back during one interview in one subject unless I did the same for all interviews in the same subject. Come the day of judgment I had to fend off letters from disappointed parents with a letter which contained a more elegant formula of 'it weren't me guv'. I can only say to critics of the system that the tutors in my time were fully aware of the consequences of saying 'yea' or 'nay' and applied themselves conscientiously to the invidious process of separating sheep from goats when so many applicants, being candidates neither for obvious selection nor for obvious rejection, shared the features of both species. In my speech to the Freshers on their first evening in college I made what for me was always my most important speech of the year. I ended by saying with real conviction that they had all been chosen on merit. 'At Trinity we discriminate neither in favour of nor against anyone. We believe that you are very lucky to be here and that we are very lucky to have you'.[10]

I participated in right of office in the appointment of new fellows – a responsibility shared with the University, where the problem was one of surfeit of qualified applicants – too many post-docs chasing too few jobs – and complicated by the fact that the Faculty's need for specialists was not necessarily the same as the College's for tutors with a wider subject hinterland. I also was involved in the selection of Professors whose chairs were attached to the College, most notably in biochemistry, the history of art and romance languages. Once I inquired sotto voce as to the identity of the most stylistically challenged member of the interviewing Panel for the first of these posts, only to be told that he was not only the holder of a prestigious Cambridge professorship but a Nobel Prize winner to boot. Polonius was wrong. The apparel doth not always proclaim the man.

Charles Clarke, when Secretary of State for Education, included me in an invitation sent to various persons in the University world to share our thoughts on the subject 'What are Universities for', to which the Secretary of State's own prefatory answer was, in perfect New Labour phraseology, 'to promote the change agenda'. We sat round a large table in the St James Plaza Hotel and were asked to make a time-limited contribution in order, the first speaker being situated on the Minister's left. Since the more garrulous academic invitees, unused as they were to the kind of limits familiar to those who appear in Court, inevitably overran, I, being situated to the Minister's right, had barely a minute left as the last contributor. I found it difficult to report on this bizarre occasion to my Governing Body. Mr Clarke, as is

---

[10] Justin Cartwright, *This Secret Garden: Oxford Revisited* (Cartwright, 2008) starts his book with a lyrical account of one of those evenings interspersed with extracts from my speech. pp 2–8 and 82.

the way of the political world, was moved on to higher things before he could make use of what, if anything, he derived from it.

In welfare – a relatively new element of the College's portfolio – I was involved through my membership of the pastoral committee, which included the deans, the college chaplain, nurse, librarian and a delegate from the University counselling service. The problems were not only the obvious ones of stress, which increased exponentially as final examinations loomed into view, but also of more irregular issues such as how to deal best with a maths student, admitted because of his intellectual precocity, at the age of 15, that is, a minor by any criterion, and how to handle the aftermath of fractured student relationships. When I had an inaugural meeting with the head of the University counselling service and said that I was not naturally attuned to the emphasis placed on its functions she said that she had some sympathy with that view. I became less sceptical as time went on.

A head of house is part Prime Minister part Monarch, an early port of call for personal news, sometimes sad – a Fellow's wife being diagnosed with cancer and, worst of all, a young law Fellow dying on her first night of a sabbatical abroad – sometimes happy – a Fellow becoming engaged to a member of staff. When the Professor of Romance Languages received a Romanian decoration we hosted the colourful official ceremony, flag, music and all, in the drawing room in the Lodgings. I had to adjust to being treated as the senior member of an extended family with the wisdom deemed to be inherent in such a post but which I was certainly not confident that I possessed.

My main focus was the students. Theirs was an undergraduate generation sometimes enlightened by gap years but not toughened by National Service, who indeed found greater solace in counselling than in religion. Life was more serious in an age of increasing student debt and growing graduate unemployment than it had been in the sixties. The class of 1968 – Tariq Ali et al – suggested that universities should be run by a cabal of students and workers. Their more sober successors sat on joint consultative committees. Their concerns were practical not philosophical: crash helmets, condom machines, Sky TV and en-suite showers.

A few found it initially difficult to adapt, not, in my view, because of the rituals of Oxford college life but simply because they were away for the first time from the family nest. I walked round the main quad with one state-school educated girl from Wales, reading law, who was acutely homesick, and wanted to quit as early as her second week. I urged her not to give up a place for which she had clearly worked so hard. I said that I was prepared to bet that come the end of term she would be sad at the thought of a temporary absence from her new friends. I was correct in my prediction. The girl in question ended up with a University prize, a place at a magic circle law firm and a Trinity fiancé.

Apart from the rare person who failed a preliminary examination, I can recall only one undergraduate who left of his own volition, in his case to manage the successful pop group Coldplay. Another, reading medicine, foolishly returned to one of the College's outlying properties brandishing a replica gun and causing predictable distress to his flatmates, unable at that hour to distinguish the fake from the real. I had to plead with the Proctors not to send him down. He is now, as a qualified doctor, an asset to the wider community. Maybe every puppy should be allowed one bite? The greatest fear of any Head of House is that during his (or her) period of office some student will commit suicide or rape or be raped. I am truly thankful that such catastrophe never occurred during my time at Trinity.

I found the students overall an impressive cohort. Man for man I thought that in intellectual terms they outranked my Magdalen undergraduate contemporaries; some of whom would not have won Oxford places in competition with the 40-years-on generation. But the comparison is an imperfect one. The most notable change from my undergraduate days was that Trinity, like all the other former all-male colleges, was completely co-ed. This greatly improved the academic standards and culture of the institution. I also observed when we had a night-time fire drill that we had spare capacity in a third or so of our rooms. In our twentieth anniversary year the female half were addressed by Mary Archer[11] at a dinner from which, to my disappointment, I was formally excluded on ground of sex.

There were remarkable persons of each gender (in that era only two were formally recognised). The female lawyer who played tennis for the University and the Welsh harp at a commemoration ball; another female lawyer who was the British ice dance champion; the male PPEist who started a project to assist Romanian orphanages; the gap year adventurer who, captured by Colombian guerrillas, bravely if rashly, escaped from their clutches, and was able to parlay this experience into an exclusive story for the *Daily Telegraph* that paid him enough to cover his fees; the female historian who, on the pretext of visiting a boyfriend, took time off to star in a BBC dramatization of Elizabeth Jane Howard's roman *fleuve The Cazalets* and, with a first in her pocket, embarked on a stellar career as, in sequence, actress, writer and barrister (mother too); the male theologian who became a professional rugby player and scored Scotland's first try in the 2004 World Cup.

A gifted young playwright scripted, and his friend directed, a play about the Oxford Martyrs, *Play the Man* – in which Durham Quad lawn, the epicentre of the College, was used as stage. I was asked to intervene to ensure that the company providing the seating adhered to the contract from which it had tried to renege not long before the opening night, on the novel pretext that the signatory to the contract had been convicted of drunken driving. By coincidence the Company which had agreed to remove the scaffolding also sought to backtrack. Both were held to their word. There was at least some advantage to the College in having a lawyer as President.

The graduates, equally impressive, came from all over the world. Trinity was a destination for Rhodes and Marshall Scholars, and through a chance meeting with the head of their programme I added Truman scholars to that list. Judith and I would entertain to Christmas lunch the handful of students who remained in College on that day. It enriched our knowledge as to how that holiday is (or is

---

[11] Scientist, Dame, Chancellor of Buckingham University, wife of Jeffrey.

not celebrated) in a variety of different countries and ensured that our family had to be on its best behaviour. I noticed that those undergraduates who had chosen, after Finals, to pursue advanced degrees in Trinity swiftly adopted a different life-style, mainly by rising about three hours earlier than had been their previous habit. Those who went out at once into the workplace suddenly had (if male) shorter hair and altered their clothing to reflect their new status. *Tempora mutantur* etc.

Any Head of House brings his own enthusiasms to the table.[12] I would partici-pate on Sunday evenings in the palavers of the Gryphon society where the Chair for the occasion would select a motion which all had to address after no more than five minutes preparation. This was an ordeal I found far more testing than making submissions to the House of Lords, not least because the participants were invited to criticise each other's contributions, in language less restrained than that of a Law Lord picking up on what was perceived to be a bad point. During my time, from this platform arose several Presidents of the Oxford Union – in one summer term we had all three senior officers (Trinity's Trinity trinity). I even represented (pro bono) one of the trio when he was charged with an electoral offence. My defeat was recorded afterwards in the CV of my undergraduate opponent (who became himself a very well regarded barrister) which is, I suppose, a form of tin plated tribute.

As a (very) ex-athlete I managed the College cuppers team, which, through sheer volume of team members (including as a last resort myself) won the trophy for five consecutive years. I encountered an Eric Liddell-type problem with a Mormon Rhodes scholar and triple jumper who for similar reasons of faith could not compete on a Sunday. I threatened, not entirely seriously, the University Athletics club with a religious discrimination suit. The club moved the event to a Thursday evening – a day not thought to be sacred to any particular belief. The moment of truth arrived, the Jonathan Edwards of Salt Lake City (his prowess known to none but the cognoscenti) sped down the runway, stylishly hopped, elegantly stepped and then jumped (barely) in agony as his hamstring snapped. Not *nul* points but *seulement un*.

I used my London contacts to re-vivify the PPE Society and Law Society by enticing speakers down to dine at High Table. I noticed PPE students' predilec-tion for the notorious over the merely successful; Jonathan A's audience was triple the size of Kenneth Baker's.[13] When Harry Woolf came to speak to the lawyers he asked to be excused dinner. I only learned a few days later that he had been called to an urgent meeting with the Lord Chancellor where he was offered the post of Lord Chief Justice.

I discovered that Gary Hart, former Senator and one time favourite for the Democratic Presidential nomination, until undermined by a single indiscretion, was engaged in research at St Anthony's, but was nonetheless a member only of

---

[12] My own enthusiasms are well summarised in the exemplary College history authored by Clare Hopkins, *Trinity: 450 Years of an Oxford College Community* (Hopkins, 2005) who doubtfully described me as 'having the highest profile' of any incoming President since Percival a century earlier, p 433.

[13] Home Secretary.

their junior not senior common room. Oxford has an affection for its own internal class distinctions. I had him elected an honorary member of Trinity's SCR – a choice which paid off in spades, not least when on the night after the Gore-Bush election in 2000 he gave a talk to the college PPE society for which he was as well qualified as anyone in the whole wide world. Gary Hart's letters stood out, if not only for that, for being all in capitals, not lower case – a feature they shared with those from Edward Fox (the Jackal).

I was able to see each of the students at termly President collections in the Lodgings, two or three times a year – a debriefing in which I could discuss in private their tutors' reports and learn about their extra-curricular activities; at the end of Michaelmas term I multi-tasked by using a five-second slot between one going out and another coming in to sign several hundred Christmas cards. There was always a risk that if someone had without notice swapped places with another, there would be a case of mistaken identity. In one instance I praised the student and said that he should be aiming for a first, only to realise to my horror that he should have been in receipt of a severe dressing down. When I apologised to his tutor, the latter replied 'Don't worry. Whatever you said, he thinks he's going to get a first – that is, alas, his problem'.

I was forever writing references. One of my fellows suggested that the body which required such references, say a global financial institution, ought to pay for the time spent in their compilation. The heretical suggestion is not without merit. The don drafts; the bank benefits. Alf Ramsey, the England manager, once said of the England midfielder Martin Peters that he was 10 years ahead of his time. I suspect that this idea is so far ahead of its time as to be without prospect of implementation. I preferred to think of provision of references as a duty owed to the students.

Early in my first term I received a visit from two persons on what was in advance an unparticularised mission but on arrival proved to be an approach as to whether I would be prepared to inform them of any student whom I thought might be suitable for a career in the secret service. Even after description of the kind of guy or gal they had in mind, I was unconvinced that I could readily identify a potential James or Jane Bond but, unlike my immediate predecessor, I had no qualms about agreeing to act as a talent spotter. By the end of my time MI5 and MI6 were publicly advertising for recruits so my skills as such were never tested. I know of at least one graduate of my era who has flourished 'over the river' (key to phrase; watch 'Spectre').

During my time Trinity never came higher than sixth in the Norrington tables. That highwater mark was described in *The Times* as a 'spectacular rise' which reads better first than second time. The table itself has lost much of any benefit that it ever had by the later entitlement of students to have their names redacted from any published list. But within my period of office in the Final Honours Schools, Trinity undergraduates came in the whole University top in 11 subjects, second in seven others, and in Law Trinity produced the top student in International Law, Administrative Law, Company Law and Tort. Two graduates were shortlisted for the All Souls Prize Fellowship – still the blue riband for recent finalists. So I was able in good conscience to tell prospective applicants and those who guided their choices that, if they had the ability and commitment, they would do as well at Trinity as anywhere else.

I had few quarrels with the student body and their representatives. Only one President of the Junior Common Room caused me any grief (as they say) and that was because the context was a proposed rent strike – a familiar cause of friction in all colleges. Will Straw, President of the Oxford Students Union,[14] took up cudgels with me when I sought to explain the realities of the college's economy, saying 'Students should not be paying for a slump in the stock market'. Yet our students were in fact subsidised, not squeezed.

I was entirely relaxed in dealing with the college's gay and lesbian officers (though I suspected in one instance that the two were having an orthodox affair of their own).[15] I did, however, rebel against the proposal that the college should only invite parents to the annual Eights Week party with the permission of their offspring. I considered that the college should pay some respect to the sacrifices that many parents would have made to ensure the best education for their children. If, as was argued, visiting parents might detect in a student's room signs of a sexual relationship of which they would disapprove, my solution, which had its own intrinsic value, was for the student to tidy up the room before the parental visit.

I arranged for the President of the JCR or a delegate to come to part of the two so-called Stated Meetings of Governing Body, at which only certain formal decisions could be taken, but my impression was that they were more interested in gaining the right to attend than in actually exploiting it. I frequented, when free, the termly dinner of the Claret Club, an all-male mainly public school educated (as of course, was I) self-selecting group but peremptorily ended the tradition of the loser of some game of counting the spines of a pineapple being obliged to drink a bottle of Claret itself after being told by one of our fellows in medicine that the exercise was seriously life-threatening.

Since little, if any, folk memory is transferred from one student generation to another, I had to be patient in handling demands for some benefit (for example more routes of access to the college after office hours) which recurred year after year and to which the same answer had necessarily to be given. But generally, with the advantage of student children of my own of the same generation, I found it easier to understand their concerns. 'Si la jeunesse savait, si la vieillesse pouvait' is a French apothegm which refers to sex, but has the capacity to be more generally applied; or to deploy an even more apposite trans-channel saying, 'tout comprendre c'est tout pardonner'.

Trinity's past reputation for academic excellence had been, as I noted in my first brief spell in the College, inconsistent. In the 1960s it was regarded (if

---

[14] Later in charge of the unsuccessful Remainers campaign.

[15] It was a generation after I had left that upped the ante by causing the LGBTQ plus rainbow flag to be substituted across the University for the College flag during the quasi-statutory month to the possible bewilderment of the passing tourists. Why not fly both?

superficially) as a college for sportsmen who couldn't get into Christ Church. By contrast its reputation for gastronomic excellence was consistently unrivalled. All colleges had Fellows who were invited to lecture abroad; but only Trinity had a chef who received such an invitation – his excellence vouched for by such as Giles Coren, who described Trinity in his column in the *Sunday Times Magazine* as a premier eating place (but added that you had to be admitted to the college first to sample its delights). Giles also repaid me by mentioning in his column that the College was looking for a domestic bursar and floating Peter Mandelson's name – a free advertisement, though one unlikely to bear fruit in the form of that particular politician. The actual fruit was Prince Charles's Treasurer. Prue Leith declined at first to believe that I had not hired an outside chef for a dinner in the Lodgings. Olga Maitland, gossip columnist for the *Daily Mail*, let her imagination rather than her memory run riot, when she wrote that we were waited on in hall by 'servants in red fronted waistcoats'. Anne Robinson,[16] Petronella Wyatt[17] and Taki[18] (who escorted socialite Jemima Khan) were others who wrote in laudatory encomia of their outing to Trinity in their weekly columns.

Every Wednesday I would invite several guests to dine at High Table, mixing rather than matching, and taking care to have a few students in to meet them beforehand for champagne in the Lodgings, partly for networking, partly to show them off. I only wish I had had the foresight to keep a diary of these visits over the decade. As it is, I must content myself with my Visitors book – an autograph hunter's dream if anyone could decipher the signatures – and with a few random impressions. I recognise that, as with the Hermitage or the Louvre, only a tithe of the collection is ever on display in this chapter – at a rough estimate my guests numbered between 200 and 250 over my 10 years. It became more a case of who's not coming to dinner rather than who was. I invited two celebrated mature students, Jonathan A[19] and the judge who presided at his trial Sir Oliver Popplewell,[20] but not at the same time. Nigel Lawson came; and after telling me that he never wrote thank you letters promptly sent me a charming one. His son Dominic came too, but I never scored a Lawson treble with domestic goddess Nigella.

On one night my guests were Baroness Helena Kennedy QC,[21] Michael Portillo[22] and Haydn Phillips, Permanent Secretary to the Lord Chancellor's department. Watching them blend so effortlessly with each other I realised that the true divisions in our political society are not so much between those of different parties but between those (a very small minority) who are inside the establishment political bubble and the rest of us outside it. When I introduced our captain

---

[16] of the Weakest Link fame.

[17] Journalist and Boris's one time girl friend.

[18] Long standing Spectator columnist of the High Life.

[19] Described in his memoir *Porridge and Passion* (Aitken, 2006) p 202.

[20] Described in his memoir *Hallmark: A Judge's Life at Oxford* (Popplewell, 2009) where references to me bulk out the script, pp 4, 20, 25, 33, 99, 181.

[21] Holder of too many prestigious posts to list but including that of Principal of Mansfield College.

[22] Tory Cabinet Minister and the Phineas Fogg of the railways.

of boats without forewarning to Matt Pinsent,[23] I realised that jaws can literally, and not merely metaphorically, drop. Despite the host of cabinet ministers, ambassadors, scholars, sportsmen and scientists whom I entertained, the only one (Matt apart) clapped out of Hall was Garth Crooks, a reasonably successful professional footballer, but clearly known more for his exploits as a regular commentator on television.

When Tessa Jowell and Patricia Hewitt and their respective spouses came, the former duo were late, prompting David Mills, Tessa's husband, to say that I'd got the monkeys but not the organ grinders. Both the Cabinet ministers, when they arrived belatedly, spent much of their time complaining about their allegedly responsible colleague the Minister for Transport. Digby Jones, then Director-General of the CBI,[24] cheerfully told me during the first course that he had failed to get a place at Trinity but at least I was able to reply truthfully that he seemed to have made a remarkable recovery from that setback. And when I was once indulging myself by compiling a notional all-star British athletic team out of my guests, I realised that Roger Bannister was only the sixth fastest miler on that list.[25]

Trinity had two main annual feasts. The first was Domus Dinner, where the fellows were expected to and did invite the great and the good. Once I had invited the Chinese ambassador, who was late. Would it cause a diplomatic incident if we started without him? Happily, one of my other guests, Sir John Kerr, then head of the FCO, was able to assuage my concerns. The second was Trinity Monday to which each student would be invited once, and the only external guests were new Heads of House, one of whom had to speak. Some were worthy of a first; others would barely have scraped a third.

I thought it useful to try to build bridges with politicians involved in education. Margaret Hodge, then Minister for Universities, was an early guest with her husband Henry[26] who used to instruct me on behalf of the Child Poverty Action Group. The Conservative shadows seemed to change with the seasons. Theresa May, Damian Green, Tim Boswell, Tim Yeo, Oliver Letwin, David Willetts, Tim Collins came in quick succession. Only Michael Gove had to cry off. Most of the aforementioned (another lawyers' catchphrase) achieved high office when the Tories were returned, some higher than others, and the first and last, or strictly, their departments, became clients.

Abdul Baginda, a graduate doctoral student, a former adviser – or spad – to Najib Razak, an up and coming Malaysian politician, brought his patron to tea. Many years later when Najib had become Prime Minister I was invited on the spur of the moment to have breakfast in his official residence in Kuala Lumpur. I had already breakfasted but decided to risk being known as 'two breakfast Beloff' in pale imitation of the role model for gastronomic doubling up 'two dinners' Goodman', solicitor supreme and Master of University College ('Univ'). Though

---

[23] Knighted as a quadruple Olympic Gold medallist.
[24] A peer and a short-term Minister in Gordon Brown's Administration.
[25] to Coe, Cram, Moorcroft, Ian Stewart and Brendan Foster.
[26] A High Court Judge.

this was a social not a power breakfast, still later he became a client whom I advised on constitutional matters, but not on the charges of corruption made against him. Mr Baginda himself became, with my Singaporean friend, Peter Koh, another sponsor of my non legal oriental adventures.

Chelsea Clinton, embarked on a one-year graduate course at Univ, her father's old college, was reported in the student press as being unhappy at what she perceived to be anti-American attitudes. I wrote to her suggesting that her impression was false and invited her to dinner. Robin Butler,[27] Master of Univ, warned me to be to sceptical about the chances of her attendance; but come she did along with Air Vice Marshall Bagnall and Andrew Roberts, the historian. She struck me as a young woman with a successful future guaranteed as much by her personality as by her parentage. By coincidence on the same night we were unveiling some paintings by a graduate student, Roma Tearne, who had proposed that the College receive them in lieu of the graduate college fee. Given that the justification for such fee was slender for a student who received no tuition from any college tutor, it seemed that her offer was at worst a good each way bet in purely economic terms. I had to explain to Ms Clinton that this was an untypical prologue to a guest night.

I was later invited to attend a meeting in London to be addressed by former President Clinton in support of his educational charity. A few of us were summoned after his address to stand sheepishly in line and have a photograph taken with the great man. This gave me the opportunity to tell him that I had had the pleasure of meeting his daughter. Naturally, I treasure the photograph itself though, it seems, a little less so than Andrew Adonis,[28] who used it that year as his Christmas card.

Private dinners in the Lodgings rather than in Hall were particularly special events. Over the decade the guests of honour included Derry Irvine, Tom Bingham, Gillian Shepherd, then Secretary of State for Education, Geoffrey Howe (who instinctively but unnecessarily wore a dinner jacket) and Ken Clarke. I also used the good offices of an alumnus who was one of his advisers to organise a visit from Charles Kennedy, newly elected leader of the Liberal Democrats with an apparently bright political future. He pulled out at the last moment on receipt of a better invitation. With the benefit of hindsight the guest of honour should have been someone who did join us – Boris Johnson, then *en deuxieme noces* (his first wife having been a Trinity undergrad). When Paloma Picasso came the Fellow sitting next to her asked her what she did. I interjected that he might not know, but his wife certainly would. Not everyone's circles intersect.

My most embarrassing tale relates to the time we entertained to dinner Princess Alexandra (married to Andrew Ogilvy, a Trinity graduate) – the lodgings vetted for security purposes by a sniffer cocker spaniel which endeared itself to the entire staff. It was a Sunday and there was a visiting preacher who had not been notified – *mea culpa* – that I would need to leave chapel promptly at 7pm.

[27] Cabinet Secretary. Peer. KG.
[28] Secretary of State for Transport in Gordon Brown's cabinet.

His sermon overran and I scampered back to the Lodgings, just as the Princess's car was arriving through the main gates. She later let slip casually and without malice aforethought how much she had welcomed the chance to be driven round Oxford for a little while so that she would not arrive in advance of the greeting party. The politeness of Princesses.

There were brief encounters, informal as well as formal. I entertained John Thaw to tea when he was filming part of the Morse series in college (a welcome increment to the college's bank account); later when his widow actress Sheila Hancock came to Domus Dinner, she described it as a 'lovely evening' only momentarily marred by being greeted by a don who kept saying 'no trouble at all' – a phrase she apparently hated.[29] I don't think it was I. Bjorn Ulvaeus of Abba brought his daughter to reconnoitre; Garret FitzGerald, the Taoiseach, unexpectedly suddenly appeared at lunch as the guest of another fellow; Algirdas Mykolas Brazauskas, who was both Prime Minister (twice) and President of newly independent Lithuania, my own guest invited to lunch on the initiative of a student from the same country, appeared to the dons' surprise with a photographer in tow to record his visit. The Chief Justice of Kazakhstan came to the lodgings with no such escort.

To brief encounters, I would add a non-encounter. Hugo Chavez wanted to visit a college. As an advance guard he sent the Venezuelan Ambassador, a cultured sophisticated author, the very smooth to President Chavez's somewhat rough. On the day of El Presidente's visit I was in Court, and missed the moment when his bodyguards, taken by surprise by the lunchtime descent of the college archivist from her eyrie in the tower, blocked her passage. The confrontation – and her identity – were speedily resolved and the Latin American caudillo showed the softer side of his character by sending her an apology and huge bouquet the next day.

For me a highpoint was reached when the (still) world record holder in the 1500m and mile, Hicham El Guerrouj, came to Iffley Road to publicise a forthcoming athletics spectacular at Crystal Palace masterminded by Alan Pascoe's[30] Fast Track. I organised a lunch party in College to which I invited, as well as Alan and Jon Ridgeon,[31] Sir Roger Bannister. After a discussion about the different conditions under which they trained and ran – Roger, cinder track, heavy spikes, one hour sessions at lunch between medical studies; Hicham, all-weather surfaces, specially fitted lightweight shoes, whole day devoted to training, sleeping, massage etc – I asked Hicham what time he thought Roger would have run had he enjoyed all Hicham's advantages; and Hicham volunteered a time just a 1/10th of a second below his own mile record. The Algerian was not only a class athlete, but a class human being. Ditto Roger. I could go on and on and on about this lunch but realise that I already have.

University as well as College life is also well lubricated by hospitality. In one's first year as Head of House one is invited to dine at the other colleges, and there

---

[29] Sheila Hancock, *The Two of Us: My Life with John Thaw* (Hancock, 2005) p 299.
[30] Multiple medallist in the 400m hurdles and successful businessman.
[31] World Championship silver medallist in the 110m hurdles and CEO of World Athletics.

is a self-selecting club, somewhat unimaginatively called the Lunch Club, founded in 1926, comprised of about 20 members, most of whom are or have been heads of house, who host each other in sequence. Roy Jenkins, the Chancellor, who once claimed that he had never in his adult life lunched alone, was generous in his invitations to his country house at East Hendred, where, in what was unconscious self-caricature, he would ensure that a decanter of claret remained filled not just for lunch, but, when his guests moved room, for afternoon tea. In the contest for his successor between three strong candidates, Neill, Bingham, Patten, I opted for Tom, wearing the baseball cap with the legend 'I'm a Binghamist' and adopting the public position 'Neill may be too old, Patten may be too young, and Bingham may be just right'. My canvassing of his cause among Oxford lawyers was described by one in the Financial Times as 'nauseating', although I am at a loss to see what is even unseemly about soliciting votes in a contested election.

I had known Chris Patten since he and Lavender, his wife, had entertained me to dinner in the Governor's Mansion in Hong Kong during one of my appearances in Court in the colony. I marvelled at the contrast between the informality of the occasion only palliated by servants who were clothed in a fashion of which Olga Maitland would have approved and the grandeur of the environment. The victor has been a strong as well as a stylish voice for the University and I was happy to support his election as an honorary Bencher of Gray's Inn, not least (though not only) because Lavender herself was a member of the Inn.

Trinity's sister Cambridge college was not a foundation of approximately equal age, but Churchill, a post-WWII foundation. Herbert Blakiston, President from 1907–38, declined to participate in the interwar enthusiasm for dark blue/light blue twinning. Trinity came late to the party and the choice of Churchill was dictated by the absence of any competitor. It was a happy choice. A representative of the fellows, and the middle and junior common rooms would attend each other's annual feasts and, as President, I could stay at Churchill in a room with all the mod cons of a well-equipped hotel. I found the difference between the two colleges added savour to the relationship. I warmed to my opposite number Sir John Boyd, former ambassador to Japan, and his wife Jill,[32] and was delighted to become acquainted with Mary Soames, Churchill's youngest child, who inherited her grandfather's penchant for cigars (though of more modest dimensions) and later graced guest nights at my invitation at both Trinity and Gray's Inn.

Trinity had an annual lecture established in memory of alumnus Richard Hillary, the author of the wartime classic *The Last Enemy*, so I was able to meet a succession of some of the best of contemporary writers. That sequence too produced a host of memories. Beryl Bainbridge, a chain smoker with barely a pause for breath, Julian Barnes, a slow methodical breakfaster, Jeanette Winterson, the openly gay novelist, who, to my surprise, kissed me on both cheeks. Vikram Seth, author of *a Suitable Boy*, saved us from any protocol problem of sleeping arrangements for

---

[32] Authoress. Their daughter Jessica became a member of Blackstone and is now a QC.

him and his male partner, by opting for the Randolph hotel in lieu of the lodgings. At the seminar he conducted on the next day a Pakistani girl student told him that she had been brought up to believe that Indians were the spawn of the devil, but, after reading his novel, she had had a damascene type conversion so that her new best friend at Oxford was Indian. It was a moment that moved me as much as it did the author.

Because the college's 450th anniversary would fall in 2005, I inaugurated a sequence of Chatham lectures in which speakers would address the theme of an aspect of the future related to their interests. Speakers included Tom Bingham, then Lord Chief Justice,[33] the Archbishop of Canterbury, the Astronomer Royal, Gary Hart and John Sulston, a Nobel prize winner. Michael Portillo, on the Future of Conservatism, only mildly blotted his copybook by observing in his opening few words that he had always regarded Pitt the Younger as the superior of the two Pitts. Incidentally Chatham, the elder, cannot have declined to send his son to Trinity because of some apprehension that it was a disadvantage for an applicant to be the offspring of an old member. It isn't true even in 2022; and it certainly wasn't true then.

During the long vacation, summer schools from UMASS, Georgia and Georgetown (a mixture of sophomore and alums) fill the rooms vacated by students – a source of temporary tension in reconciling the need to maximise the use of the plant for the former with protection of the academic interests of the latter. I enjoyed meeting these visitors, when I was on site, at their first and last dinner (sometimes both) recycling the same welcome or farewell speech – 'Pitt the elder ensured that the French would not govern America, Lord North that the English would not do so either' and submitting myself (with barely concealed enthusiasm) to having selfies taken with those who wished for such a memento of their Trinity time. A prestigious group – last in the sequence whose departure coincided with the first intimations of autumn – was of the Smithsonians, highly cultured, but to a man and woman senior citizens. One elderly lady tripped down the step from High Table after dinner and needed hospital treatment. Conscious of the American appetite for personal injury claims, I invested a judicious portion of the college funds in a large bouquet accompanied by a note as solicitous as I could make it without admitting responsibility. The limitation period expired before the end of my Presidency.

There was constant contact with old members – annual Trinity Society weekends, gaudies for different generations with the default gap of seven years shrinking as alumni crossed the river Styx. Trinity graduates were prominent in Livery companies, five of which had Trinity Wardens or holders of equivalent posts during my time. I was expected to sing for what could only be described with exaggerated understatement as my supper at their major feasts of the year, so

---

[33] Lord Bingham, *The Business of Judging* (Bingham, 2011) p 274ff has the entire text.

gaining access to ancestral halls, the Guildhall included, containing treasures all too rarely accessible to the public.

On one occasion the Master, Philip Keevil, had gone upmarket and invited Theresa May to do the honours. She was delayed on Parliamentary duties and Philip warned me that I might have to come off the bench to fill her (famously kitten) shoes. Luckily, she arrived at the last minute so saving me from embarrassment and the diners from disappointment. Philip was also a pillar of the Trinity boat club, the institution which unquestionably commanded the greatest loyalty among alumni. He had entertained me to a club Thameside lunch, only interrupted by an urgent call to tell Philip that his car was being slowly submerged by a rising tide. Alas our one-time cordial relationship was ruptured in circumstances I describe below.

Trinity was also well represented in the diplomatic corps. When I gave talks to an overseas branch of the Oxford or Trinity Societies I could sometimes find myself housed in the Embassy. In Stockholm, Andrew Colvin took Judith and me out to dine. The other guests included Hans Blix, the official who failed to discover any WMD in Iraq, and David Steel who, when Liberal leader, failed to discover the misconduct of Cyril Smith. David in his prime once asked his party to prepare for Government. Now he was visibly disconsolate when outvoted on whether we needed to cap the fine meal with dessert. How far can horizons shrink?

When alumni reached the age of 70 (and at quinquennial intervals thereafter) I would send them birthday cards, which elicited responses, always cordial, sometimes enlivened with reminiscences of bygone days, and sometimes containing, more rarely, a pre-emptive strike against a later request for donations.

Fundraising had indeed already become an expected part of a President's duties – I had only one staff member dedicated to the task; whereas now there is a development fellow and an office of five. I thought that fundraising efforts should focus on the 450th anniversary of Trinity's foundation and sent out a carefully crafted advocate's letter to old members arguing that their support could guarantee the College a future as glorious as I depicted its past. The College meanwhile devised a special brochure for lawyers in which I appeared on the cover along with graduates Selborne, Lord Chancellor, Goddard, Lord Chief Justice and the constitutional scholar, Dicey, former fellow. As with a favourite 11-plus question juxtaposing one vegetable with three fruit, it required no great intellect to identify the odd one out in that quartet.

Every two years, along with other Heads of House, I would travel in the Easter vacation to meet old members in New York, initially at the United Nations, later at the Waldorf Astoria, where the college standard would be displayed, and alumni would congregate in the vicinity in the manner of troops preparing for battle in the middle ages. All heads prayed that one or more of their college's alumni would have become a dot.com trillionaire, or international hedge fund manager, Trinity seemed to produce the worthy rather than the wealthy – the chaplain to the US navy and a sculptor in wire from a mid-western state. I was able off the back of my international practice or invitations to lecture overseas, to hold meetings with alumni on the west as well as the east coast of the USA, in Canada, Australia, New Zealand,

Japan, Hong Kong, Singapore, Malaysia and Thailand, as well, of course, in various places in England, sometimes as a guest of the local branch of the Oxford Society with the bonus on one occasion of a lunch at Rick Stein's restaurant in Padstow, after which it hardly mattered what I said in praise of the alma mater.

I wonder whether fundraising owes more to good luck than to good management. During my time an engineering fellowship was endowed by Robert and Julia Hunt-Grubbe, parents of one of the last undergraduates to read biology at the College (and for that role felicitously named) and a law fellowship by Wyatt Haskell, a successful Atlanta lawyer,[34] nephew of Wyatt Rushton, an undergraduate who died en route to serve in the First World War. The Shaw foundation gave a hundred thousand pounds towards a maths fellowship after a granddaughter of the celebrated Hong Kong movie tycoon studied at the college.

I discovered serendipitously that Gillian, widow of John Sutro, an alumnus who was part of Evelyn Waugh's Oxford set, had retired to Monte Carlo. Gillian, an offshoot on one side of the Gamage family, was an exquisite model.[35] She was also a woman of some means. As my role as the IAAF's doping prosecutor took me frequently to Monaco, I got in touch with her, and we bonded over several lunches that lasted so long that I was in constant risk of missing my return flight. Gillian had known many of the cultural icons of the early twentieth century, from Picasso to Cocteau, Graham Greene to Somerset Maugham, Diaghilev to Lawrence Olivier. On the last occasion I met her she said she had a little present for me which was wrapped untidily in a brown paper bag. When I opened the bag, I found it was a first edition of Evelyn Waugh's *Ordeal of Gilbert Pinfold* inscribed to Gillian herself.

I ascertained that Gillian was torn between leaving her estate to the family of her Hungarian lover, the painter Vertès, and to the College in memory of her late husband. After (and maybe in part as a result of) our conversations she left Trinity about four million pounds and her personal archive and library. The archive (which included a volume in which she pasted press cuttings about her various other lovers with annotations as to how she ended the relationships) was too large for the College to process so I negotiated an arrangement by which Trinity shared ownership with the Bodleian, but the Bodleian took on responsibility for cataloguing, editing and display – a task now professionally completed. To mark Gillian's generosity, I had a room in College refurbished and redecorated, with space to house items from Gillian's collection, which I immensely enjoyed selecting. One wall holds photographs of a youthful Gillian and John. The Sutro room was opened in the anniversary year by Princess Alexandra.

I found out that Wafic Said, who had endowed the business school which bears his name, had not been offered an honorary fellowship at any College. I thought this omission both discourteous and negligent. Through the good offices of

---

[34] With his delightful wife Susan we were entertained at their home when Wyatt solicited four speeches from me in a single evening.

[35] She features prominently as the best friend of the subject in Nicholas Shakespeare's *Priscilla* (Shakespeare, 2013) the author's aunt. See esp Ch 7, 'Gillian'.

Charles Gray,[36] who had represented Wafic in a libel action, I met him – another encounter out of which I derived great personal pleasure since his wealth was equalled by his charm – and organised an honorary fellowship for him. He too enhanced the College's funds as well as creating a link with one of Oxford's most prestigious modern institutions. In my last term we were invited to a dance in Wafic's country house the night after we had attended the College's own biennial ball. Only the excellence of the hospitality and my sense of obligation kept me, no dancing king, awake.

Nigel Armstrong-Flemming wrote to me saying that he believed that he had been admitted to Trinity but that, unbeknown to him, his parents had, for whatever reason, declined the offer. Upon investigation this curious and melancholy tale proved to be true. In consequence he became constructively a most loyal alumnus – and provided money for the housing of the college archives.

In my last year Verne Grinstead, another old member, introduced me to Geoffrey de Jager, a South African with a pronounced philanthropic streak, which, during my successor's time, benefitted the college, with among other things, endowment of a language fellowship in his wife's name. He was also a patron of the charity Classics for All and the Oxford Philharmonia and became one of the most dedicated and visible of Trinity's honorary fellows, as well as a Trinity parent.

The College also embarked on a series of telethons using current students to make contacts with old members, covertly, if not overtly, soliciting donations. This was an enterprise fraught with some peril. One old member said to the student telephonist 'What you are trying to do is to raise money to fund the kind of student who will replace people like me' – touché. We also instituted the William Pitt Society for alumni who had pledged to leave money to the College in their wills. This involved a degree of trust, not required for the Bathurst Society (named after one of the College's longest-serving presidents) which was for alumni who had already given money. Each cohort was rewarded with an annual lunch – the gamble for Pitt Society members, unless they were very young, was not considerable.

Some prosperous old members, despite our excellent personal relationships, declined to make donations because their sons had been refused college places. Ham Richardson, former Wimbledon semi-finalist and part of the Vicks family, entertained me royally in his Manhattan apartment (though insisting I made two speeches because my first was too short – an unusual criticism). He was reared in the tradition of alumni preference, alien to the British tradition. Sir Tommy Macpherson (three MCs, three Croix de Guerre, an international in both athletics and rugby) fell into the same category. Because of the friction which had been caused during the time of my immediate predecessor, I failed in my effort to have Tommy made an honorary fellow, an omission finally rectified by my successor. Arnold Goodman recollected in his memoirs weeping (internally only) in the Senior Common Room at the news that Mr Crust of Bread's child had been

---

[36] High Court Judge, another Trinitarian.

admitted in preference to Sir John Moneybags' grandson,[37] a reaction which might be silently shared by not a few Heads of House. Arnold once invited Judith and me to dinner over the Christmas period explaining that we required a retreat from the seasonal pressures, where the other guest was Clarissa Eden, widow of the former Prime Minister. As a pair they resembled Bottom and Titania. Arnold's favourite phrase was 'He's an absolute villain' but I cannot remember in respect of whom he deployed it on that festive occasion.

I was, alas, unable to make use of my relationship with Bruce Buck, to persuade Roman Abramovich that there are only so many wives, yachts and football clubs that one can buy, and that an honorary fellowship of an historic Oxford college purchased for only a few million pounds would add a touch of class to a CV which was a mixture of shade and light.

Richard Branson rang me directly to seek confirmation of the opinion, which I had given by the orthodox route to his solicitors, about his chances to run the national lottery. He let slip that his grandfather Mr Justice Branson was a Trinity graduate. Envisaging the possibility of a college benefaction – the Virgin suite? – I checked on the internet only to discover that the Trinity was the Cambridge version. If I said that I was disappointed, I would be guilty of meiosis.

A plan put to me by Vittorio Radice, the ebullient retailer, for marketing a joint Trinity/Selfridges brand (or was it to be the other way round?) perished on his departure from the department store. Nor did a germinating relationship between the college and Lord Paul of Caparo Industries, who had plans to establish a technology institute in his native India, produce a harvest.

Appreciating that present members of the college community were unlikely to have the wherewithal to make a financial contribution to the appeal, I procured from Dave Bedford[38] three places for the London Marathon. One undergraduate, one fellow and one member of the staff completed the course raising money for the College, itself a charity, from sponsorship by affluent, if less athletic alumni. I also obtained sponsorship for the College law society and Boat Club from Allen and Overy and Addleshaws and other funding for events from Freshfields and Denton Wilde Sapte, which had the ancillary benefit of cementing my professional relationship with these four firms; and sponsorship of the College Music Society by Gillian Howard, a doughty employment solicitor who also relocated an annual law lecture in her mother's name from UCL to Trinity, funded an essay prize and donated a piano.

The first four bonuses were the product of design; the fifth of pure chance. I had been the after-dinner speaker at the Employment Bar Association's annual dinner and Gillian claimed she had been impressed not so much by my speech itself as by my conversation with her afterwards. Would that it was always so easy to find funds for worthy causes!

One option for some Colleges is to change the College's name in exchange for some gargantuan sum. Trump College? Maybe on first, let alone second, thoughts

---

[37] Arnold Goodman, *Tell Them I'm On My Way* (Goodman, 1993) p 439.
[38] Former world record holder for 10,000m.

not. That option was foreclosed to Trinity in Oxford or Cambridge as it would be, for like reasons, to Jesus. All in all, I raised – or more precisely – there was raised during my time about 10 million pounds, a pass, if not a starred achievement.

I was conscious that in the Wroxton estate, around which I travelled every other year in a tractor-driven cart to meet those who farmed and managed it, and enjoyed en route an *al fresco dejeuner sur l'herbe*, the College had an asset which would generate, though after my time, a substantial sum when part would be sold off for development required by the bulging town of Banbury. This compensated, if only in part, for the fact that 30 years or so before, the College had to meet some short-term expense and sold Wroxton Abbey to Farleigh Dickinson University (New Jersey) which has been converted into its overseas campus and would have been a marvellous money-making property. Still it's no use crying over spilt mortar.

I realised early on that, if I was to retain a practice while satisfactorily fulfilling my presidential role, I would have little time for involvement in University governance. I dutifully attended the meetings of the Conference of Colleges where most Heads of House were chaperoned by their bursars, in case they put a word wrong. There were continued issues about whether the richer colleges should subsidise the poorer. Trinity, positioned just above the middle in terms of its estate, was a modest giver, so enjoying a sense of altruistic virtue but at only minimal expense. More complex was the issue as to whether Colleges or the University should have first call on potential alumni donors; sophisticated protocols were put in place to regularise the system. Part of the time of the Conference was spent criticising the Vice Chancellor behind his back and once a term repeating it, if more decorously, to his face. The Colleges' relationship with the University (somewhat pejoratively known because of its location as Wellington Square), was not dissimilar to that of the States with Washington DC in the USA.

I did become a member of the Ethics in Donations Committee, which involved interesting moral speculation about whether the University should accept money from persons or bodies who had not, however, as yet indicated any intention to make a donation – a paradigm academic exercise. My service predated the era of campaigns to remove recognition of benefactors of an earlier era whose deeds or acts were at odds with modern mores; many would have failed this arbitrary and anachronistic test. Explanation is preferable to eradication. One cannot cancel the past.

I was inevitably a member of the Conference of Colleges legal panel (chairing it for one term) which consisted of dons specialising in a range of subjects, property, employment, human rights law amongst them, and provided a challenge to the University's own legal adviser who was not so variously equipped. I also drafted, with Simon Whitaker, law fellow at St John's, a student/college contract which contained the minimum obligation for the college, and the maximum for the student, as well as with Nick Bamford, law fellow at Queen's, a template for Convention compliant disciplinary processes. Trinity undergraduates, given the option, sensibly preferred the summary, but swift, justice meted out by the Deans. I became too a de facto neighbourhood law centre for other heads of house.

As President I would be invited to the annual Encaenia, high point of the Oxford social calendar, when honorary degrees were conferred on those perceived by the University establishment to be the greatest and the best. After partaking of Lord Crewe's benefaction – peaches and champagne – we would process berobed down Broad Street towards the Sheldonian. I would prudently peel off into the Trinity lodge to avoid the discomfort – once experienced never forgotten – of sitting in the upper rows of Wren's masterpiece, not designed for those with dodgy backs. At the appropriate moment when the ceremony was over, the Latin encomia duly delivered by the Public Orator, the degrees duly conferred, I would rejoin the dignatories destined for the lavish lunch in All Souls' Codrington Library. With scarcely an intermission it was off to the Vice Chancellor's Garden party in a college with gardens large enough to contain the madding crowd – the foot soldiers now able to mix with the officers – and so to bed.

When Nelson Mandela came to give a lecture, his reception was held in Examination Schools. I noticed that rather than circulating among the dons, he chose to thank all the serving staff in turn. Avid to make contact I managed to insert myself in the line of waiters and, by this shameless tactic, am able to say that I shook the great man's hand.

I was astonished to read in the broadsheets that I was a potential successor to Colin Lucas for the position of Vice Chancellor. Indeed according to the *Daily Telegraph* I was the bookies' favourite, placing professional scribblers a good deal lower in the prophecy stakes than Nostradamus. The student interviewed by *The Times* about the possibility expressed reservations so strong that he preferred to remain anonymous.

I did, however, defend Oxford in a public forum. When the Dearing report recommended an abolition of the special grant given to Oxford and Cambridge as collegiate universities, together with the far more formidable figure of Roy Jenkins – Robin to his Batman – I lobbied Tony Blair at a reception in Number 10. To our remonstrances the Prime Minister gave a politician's non-apologetic expression of regret. Later after Gordon Brown accused Magdalen of class bias against Laura Spence, I argued in a letter to the *Daily Telegraph* that such ministerial references were triply misconceived.

> They deter able pupils from non-traditional backgrounds from applying to Oxford by encouraging a false belief that such pupils will not have a fair crack of the whip. They alarm able pupils from traditional backgrounds by appearing to suggest that the Government is coercing Oxford to discriminate against them. And they unjustly attribute to academics prejudices from which they are notably free.

At the Headmasters' Conference in St Andrews in 2004 I gave the keynote speech at the invitation of Martin Stephens, whose sixth form I had addressed when he was headmaster of Manchester Grammar School, and with whom I had discussed collaborative efforts between school and college to prepare potential Oxbridge candidates from local state schools. I defended our admissions process and deployed a borrowed soundbite but a predictable headline 'get your tanks off our lawn' at a moment when the Government appeared to be threatening penalties for institutions which did not meet quotas of state school educated entrants.

As a result, I enjoyed what Andy Warhol, the American pop artist, called the 15 minutes of celebrity to which every human being is entitled – commissioned by Boris Johnson to write a diary of my week for the *Spectator*, profiled in the *Sunday Times* by Jasper Gerard who, while 98 per cent faithful to his promise of verbatim quotes, by sinuous rearrangement made them mere footnotes to his own acidulous comments. I was interviewed by the BBC's John Humphreys and – with my crème de la crème PA Yvonne[39] – chauffeured Sky-wards to be interrogated by Adam Boulton, sandwiched between Oliver Letwin and former Formula One world champion Jackie Stewart who was almost late – he had driven himself.

The *Daily Telegraph* applauded my 'silky skills', the *Guardian* assailed my 'raucous … combative remarks'. To the *Observer* I was a humbug[40] – to the *Sunday Telegraph* a hero. The then Vice-Chancellor reflected to me, 'I am struck by the ability of the media … to shape a story to suit their present preoccupations'. Quite so. I was stood down from a *Newsnight* discussion about the appointment of the Office for Fair Access, sobriquet Offtoff (the least popular public official since the hangman was made redundant?), because the Minister wanted not only star, but solo billing. Although I was described as 'the most articulate proponent'[41] of the case for Oxford going private that was never either my proposal or my prophecy. Indeed I had urged fidelity to 'the traditions of the founders of the colleges whose concern was imparting education and its ideals to those with capacity to absorb them'.

I did seek, together with the Principal of Somerville, to resurrect the proposal that an honorary degree should be conferred on Margaret Thatcher which had – to my mind unwisely – been voted down in 1982 by dons dissatisfied with her educational policies. It seemed to me to be ill-considered that an Oxford graduate who had reached the top of the domestic political tree should not be honoured in right of that fact alone. Roy Jenkins, recognising that Tony Blair might equally be denied the honour, suggested that he (Tony) could be in a double bill with James Mackay, the long-serving Tory Lord Chancellor which would have been patently asymmetrical. Brian Mawhinney[42] told me that it was unlikely that Margaret Thatcher would even be interested. The notion fizzled out shortly after take-off. So, no LLD hons for David, Theresa and Boris or maybe in the fulness of time, who knows, Rish, Liz, or Keir?

The major crisis during my term of office occurred when the Blairs' eldest son Euan applied to Trinity. By chance on an open day I had bumped into him in the front quad when a whimsical conversation ensued. Blair fils, 'I think you know my mother'. I, 'I believe I know your father too'. I invited him into the Lodgings to sing the College's praises. I naively thought that it would hardly harm the college to be

---

[39] So described in a *Times* supplement of that name.
[40] Will Hutton, a future Principal of Hertford, wrote of 'the crusty innocence of Beloff's law'; whatever that meant.
[41] Robert Stevens, *University to Uni* (Stevens, 2005) p 168.
[42] Tory Party Chairman.

the choice of the Prime Minister's eldest offspring; and did not fully foresee the opening it would provide for the more malevolent members of the media. When I told governing body about his application and reminded them of the need for confidentiality, the main interest voiced was in what subject he intended to read.

The Blairs themselves complained to the Press Complaints Commission over a piece in the *Daily Telegraph*'s diary column, Peterborough, referring to the application which inevitably linked it – as did the *Daily Mail* – with the fact that Cherie and I were professional colleagues. The PCC found for the Blairs[43] and agreed that it was an invasion of their son's privacy. The *Guardian* also self virtuously referred itself to the same body for quoting my own revelation of his application which I had made in a vain effort to forestall captious criticism. In the absence of any actual complaint the PCC took that matter no further.

Invasion of privacy was one thing, the imputation that he was being fast-tracked quite another. Euan did in fact win a conditional place subject to satisfactory A level results. By unhappy mischance his offer coincided with the turning down of the second son of Philip Keevil, who was co-chair of the College's anniversary committee. Not only did Mr Keevil (after an apoplectic telephone call) resign from the committee but he withdrew his promise of kickstarting the appeal by his own substantial contribution. I must be the only head of house whose first achievement in organised fundraising was to lose £100,000. Ephraim Hardcastle in the *Daily Mail* added a fresh twist to the story by quoting dons (unnamed and probably fictional) as speculating as to whether the public revelation of the failure of the benefactor's son was designed to provide a smokescreen for the smuggling in of the Prime Minister's. 'Just imagine (they say) if a Prime Minister's son is offered a place at Trinity. What better riposte for Lord Beloff (sic) after the inevitable (and justified) cries of nepotism and cronyism than the tale of Mr Keevil.'

I had to defend the position that an elite academic education has to be reserved for an academic elite. In an article in *The Times* I explained 'We are entitled to take risks, to prefer the uncut stone, which may be a diamond over a polished semi-precious gem' to reinforce the point that it was academic potential which the College was seeking to identify. Though the broadsheet itself in its lead editorial, 'Appeal for Oxford. But money should not buy preferment for the fundraisers', defended my stance, I encountered further criticism from other quarters. The author and historian AN Wilson riposted in the *Daily Telegraph* in a piece entitled 'Mean spirit at Trinity';[44] calling my piece 'odious' adding, for good measure, that I was guilty of use of 'committee-speak and cliché' and arguing 'If Oxford had the courage it would glory in the benefactions of its old members'. When one journalist suggested that I protested too much I was provoked to respond that even in a trial by media a protestation of innocence should not be taken as a confession of guilt.

---

[43] Paul Scott, *Tony and Cherie. Behind the Scenes in Downing Street* (Scott, 2007) p 139.
[44] *Daily Telegraph* 23 December 2001.

The last chapter had yet to be written. The young Blair narrowly missed the grade of one of his A levels and could not take up his place. I was anxious to be able to let this outcome be publicly known in order to bury as soon as possible and once and for all the canard of favouritism. But Downing Street asked me to stay my hand again on privacy grounds and, somewhat reluctantly, I did so. The more positive story which appeared shortly afterwards in the media was on Euan's success in winning a place at Bristol. There was a happy sequel. Euan married a Trinity graduate; if you can't join them, join with them. With the benefit of hindsight, I suspect that the problems with security had Euan come to Trinity would have outweighed any notional benefit from the publicity, though given his later entrepreneurial success in proseletysing apprenticeships, I do wonder idly whether, as an old member he might have endowed, say, a Blair politics fellowship.

On a lesser scale another actual old member Keith Topley, a Master of the High Court, withdrew his support for the Boat Club as a protest against the College accepting a gift from Mohammad al Fayed of an eight which bore the Harrods crest. That was more a trickle than a tsunami.

I survived this tale of two crises and looked to the future. Trinity's 450th anniversary, in 2005, coincided with that of its adjacent foundation St John's. With the assistance of Robert Fellowes, her private secretary, Michael Peat, her former treasurer, and Robert Janvrin, her press secretary (respectively parent, alumnus and guest) I had all my minor pieces in place, but no Queen. In the event the College had to be satisfied with her message of goodwill (unsigned – the convention for informal letters) and a visit from the Prince of Wales.[45] He spent precisely one hour with us with not a second wasted as he gave a masterclass in meeting and greeting before leaving, like Alice through the looking glass via the narrow gate which separates Trinity from St John's to replicate (I assume – I was not there) similar diplomatic skills on the other side of the wall.

Michael Peat himself had invited me to a small lunch party in Buckingham Palace on what was essentially a purely social occasion. Not so the lunch I had in the same prime venue when Lord Luce, the then Lord Chamberlain, invited me to talk not of cabbages but of kings and on sundry matters royal; he later came to College to discuss with a quartet of selected members of staff and students the perception they had of the royal family – a kind of mini Gallup poll. Republicanism had no apparent toehold in Trinity.

The sesquitercentenary feast was attended, among others, by a former Foreign Secretary, England's second senior Law Lord, prize-winning novelist, PD James, actor Edward Fox, two Olympic gold medallists and Tom Graveney, President of the MCC. To match spiritual with secular, a Roman Catholic mass was held in

---

[45] I had once before met him at a reception at Clarence House to celebrate the opening of the Islamic Centre at the University. The South African High Commissioner with whom I had been chatting suddenly asked me if I had spoken to the Prince and when I demurred literally dragged me across the room. The Prince when apprised of my identity asked simply 'How are things at Oxford?' but time did not permit me to give a sensible answer or him to listen to one.

Chapel, conducted by the Archbishop Emeritus of Paris, during which he read out a message of congratulations from the newly elected Pope Benedict, a fan of Newman's theology. This had been brokered by one of our graduates, Mark Pellew, the British Ambassador to the Holy See.[46] Given that the college had been founded with the spoils of expropriation of the monasteries, the occasion had an intriguing resonance. The Clerk of Works was on tenterhooks during the Mass in case the incense should set off the smoke alarms in Chapel. The Domestic Bursar was amused when at breakfast the next morning the Cardinal said, after some hesitation, that he might relax his usual dietary rules and partake of a sausage.

Another old member, Ian Flintoff, wrote and produced a lawns play based on the College's history, preceded by a ceremony in which I conferred honorary membership of the Common Room on Martin O'Malley, then Mayor of Baltimore and later himself, when Governor of Maryland, a short-lived aspirant to the Democratic presidential nomination in 2016. Two Trinitarians, the Calvert brothers, were Maryland's founders, and in 2003 I had written to Mayor O'Malley a speculative letter asking if I could pay him a visit, without any expectation of a reply. In fact, I received a warm invitation, and when I arrived at his office, realised why – two large portraits of the brothers were prominently displayed at its entrance. Over a working lunch we swapped aims; mine to double the number of firsts, his to halve the number of murders. In 2005 the Mayor bravely attended the play's first act, which must have been incomprehensible to him, before retreating to a nearby pub.

Anne Robinson more than filled Jeremy Paxman's shoes in presiding over a college quiz show challenge pitting a quartet of golden oldies (or silverbacks?) against the pick of the current Trinity crop. I committed an almost fatal faux pas which almost prevented the curtain rising on the occasion at all by asking Anne on her arrival whether she wished to change, to which she replied curtly and with good reason 'I have changed'. I was clearly the weakest link.

On Judith's imaginative suggestion Sir Roger Norrington, son of the former President and celebrated conductor, agreed, with a barely sufficient three years' notice, to conduct a musical item with an orchestra of present and old members. Nigel Davenport, an alumnus actor, and Claire Booth, an alumna singer, added recitation and melody to the soiree.

The anniversary year seemed to be an obvious moment for me to leave the groves of academe and reinvigorate my practice at the Bar. Governing Body, however, thought it inconvenient for me to leave at the end of the calendar year rather than the end of the academic year. So I bargained with them to take a sabbatical during Hilary term 2006 as if I were a genuine academic. Serendipitously I was invited to give the Distinguished Alumni Lecture at the University of Wellington and to

---

[46] He and his wife Jill, a friend from our teenage years, held a Trinity reception in their Vatican villa, flanked by the Aurelian wall, as well as procuring an invitation to a party at the Villa Wolkonsky, later home of my successor at Trinity, Sir Ivor Roberts, the British Ambassador in Rome.

arbitrate for CAS at the Melbourne Commonwealth Games, engagements which paid for most of the travel. Starting in Singapore and returning via Los Angeles, San Francisco and New York, I met alumni in Asia, the Antipodes and America so the College may have benefitted that term more from my absence that it would have from my presence.

My appointment as President had opened up many doors; as I recount later[47] I had as a C-list academic celebrity a full social calendar beyond the dreaming spires. I nonetheless was able to maintain a toehold in practice, which I had volunteered to give up as a price to pay for the office. As I anticipated, the offer was declined. Oxford Fellows prefer the light touch to the heavy hand.

Trinity's Governing Body conventionally meets on Wednesdays: I decided that it would become my committee day, whether Bursarial, Investment, Tutorial, Joint Consultative or Equality. (For Melina Mercouri, it was 'never on a Sunday', for me, 'never on a Wednesday'.) This neatly bisected the week. As a result, I would accept no brief in term (in Oxford nought to ninth week) that was estimated to last more than two days, and then, at solicitors' acceptance of the risk of my premature departure. I never missed a College meeting in eight years because of a double booking, except once when Mohamed Al Fayed, who overvalued my services, made a handsome contribution of £50,000 to the College bursary scheme as the charge for buying me out, so that I could appear for him in the House of Lords.[48] (No, I must confess, I did earn a fee too; and, no, I was not surprised, or even aggrieved, by how swiftly my colleagues accepted the bargain.).

On one occasion I finished my submissions in the Lords at 1pm and dashed out to a car already in gear, so as to arrive at a Bursarial Committee at 2.15pm; on another occasion it was Strasbourg in the morning followed by an airport dash, and the same committee in the afternoon. No one at Trinity knew how close I, even if potentially betrayed by a certain breathlessness, had come to being late. Least said, soonest mended. Most strikingly I once flew to Hong Kong on Saturday night so as to appear for the Hong Kong Government in the Court of Final Appeal on Monday; gave a talk to the Hong Kong Bar Association on the evening after the hearing concluded; and flew back overnight. I was a little discomforted to discover that no one in college had noticed that I had not been there. So much for the power of the Presidency.

Much was owed to the indulgence of my judicial friends, who would often sit early or late in order for me to complete my submissions or release me before close of play to race off to some college event. I was grateful for the Oxford Tube, which links province and capital on a 24-hour basis: I caught it often after a Guest Night if I couldn't cadge a London bound lift in a chauffeur-driven car. I lured a few clients to Trinity for consultations with the promise of lunch and had the advantage of access to libraries on my doorstep, matching any in the Inns of Court.[49]

---

[47] Chapter 12 'Odds and Sods'.
[48] [2000] 1 AC 595.
[49] See my article 'A Tale of two Cities' Graya 118 p 13ff.

I twice acted for other colleges, failing to persuade the Visitor's delegate that an undergraduate from overseas had been lawfully sent down by St Anne's, a double blow to the college since the father of the young man in question had been identified as the possible source of a major benefaction, but succeeding in fending off a claim of a different sort made against St Peter's. I also gave advice to St Hilda's, at the time wrestling with the problems of advancing into the new millennium by becoming co-educational, against a vociferous rearguard action by those who cherished its uniqueness as a women-only college.

Regrets? I've had a few; but only in the sense that you can't have every chocolate in the box. I had advised on a constitutional issue in Malawi, where the opposition had frustrated the Government by absenting themselves from the legislature so ensuring that the body was never quorate. Unfortunately, the hearing was fixed for the first week of my first term. It was Patrick Elias[50] who took my place on the road to Lusaka.

I couldn't fly the Government's flag in *Pinochet*; I had to turn down briefs in Malaysia to represent the once and future Deputy Prime Minister, Anwar, and another in the Seychelles. Indeed I rejected a feeler from a fellow arbitrator in a commercial case held in Geneva to join the Seychelles Court of Appeal, though tempted by the vision of spending my declining years dispensing justice under the palm trees. I had to cast away a king's ransom because the first day of a trial in Hong Kong, set down for six days, clashed with Domus Dinner. It was certainly the most expensive dinner I've (or perhaps anyone) has ever eaten. The case inevitably lasted only three days.

I appeared nonetheless during my Oxford decade in 80 reported cases of varying importance. In a case arising out of a charge of unlawful gaming the key issue was whether teddy bears were 'tokens' and hence non-monetary prizes. Lord Hope records in his diary that 'One of the teddy bears had been brought along for the hearing, much to Tony Lloyd's delight'[51] – a delight which led to him taking custody of the bear, which, whether token or not, was certainly not a bribe.

Setting myself a target of not, while at Trinity, earning less in any year from my practice than the salary of the Lord Chief Justice, the highest-paid judge, I never came near to falling below it. But I regarded my bar earnings (at any rate part of them) as held in trust for the college. Without Governing Body's permission I would have had to rely on my President's salary. I felt a duty in consequence to give the College and its members something tangible so I set up a small charitable (The Troy) trust, in a form which prohibited any subsequent backsliding on my part. Over the years I used this vehicle to set up the Max Beloff History Scholarship (modestly enhanced by contributions from two miscreant publishers of inadvertent libels on me), to buy for the Boat Club a Women's IV – the *Judith Beloff* – to provide picnics and t-shirts for my beloved Track and Field Cuppers winning teams, but also to make grants to various Trinity Societies, clubs and the choir,

---

[50] Lord Justice.
[51] [1999] AC 247. Lord Hope Diaries, *House of Lords 1996–2009* (Hope, 2018) p 47. Tony himself was an OE.

and (anonymously) gifts to individual students who had achieved some particular success, or who were suffering particular financial hardship.

Under the stewardship of canny Scottish financial advisers the fund was still larger at the time of my departure than of my arrival so I endowed the Michael and Judith Beloff scholarship for a graduate student to study the BCL at Trinity with a preference to be given to those who wished to practise at the bar of England and Wales, in light of which donation I was made a member of the Vice Chancellor's Circle. I was particularly pleased that out of a cohort of outstanding young scholars one, AJ Ratan, later achieved a tenancy at Blackstone. The first and most successful was Tom Blomfield, later founder of Monzo bank and a member of the *Sunday Times* Rich List.

I was also invited by Chris Patten to become a patron of the University's extraordinarily successful appeal. It was decided that, as a matter of form, there should be at any rate one meeting of this body, albeit it had no executive function. It was held in Spencer House in Park Lane. Colin Lucas, erstwhile Master of Balliol and Vice-Chancellor, and I, as an in-house duo, sat somewhat out of place amongst a cohort of the super-rich benefactors, business people and philanthropists Vivien Clore, David Tang and an alumnus who appeared to own a sizeable part of Brazil. On a tour round this historic home the wife of James Martin (dressed informally in an unremarkable tweed jacket) who had endowed a school to study the problems of the twenty-first century, spotting a Picasso on the wall said with unconscious innocence, 'We have one of those at home'. Colin and I at least could not claim the same; the other attendees probably could.

All good things had to come to an end. In our last summer term, through the good offices of the Vice Chancellor, Trinity hosted the annual garden party for Encaenia, and I enjoyed a host of farewell parties accompanied by an eclectic series of gifts – a cake baked by the Social Secretaries of the MCR, a Slovakian straw doll from one graduate, a bottle of Scotch from another, a Trinity biro from the Tutorial Committee, an elegantly packaged shoe cleaning kit from a pair of medical twins, a scroll expertly organised by the steward and signed by the domestic staff in nine different languages, a carved wooden bench from the other staff, an inscribed tankard from Vincents, a leather-bound book with my initials embossed containing a variety of generous messages from the Junior Common Room. The old members decided to commemorate me by inaugurating an after-dinner speaking prize and the College Law Society did so by giving my name to its annual dinner.[52]

By convention I played no part in the election of my successor. My PA, Yvonne Cavanagh, tasked by the Governing Body to administer the process managed to maintain an impermeable Chinese wall so that my only inkling of the runners and riders was to observe the occasional (fairly) well known public figure in front quad casing the joint. On the day of the short list interviews Judith and I were politely

---

[52] Giving me the task of soliciting speakers for which I made full use of my upmarket legal connections, mainly in the new Supreme Court, so as not to devalue the coinage.

invited to make ourselves scarce. I left on the bed in the main lodgings bedroom a large cut out of Jeffrey Archer with the advertising slogan Absolute Thriller, which I thought might provide an unusual test of any candidate's imperturbability.

When I was appointed, the fashionable pool for potential heads of house was still former civil servants or diplomats (all conveniently retired at 60 with the prospect because of the then typical provisions of college statutes of no more than a decade in situ in the lodgings). After my departure media folk and lawyers became the fresh flavour.[53] Curiously the choice of lawyers fell on silks rather than judges.[54] I know of at least three judges in the Court of Appeal who did not even make a short list.[55] I was astonished to see that the very fellow who had the year before canvassed my views about the eligibility of a judicial candidate for one Cambridge college had himself been appointed Master. CP Snow thou shouldst be living at such hour.

Tom Bingham in his message of congratulations on my election said that he hoped my reign would be 'happy and glorious'. Happy it certainly was. Glorious it is for others to judge. After all I had instituted no major policy initiative. I had left no new buildings – I shied away from spending a decade on a construction site. But if I left no ideological or physical trace of my term in office (apart from having commissioned chairs in place of benches in Hall in the interest of female mobility and decorum), I made some mark. And at least on the staircase in Blackwell's bookshop, leading down to the Norrington Room, I appear in a photograph, inspired by a predecessor print of several decades before, of Oxford figures including such as Richard Dawkins and Phillip Pullman, in which my pleasure is only slightly diminished by the fact that I am described as Master, the title of the head of the far grander Cambridge college of the same name. In a profile in the *Oxford Times Magazine* on the eve of my demitting office, the writer said 'His students love him to bits'.[56] If that were indeed so, it would be enough.

On my departure, I was commissioned to write an article for the *Spectator* by its editor Matt D'Ancona which I entitled 'Goodbye to all that'. In it I proclaimed my unashamed pride in the University. 'It is the combination of three factors – higher admissions standards, a more intimate system of tuition by dedicated dons, and more intensive work – which give graduates of the two ancient Universities their dominance in so many areas of national life'. Whether this is for better or for worse others continue to debate.

---

[53] See my article in the *Oldie* in October 2019, 'Oxbridge Heads and Tales'.

[54] The prohibition of age discrimination has allowed some colleges to appoint distinguished persons approaching their eighth decade. While I do not think that a Head of House need be 'down wid da kidz' I do think that such age gap between him or her and the students alters the relationship and not necessarily always for the better.

[55] Pembroke, Oxford, has bucked that trend in 2020 by appointing Lord Justice Ryder.

[56] Linora Lawrence 'Farewell to Trinity' July 2006.

7

Second Time Round the Track

In *Twelfth Night* the restless Count Orsino says to his court musicians 'Enough no more; Tis not so sweet now as it was before'. On my return to full-time practice, after one decade's absence, I echoed the second sentiment, if faintly, without, until another decade later, seeking to implement the first.

In the very year 1996 when I moved from court to college I was ranked in the Chambers directory as one of the top three stars of the Bar along with Gordon Pollock and Jonathan S and, depending on how one interpreted the layout of the table, predictably my own preference, as numero uno. The number one or even number two or three spot, is enjoyed by only a handful of barristers (or tennis players or golfers or boxers or snooker players or etc etc) in their careers, but it's to be treasured while it lasts for that very reason.

But the moment, if golden, was transient, and given my career change inevitably never to be recaptured. By the time of my return, if, in Counsels' clan I had not quite as Frank Sinatra sang in *High Society*, 'become the forgotten man', other younger barristers had carved out starry careers in the areas in which I had once flourished; notably David shortly to be ennobled Pannick QC. Was I to be remembered only as a Perugino to his forensic Raphael, or (even less attractively) an envious Salieri to his forensic Mozart?[1]

No longer an automatic choice as first violin, I had nonetheless no wish to accept a perpetual role as second fiddle or to stigmatise my sojourn among the dreaming spires to prove less a case of *reculer pour mieux sauter* than *reculer pour moins sauter*. But now any superiority would no longer be effortless – the quality ascribed by Herbert Asquith to Balliol, not Trinity (or Magdalen) men. On the contrary it would demand qualities of maximum effort and eternal vigilance. To cite Frank once more 'Let me try again'.

When in 2008 I was given my lifetime achievement award at the annual Chambers Directory Awards, at a ceremony at Grosvenor House (along with the even older Pat Neill), I thought pessimistically that it recognised our past achievements rather than our current standing. In the directories – Chambers Directory was no longer the only kid on the block – I was sometimes referred to as a 'Senior statesman' and once in a newspaper report, a little woundingly, as a 'veteran barrister'.

---

[1] Our friendship and mutual respect survived intact and for several years we battled round the globe not only in London but in Hong Kong, Trinidad and the BVI; and if he won more of our encounters, I at least won the last of them.

One obstacle in my path was that many of my previous solictor contacts had either retired or ascended to the roles of senior or managing partners and were no longer the bestowers of bounty on the Bar.

Another obstacle was a growing tendency to pigeonhole barristers into ever narrower specialities. In my time I had featured in a dozen lists of leading counsel in various areas from agriculture and arbitration via immigration and insurance through to sport and telecommunications. But no longer could I be sold as an expert in both defamation and scuttling – or indeed in either. I was marketed as an administrative and sports lawyer – and my occasional forays into other areas were just that – occasional. I never appeared again in the ECJ and only once more in the ECtHR.[2]

Sir John Foster used to say that any proficient advocate could turn his hand to a case in any field of law with an up-to-date copy of Halsbury's Laws of England to hand. I doubt that that was ever wholly true even for a forensic giant like Sir John. I do think, nonetheless, that there is benefit in not over concentrating on a single speciality and recognising the advantages of cross-fertilisation. But that is not the view of the market for which, nowadays, it is all about horses for courses. At least administrative law itself covered a multitude of sins so that the restriction on the instructions for which I might be tendered was more apparent than real.

Yet, another obstacle was national advocacy protectionism. When so much of the map of the world was painted red and the Privy Council was an Imperial Court of Final Appeal there were also many opportunities open to English advocates in common law countries. Reading the memoir of Lord Elwyn Jones, a former Lord Chancellor and a near neighbour of my parents in Brighton, I was very impressed that he had once appeared in a court in Ethiopia, a country with its own Emperor. But since that far off era, closed or closing shops developed in smaller jurisdictions once open to English travelling tongues, and restrictive rules of admission became the new normal. There are a number of law reports in Hong Kong and Singapore in which my admission to plead a case was successfully contested by local lawyers. The adverse judgment was only partly alleviated by the standard formula that I was of course an acknowledged expert in the field of … blah blah blah etc.

Because of such factors few instructions and no more briefs arrived from Asia, except from Hong Kong itself. Even thence what was once a stream had become a streamlet. Courtesy calls on the Attorney-General and invitations to lecture the Government legal service belonged to my pre-Trinity era. Other newer counsel could enjoy the pleasures of Cathay Pacific (first class) and a suite with a panoramic view in the Shangri-La.

I did once joust in the multi-national Hong Kong Court of Final Appeal, then still located incongruously in the small, elegant, former French mission building, against Jonathan S.[3] I was forced to reject, with some specious excuse, his invitation to dine to while away the time before the due date for our case. I was reluctant to reveal to him that I was about to fly off for an all-expenses paid weekend in

---

[2] Application no. 8139/09.
[3] 2009 HKCFAR 68.

Doha to speak at a sports law forum, though I am uncertain as to whether he would have taken this as a sign of over confidence or of surrender. Only the fact that my junior Michael Thomas QC was on the same excursion provided some defence against the charge that this was not the best way to prepare for the hearing. We might have lost the case anyway.

Singapore, characteristically a law unto itself, exceptionally liberalised its rules as to rights of audience but not enough for me to be admitted to argue a case about the capacity of a final court of appeal to overrule itself. My application, successful at first instance, was rejected in the Court of Appeal on the usual basis that local counsel was more than competent – not, at any rate expressly, on the basis that I was less than competent. The Court did, however, allow me to sit in Court and play the junior's time-honoured role of handing up wholly indecipherable notes on post-its to the advocate on his feet. At least I did better than Cherie Booth who, once instructed in a case in Malaysia, flew out to conduct it and was not only refused admission but actually exiled to the gallery.

I was also on the recommendation of Davinder Singh[4] made a member of the Singapore International Council of Mediators despite my inability to indicate in the standard form any training or experience in this new form of dispute resolution. On the standard forms later required for my reappointment I simply referred back to my initial form. My ability in this area was never put to the test.

If for me it was closing time in the gardens of the East I now had to look westward where the land was brighter. In Trinidad, I had an uncovenanted bonus when sometime junior Anand Ramlogan, an endlessly inventive lawyer, became a youthful Attorney-General and showered me with instructions to advise on a number of constitutional cases involving officers such as the President, the Prime Minister, the Senior Judiciary and issues such as capital punishment, gay marriage, and Trinidad's membership of the Eastern Caribbean Court of Final Appeal.

My last was my most interesting Trinidad case. Its context was a statutory amnesty given to all persons accused of other than what were colloquially known as blood crimes – murder, rape and the like – which had not been brought to trial within 10 years from charge. The rational policy objective was to clear the huge backlog of criminal cases and make a fresh start. Just when the Act was about to come into force by Presidential proclamation, an astute journalist noticed that this would mean that my client, not accused of any blood crime, but of corruption and bribery in connection with the construction of Trinidad's new Piarco airport (which he stoutly denied) and who had already undergone old-style committal proceedings lasting more than 100 days, would not have to face trial.

In response the Government introduced, and Parliament rushed through, emergency legislation. On its face it was of general application but – which was

---

[4] SC. Senior Partner of Drew and Napier before setting up his own firm. Inductee to Asia's Legal Hall of Fame. I had led him in a case for the Jurong Town Corporation where our opponent, the solitary opposition MP Ben Jereyatnam suddenly told the Arbitrator that he had parliamentary duties to attend to, and walked out of the hearing room without so much as a by your leave. A cool cat by any standard …

the essence of my client's appeal – in fact ad hominem – deliberately targeted at him, and for that reason unconstitutional on a number of grounds. I fought side by side in the local courts with the passionate Ed Fitzgerald QC, playing the cerebral Laurel to his ebullient Hardy. The Privy Council rejected our client's final appeal, essentially on the basis that the motivation for the legislation was not a subject which it could properly consider[5] and so saved itself the need to do so. It did, however, suggest that the Director of Public Prosecutions had involved himself too closely in the promotion of the Act, an issue on which my client had the benefit of input from Sir Keir Starmer[6] who had held a similar position in England before he plunged into the perilous pond of politics.

I acquired one new regular client, the Financial Services Commission of the British Virgin Islands (BVI).[7] I soon discovered that reaching the BVI is somewhat like trying to get to Cambridge from Oxford. There are a series of options – none of them satisfactory. Either one starts in Antigua, and then proceeds by a series of hops touching down in every island in between – and there are not a few – or one risks going via New York but with the benefit of only one further stop in Puerto Rico. When I experimented with the latter route my plane from Gatwick was two hours late taking off, giving me minimal time to circumvent US Immigration. I found myself behind a young woman who shamelessly queue jumped. Nothing ventured nothing won, I followed in her wake shouting 'I'm with her' trying to convey the impression that we were a married couple off on honeymoon. We were the last two to board the onward flight; but board it we did. Leaving the islands once proved as problematic as arriving at them when there was a volcanic eruption in Iceland causing havoc in the international skies with a cloud of ash. This cloud did have a silver lining since on my return I was asked to advise a number of aviation stakeholders as to whether they had any right to compensation and from whom for the damage to their profits.

More agreeable was a flight from BVI to Trinidad in a private jet. David Pannick and I were fortuitously against each other in both jurisdictions. In the BVI I was for the public authority the FSC, David for a corporate body under investigation. In Trinidad David was for the Attorney General and I for the client I shared with Ed Fitzgerald. It was our private clients who chartered and paid for the jet. Moral (trite): publicly funded work pays less well than privately funded work.

In Cayman, my client had been refused on safety grounds a licence to operate a helicopter service. Visiting the helipad for an initial consultation I declined my client's invitation to take a helicopter trip. I do not relish putting all my eggs on one propeller which has never seemed to me to be quite enough. When we paid a formal site visit during the hearing itself I noted that the Judge declined a similar invitation. Site visits are often helpful but there's no need to exaggerate.

---

[5] [2016] UKPC 2.
[6] QC DPP KBE MP PC, Leader of the Labour party in chronological order.
[7] After I had retired I was invited to return to the BVI to give some continuing advocacy education to the local presenters of the FSC, which offer I rejected with only a tinge of regret.

On that occasion my Senior Clerk had arranged for me to meet the former Premier McKeeva Bush who was the object of serious allegations of impropriety. The barrister, like the cobbler, should stick to his last – or in his case schtick. I explained that I was no criminal lawyer. He turned in the end to Sir Geoffrey Cox QC, former Attorney-General, whose riches, if not concomitantly his reputation, profited from the brief.

At home I had been unable to take full advantage of the growth in human rights litigation after the coming into force of the Human Rights Act in October 2000. My only major human rights case in the House of Lords[8] was as untypical as could be devised; did the duty of purchasers of glebe land[9] to pay for the repairs of the local parish church (a lurking mediaeval legacy rightly recognised to be ripe for reform) violate the unwary owners' property rights? Property claims also featured in an unsuccessful effort by some of the shareholders in Northern Rock to be compensated for its collapse.[10]

Nonetheless it was by no means, if indeed at all, doom and gloom. There were many highlights. I had to advise the father of Stellios Haji-Iannou, founder of EasyJet, and flew to Monte Carlo where he had a sumptuous flat above the no less sumptuous hotel in the casino square. My mother had instilled in me a preference for what she perceived to be the superior safety records of national carriers over budget airlines so I flew by BA rather than EasyJet. This appeared to concern my solicitors more than my client. When I appeared in the Court of Appeal to plead his cause[11] I was unable to stay for a third day – the case having overrun, leading Lord Justice Brooke to quip that my client had obviously been unable to afford me further – a quip that I feigned to take in good heart.

My last case to end in Strasbourg involved Abu Othman, known as Abu Qatada, reputed to be Osama Bin Laden's vicar in England and temporarily anonymised as 00 in the law report. The Home Office wished to deport him to Jordan; but, although it was not in issue that he was a threat to British national security, his deportation was said to be blocked on human rights grounds.

The problem about how to deal with foreign terrorists was a recurrent one. Unless they could be convicted of a criminal offence they could not be imprisoned. Because of the Chahal case (in which I was involved both in the domestic courts[12] and before the European Commission of Human Rights)[13] there could be no deportation to countries where there was the risk of violations of Article 3 of the Convention in various forms of inhuman or degrading treatment. Because of the Belmarsh case they could not be detained when their English equivalents were not. Control orders were insufficient to control them. David Seymour, senior legal

---

[8] [2004] I AC 546.

[9] An area of land within an ecclesiastical parish used to support a parish priest.

[10] NLJ 20 February 2009.

[11] [2006] All ER (D)100.

[12] [1995] 1 WLR 526.

[13] 224/14/93 until Nick Lyell the Attorney-General deposed me in favour of himself, a substitution which was not, I was told, entirely to the liking of the Treasury Solicitors department. In the event he did no worse than me but also no better.

adviser to the Home Office, told me that this, the fourth, was also the last throw of the Government's dice. In the House of Lords we succeeded.[14] But represented by Edward Fitzgerald, instructed by Gareth Pierce, two of the doughtiest civil liberties lawyers, Abu Qatada won the replay in Strasbourg on the basis that evidence against him might be tainted by torture. Eventually he was sent back to Jordan after the then Home Secretary, Theresa May, had personally secured a guarantee from the Jordanians that no such testimony would be relied on against him. In consequence terrorist charges against him were dismissed for lack of evidence. In the long run he was the only winner.

I had previously been vetted for clearance in connection with national security matters and, as a citizen, was hugely impressed by the depth of scrutiny. Not only did I have to identify friends and colleagues from Dragon days onwards for interview (yet how many, if any, prep school boys can spot a potential fellow traveller down revolutionary road?) but enquiries were made of my wife's sister's Swedish husband. I guess that the officials got small change from him, a stolid Scandinavian psychiatrist.

To balance my litigation ledger I was, however, instructed to challenge the decision of the Home Secretary to cancel the British passport and refuse an application for a new one of a student who had already been subject of a travel measure under the Act colloquially known as TPIM 2011 because of suspected terrorist-related activities. The maximum duration of such measure was two years. The constitutional issue was whether the prerogative could be used to prolong so legislatively limited a period. The client, known only by his initials being subject to an anonymity order, became even less visible when he disappeared before the issue could be tested – not much of a vote of confidence in his leading counsel. David Cameron, who had vowed in Parliament to introduce new legislation if the challenge had succeeded, was spared the need to embark on such exercise.

On several occasions I visited Michael Gove in his eyrie in the Department of Education decorated by portraits of Lenin and Margaret Thatcher, unlikely bedfellows. Before the first consultation started, with Dominic Cummings, one of his special advisers, standing watchfully in the background, I disconcerted Michael by tendering his biography of Michael Portillo for autograph, so doubling up author and subject on the same flyleaf. After the consultation ended I gave him some informal suggestions on ex-President of the Union terms for the speech he was crafting for the *Leveson* inquiry – not those which prompted Lord Justice Leveson to say acerbically he did 'not need to be told about the importance of free speech'. I also fended off a challenge to the establishment of an Academy (to be sponsored by University College), a cause supported by Michael Gove but instigated by his predecessor.[15]

Other issues which crossed my desk or appeared on my screen included the future of the World Service and the terms of the BBC's new charter; Nick Clegg's

---

[14] [2010] 2 AC 110 Lord Hope's diaries, House of Lords, p 356 'The advocates were on the whole very good'. Whose performance was it which prompted the critical qualification 'on the whole'?

[15] [2010] PTSR 749 discussed in Andrew Adonis, *Education, Education, Education* p 110. The case turned on the reach of European procurement law. He calls me 'one of England's best public law barristers'. Did he mean public *school* barristers?

proposal for free meals for primary schoolchildren; the ownership of tapes made by the speech therapist of the late Princess of Wales; and, of more popular, if not private significance, the rights to Ian Fleming's *Thunderball*; and the return of assets to the Arab spring countries, about which my advice was discussed in Parliament.

I advised the Garrick on the legality, not the morality, of maintenance of their bar to female membership. I was not myself a member so I did not have the opportunity to resign from the club as did Anthony Lester who appears somewhat belatedly to have recognised after many years subscription that it was an all-male institution. Peter Jay was leader of the pack which disagreed with my freely available analysis. The Club conservatives gave me an excellent dinner chaired by Peter Riddell[16] to celebrate their victory over the forces of progress, on whose side – as I made clear – I was certainly myself aligned. I had earlier advised the Oxford and Cambridge Club that, a century after women had first become members of the older of the two universities, the time had come, in law as well as fact, to admit alumnae as well as alumni to all, not only part, of the club's sombre facilities. I predict the Garrick will follow its example sooner rather than later, though not soon enough.

I advised the Law Society that the legal profession could no longer claim exceptionalism and that the standard of proof for disciplinary offences should become the civil, not the criminal standard. Like Daniel in the Lions' den I had to defend my position in a meeting convened for that purpose to a largely hostile audience. Since the Bar Council had taken the same step at least I could not be accused of hypocrisy.

I was still instructed by a galaxy of regulators adding Ofwat (clean rivers) to Ofgem and Ofcom, by Big Pharma, the Pharmacists Association and NICE, by the CAA and regional airports, by the Electoral Commission, and wealthy ex-pats seeking to ensure their right to vote and by various government departments, some of whose problems were more entertaining than others. Should Job Centres advertise vacancies in the adult entertainment industry? What the answer was to this question of national importance I cannot now for the life of me recall.

Despite these excursions abroad and alarums at home I increasingly realised that I was operating more on the basis of experience than of enthusiasm. Blackstone Chambers enticed year by year outstanding new juniors, all of whom had undergone a rigorous pupillage with at least four different pupil masters (or supervisors as they were now more gently termed) and passed through, as did all candidates for tenancies, the scrutiny of a not so gently named 'barbed wire' committee. In providing advice or opinions I sometimes became more an editor of my juniors' first draft than an author. All of them swiftly learned my eccentric aversion to ending any text with an odd number (other than five). For my submissions in Court I would usually give my juniors guidelines and then translate their product into something that was recognisable – to me at any rate – as a script in

---

[16] Kt Commissioner, for Public Appointments.

my style. But I never, never, simply read out a document into which I had had no input.[17]

The times they were a changin' in other ways too, making professional life simply less fun. Emails had sprouted like weeds. Not only did accessing them take up excessive time, but because of them the previous pace of the law had accelerated. With increasing frequency no hard copy papers were delivered, so neatly transferring the duty to provide physical bundles from solicitor to counsel who had to organise the printing in chambers. Advices could now be sought instantaneously (irrespective of need). In my early days at the Bar I often encountered in unedited correspondence files a solicitor's excuse to an impatient client that 'papers are with counsel' which was sometimes pure fiction requiring on counsel's side a gritting of teeth – never bite the hand that feeds you. Now papers could be with counsel metaphorically at the drop of a hat, literally at the press of a button. IT operators in chambers devised ever more elaborate ways of ensuring security – all doubtless highly necessary but all of which ate into the fleeting hour; and don't speak to me of the GDPR.

But there were other diversions from pure or impure practice. In 1978 I had been lunching with two of the circuit judges at the Bloomsbury and Marylebone County Court, where I was administering what purported to be justice, when I was asked to take a telephone call from Gordon Slynn, that year's Treasurer of Gray's Inn. He told me that I had been elected a bencher, a member of the Inn's governing body. I had no advance inkling of my election, although, as I learned later, the fact that I had recently been asked for a photograph by the Treasury Office was a clue for the cognoscenti. It was only seven years since I had taken silk, then the minimum period prior to election, since lowered to three to inject youth into administration. I was embarrassed to tell my fellow lunchers since circuit judges were then not eligible ever to become benchers under another rule since sensibly abolished.

In becoming a bencher one crosses a legal Rubicon. Out of court one mingles on first name terms with judges (though I still called Geoffrey Lane LCJ 'Chief' just to be on the safe side). In court one may not be given more favourable treatment when appearing before a fellow bencher, but one may at least feel that any more testing treatment is not (necessarily) the product of personal antipathy.

The ranking of benchers is dictated by the date of one's election. I was for that reason just one place ahead of Kenneth Clarke. Even the spiritual cannot override the secular rule. When the Archbishop of York, John Sentamu,[18] an honorary bencher, came to a service in chapel, to my embarrassment, even in those circumstances he too joined the queue several places below me.

Each year the benchers elect a new cohort and each year also, oscillating between bar and bench, a Treasurer and Vice Treasurer (the heir apparent). While

---

[17] Sometimes solicitors said they only wanted my signature on my juniors' or even their own draft on the basis that it would strengthen their defence if they were ever to be sued by their clients for negligence. But I had my own interest in protecting Brand Beloff (if such it was) which also led to instructions to give advice on aspects of English law in other jurisdictions.

[18] A fellow bencher once canvassed with me the notion of a race discrimination suit when Sentamu was not elevated to the see of Canterbury. The notion was not further developed.

I was at Trinity I was in practical terms out of play to join the race. But in my second last year there Alan Ward[19] asked if I could stand as his deputy – again just too early but an indication that I was thought papabile by the powers that be.

When the Treasurership was contested, sometimes the defeated candidate tended to slink away from the Inn, a little like a rutting stag who had lost the *jus primae noctis* to a more powerful rival and quit the herd. It was better to avoid such contests and carve up the succession. Robin Jacob,[20] a potential rival from my generation, whom I claim to remember from our call night singing in his cups about his big bamboo,[21] flatteringly told me I could choose my time, and I duly became what he revelled in calling his 'Vice'. I had already negotiated with Mark Waller[22] to precede him in that post. We each had an elderly mother who would wish to see her son become Treasurer, Mark's because her husband had done so, mine because her father would never have believed it. My mother was slightly older than Mark's so I got first dibs. Each mother lived long enough to see her son achieve her (and his) ambition.

I was fortunate that it was only after my election that a rule was introduced making service on the Inn's management committee (the body that does the real work) a precondition for candidacy. I had only been Master of Moots so as to honour my bencher's undertaking to serve the Inn in some capacity, and not just to enjoy its social life – an undertaking sometimes honoured more in the breach than in the observance. I once, in Robin's absence, had to preside at Pension, the Inn's name for the governing body's meeting, when I banged my gavel and observed superfluously that this was not a coup d'état but a dress rehearsal.

'What do you do?' is an orthodox conversational opening gambit, as the Inn's Preacher Roger Holloway[23] observed in the last of his 2008 Mattins sermons. It is one that Treasurers are often asked but never accustomed to answer, at any rate in print. There is no CV particular to the office, but being Head of House at Oxford (or even Cambridge) comes as close as any, though the scale is different. You get a flat, not lodgings, you are in post for a year, not a decade, you have a garden view but not your own garden and you are called Master Treasurer, not Master (or Warden, Rector, President, Dean, Principal or Provost as the case may be). For me to do one (Gray's) after the other (Trinity) was like using a decompression chamber after a deep sea dive.[24]

The year starts with an introduction by the Under Treasurer to the serried ranks of the staff (a little like a Cabinet Minister entering his or her new department, but, on reflection, not very like). The chief demands are on stomach and larynx: all ex-Treasurers should be given a subscription to Weightwatchers. During term time there are often back-to-back dinners (moot night, mixed messes, debate

---

[19] Lord Justice.

[20] Lord Justice.

[21] Robin disputes my recollection. Perhaps it was I who was in my cups.

[22] Lord Justice.

[23] Described in his *Times* obituary as a soldier, big game hunter, wine merchant as well as priest. In short – not your typical Barbara Pym vicar, his sermons were as unconventional as he. The first one he preached during my Treasureship was on prostitution.

[24] MJBQC 'A year in a Treasurer's Life, Graya no 122 p 85.

nights, guest nights). You feed away as well as home (Grand Day at three other Inns), and enjoy the enticing free lunches throughout the year. (The fact that my chambers, Blackstone, were as far away from hall as any set in the confines of the Inns of Court could be, at least compelled a brisk walk – brisker before than after.)

There are speeches to be made and, indeed, non-speeches, a modern euphemism for the succinct flattery of ones' guests, commenting evening-end on their wit, charm, intelligence and rare physical beauty. There are speeches sad – at the departure of valued members of staff – speeches inspirational – at student weekends – and speeches gay (in the original sense of the word) to celebrate some Gray's Innachievement.

The elevation of benchers to the great Pension in the sky engages the duty to read a lesson: how to do it audibly is itself a lesson learned from regular attendance at Mattins. Speakers from outside must be introduced (thanks can be left to others – it's safer that way); indeed speakers as well as guests have to be lured by promise of stimulating company in an historic hall: Though it had to be rebuilt after wartime bombing, the spars in the surviving gallery are said to be rescued from the wrecks of the Spanish Armada.

For mixed messes I invited several well-known speakers (Jonathan A, Norman Lamont, Christopher Meyer,[25] John Wadham[26]) and one so covertly known that his visit could not even be advertised, John Scarlett, the Head of MI6. The visit of Chelsea's Bruce Buck with his gift of 125 club baseball caps (there's tactical skill for you) generated a photograph which appeared in *Graya News* (circulation 5,000 maximum) and the Stamford Bridge programme for Chelsea v Liverpool (circulation 60,000 minimum).

In particular for Grand Day the Treasurer compiles a list of the great and the good (to be firmly distinguished from London-Lite celebs) with a sideways competitive glance at the other Inns' invitees (do two Knights of the Garter outrank one royal?).

The Treasurer must find a preacher for the established Mulligan sermon (my Oxford contacts to the rescue – come in the Bishop, Richard Harries) and an inaugural Birkenhead Lecturer: no need for any Dick or Harry but our own Tom Bingham the only possible choice.

Musical entertainment survives for the odd Friday night dinner. I used my Trinity connection to attract a barbershop ensemble including two ambassadors and a consultant surgeon, who had performed in their time for President Reagan in the White House, so were not unused to still more ('surely you mean less?' – Ed) significant audiences.

Above all there are the four call nights, in which to exercise the only function that the Treasurer has wired into the legal system, converting the BVC – fledglings – students whom the Treasurer may have met in his travels around the country at various Inn events[27] – into earnest seekers after the holy grail of pupillage.

---

[25] UK Ambassador to the USA.
[26] Legal Adviser to Liberty.
[27] In my year Bristol, Leeds, Guildford, Nottingham, Cambridge.

There is formal ceremony with the callees one by one being inducted with the Treasurer's mantra 'I hereby call you to the Bar and do publish you barrister', and after, not before, a handshake.[28] Then there is the Treasurer's speech by convention, a blend of congratulations on the journey made and warnings about the journey to come, culminating with a reminder that the Bar is an honourable profession. After my first one the Under Treasurer came up to me and said in a military phrase 'That was a senior speech'. I misheard him and mistook what was intended as a compliment to be an accusation that I had uttered some obscenity. Many callees become Gray's alumnae abroad to be nurtured; an offshoot of travel for other purposes when Treasurer to Guernsey and Isle of Man, when 'Vice' to Hong Kong, Kuala Lumpur, Singapore.

Then there are the Committees: Management Committee fortnightly, expertly chaired by another bencher (in my year my former fag at Eton Michael Burton, more used to taking instructions from than giving them to me, but equally adept at either) where the Treasurer's role is monarchical, to warn, encourage and advise; and Pension monthly where the role is more Presidential, to ensure that the heat of debate casts light appropriate to the significance of the issue (dress code at Grand Day as against a rethink of the role of the Inns). For my Grand Day, not wishing to put my male guests to the expense of hiring a tail coat and accoutrements, I proposed dinner jackets only, a break with tradition not since reprised and one which I only achieved with the support of Terry Etherton,[29] temporarily given for his benign consensual radicalism the nick name 'Red Tel'.

There were monthly COIC (Council of the Inns of Court) sessions where the four Inns representatives confront (usually in harmony) the serried ranks of the regulators. Glory of glories, the Treasurer's Reception (pray for sun), one and a half hours of handshaking (antibacterial squirt and arnica recommended),[30] one and a half hours relaxed recovery with daughter Natasha stepping at virtually no notice into the shoes of wife, rendered hors de combat by an accidental fall. In pre-Christmas mode there is the annual Thespian Miscellany – an occasion to make a fool of oneself but this time officially. My putative contribution, a political pastiche 'The Eton Voting Song', was returned with the comment 'Don't call us, we'll call you'.

Disciplinary issues arise for applicants, students and barristers, each with their complex and different procedures. They posed no easy questions: should a teenage peccadillo disqualify someone from entry into the profession forever?[31] After all Barack Obama had recently confessed (un-Clinton like) to dabbling in drugs as a young man and, as Bruce Forsyth might have said, 'didn't he do well'?

In the best traditions of the Bar those whose cases require a hearing are both prosecuted and defended by our own QCs pro bono, displaying wisdom and

---

[28] in pre-Covid days.
[29] Master of the Rolls and a Life Peer.
[30] again, in pre-Covid days.
[31] I discuss this issue further in chapter 11, 'Judge Not Lest Ye Be Judged'.

forensic skills for which they could – and no doubt do – charge a fortune down at the Bailey. Sometimes the Treasurer is required by an order of an external body to issue a reprimand to a senior member, for which sanction Atkin's Court Forms provide, alas, no precedent, and the fallback position of the beleaguered house-master at a minor public school ('I don't like your general attitude') seems to fall woefully short of the mark. Time for some creative oratory …

Finally – in reality it should be firstly – there is the bilateral relationship, criti-cal to the Inn's wellbeing, that of Treasurer and Under Treasurer; meetings almost daily in which a response to issues, personal, political and practical are cordially plotted and an agenda set for the monthly meetings of governing body. My year was a year of two Under Treasurers, both former army officers of distinction, David Jenkins and his successor Tony Faith. In 1 Corinthians 13:13 it is pronounced 'And now abideth faith, hope, charity, these three; but the greatest of these is charity'. For me for two terms the greatest of these was Faith.

The Treasurer's is a demanding schedule for a busy practitioner (and even, dare I say it, for a Judge with a timetable disciplined by the MoJ). On one memorable occasion I had to ask my judge (fortunately a Gray's Inn bencher) to rise early so that I could change costume, read a lesson at a memorial service, exit at solemn pace, mutating to a frenzied rush, to a car in South Square, whence I was chauffeured to the Reform Club where I had to preside over an annual meeting of the advisory panel of ANA (Japan's major airline) and make an introductory humorous address, the jokes of which could *not* be Lost in Translation. Management Committee as per usual at 8.30 prompt next morning, before resuming Court battle at 10.

Unlike that of the Policeman in *Pirates of Penzance*, my Treasurer's lot *was* truly a happy one. It was not enough to be; one must do as well. As the old *News of the World* used (wrongly) to say 'All human life is here'. But on 31 December after ascent to the top of the ladder you promptly tumble down, taking your subordinate place in the nominal list of Benchers, your only material legacy being the mandatory coat of arms. In an institutional after life I remained an adviser to the Treasurer on possible honorary benchers. But having in my own springtime as a bencher suggested that it was premature to offer that status to Mikhail Gorbachev, in my autumn I failed to procure it for either Hilary Clinton or Michelle Obama for each of whom another Inn had made a first bid, neither to date successful.

But the Treasurership was a time-limited post. Could I find an outlet of a more permanent kind? I had become used to conflation with my father. However, when in 2003 journalists in the *Daily Telegraph* described me on three occasions as a knight,[32] I wrote to Charles Moore,[32] the then editor, saying 'A single reference is a source of amusement; a second a source of embarrassment; and a third a source of annoyance'. I was admittedly a trifle concerned that a circular to his staff along

---

[32] Lord Moore of Etchingham.

the lines of 'Michael Beloff wishes it to be known that he is not a knight' would be catnip to *Private Eye*. Charles efficiently stemmed the flow of miswrites without exposing me to any obloquy.

My father had himself progressed beyond a knighthood to a life peerage.[33] As my own career nudged me into the public eye friends from all three major parties suggested that I might be interested in emulating him.[34] It remained an article of faith for me that, while in practice at the Bar, I should eschew any formal political attachment so no, not then. But as my decade at Trinity came towards its end, and partly stimulated by the teasing title of a piece about me in the *Financial Times Magazine*,[35] I wondered whether I should propose myself as what was popularly if inaccurately called 'a People's Peer'. I canvassed the views of Robin Butler, who agreed to be a referee and solicited further support from my usual patrons Tom Bingham and David Williams. I added the Head Mistress of King Edward VI Birmingham, whom I had met when speaking at the annual meeting of the National Association of Grammar Schools and my own PA, Yvonne Cavanagh, for insight into my activities at Trinity.

Invited to a lunch with Lord Kingsland, the conservative shadow Lord Chancellor, with whom my wife had become friends when both were reading for the Bar at Lincoln's Inn, I was mildly embarrassed when he said that *he* thought I should become a Peer. I had to explain that I would only be interested in sitting on the cross benches and somewhat sheepishly that I had already set the process in motion. The months passed and from time to time I received a letter saying that I was still under serious consideration. Finally, I was summoned to an interview with Lord Stevenson of Cottenham, in charge of the appointment procedure. But then, after a further gap, I received a short letter saying that the Prime Minister, then Gordon Brown, would not be putting my name forward ... 'More fool they' wrote Robin Butler consolingly, if charitably. But given that David Pannick had recently been appointed and Anthony Lester and Harry Woolf had long been peers I was not that surprised. For the second chamber four players from one set of chambers might have seemed a little *de trop*.

Lord Kingsland, however, was not satisfied and said he would pursue my cause. I was sitting in my hotel in Guernsey during one of my week's sittings in the Court of Appeal when I read in *The Times* of his sudden death. My immediate and utterly unworthy thought was – bang goes my chance. I had, like some Warren Gatland, reshuffled my pack; seeking to provide from a fresh perspective not just a resumé but a record. In my new support team[36] were a former Canadian ambassador to

---

[33] At the same time as I took silk, prompting a paragraph by Albany in the *Sunday Telegraph* headlined 'Silk and Ermine'.

[34] Although each held a senior position I had no reason to believe that these were other than casual approaches.

[35] Julia Llewellyn-Smith 'Without Peerage, 30 June 2002'.

[36] I was told that all traces of my previous application would have been destroyed as confidential.

the United Nations, a senior member of the IOC (both of whom colleagues on CAS), a serving Law Lord with whom I had had many a joust when he was at the bar, a female bencher of Gray's Inn familiar with my work there, the Bailiff of Jersey, for my judicial role, and Rabinder Singh to signal and support my commitment to diversity. The outcome was, however, the same and the rejection letter arrived more swiftly than before. The Chair of the Appointment Commission at that time was Michael Jay, former head of the Foreign Office, whom I had thought might succeed me as President of Trinity but who was in fact earlier pipped to the post by Ivor Roberts, his junior in the diplomatic hierarchy. There was coincidence but of course no connection between our two rejections.

I had in fact a third extremely long shot. Bill Cash,[37] concerned that some balance was needed in the all but wholly Remainer second chamber, proposed to Boris Johnson that he put me in his list of working peers. Although he told me that Boris had commended him for his proposal, nothing came of it. Boris had once, spotting me at the annual Hong Kong dinner, where, when Mayor of London, he was the guest speaker, called out 'And there's the great Lord Beloff'. Maybe, never by reputation a man for detail, the PM thought I was already a peer; there are so many of them. Be that as it may, there were not to be two Lord Beloffs and my right to sit on the steps of the throne as the eldest son of a peer, only once exploited, died with my father.

Turning elsewhere and less ambitiously I put myself forward as a candidate for the second iteration of the Judicial Appointments Commission, then chaired by an old Etonian. Here I felt I was on stronger ground. I had been an early proponent of the need for such a Commission; I had been a Judge myself; I had served on the Senior Salaries Review Body (SSRB) (more of both later), I had acted professionally for all the bodies involved in the battle against race and sex discrimination. I had sat with the Chair of the interviewing panel on another appointment commission and I knew well the senior judge, another panel member. At the end of the interview I had, to my mild surprise, to prompt the panel to ask me what I thought was the most important question – what were the key judicial qualities? In the end I lost out to a far junior barrister, who ticked the one box that I could never have ticked. He was of a validated ethnic minority. Neither being a Jew or an Old Etonian helped me this time round.

None of these side roads off the main highway were open so on my seventieth birthday I wrote a letter to my Senior Clerk, suggesting that the time had come for me to scale back substantially and concentrate more on authorship, less on advocacy. He treated it as some kind of belated April Fool. And after a few half-hearted efforts to show that I meant what I said by turning down a bare handful of instructions, I rolled over. For a few more years at least it was back to the Bar for me.

---

[37] Former shadow Attorney-General and constant Europhobe.

8

Politics and the Law

My interest in politics led me naturally towards administrative law, whose purpose is to keep the powers of government within their legal bounds. It was both fortunate and fortuitous that I was called to the Bar in the decade in which the green shoots of review reappeared after a long winter in which the judiciary had adopted a measure of self-restraint – explicable during the Second World War (when it saw the interests of the state as paramount) and only marginally less understandable during the time in office of the socialist post-war administrations (when it shrank from appearing to be a class opposition). But from the swinging sixties onward the pace of judicial intervention accelerated, reflected in the novel vocabulary of public law (designed to differentiate it clearly from private law) and judicial review (given concrete form in new procedures).

In a lecture I gave in 1997[1] I advanced the argument that 'imperceptibly in Great Britain – there is developing a constitutional court, even a Supreme Court'. At that stage I was agnostic about the development, ending with the observation that 'essentially of its own volition the power of the English judiciary has increased and is increasing. It is not my case that it ought to be diminished; it is only that the phenomenon be recognised'. Influenced maybe by the fact that I had more time for reflection sitting in an ivory tower in Oxford, rather than standing in the front row in London, I did become something of a sceptic about the process, adopting the position more generally associated with Jonathan S and elaborated by him in a series of addresses over a decade and more, culminating in his elegant and much-discussed Reith Lectures in 2019.

In a later lecture in 2003 I summarised the trend:

> My thesis is that one of the most profound recent changes in the constitution results not from the designs, benign or brutal, of Thatcherite Tory or New Labour, but from the activities of a third branch of government, the judiciary, which has itself not only to a substantial extent exercised control over the executive, but even infringed the sovereignty of Parliament, an impregnable given for those reared in the traditions of Blackstone and Dicey.

The passage was quoted by the then Home Secretary, David Blunkett[2] in his assault on what he perceived to be hyperactive judges; in his view abstinence had been replaced by overreach.[3]

---

[1] John Kelly memorial lecture, 'The Irish Jurist'. Vol.XXX 1998 p.1.
[2] In a speech to the Institute for the Study of Civil Society in October 2001.
[3] Two years later David Blunkett overreached himself in a personalised attack on my old friend and former Chambers colleague Andrew Collins who had offended the Minister over an asylum case.

There were several reasons for this control creep, which has continued despite the 'Blunkett' critique – the increasing inability of Her Majesty's opposition (or rebel backbenchers) effectively to corral the activities of the executive especially during the decade long Thatcher and Blair administrations;[4] the accession of the United Kingdom to the Common Market and the consequent, if only slowly appreciated, paramountcy of Community law over national law and, finally, the enactment into that national law of the ECHR. Lord Neuberger even threw into the explanatory mix 'the irreverent psychology of the baby boomer judiciary … judges educated in the rebellious and liberal seventies replacing those brought up in the conformist and respectful sixties.'[5]

A paradigm example of the latter category was Clan leader and man of Trinity, Sir William 'Bill' Macpherson,[6] whose ratio of refusal to grant of leave (since his time renamed permission) to pursue an application for judicial review was statistically proven to be the highest among judges of his era. He used an unusual sense to detect merit or lack of merit in an application. In a case about a ban on oral snuff marketed by US Tobacco, he said 'Mr Beloff, my nostrils always tell me when there has been unfairness, and my nostrils have not troubled me in this case'. (Actually, his nose must have been blocked on that occasion since US Tobacco ultimately won the case in front of Peter Taylor.[7])

Despite the efforts of the likes of Bill, the resolution of many issues with a political penumbra has migrated from Parliament to the Courts. Analysing some provision in the Hague Visby rules or the dimensions of the concept of equitable estoppel, judges are unlikely in consequence of either nature or nurture, ethnicity or education, genes or gender, to approach the legal issue with any form of inherent preconception. However, the same is not the case when what has to be decided was whether the qualification to some fundamental human right was proportionate, a matter on which Parliamentarians, or members of the public, could equally have reasonable views. To give but one example out of many, in 2021 the Supreme Court held that the right to protest could justify obstruction of the highway. It is debatable that this is an issue on which the JSCs are uniquely qualified to pronounce.[8]

Judges can rightly claim that it was Parliament which entrusted them with the responsibility by incorporating the Convention and the successive European treaties;[9] but that is not a complete answer since they showed for the most part an

He quoted both Bill Wade and me in his general support prompting Anthony Lester in Lords to say that he had checked with both of us and thought that our earlier observations, unrelated to the particular case, had been wrongly extrapolated.

[4] though in the latter part of 2021 backbenchers got back their mojo vis a vis Bojo.

[5] In his speech at the Trinity Michael Beloff Law Society dinner in 2009.

[6] Best known for identifying institutional racism in the police in his report in the Stephen Lawrence enquiry.

[7] Bill's *Times* obituary said that he put me 'firmly in my place' – but with two bounds I was free 1992 QB 353.

[8] And as members of Extinction Rebellion and Insulate Britain glue themselves to the motorways frustrated drivers have a different perspective.

[9] Elegantly expressed by Tom Bingham 'I do not in particular accept the distinction which he drew between democratic institutions and the courts. It is of course true that the judges in this country

equal appetite for activism in common law judicial review. Anyone who has sat as a judge knows the temptation of moulding a law which is plastic rather than steel to achieve what he, whether instinctively or intellectually, considers to be the just result.

In some of the major cases which have attracted headlines in recent years, because judges had proceeded down a route adverse to the wishes of the Government of the day, there were respectable arguments espoused by respected lawyers which, if adopted could have led to a different result. In Miller One where the Supreme Court held that Article 50 of the EU Treaty could only be triggered by a parliamentary vote there were three dissenters. In Miller Two where the Supreme Court unanimously held Boris Johnson's proroguing of Parliament to be unlawful, they overturned a contrary decision by a Court which included the Lord Chief Justice and the President of the Queen's Bench Division. In Belmarsh where the House of Lords held that the detention of terrorists from overseas would be unlawful if domestic terrorists were not subject to the same treatment, it reversed a decision of a Court of Appeal presided over by Lord Woolf, a famously liberal judge. The decisions of an apex court are binding because they are final, not because they are infallible. Lord Reed has succeeded Baroness Hale alias, Spiderwoman, as the President of the Supreme Court. For anyone who doubts that personalities can affect precedents, I can only say 'Watch this space'.

As a commentator (and citizen) I was less than a whole-hearted enthusiast about the merits of this constitutional recalibration, not least because it exposes judges to the threat of political intervention in their appointment.[10] I was about to send out copies of my Atkin lecture, making that very point, to my political and legal friends, when the wife of Trinity's Estates Bursar, who had an advance copy, noticed that the title page had been inscribed with the words 'Legal Protection of Same Sex relationships in Australia'a less immediately relevant subject'. The publishers sent me a fresh batch and waived the printers' fee.

In another paper, delivered at the Commonwealth Law Conference in Kuala Lumpur in 1999, I prophesied that 'If judges go too far, wholly unnecessary friction between judiciary and executive will come to pass' as indeed it has. It was as well that the organisers of that generously funded conference had required papers in advance because the platform which I shared with Beverley McLachlan, Chief Justice of Canada, allowed us a mere three minutes each to say our piece.

However, as a practitioner I revelled in the very same development. The pleasure of public law is that it is less concerned than is private law with technical issues

---

are not elected and are not answerable to Parliament. It is also, of course, true that Parliament, the executive and the courts have different functions. But the function of independent judges charged to interpret and apply the law is universally recognised as a cardinal feature of the modern democratic state, a cornerstone of the rule of law itself'.

[10] To avoid which I proposed the creation of a Judicial Appointments Commission in my 1999 Atkin Lecture 'Neither cloistered nor virtuous? Judges and their Independence in the New Millennium' (2000) *Denning Law Journal*, as acknowledged by its first Chair Baroness Prashar, in her essay in 'Judicial Appointments; Balancing Independence, Accountability and Legitimacy' at p 43.

and more with broad principle. Indeed, despite the weighty tomes devoted to the subject, as Lord Cooke of Thorndon observed, at its root administrative law is simply concerned with ensuring that public authorities act lawfully, fairly and reasonably. It covered a vast spectrum of topics for my engagement ranging from the treatment of suspected terrorists to the designation of house numbers in an urban road.

Many of the issues with which I most enjoyed involvement were not only those with a political context, but those with a political core.

In 1988 I represented the Ministry of Defence when the TGWU sought to restrain an order privatising one of the royal docks on the grounds of inadequate consultation. In his memoir the judge[11] described it as a case of 'considerable political sensitivity'. As he explained Margaret Thatcher was currently considering the date of a General Election. It would not have suited her to have a government measure injuncted at the outset of an election campaign. He noted that it was comforting that, despite the Government's obvious interest in the case, no one had come up to him and murmured 'you know what's expected don't you' (I would have been astonished, if anyone had!). A relieved Minister of State, Archie Hamilton, hosted a party for the successful legal team at the department. Years later when Harriet Harman came to dine prior to speaking to the Trinity PPE Society I was relieved that she was not accompanied by her husband, Jack Dromey MP, whom I had had vigorously to cross-examine during the hearing.

I once had to advise on whether there were any legal inhibitions on the adoption by the new party created by the so-called Gang of Four, exiles from the Labour party, of the name 'Social Democrat'. My solicitor, Piers Coleman, an election law expert, recalls in an e-mail: 'I remember a very learned opinion that you provided (and sometimes you used to type your opinion manually as we spoke) in which I came across the word 'fissiparous' for the first time'.

Later when the Social Democrats (or most of them) merged with the Liberals the issues of potentially confusing nomenclature arose in an actual and not merely theoretical context.

In the 1994 European Parliamentary Election for Devon and East Plymouth Constituency held on 9 June, my client the Liberal Democrat candidate, Mr Sanders, was defeated by a Mr Huggett who had cleverly described himself as a 'Literal democrat'. The returning officer held that Mr Huggett's nomination paper was valid because it was good in form and complied with the relevant rules, a decision challenged by Mr Sanders. Jeremy Thorpe had himself been called to the Bar by the Middle Temple and he proposed that he don wig and gown (for the first time) and sit behind me in the junior's row. I feared that this might inject a further element of farce into the proceedings and tactfully persuaded him to attend as a member of the public, dressed in an ordinary suit, a few rows back.

---

[11] Peter Millett, *As in Memory Long* (Millett, 2015) pp 148–49.

The election court presided over by Mr Justice Dyson dismissed the claim though, after and in the light of his judgment, the law was actually changed by legislation to prevent a repetition of such political passing off – too late alas for Mr Sanders.[12]

I advised the EOC that all women shortlists for parliamentary constituencies, introduced by the Labour Party, were lawful. Armoured with better advice from Anthony Lester and David Pannick the Commission supported two men who successfully challenged the practice in an employment tribunal. Nonetheless it was later reinstated by new Labour. Where Parliament is sovereign, a government with a large majority is usually able to do what it likes.

Shortly before the General Election of 1997 I was instructed by Wedlake Bell, together with and on the recommendation of Rabinder Singh,[13] then a junior at 4/5 Gray's Inn Square, to advise the Labour party about the legality of the plans of Gordon Brown, then Shadow Chancellor, to impose a Windfall tax on what were deemed to be excessive profits made by the utility companies privatised under the Conservatives. It was thought essential that the tax, the means by which funds could be provided for Labour's most ambitious commitment to get a quarter of a million unemployed young people back to work, could raise money swiftly. It had therefore to avoid legal challenge, in particular one based on European Community law or the ECHR, not least because other tax and spend options had been closed off by the Blair-Brown duumvirate.

Secrecy was paramount. Any premature leak could generate a pre-emptive strike from both political opponents and the vulnerable utilities. There was to be no unnecessary paper trail. Our instructions came from the John Smith Institute. Ed Balls,[14] Brown's vicar on earth, together with Geoffrey Robinson, the million-aire Labour MP, came to my Chambers to explain precisely what the plan involved. Geoffrey wrote later

> There was no problem in welcoming Michael to our team. He was thought to be sympa-thetic to New Labour and had been described by Jeffrey Archer, with the flight of the modern novelist's imagination, as having 'the mind of a planet'. In fact, despite such an endorsement Michael is widely regarded as one of the best barristers in the country.[15]

I could forgive the 'despite' more easily than Jeffrey.

The pressure group Aims of Industry had commissioned three barristers at Brick Court Chambers to give an opinion on the tax adverse to ours. Barristers

---

[12] (1995) 92(3) LSG 37. John Dyson reveals in his memoir *A Judge's Journey* (Dyson, 2019) that he had been reluctant to find against us, pp 104–05.

[13] Inter alia, author of *The Unity of the Law.*

[14] MP Secretary of State for Education, dancer and chef.

[15] *The Unconventional Minister: My Life Inside New Labour* (Robinson, 2000); see too Hugh Pym and Nick Kochan, *Gordon Brown: The First Year in Power* (Pym and Kochan, 1998) pp 43–47, Francis Beckett and David Hencke, *The Survivor: Tony Blair in War and Peace* (Beckett and Hencke, 2005) p 214 which explained 'Brown devoted a lot of effort to making the tax legally watertight. The key to this was the head of Cherie Booth's old chambers, Michael Beloff QC'.

are often – and properly – asked to provide the best arguments in favour of a client's proposed course of action, rather than objective analysis reflecting their own expert views. Their opinion, promptly trumpeted by Michael Heseltine, travelled over the same ground as mine and Rabinder's but added a fresh point on state aids. To this we next provided a rebuttal.

As a result, we were able to give the proposed Windfall tax a clean bill of health – at any rate as far as the law was concerned. We had agreed to change a cautious 'should' with reference to the chance of a successful ECHR challenge into a 'would' since the Convention had not yet been incorporated into English law (although its proposed incorporation was another New Labour flagship policy) and our opinion was published to the media. The *Guardian* broke the story with a front-page headline 'Labour windfall tax is legally watertight. Tories caught off guard as emphatic ruling blunts attack'. Despite various threats the challenge never materialised. The Windfall tax was duly enacted.

Once in Government Geoffrey Robinson encountered personal and political problems of his own when the media learned of the existence of a Robinson family offshore trust. Sir Gordon Downey was asked to investigate whether he should have declared the trust in the Commons register of members' interests. Robinson said he decided that 'a high-level legal opinion should be sought'.[16] I visited him in his Millbank eyrie to discuss the matter. He apologised for not offering me his Ministerial car to take me back to Chambers since, in particular at that time, if a member of the paparazzi had snapped me in the passenger seat, the optics would not have been good. In due course I advised him that registration was not required under either key clause in the MPs' Code of Conduct;[17] and Sir Gordon came to the same conclusion.[18] Unfortunately, Sir Gordon also said that had he been consulted he would have advised registration. My involvement in the matter resulted in a prolonged dispute with the *Sunday Times*.[19]

The demarcation of constituency boundaries is vital for Parliamentary candidates. Their natural concern is to ensure that the maximum number of voters sympathetic to their party live in the seat where they are standing. I first encountered Tessa Jowell[20] when (successfully) representing her in a dispute over the limits of her South Southwark seat. Later I was instructed by the Electoral Commission to resist Ed Ball's challenge to an unfavourable redrawing of his Northern Normanton seat. In the end he withdrew the challenge, depriving me of the chance to bisect Michael Heseltine's party conference jibe at the Labour Party's economic policy, 'It's not even Brown's, *it's Balls*'.

[16] Robinson p 218.

[17] Robinson ditto.

[18] Tom Bower, *The Paymaster* (Bower, 2001) p 171. 'To his good fortune the Committee was impressed by the evidence provided from a leading Lawyer'.

[19] See chapter nine, 'Good Names and Bad'. No such controversy attended the opinion authored by me and Dinah Rose on 2002 which was Appendix 25 to what proved to be only one of the several reports into the conduct of Keith Vaz, then MP, by the Select Committee on Standards and Privileges HC 605–11.

[20] Minister for the Olympics, Life Peeress.

The lawfulness of funds is vital not simply for candidates but for their parties. Three times I had to consider for the Electoral Commission whether the monies received by three different parties were tainted.

First, in the run-up to the 2005 election the Liberal Democrats received their largest ever gift from a company – £2.4 million – controlled by a Michael Brown, a convicted fraudster. The advice of me and my junior Jane Collier was that the law as it stood prohibited donations from foreigners within whose definition Mr Brown did not fall, but not from fraudster, within which he did. Nonetheless, without questioning our advice, in a report laid before Parliament, the Parliamentary and Health Service Ombudsman found that the Electoral Commission's inquiry into the facts 'fell significantly short'.

Second, in the run-up to the 2010 election the Conservatives received a £5.1 million donation from Bearwood Corporate Services, a company which Lord Ashcroft controlled. Again, mine and Jane's advice was that allegations that Bearwood was not carrying on business in the UK rendering it ineligible to donate money to political parties were not made out.

It was not my first encounter with Lord Ashcroft. He was in 2001 in dispute with the British Government over whether the tax exemptions for public investment companies applied to his company Carlisle Holdings. As he tells the tale

> The British Government, still desperate to pursue its anti-Ashcroft agenda instructed Michael Beloff QC to examine the issue. He too qualified his advice to such an extent that the British Government was unable to get what it wanted. [Clare] Short, I am told, was left on the point of apoplexy with her latest plan to 'Get Ashcroft' in tatters.[21]

I am myself unaware of Ms Short's reaction (if any) to my advice.

Third, in the run-up to the 2015 election, UKIP had received over £1 million from a single donor, one Alan Brown – no relation to Michael. During a short period when he gave the party almost £350,000, he was not on the Electoral Register and disqualified in consequence as a donor. The Electoral Commission, whom I again represented, argued that he should forfeit the entire amount. The majority of the Supreme Court considered otherwise and by a bare majority of 4-3 restored the judgment of the District Judge who had ordered a forfeiture of only a little over £17,000.[22]

The case is especially memorable in point of law for two features. First the minority used language which verged on the unjudicial in its criticism of the majority's reasoning. As Lord Simon Brown put it

> On the Commission's forfeiture application the Senior District Judge allowed UKIP to keep almost all of the £350,000 odd total of impermissible donations it had accepted from Mr Brown. In common with the Court of Appeal – although not, as now appears, with the majority of this Court – I find that a surprising and unsatisfactory outcome to this regrettable affair.

[21] M Ashcroft, *Dirty politics Dirty times* (Ashcroft, 2009) p 265.
[22] [2011] AC 496.

Second, one Supreme Court Justice, John Dyson, who did *not* sit on the appeal, subjected the majority judgment in a public speech to a compelling critique.[23] (Yes, I would say that wouldn't I?)

But the case is memorable in point of fact for something more. Had UKIP had to return the full amount of the impermissible payment it would not have survived; and – as I suggested to Nigel Farage when he came to address the Political Committee of the Reform Club[24] – we might never have heard of him again. In a curious footnote to this story, shortly after the 2017 election, one of my clerks was telephoned to ask if I could give advice as to whether, given the Brexit Party's recent success in terms of votes, its leader, none other than Nigel Farage reborn, ought to have been put in the House of Lords. There was no follow up to the inquiry, possibly because my role in the UKIP case had been belatedly unearthed, possibly not.

My most exotic political case came with my appearance before the Privileges Committee in the House of Lords, sitting in the Moses room, in a vain attempt to postpone the expulsion of the hereditary peers on the basis that the Royal Writ of Summons entitled them to retain their seat for the duration of the Parliamentary session.[25] Lord Cranborne, one of the Committee, had, after a talk a few nights before to the Trinity PPE Society, given me a lift back to London but, with the utmost tact, had not disclosed that he was to sit on the Committee.

At a time when all peers, hereditary or life, had the vote, Colin Moynihan,[26] another member of the Oxford Union mafia, telephoned me with a speculative enquiry as to whether I might be in a position to assist him over an issue as to who was to hold the hereditary Moynihan title. (The problem was caused by the number of the third Baron's marriages and questions over the parentage and legitimacy of his sons Andrew and Daniel.) Without my assistance the Committee of Privileges ruled in his favour.

My last flurries in this area were grace of Bill Cash. Bill had been one of the MPs found guilty by Sir Thomas Legg of breaching the rules on MPs' expenses. On the recommendation of Pat Neill, Bill instructed me to conduct his appeal which I did with an exonerating outcome. Several years later David Cameron, newly installed in No.10, tried to neuter the 1922 Committee of Backbench MPs by allowing Ministers not only to attend but to vote, claiming that there was a need to preserve 'unity' and 'harmony' when the party was in a coalition government. Bill sought my advice on whether such change would be lawful. Furnished with my opinion, he met in Downing Street with the key leadership figures involved and threatened Court action if they went ahead. Mr Cameron climbed down. The story

---

[23] Published in *Justice: Continuity and Change* (Dyson, 2018) pp 128–33.

[24] The warm reaction he received from the audience was to me an early intimation that Brexit might indeed happen.

[25] 2002 1 AC 109. My submissions are recorded in HL paper 106-1.

[26] Olympic cox, businessman and Chairman of the British Olympic Association.

behind it was only revealed by Bill at the ninetieth-anniversary celebrations for the Committee, where Mr Cameron, with a politician's guile, urged backbenchers to 'stick to their guns'.[27]

In July 2021 the same Committee's Executive Committee held a dinner in honour of Bill at the Carlton Club. In his speech,[28] he referred to 'my essential role and how I had bypassed a grandchildren's birthday party … on a lovely weekend'. 'Oh yes' in the words of Maurice Chevalier I too 'remember it well', if only for Bill's spirited driving, when he collected me at Oxford, en route from his northern constituency to deposit me in Gray's Inn, more characteristic of Lewis than of Alexander Hamilton.

In 2015 I was asked by Bill to advise for onward transmission to the 1922 Committee on the role it might play in the event that there was no decisive outcome to the General Election due to be held on 7 May. Since there was a decisive outcome, my advice became irrelevant to the nation's future – and to anything else.

In 2019 the Conservative Party was becoming increasingly concerned about its electoral prospects if Theresa May remained in Downing Street. She had, however, won a vote of confidence by her party which, on one interpretation of the party's constitution, prevented another challenge being mounted within 12 months, that is to say prior to 12 December 2019. On Bill's initiative once more I was instructed to advise him, again for onward transmission to the 1922 Committee, whether that interpretation was correct. I concluded that it was not. I was next asked to advise on any amendments to the Procedure Rules which would enable the Parliamentary party to set in motion an earlier vote of confidence in Mrs May. In the event she decided to step down before any fresh challenge could be made.[29] Spike Milligan once wrote a piece entitled 'Hitler – my part in his downfall'. I cannot make the same claim about Theresa May since she fell on her own sword.

Brexit provided the backcloth to another potential case involving one of Mrs May's senior colleagues, Liz Truss, the first woman ever to be Lord Chancellor. Three senior judges in the Court of Appeal held that to trigger Article 50 so as to start the UK's withdrawal from the European Union required a parliamentary vote and not simply a governmental decision. In consequence, they were notoriously stigmatised by the *Daily Mail* as 'Enemies of the People' and subjected in the same journal to highly personalised attacks. I was asked to advise the Bonavero Institute of Human Rights, located in Mansfield College, Oxford (whose Principal, (Baroness) Helena Kennedy QC, had recommended me for the role) as to whether Ms Truss was in breach of her constitutional duty to defend the judiciary.

---

[27] For the detail of the inside story see Isabel Hardman 'The Court threat that stopped David Cameron from abolishing the 1922 Committee'. Coffee House 23 April 2013. See too David Cameron *For the Record* (Cameron, 2019). Some even threatened legal action pp 238–9.

[28] This comes from Bill. I was not there and, of course, have never been a member of the 1922 Committee.

[29] See too Anthony Seldon, *May at No.10* (Seldon, 2019) pp 611–612.

The question was the subject of much public debate. On the one side, there were those who believed that the breach was clear but that, because of its subject matter, it would be impossible to find a judge sufficiently free from the appearance of bias to decide it. On the other side there were those who believed that an appropriate judge could be found but would on balance be unlikely to rule against Ms Truss. Certainly, Ms Truss's initial reaction was arguably inadequate. But her second public statement, which appeared to owe much to the draftsmanship of Lord Keen of Ellie QC, a Blackstone colleague turned government law officer, did seem no less arguably to hit the proper mark. It was a case whose presentation I would have relished (what constitutional lawyer would not?), but it was not pursued. So I cannot claim 'Liz Truss, my part in her downfall' either. History records that she has in fact risen relentlessly.

Once Brexit was underway the next question was how to get it done. Here Bill recruited me as part of a team of Boris's background boys simply to test for legal strength the obstacles put by parliamentary Remainers in the path of the Government's wish to give effect to the result of the 2016 referendum. In the end Boris's comprehensive election victory in 2019 itself removed those obstacles. The law and politics can overlap; but in the end politics can often outflank the law.

My disinclination publicly to align myself with any particular party certainly did not dissuade solicitors for those parties from instructing me in political cases; and over the years I have advised and acted for all three major parties as well as for bodies with a particular political agenda, ranging from Charter 88, through to the Freedom Association, founded by Trinity graduate Norris McWhirter after the murder of his brother Ross. A by-product of this promiscuity in my lay clients was my ability, for better or for worse, to see and understand both sides of a political argument. Or maybe it was the cause? Whichever it was I have become unaligned, a classic potential floating voter and importantly not seen as umbilically committed to any one faction, with pals on all points (and none) on the political spectrum…

And as I later explain[30] that is, for a member of the Bar, just as it should be.

---

[30] Chapter 14, 'The Art of Advocacy'.

9

Good Names and Bad

My time in the law has spanned the decline and fall of the major libel action. The pleading complexities have been smoothed out. Statutory reform, judicial creativity and the incorporation of the Convention have elevated the claims of free speech to heights approximating to, if not yet emulating, those of the first amendment of the US constitution and have seriously curbed the amount of available damages. Juries have been all but expelled from libel litigation. In-house lawyers are astute to ensure that articles which generate a cloud of suspicion are sanitised, if not wholly convincingly, by phrases expressly disavowing any specific allegation against any particular individual, such as 'there is no suggestion of any wrongdoing by X,' when 99 per cent of the time the whole purpose of the piece was to hint at such possibility (without of course upgrading it to an actual allegation): indeed, the article itself would often lack point in its absence.

Cases, when brought, often settle in equally queasy and oddly constructed statements in open court in which the offending defendant says that his libel was never intended to mean what it all too obviously did mean. Only squabbles between local political rivals or umbrage taken by minor royals or reckless celebrities who believe, not necessarily correctly, that all publicity is good publicity, keep that branch of the law alive at all. For what were once known as niche libel sets, invasion of privacy, until recently in itself an unprotected right, is now the name of the media lawyer's legal game.

My first encounter with libel was as a victim. As President of the Union I was twice grossly defamed in two issues of the same undergraduate ephemeral *Oxford Circus*, the former alleging that my ambition had left me mentally disturbed, the latter advancing a barely concealed anti-Semitic slur. Having not yet embarked upon my law degree, I was not fully aware of the opportunities either might provide for financial compensation and after a while I both forgave and forgot. One defamer became an MP; the other a Circuit Judge, and I would count both as my friends.

Oxford students – and I suspect not only they – seem to see themselves as living in (to borrow Lord Atkin's famous phrase) an Alsatia where the Queen's writ does not run and only Proctors prosecute. When President of Trinity I had to plead with the father not to sue when his daughter's return to the University after failing her preliminary examinations had been indefensibly attributed by *Cherwell* to a paternal bribe. My skimpy argument was that, if he did, his daughter might, throughout the balance of her university career, carry the stigma of being responsible for the demise of the University's oldest student journal. Whether for that or some other reason he held off, allowing *Cherwell* to celebrate its centenary in 2020.

My libel reading for the *Observer*[1] – my first practical, as distinct from personal, experience of defamation – was facilitated by its location. The *Observer* was then housed in Tudor Street, just east of the Temple. It was easy for me on a Friday evening to walk a short distance to take a first look at the proposed features, and then spend Saturday monitoring the news reports from the first edition winging its way to outer Hebrides or the Scilly Isles through to the last destined for its metropolitan readership.

Its location had no impact on my proficiency. I was far short of perfect at this part-time job. I had a variable view as to what was or was not defamatory, and of the boundaries of justification and fair comment, and an equally variable view as to whether foreigners ever sued in English Courts. (This was before the golden age of libel tourism.) If someone one week wrote a story that a high-ranked former Nazi was living in palatial splendour in Peru, I would worry about how the *Observer* could prove their case if a writ arrived, so suspending all action by the printers to the great annoyance of the writer. The next week I would casually waive through a story accusing some African politician of corruption only to be told within days that a letter before action was already in the post. I was more popular with the journalists than with the business managers since I let through some risky pieces; one suggesting – I summarise crudely – that Marmite kills. That would have been an expensive settlement had not Sir James Goldsmith, whose company was brand owner, dropped his suit, as a precondition for discussing his possible purchase of the *Observer* itself.[2]

The whole experience left me with a somewhat equivocal view about journalists. They seemed to care as much about the prominence of their names under their by-lines as they did about their role as the people's watchdogs, though I must acknowledge that it could equally, fairly or unfairly, be said that barristers care as much about their fees as about their role as promoters of the rule of law. I acted for the *Observer* on several occasions, sometimes defending my own decisions to let a story through. On one occasion, when I did not, Edwina Currie had sued the newspaper's weekend magazine for inadvertently naming her in an article about a film featuring a female politician who murdered her husband. The *Observer* briefed George Carman who, in his cross-examination, produced another newspaper's photograph of Edwina in her underwear. This time the rabbit out of the hat bit the conjuror. The editor commented 'I wished afterwards that I had allowed Michael Beloff to handle the case as he had offered to do'.[3] Would any other editor ever have said the same?

---

[1] Jeremy Lewis, *David Astor* (Lewis, 2016) p 281.
[2] (Trelford, 2017) p 173.
[3] Ibid, p 288.

One uncovenanted bonus of my *Observer* role arose from the concern of the editor, David Astor, about the implications of Michael Foot's trade union bill.[4] He commissioned me to write an essay setting the bill in the context of journalists' restrictive practices headlined 'Closed Shop – the Story Fleet Street Doesn't Tell' and spread over two full pages. It provoked angry letters from Foot himself and the senior official of the NUJ to which I was given space to respond. Oddly, neither had suggested that for a member of the bar to write about a profession's protective rules was a paradigm instance of a pot calling the kettle black.

Many libel cases in which I was involved never came to court. *Time* magazine settled with my client Mr Papandreou, the socialist Prime Minister of Greece. Others did not even reach the stage of formal instructions. Davinder Singh rang me when Lee Kwan Yew had made some harsh remarks which threatened Singapore's relationship with Malaysia, but the dispute resolved itself by political, not legal, means.

However, I did appear in five libel trials. In the first, I was instructed on behalf of a Harley Street physician Dr Gee, accused by *That's Life*, the BBC consumer affairs programme, of endangering the lives of his female patients by use of an amphetamine-based slimming therapy. I had two actual juniors, with Dr Gee's son, an extremely clever commercial lawyer, who had recommended me for the case, acting as an unofficial third, sometimes, but not always, a bonus for the official team. The BBC had instructed Andrew Rankin, my erstwhile leader, who was renowned for his powers of cross-examination. The doctors who had contributed to the programme were represented by the talented Wykehamist-Etonian colour combo Gray (Charles) leader[5] and Browne (Desmond)[6] junior, who were forced to play a muzzled role since almost the entire hearing was taken up with the sparring match between the all but irresistible force (Rankin) colliding with the utterly immovable object (Dr Gee).

After two weeks Rankin sought to suggest to the good doctor that he had a sideline in running an abortion clinic in France. The Judge, none other than Mr Justice Croom-Johnson, considered the question to be irrelevant and prejudicial and, since it was by now becoming clearer that the outcome was likely to turn on expert evidence as to the virtues (or vices) of the therapy, he discharged the jury. At one stage Rankin, unable to penetrate the doctor's defences, turned to a new article relied on by the latter and expostulated 'But it's in (sotto voce expletive deleted) Japanese'. The hearing was briefly interrupted when the Court usher suffered a temporary epileptic fit. There was an apocryphal story that when another court official leaned over him and asked if he needed a doctor, the usher replied 'Anyone but Dr Gee'.

---

[4] Discussed in Nora Beloff's book 'Freedom Under Foot' (Beloff, 1976).
[5] My mother occasionally came to the hearing, not to listen to me, but to admire Charles's good looks.
[6] QC, Chairman of the Bar Council and Treasurer of Gray's Inn.

The case, manna from heaven for the legal correspondent of the *British Medical Journal*, lasted 97 days by which time the Defendants had yet to open their case and the prolonged looked set to be the eternal. But then suddenly the BBC threw their hand in, forking out what was the largest libel damages ever paid at that time, as recorded in the *Guinness Book of Records*. The outcome contributed to the resignation of the then Director-General.[7] The pressure had so affected *me* that I had started to draft a letter to my instructing solicitor seeking to withdraw from the case and offering my fees to Dr Gee. I do not believe I would ever have sent it; but it was my own special therapy.

In my second major case I acted for the *Sunday People*[8] when its drama critic, Nina Myskow, was alleged to have confused fact and opinion in suggesting that the actress Charlotte Cornwell, half-sister of John le Carré, in the part of a clapped out rock star, in the TV play *No Excuses* must 'have been living down a sewer for the last decade' and was therefore no better than the unlovely character she played. Before the jury I described the play as 'a desert of darkness punctuated by oases of sheer nastiness'. The press reporting of the case itself failed to appreciate the legal subtleties of the defence of fair comment since it concentrated on the observation also made in the review that the actress's 'bum was too big'.

I had to cross-examine the prominent thespian Ian McKellen whose evidence, adduced to illustrate the difference between a role and the actor who played it, instanced his own performance in an Edward Bond play as an ancient Briton who had to simulate being buggered by a Roman soldier. Given his subsequent coming out as a vigorous campaigner for gay rights, I now wonder whether that part of his testimony was a deliberate tease or dare. Ms Cornwell was awarded £12,000.

The trial judge, the late Mr Justice Michael Davies, himself no stranger to the art of playing to the Press, had been so solicitous of Ms Cornwell that his partisan behaviour constituted the third of our grounds of appeal, although only parts of it were transparent on the transcript. The rest, consisting of his facial expressions which themselves spoke volumes, were unprovable at the appellate court in the absence of video footage. When on the eve of the appeal itself, I received a message via my clerk that the Court of Appeal wished me to concentrate on the first two grounds, including that Mr McKellen's evidence was inadmissible, I realised that we would win.[9] The Court of Appeal would obviously strive might and main to prevent the third point being gratuitously argued. And so it came to pass. The appeal was duly won and a retrial ordered.

The *Sunday People* politely informed me that it intended to instruct a new leader since Ms Cornwell ought not to have the benefit of familiarity with opposing counsel's style or likely questions. Gareth Williams QC[10] took on my role. Ms Cornwell was awarded £10,000. I could not resist writing to Gareth, that the

[7] 'Record libel damages for doctor' *Glasgow Herald* (3 March 1985).

[8] Adam Raphael, *Grotesque Libels* (Raphael, 1993) covers the case in all its twists and turns at pp 178–184.

[9] And we did! [1987] 1 WLR 630.

[10] Attorney-General and Leader of the House of Lords in the Blair administrations.

gap in the damages awarded first and second time round reflected the gap in our forensic abilities.

One academic, giving the case more weight than it could reasonably bear, wrote:

> It is worth noting that according to the law report, counsel for the defendant on the appeal, Mr Michael Beloff QC, ... suggested that the courts were not the place to deal with someone's sense of grievance that another person had been rude in print about their bottom.[11]

The proof of that particular pudding was in the eating. Ms Cornwell's victory was pyrrhic, her costs far exceeding her damages.

My third case involved the so-called Godmother of Broadwater Farm, Dolly Kiffin,[12] alleged to have buried certain documents in her mother's grave in Jamaica in order to avoid scrutiny by the district auditor. She recovered a modest sum of damages but was subsequently charged on essentially the same facts and found guilty of perverting the course of justice. Curiously I, with my junior and former pupil Andy Nicol,[13] had done better for her in the civil case where the defendant's newspaper only had to establish truth of the allegation on the balance of probabilities, than had her defence counsel in the criminal proceedings, when prosecution had to make good its case beyond reasonable doubt.[14] I would like to pretend that this was all due to my advocacy; but it is far more likely to have been down to the vagaries of juries.

I had a retainer for Associated Newspapers, in the days when such things were permitted. In my fourth case, I had to defend with the assistance of my junior, Victoria Sharp, the allegation made by the *Mail on Sunday* that the plaintiff retailers were offering for purchase food well past its sell-buy date. Our defence crashed and burned through lack of compelling evidence and a hyperbolic expert for whom the judge, Mr (later Lord) Justice Brooke, displayed ill-concealed dislike, overruling my objections, in the jury's absence, to what we saw as his less than neutral behaviour.

My opponent, David Eady QC,[15] normally the most courteous of opponents, refused on instruction to provide me with any indication of which witnesses he would be calling when, which inevitably dislocated my preparation. Damages of £450,000 were awarded against the newspaper which far outstripped those awarded to Dr Gee only a few years earlier. The editor, Stuart Steven, wrote me an encouraging letter in the aftermath, acquitting me of responsibility for the omnishambles.

---

[11] Heerey J 'The Biter Bit' *University of Tasmania Law Review* Vol 11, 1992 at p 21. The case features too in Veronica Bailey's Cape Case law book on contract, tort and property. I prefer the *Daily Mail* summary, 'Rock actress given the bum's rush'.

[12] Real name, Menzies Kiffin, director of the North London-based Broadwater Farm Youth Association.

[13] Whose career on the High Court bench concluded spectacularly with the *Depp v The Sun* trial.

[14] The judge took account of her libel damages in ordering her to pay the prosecution costs. David Hooper, *Reputations Under Fire* (Hooper, 2000) p 229.

[15] Mr Justice Eady.

The owners, counting the cost (and costs) took a more business-like approach, and my career as a newspaper libel lawyer seemed to have come to an end.

But not as it turned out my career as a libel lawyer, because my fifth and last case was, depending on one's point of view, my most famous or infamous. I was instructed by William Garnett of Bates Wells and Braithwaite[16] to represent Gillian Taylforth, soap star of Eastenders, in her case against *The Sun* which had accused her, as a result of a police tip-off, of giving her boyfriend, Geoff Knights, a blow job on a slip road off the A1 (what I have subsequently taken to calling, more decorously, 'A stationary traffic offence').[17]

On the first day of the trial, as Gillian recalls it

> George Carman started trying to introduce any number of new arguments and Michael Beloff got them all thrown out. I was impressed by his performance; he seemed to be right on top of everything and running rings around the Sun's team.[18]

On the second day of the trial a reconstruction took place in the car park in the precincts of the Royal Courts of Justice in order to demonstrate whether or not it was actually possible to perform the alleged act in a Range Rover. Gillian and her boyfriend, Geoff Knight, and then two *Sun* reporters acted out their rival versions. The somewhat unhelpful conclusion was that it all depended upon whether the seat belt (and, for that matter, the boyfriend's trouser zip) was (or was not) undone.

Gillian, demurely dressed for the part of a distressed Plaintiff, survived all the barbs initially thrown at her by George Carman. But then in mid-trial, the defence team disclosed a video taken at a party which showed Gillian sucking a beer bottle and saying saucily 'I give good head'. My junior Richard Parkes[19] rang me late at night. Houston we had a problem. Our efforts next morning to persuade the judge, Mr Justice Drake, to exclude it, on the basis that words spoken at a private party were no more a guide to public behaviour than words spoken in an after-dinner speech at a rugby club social, fell on deaf ears. And Gillian's vulnerability to George's cross-examination was increased by the contrast he effectively drew between the pose, not far distant from that of a vestal virgin which she had adopted in her earlier session in the witness box, and what he claimed to be the real Gillian revealed in the video.

Our case that Mr Knight's admitted opening of his trousers was to relieve the pain induced by a bout of pancreatitis, supported though it was by medical evidence, did not convince the jury despite (maybe because of?) my beta minus

---

[16] And a member of the powerful Jay clan.

[17] The case is discussed by Gillian in *Kathy and Me* (Taylforth, 1996) pp 157–84; by George's son Dominic Carman in his filial biography *No Ordinary Man* (Carman, 2002) pp 176–82 and in (Hooper, 2000) pp 262–68.

[18] (Taylforth, 1996) p 159.

[19] His Honour Judge Parkes QC.

jest in my closing speech that 'All men who want sex open their trousers; but not all men who open their trousers want sex'. This did no more than provide a quote for the court reporters, although David Hooper in his analysis of the trial said the point had 'some force'.[20]

The impact of the video evidence at the time it surfaced was, of course, far greater than it would have been had our team known of it in advance, when we could have softened its edges in examination in chief. It has been often suggested that George deliberately, and unethically, in this, and indeed in other cases, kept such material under lock and key until the moment when it would have maximum effect. In the signature phrase of Francis Urquart,[21] 'Others might think that, but I couldn't possibly comment'. Hooper noted that I had, as he put it 'very properly and with great prescience warned her before the action about Carman's reputation for finding skeletons in the cupboards'[22] – as anyone familiar with George's track record would have done. I am convinced that but for the video we would have won – and all the members of the Bar involved in the case apart from ever-cautious George have privately indicated that they agreed with me. As it was, we lost but only on a majority verdict of 10-2. So, the case which gave a new meaning to the phrase 'motorway madness' went to the wire. Fortunately, the verdict did Gillian no longer-term damage. She later had a starring role in another soap, *Footballers' Wives*.

There were divided views as to whether I should have accepted the brief at all, and whether my standing at the Bar was enhanced or damaged by my involvement. George's son thought that I had been unwise to venture into pastures new. 'Although a most eloquent and witty speaker, he was not a regular in the libel courts, preferring to address the more cerebral points of law in the House of Lords'[23] and convincingly commented that my description of the badinage on the video as 'Rabelaisian humour flew over the heads of the jury' and was not 'the hallmark of a jury advocate'.[24] What is certain is that the case gave me far greater publicity than all my other cases rolled into one;[25] and it was some comfort that neither my client nor my solicitor blamed me for the outcome.

The trial was twice reprised on television. The first for which I was asked to provide some background on the somewhat euphemistic pretext that the programme, to be broadcast on a history channel, would shed light on the social morality of the 1990s, the second more honestly advertised as 'the libel trial that had Britain agog', in which I was described as 'a rangy Old Etonian'. Rangy – moi? The commentator should have gone to Specsavers. There were no BAFTA awards for the actors who played me.

---

[20] (Hooper, 2000) p 264. 'A case blown out of all proportion', pp 262–68.
[21] The malevolent star of the televised political drama *House of Cards*.
[22] (Hooper, 2000) p 268. His source was Gillian, not I. Taylforth, p 148.
[23] (Carman, 2002) p 177.
[24] Ibid, p 181.
[25] George and I featured by name in a Jak cartoon which showed us leaving the Royal Court and saying 'it's so popular that we're thinking of taking it up to the West End'.

Curiously I had, totting up all the days spent in court in my quintet of libel trials, more libel experience than many barristers located in specialist chambers.[26] After all most libel cases settle; the outcome, especially when jury trials were the norm, was uncertain; the potential costs substantial. Oscar Beuselink, one of the senior ranks of specialist libel solicitors, who never instructed me himself, said in an interview 'he's a bit like an undertaker on his holiday but he's still very good'. I am uncertain about what sparked the metaphor.

My role in advising Geoffrey Robinson over his offshore family trust[27] led to a bizarre skirmish between the *Sunday Times* and myself. The newspaper reported that it had been a 'bad week' for me because of my omission to advise Robinson that he would have been wise, even if not required, to register the trust. I immediately wrote to correct the false impression that I had been in any way involved in that original decision not to register.

Reluctant to take any step back, the newspaper switched its line of fire and then criticised me for advising on the meaning of the Ministerial code which was not strictly a matter of law. In another rapid response I pointed out that my advice had expressly recognised that very point in its last paragraph where I wrote that I was assuming that the interpretation of the Code would be governed by the same rules as the interpretation of any similar legal document.

That was not enough for the ever-obdurate weekend broadsheet. It now suggested that the disclaimer should have been placed at the start rather than at the end of my advice. Tired of this seemingly interminable correspondence I wilted; and issued no writ. Later the *Sunday Times'* solicitor, with whom I had collaborated for other clients, told me informally that had I sued the newspaper would necessarily have settled. Another lost chance for some work-free income!

I contented myself with writing an article the gist of which was to ask if I, a lawyer with some considerable experience of libel, could be dissuaded from taking up arms against a powerful organ of the media, what chance was there for a layman, similarly defamed. Trinity's English Fellow, Dinah Birch,[28] the wisest of wise women, read it, complimented me on its prose style but advised me not to seek an outlet for its publication because I would simply make myself a perpetual target in the future. I took her advice.

While not a perpetual target, I did become a target once more, this time arising out of my role as President of Trinity, for the *Daily Mail's* resident hatchet hack Geoffrey Levy. The insults about my appearance ('rather straggly really with a beard') and clothing ('slippers or shoes with Velcro straps'), the effort to tar me with the brush of some of my more notorious clients at the Bar, the criticisms of my personality, which came from a 'fellow lawyer' who (if he or she existed) was

---

[26] I also spent more days in court in my trio of scuttling cases than many members of the Admiralty Bar have ever done.

[27] See chapter eight, 'Politics and the Law'.

[28] Editor of the *Oxford Companion to English Literature* and a Professor of English Literature at Liverpool University.

not apparently prepared to go on the record, could be ignored as mere garnish. The meat of the article was based on an interview with Philip Keevil[29] to the effect that his son had been refused a place deliberately to open one up for Euan Blair.[30]

Levy added by way of journalistic surmise that I had caused embarrassment to both the young Keevil and the young Blair by revealing the fact of their applications, matters already widely reported in the press. I had been given no opportunity to respond in advance. By way of excuse for breach of this usual convention Mr Levy reported that I was at the Henley regatta enjoying myself so much that I had switched off my mobile (a device which I did not at that time even own). Mr Keevil was further quoted about what the newspaper was pleased to call 'an unsavoury situation' as saying that he believed 'that one day Michael Beloff will destroy himself'. I am still striving to postpone that evil day. Despite the urging of some of my fellowship I was again not tempted into counterattack.

I have always advised clients, angry at some baseless accusation or unfair comment, to sleep on it, preferably for weeks not days, when the passage of time will add perspective to soften the hurt. Libel law is a quicksand; those who believe that there is gold at the rainbow's end too often have to be contented with, at best, brass. If there is one certainty it is that the issue of proceedings will add a fresh spark to what may be the dying embers of the original slur. I could hardly not follow my own advice.

Sometimes of course, over and above such salutary considerations, there is simply no prospect of success. During Mitt Romney's tilt at the Presidency of the USA in 2012 the BBC planned a programme on the Church of the Latter Day Saints (or Mormons) which it was feared might damage Mr Romney's chances in the election. Their senior legal adviser, a Yale graduate whose courteous demeanour and gentlemanly style was as far removed as could be imagined from that of the stereotypical American aggressive attorney, beloved of legal soaps, flew from Salt Lake City to ask whether the programme could be injuncted. It is a basic principle of English libel law, known to any first-year student, that no injunction will be granted if those responsible intend to defend a claim on the grounds that the allegations said to be defamatory were true. I added to my formal advice an informal observation that it was unlikely in the extreme that a programme by an English broadcaster would make the slightest impression, good or bad, on the American electorate. It weren't the BBC wot lost it for Mitt Romney

Another case which raised reputational issues gave me the opportunity to represent Oxford University. Andrew Malcolm, author of a philosophical treatise entitled *Making Names*, brought a successful action for breach of contract by the University Press in refusing to publish it. He has described the saga at length in another book entitled *The Remedy*. The claim was ultimately resolved by a consent order. However, Mr Malcolm took fresh proceedings in the Chancery

---

[29] There is a fuller account of the background in chapter six 'Transition to Trinity'.
[30] Ibid.

Division of the High Court alleging that the order had been breached by Dr Alan Ryan, an Oxford contemporary of mine in our far off undergraduate days, who became Warden of New College at exactly the same time as I became President of Trinity. He had expressed himself in highly critical terms about Mr Malcolm's thesis.

There was an initial problem in ensuring that the Chancery Judge appointed to handle this new case was not an Oxford graduate – a problem less easy to resolve than one might at first sight imagine. Lightman J finally appointed was of the Light rather than the Dark blue species. He dismissed Mr Malcolm's application, holding

> It would be wrong, to construe the Consent Order (as he wishes) as effective to muzzle academic freedom of expression and debate and censor any disparagement of the Work by academics at the University unless such disparagement is prompted or authorised by the University.

The case proved to be a right true end to my career as a litigation libel lawyer.[31] By the time I returned to full-time practice in 2006 the caravan had moved on and I was no longer aboard it.

---

[31] And instructions to advise on such matters, mainly from oversea law firms, dwindled pro tanto.

Captain and Chronicler.
Eton 1960.

Sans wig, sans gown but otherwise all ready to be made a silk.
Temple, 1981.

The cartoon is inspired by the libel case *Gillian Taylforth v Sun Newspapers Ltd* pitted MJBQC against George Carman QC. Jury score Carman 10 MJBQC 2 – close but no cigar.

Inside (and outside) The Royal Courts Of Justice, 1994.

Magdalen College Moot celebrating the college's 550th Anniversary.

Flanked by two student advocates, from left to right Jonathan Sumption QC, Justice Souter of the US Supreme Court, Lord Browne-Wilkinson, Senior Law Lord, Justice Breyer of the US Supreme Court, and MJBQC – all Magdalenses. The judicial trio might properly be called in the hallowed phrase 'a strong court'

Magdalen, Oxford 1998.

MJBQC with two legends of the mile. Hicham El Guerrouj is the current world record holder. The other needs no identification, at any rate in more than four minutes.

Trinity, Oxford, 2000.

The President and the Prince. A royal visit to celebrate Trinity's 450th anniversary.

Trinity, Oxford, 2005

An a la carte ensemble of Oxford worthies reprising an earlier version of 1950
Blackwells, Oxford, 2004.

MJBQC as Vice Treasurer escorting the Sultan of Brunei to his daughter's call to the bar.

Gray's Inn, 2007.

Flying the flag for London 2012. Tessa Jowell (Minister for the Olympics) MJBQC, Boris Johnson (Mayor of London).

The Bird's Nest, Beijing, 2008.

Dress down Grand day. MJBQC as Treasurer, and Judith, await the arrival of the Inn's guests.
Grays Inn, 2008.

MJBQC receives a lifetime achievement award from Clive Anderson and the sponsor's representative.
Only a decade's hard labour still to go!!…
Grosvenor House Hotel, 2009

MJBQC in the robes of a Judge of the Court of Appeal in Guernsey. Unlike in Jersey toques are worn in Court at the start and end of hearings.

St Peter's Port, Guernsey, 2009.

The 26th President of Trinity (founded in 1550) with the 42nd President of the USA (created in 1776).

Gems Foundation London 2013.

MJBQC (best time 10.4 secs 100 yards) with Usain Bolt (best time 9.58 secs. 100 metres – the world record) The Airport, Beijing, 2015.

MJBQC addresses the Privy Council in *Mexico Infrastructure Finance LLC v Corporation of Hamilton* [2019] UKPC 2

Note the Vincent's tie and the label badge of the Court of Arbitration for Sport. The Pop socks are off screen. These three good luck charms worked on this occasion with a 3-2 win over none other than Lord Pannick QC.

Supreme Court, 2018.

Sir Anthony Seldon, Vice-Chancellor, greets MJBQC after his receipt of an honorary degree from the University of Buckingham of which Max (Lord Beloff) was the founding father. Was this an example of posthumous nepotism?

Buckingham, 2017.

10

My Sporting Life

My life as a sports lawyer has been a substitute for the real thing. Unlike Marlon Brando's character in *On the Waterfront* I could never 'have been a contender' in any sport. The evidence proves beyond reasonable doubt that I was better equipped to be a worker by brain than by body. The high points in my athletic career were more Chilterns than Himalayas.[1] Winner of the 100 yards in those far off pre-metric days at Eton,[2] I came fourth in the Berks, Bucks and Oxon 40–50 age group 400m, just one short of a podium place, but when fourth was also last. I was a guinea pig in the *Sunday Times* campaign to domesticate the transatlantic jogging craze, which earned me a half-page story with photographs in the sports section[3] optimistically entitled 'The Man who was Transformed'. In the – and my – first London marathon, when the site of what is now Canary Wharf still bore the ravages of war, I overtook the legendary British lion JPR Williams. In my second and last I was overtaken in the Mall by six men dressed up as a caterpillar. The only other time I travelled the marathon course from Greenwich to the Mall was courtesy of Dave Bedford in one of those open jeeps which follow the leading runners, in my case, female, which gave me an unusual perspective on this national festival.

In Oxford I sporadically participated in a race over two miles in Cutteslowe Park, named after the Indian spiritual leader Sri Chinmoy:[4] the results were recorded in *Athletics Weekly* where I appear, under the guise of Beloss, Belove and Beloof.[5] Eventually my Achilles tendon proved to be my Achilles heel. Games over.

---

[1] And in other sports even lower. I was the Chelmsford and District tennis mixed doubles champion in 1959. The event is not to be equiparated to a Grand Slam, and my partner must have had all the talents of an Emma Raducanu to carry me through that far.

[2] While at Oxford, as anchor man of a relay squad containing Metcalfe, Hogan and Archer which was competing in a match against my old school, I was roundly outsprinted by my schoolboy opposite number. Libraries and lethargy had taken their toll despite Jeffrey's stentorian coaching shouts of 'Knees, Knees, Knees'. He said later 'Michael knows a great deal about athletics but he doesn't understand the pain of international competition' – or even, he could have added, the pain of fun runs. In Charles Hollander's book celebrating Brick Chambers centenary there is a statement that Jonathan A used to accompany Jeffrey and me on our training runs, p 61 fn 96. This fiction is stranger than truth. Jonathan's penchant was for indoor sport.

[3] Issue of 19 December 1976.

[4] Whose application of the precept *mens sana in corpore sana* ranged from meditation to marathon running.

[5] In the same greensward I ventured into Park Runs where I was accompanied by the back marker whom the organisers employed to look after any stragglers who might not survive the ordeal – the precautionary principle in practice. In London I took annually the underground to Golders Green so

I have already described how I was deflected from my hopes of an athletics blue by my encounter with Adrian Metcalfe.[6] Some years later, when I was making my tentative way at the Bar, I was telephoned by Adrian, the founder member of the International Athletes Club (IAC), a pressure group formed by athletes to battle for a degree of control of their sport against those caricatured by Will Carling, the England Rugby Captain, as old farts. Adrian was seeking advice that would certainly be cheap and possibly be cheerful.

The Amateur Athletics Association (AAA) had sold all the TV rights for Athletics in Great Britain to the BBC. The IAC had organised, with sponsorship by Coca Cola, a meeting with athletes from around the world competing not as part of a team but as individuals, then a novel, now a conventional formula, which it wished to have broadcast on ITV. I went to the AAA's AGM presided over by Harold Abrahams,[7] to provide a soupcon of legal support to two club officers, Olympic gold medallists David Hemery[8] and Mary Peters.[9] The *Evening Standard* published a photograph of the three of us – two of whom at any rate must have been recognised by its readership. The IAC lost the battle but won the war, though not for that year: for the future the fixture was assigned to the commercial channel.

In right of my efforts, I was elected an honorary member of the Club.[10] It was something of a backhanded or backfooted compliment since the other honorary member was John Cleese, celebrated for his funny walks. More importantly my clerks were enabled, with that gift for exaggeration which is essential to their occupation, from that day forth to market me as a 'well-established sports lawyer'. It was only as a lawyer that I later became first a member (and later Vice-President along with Roger Bannister) of the Achilles Club, ordinarily reserved to Oxbridge athletic blues.[11]

Sports law was, in the 1960s, a barely recognised discipline. Few, if any, sports generated the money today available to top stars. Tennis and athletics, now major income providers, were still essentially amateur; and football had only recently broken through the £100 a week cap on wages. In a more deferential society, the notion of challenging decisions of sporting regulators was all but unknown; the *Eastham* case (where the transfer and retention system of the FA was held to be in restraint of trade) was a rare exception. Judges felt that sporting disputes,

---

as to jog through the intervening London parks and end up at my house in Holland Park. I chose the longest day of the year because it gave me a sporting chance of concluding my journey before sunset. My knee proved to be my Achilles heel. I'm now officially forever 'off Games'.

[6] See Chapter 3 'Oxford Blueless'.

[7] His 100m victory in the Paris Olympics of 1924 was a highlight of the Oscar winning film *Chariots of Fire*.

[8] David Hemery, *Another Hurdle* (Hemery, 1976) pp 198–200.

[9] Dame CH LG as honours for her outstanding services to the community in Northern Ireland. She was one of the star speakers at a series of lectures on sports law that I co-organised to be held in the precincts of the Supreme Court which were introduced by Nick Phillips, the Court's first President, along with an exhibition to celebrate London 2012.

[10] And got the tracksuit, if not the t-shirt, given to me by Dave Bedford.

[11] And was also a very odd man out in a long line of internationals when chosen – a prerogative of the away team captain as the guest of honour and speaker at the post-match track and field blues dinner.

now multiplying because of the money at stake, ought, if possible, to be determined within the sport. In a classic statement in *McInnes v Onslow Fane* (in which I appeared for the applicant against Alan Moses)[12] Sir Robert Megarry, Vice Chancellor, said

> I think that the Courts should be slow to allow implied obligations to be fair to be used as a measure of bringing before the Courts for review honest decisions of bodies exercising jurisdiction over sporting and other activities which those bodies are far better fitted to judge than the Courts.[13]

To this day arbitration with the advantages of procedural flexibility, speedier resolution, shorter hearings, sports-specialist arbitrators and privacy is the favoured forum for adjudicating on such disputes, even those with a considerable legal content.[14] Courts of law are long stops rather than wicket keepers.

I was fortunate to be in practice when sport and law first significantly interacted. Enjoying a head (but not a false) start I received many journalistic accolades and was described by a specialist academic as a 'founding father' of sports law.[15]

My life as a sporting lawyer has been bifurcated; first as adviser and advocate; second as arbitrator – the second following on from the first with only a modest degree of overlap. Arguing a case requires a monocular focus; as an arbitrator one must keep both eyes open. A key issue, which has had increasing salience, is where the boundary should be drawn between men's and women's participation in sports. The Sex Discrimination Act 1975 had a section with a sports exclusion clause which allowed discrimination in competitive activity where the average man had physical advantages over the average woman. I represented the British Judo Association (BJA) where two of my witnesses, Olympic medallists both, staged an impromptu and unscripted display before an astonished industrial tribunal, in an unsuccessful endeavour to establish that the clause applied to female referees as well as to female participants.[16] When the claimant, Belinda Petty, died in July 2020 *The Times* obituary called this a 'landmark equal opportunities case' and devoted most of its article to a description of the Tribunal hearing, describing me, somewhat curiously in the circumstances, as a human rights lawyer.

I was equally unsuccessful in trying to preserve the Professional Footballers Association (PFA) Annual Dinner as an All-Male event – a tradition which the

---

[12] Lord Justice Moses and first Chairman of IPSO, the press regulator.

[13] [1978] 1 WLR 1520.

[14] See my CIArb Alexander Lecture 'ADR in Sport', which I delivered, like a pantomime horse, in tandem with Sir Philip (former Lord Justice) Otton.

[15] Jack Anderson, *Modern Sports Law* (Anderson, 2010) para 1.23. The indefinite article was used since I was bracketed with Edward Grayson DNB, a venerable junior whose own disorganised but enthusiastic book *The Law and Sport* was first in the field, preceding my own more structured *Sports Law*. In a cultural flight of fancy I liken Edward to Cimabue, the last pre-Renaissance religious painter, and myself to Giotto who first recognised perspective. I was also described in the *Daily Telegraph* in 2011 as 'probably the most eminent sports lawyer in the world', by the *Guardian* in 2012 as 'the go to man for sporting disputes' and by *The Times* in 2016 as 'by far the UK's and maybe the world's most distinguished specialist in sports law' and by the *Daily Telegraph* in 2016 as 'the silkiest assassin in sport'. Whatever bias there may have been in these assessments, it was at any rate not political.

[16] Which I lost on appeal as well, [1981] ICR 660.

female claimant, Rachel Anderson, an agent, asserted denied her networking opportunities. Her triumph was many years later celebrated in the *Daily Mail*.[17] I attended the dinner where I met Arsène Wenger and members of his Arsenal team, then at the height of their powers.[18] The after-dinner speeches brought a blush to my ears. Who knows what they would have done to the ears of the hypothetical maiden? I plumbed the depths of failure in *Saunders v Richmond BC*,[19] when a claim that the Borough had discriminated against a woman applicant for the post of golf professional was roundly dismissed, even though the Borough's letter acknowledging her application started 'Dear Sir'.

In a paper at the Bar Conference, I frivolously suggested that the exclusion clause could be repealed; if any woman wanted to chance her arm (or leg) by competing with or against men she should be allowed to do so. But such a simple solution is at odds with nature,[20] and the complexity of the issue was highlighted by the later debate over intersex athletes. I was invited by Arne Lundquist, chief medical adviser to the International Federation of Athletics Associations (IAAF), to a two-day multi-disciplinary conference in Nyon to provide a legal rights perspective; and a few years later by Richard Blodgett, who held the same position in the IOC, to another conference in Lausanne with a similar theme. The intersex athlete attendees, indistinguishable in their outward appearance from women, were remarkably undogmatic about the solution to this vexed problem, which affects transgender athletes too – at any rate those born male who switch to female.

I was not myself formally (though I was informally) involved in either of the two CAS cases, those of Dutee Chand and Caster Semenya, which led CAS to rule that women with unusually high levels of testosterone[21] should undergo therapy to reduce those levels as the price to pay for participation in women's athletic events. I was, however, involved in the drafting of the regulations designed to reflect those decisions, now under scrutiny by the ECtHR. I continue to believe that biology should trump identity in the sphere of sport. Minority rights, important though they are, cannot always prevail over the rights of the majority.

Whether disabled athletes who use prosthetics should be able to compete in the Olympic as well as in the Paralympic Games raises further questions as to what is meant by equal treatment in sport. The IAAF wanted to instruct me to defend claims brought before CAS by the South African sprinter Oscar Pistorius who wished to run in both Games, but as a serving arbitrator I was by then ineligible to accept the brief. The IAAF lost the case; Mr Pistorius ran in the London Olympics,

---

[17] 'The woman who took on the PFA and won! 22 years ago Gordon Taylor told football agent Rachel Anderson she was banned from an awards dinner. Her crime? Being a woman'.

[18] 'Those were the days my friend we thought they'd never end'. But they did.

[19] [1978] ICR 75.

[20] I cannot help but note that in swimming the pace of female improvement has meant that times which half a century ago would have won medals in men's events are only sufficient to win them in women's events. I teased Mike Wenden, double Olympic sprint champion in Mexico city, with this at a reception in Melbourne in 2006. 'Yes', he conceded 'But look at their shoulders'.

[21] Where to draw the line is still a vexed question.

but his sporting career came to a halt when he was sentenced to a long term of imprisonment after conviction for the homicide of his girlfriend. The difference between the able-bodied athlete and the user of prosthetics was indisputable; its consequences less clear. Because of this uncertainty I later advised the IAAF to alter the burden of proof in its regulations by requiring an athlete who used prosthetics to prove that they did not give an advantage rather than the IAAF to prove that they did. I declined appointment by the IAAF as an arbitrator to defend the new regulation since I would certainly have been at least apparently biased. In 2020 a CAS panel ruled, contrary to my view, the alteration to be unlawful.

Age discrimination in sport is tolerable since it gives to persons of either biological sex the chance to compete with and against persons in their own age group, neither too old or too young as the case might be. But not all beneficiaries want that protection. Greg Hutchings, sometime multi-million pound boss of Tomkins, a talented hockey player, wanted to represent his country in the age group below his own. I could find no way for him to achieve this unusual goal. Greg was never a reticent risk taker. I overheard him at one of the Archers' champagne and shepherd's pie parties tell Mrs Thatcher that he admired the way in which she bounced back from her mistakes. 'What mistakes?' she witheringly retorted.

My membership of the IAC put me in pole position for cases involving track and field athletes. Some issues had a politico-legal dimension, notably on whether or not a threatened ban by Mrs Thatcher on British athletes competing in the Moscow Olympics would be judicially reviewable. No ban could have been effective without legislation. Law is one thing, guidance quite another. The athletes ignored her recommendation not to go, and won four track and field gold medals. For the next Olympic cycle I advised on the implications of the South African barefoot distance runner Zola Budd's fast track admission to the United Kingdom. She did run for Great Britain in the 1984 Los Angeles Olympics, notoriously tripping the American favourite for the women's 1500m and putting both out of the hunt for medals.

I represented Dave Bedford in a libel action against the *Daily Telegraph*. The newspaper reported that he had been prosecuted for driving a car under the influence of drugs, whereas he had (more plausibly) only been under the influence of beer. The *Telegraph* settled at the door of the court and we went off to spend some of the money on a celebration lunch at which still greater quantities of better alcohol were consumed. I also advised Seb Coe about another libel in the same journal. Both Dave and Seb were to play important parts in my later development as a sports law specialist.

I represented Tessa Sanderson, javelineer and another gold medal Olympian, accused of breaching the AAA rules by receiving modest remuneration in a brown envelope for her participation in a meet in Gateshead. Such undercover payments to elite athletes were par for the course in those distant days. Now the payments are both larger and legitimate.

The drugs issue came to the fore, fuelled by Ben Johnson's 'triumph' in the Seoul Olympics in 1988. The IAAF instructed me to prosecute in a number of high profile doping cases: Butch Reynolds, Katerine Krabbe, Dennis Mitchell,

Mary Decker Slaney, Merlene Ottey, Javier Sotomayor and Dean Capobianco, with the exception of the last named, all Olympic or World Champions or World Record Holders – part of the crème de la crème of global track and field.

The venues for the first two and last five of my magnificent seven cases were markedly different. The former were held in cramped quarters behind Harrods in Knightsbridge; the latter in a spacious conference room in Monte Carlo where the IAAF had now relocated for fiscal rather than climatic reasons. The move to the Med had been initially inspired by the resentment felt by Primo Nebiolo, the late President of the IAAF, of Lord Denning's decision that the ban on Taiwanese athletes from IAAF competitions was invalid under English law.[22] Primo wanted the IAAF to be subject to the Monagasque law, impenetrable to all but a few local attorneys.

Common to all those cases up to 1999 was the Chairmanship of Lauri Tarasti, a former Justice of the Supreme Administrative Court of Finland.[23] He was a presider whose desire to reach a swift (and sure) result led him to organise some of the most remarkable schedules in my five decades in practice. In the Reynolds hearing (held, as was usual for the IAAF tribunal, at weekends) we sat on the first day between 9am and 11pm with only short breaks for refreshment, relief or recreation – and might have sat longer had I not intervened to support the plea of my jet-lagged American opponent for an overnight adjournment. I was concerned that any verdict might be challenged for breach of natural justice – to counsel! The Attorney in question suffered from an additional disadvantage. He had prosecuted Reynolds on behalf of US Track and Field before the *national* disciplinary body but now had to defend, before the *international* equivalent, the decision of that very body which had acquitted the athlete – not the easiest of exercises, and one which defeated even his talents.

Ignoring his loss in London Reynolds later sought damages against the IAAF in the US. Although he was no more successful there, it was that experience, which led CAS, in anticipation of the Atlanta Olympics in 1996, to set up the first of its ad hoc panels to adjudicate on games-related disputes to the exclusion of the local courts, a novelty which proved greatly to my benefit.

Defendants charged with doping offences lacked little in imagination. Dennis Mitchell, the American relay runner, attributed the unnaturally high levels of testosterone in his bodily fluids to a combination of energetic sex, boastfully described as a birthday present for his wife, and excessive lager; Javier Sotomayor, the world record holder for the high jump, claimed that the cocaine found in his sample was the result of American corruption of the Canadian laboratory officials. He produced a statement in his support from President Fidel Castro. It was a long statement. The weight given to it by the Tribunal was in inverse proportion to its length.

---

[22] Taiwan, under the compromise name Chinese Taipei, is still a member of World Athletics. International Sports Governing Bodies (SGBs) nowadays prefer to maximise their membership and to smooth over geo-political problems.

[23] In an autobiographical essay entitled 'Personal experiences in Sports Law' Lauri wrote 'The IAAF was also represented by Attorneys. One who particularly comes to mind is Mr Michael Beloff. The sharp minded English lawyer who became one of the foremost names in international sports law'.

It was not only track and field athletes who produced such exotic defences. Petr Korda, the Czech tennis star, claimed before a CAS tribunal on which I sat[24] that there must have been steroids in his Bolognese sauce served in his favourite restaurant in Wimbledon – not, as might have been a fitting fortuity, part of the 'Fasta Pasta' chain.

One case which fell to be decided in the wake of the Athens Olympics 2004 but did not involve any potential alteration of the results involved the two Greek sprinters, Kostas Kenteris and Ekaterina Thanou – both national poster icons for the Games as prospective medallists. Their whereabouts in the run up to the Games sparked a magical mystery tour. The drug testers sought them here, they sought them there, they sought them everywhere. Emulating the Scarlet Pimpernel, the sprinters were never in the place where they had said they would be, giving a new twist to the phrase a quick getaway.

Finally, on the eve of the Games, when they returned to (if they had indeed ever left) their native land they were summoned to present themselves for a drugs test in the Olympic village. Once more they failed to appear. Their explanation was that they had been victims of a motorcycle accident and hospitalised en route to the test venue. This excited, in the absence of any corroborating evidence, a widespread measure of incredulity. For the athletes, discretion was the better part of valour; and, after a hearing before the IOC Disciplinary Commission, they announced that they would not contest their events 'in the interests of the country'.

The missed test in Athens was, however, the third of the summer for each, and under the athletics equivalent of the 'three strikes and you're out' rule of criminal law they were both provisionally suspended by the IAAF. The next year the Greek Federation cleared them. In reaction the IAAF exercised their right to appeal under a rule designed to allow review of suspect 'home town' decisions. I was briefed by the IAAF to prosecute. The charge was not the lesser one of simple failure to appear for a third test but the greater one of deliberate evasion. On the first day of the hearing I had to cross-examine Ms Thanou. The Greek Federation had put her first in the firing line on the basis that, as Rudyard Kipling suggests, the female of the species is more deadly than the male. However, shortly before the bell was to sound for round two of the adjourned hearing, I was told in the departure lounge at Heathrow that the IAAF had settled the case by accepting a plea of guilty by both runners to the lesser charge. The IAAF had shot my fox and indeed my vixen. I felt aggrieved to have been denied the chance to try to expose both as cheats. The arbitrator, Alan Sullivan QC, who had flown all the way from Australia to preside over the case and had to make an unexpectedly prompt return journey had a still more legitimate cause for complaint.

The saga had not, however, come to an end. The wheels of justice in Greece ground slowly, but both athletes were eventually tried for faking the motorcycle accident and making false statements to the police. They were initially convicted of perjury. Finally, by which time the whole issue had all but vanished into the

---

[24] 99/A/223.

oubliette of history, the guilty verdict was overturned on appeal. But neither athlete ever ran in a major competition after Athens.

I defended as well as prosecuted athletes faced with drug-related charges.[25] When sprinter Dwain Chambers proclaimed his innocence I had to argue that the artificially concocted product which he had taken had not been sufficiently tested on just a single monkey which I caricatured as 'that poor unfortunate primate' to justify the finding that it fell within the category of prohibited substances. Dwain was found guilty and suspended for several years. He later returned to the track, admitted his guilt and became a powerful advocate of drug-free sport. In an autographed flyleaf to his own memoir *Race Against Me* he wrote 'We've both come a long way'.

I took an unheralded call in Blackstone Chambers from a train in Estonia. The caller asked me whether I would be prepared to act for seven Russian female athletes accused of doping offences. I found out that all had provided clean urine samples in different places but traceable to a single source. The explanation could only be organised manipulation. I received a courteous letter written in English from one of the misguided seven Olympians, Svetllana Cherkasova, reluctantly accepting my doleful assessment. All were duly sanctioned. This was the first, but not the last, time that I was to confront issues of doping in Russia.

Notably, shortly before the Pyonchang Winter Olympics in 2018 I was appointed as a sole arbitrator in an appeal involving a group of Russian stars of slope and rink who had been barred from the competition for alleged doping offences. I was immediately challenged for lack of apparent independence and impartiality. The appellants then embarked on a bizarre merry-go-round of forum shopping, first in the Swiss courts and then before the CAS ad hoc panel, both of which lacked jurisdiction. So, force majeure, in a volte face they withdrew their objection to me. The Games had already started; an urgent decision was needed; I sacrificed my weekend to draft an award only to be informed on Monday morning that the appeal had been withdrawn. Much Ado about what was claimed to be Nothing had been followed by A Comedy of Errors. For me it was an extraordinary Winter's Tale.

By far the most important defence I ever mounted was that of Christine Ohuruogu, the 400 metre runner,[26] who had missed three out-of-competition tests and was, on the basis of the British Olympic Association's rule, ineligible to be a member of a British Olympic team. I was in Osaka for the 2007 World Athletics Championships, sitting next to Ed Warner, Chairman of UK Athletics. When Christine won the final, in a fit of patriotic enthusiasm I turned to Ed and said 'If she challenges the ban I'll represent her for nothing'.[27] A lawyer offering to

---

[25] Footballers too including Adrian Mutu, the Romanian striker, who was dismissed by Chelsea for doping and Mark Bosnich, Manchester United's Australian goalkeeper, who ran what later became a fashionable defence that it was his girlfriend who had spiked his drink. He was ahead of his time and the FA disciplinary body did not believe him. He had not helped his case by failing to appear on the originally scheduled date for the hearing.

[26] Double world champion and the UK's most medalled athlete.

[27] See my profile in *Athletics Weekly* titled 'Ohuruogu's Legal Aid'.

do something for nothing is a rare beast. Some intra-stadium bush telegraph must have been at work. Within five minutes her agent Ricky Simms approached me and asked whether I would be as good as my word. I drafted in my son Rupert[28] as one of my two juniors. Thrice no fee is still value for money. Christine's appeal succeeded and I had the unique experience of watching from the stands in the Birds Nest in Beijing in 2008 where she won Britain's only athletic gold, but where she would not have even been but for our success. I had to explain to my alarmed CAS colleagues sitting with me why I had succumbed to what they must have thought was an inexplicable bout of hysteria.

There are two postscripts to that tale. In 2015 there was a TV religious programme about Christine, by now Great Britain's most medalled female athlete, and a devout Christian. The narrator, Fern Britton, told the story of her ban and said 'Christine then prayed for a miracle. Fortunately watching her gold medal win in Osaka[29] and possibly answering her prayers was an ally who happened to be a top sports barrister'. And – mirabile dictu – at that very point a shot of my face in Blackstone Chambers appeared on the screen. Christine is now herself embarked on a legal education. My special trophy is her autographed T-shirt.

In the same year where I had been at the Beijing World Athletics Championships as a Chair of the IAAF Ethics Commission I boarded an earlier than scheduled airport bus from the IAAF hotel, to avoid a crush at immigrational control. On arrival I found that another dawn rider was none other than Usain Bolt, fresh from his usual triple sprint triumphs but insouciantly imperilling those valuable legs by riding around on a segway. He was another client of Ricky Simms. Noting my awestruck expression Ricky asked if I'd like to be introduced. You can guess my answer. I enjoyed several minutes chat and – be still my beating heart – a photograph taken by Ricky which I still lose no opportunity, however weak the excuse, to email to acquaintances, however distant.

Because of my role in these various doping cases, whether prosecutor, defender or arbitrator, I was invited by the Colins Blakemore[30] and Moynihan to sit on committees investigating ways to contain the drug culture in sport. For that very reason I thought it better to refuse. Several years later I was therefore free to advise the World Anti-doping Agency (WADA) that the BOA's rule that no sports persons convicted of a breach of the WADA Code could represent Team Britain in the 2012 Olympics, even if their period of ineligibility had expired, violated the rule against double jeopardy. I received a grateful call from David Howman, the then CEO of WADA, and my Carling black label type encomium in *Sports Telegraph* after the rule was withdrawn.

Drug testing in and out of competition is the price properly to be paid by elite athletes. Arguably less obvious is the need to subject participants in a team sport, such as football, where the use of other than recreational drugs is less prevalent and

---

[28] The other was Jane Mulcahy, now QC and a prominent sports lawyer in her own right, as is Rupert.
[29] Actually Berlin.
[30] Oxford Professor of Neurobiology Kt.

the benefit to be gained from doping (improvement of stamina and strength apart) not clear cut. The Professional Footballers Federation (PFF) asked me whether the need for top players to provide their whereabouts for an hour every day amounted to a form of house arrest. It is not easy for sports governing bodies (SGBs) to strike the right balance.

It was not only drug-related restrictions imposed by SGBs against which sports people chafed. As a junior to Colin Ross-Munro QC I acted for George Best in search of a way round FA Regulations so that he could be released from his contract with Fulham to play in the North American Soccer League (NASL), where many English football superstars went to fade profitably away. Our victory was another pyrrhic one. Best's best days were behind him. A fanzine summarised the denouement.[31]

> In 1977 the 'fifth Beatle' joined the LA Aztecs (who were part owned by Elton John). And the stories about booze, betting and birds crossed the Atlantic with him. He was promptly traded to the Fort Lauderdale strikers, where he became embroiled in a huffing, puffing, shirt flinging feud with manager Ron Newman, who called Best 'a selfish son of a bitch'.

John Conteh, world light heavyweight champion, spent almost as much time in Court as in the ring.[32] While the *Evening Standard* wondered where John had gone to ground, Stanley Brodie and I were appearing before the duty judge Walton J, sitting in his suburban garden, conventionally ornamented with a stone gnome, in an ambitious but vain attempt to stop a forthcoming bout from being, in John's absence, labelled a world championship.

I was struck by the trite thought that whereas John, as a sportsman, was at the summit of his necessarily short career, I, whose tools of trade were mind and tongue not physique and fists, could hope for better future things. In my second London marathon I passed John at the 16-mile mark, partial proof of my earlier reflection. John's case established that where similar issues (here of contract) were ventilated before both a Court of Law and a sporting tribunal, the former took precedence as a forum.[33] Some consolation to his lawyers if none to their client who wanted to win, and couldn't care less where.

John was not my only boxing client. I represented Jim Watt, world light heavyweight champion and Lennox Lewis, world heavyweight champion, whose complaint was remarkably similar to John's, but was similarly met with a judicial KO. I also saw Frank Bruno in Chambers, who wanted his licence restored by the British Boxing Board of Control (BBBC). For his visit I commandeered a particularly sturdy chair. I entertained hope that the case might come before Harry Woolf so my client could use his favourite phrase 'Know what I mean Harry', originally directed at the BBC boxing commentator Harry Carpenter. In the event Bruno got his licence back without a contest.

---

[31] *Tales of NASL.*
[32] Discussed in his ghosted autobiography 'I Conteh' where he commented astringently, 'legal advisers percentages don't come any lower than managers or promoters', p 68.
[33] *TLR* 5 June and 25 June 1975.

On a matter of more general importance, I advised the BBBC not to contest the Court of Appeal decision in *Watson* which held it liable in negligence for failure to ensure adequate ringside medical attention. Lord Scott, a former Cambridge boxing blue, told me that had he been on a panel in the House of Lords he would have voted in favour of the BBBC.[34] But would his colleagues have taken such a robust stance?

It was not only individuals who found themselves at odds with the sports regulators. In 1995, Tottenham Hotspur ('Spurs') were charged with various offences against the FA Rules by making undercover payments to players in addition to their declared signing on fees. The alleged offences had occurred under previous ownership, but the powers that be decided that Spurs should nonetheless be punished. Despite the Club's use of the services of Tony Grabiner, the FA expelled Spurs from the 1995–96 FA Cup, and docked them 12 points. Given their notoriously uneven form in the Premier League, this put them at risk of relegation with all the dire consequences in terms of money and reputation involved.

Alan (later Lord) Sugar, their then majority shareholder, had not made one of the biggest fortunes in Britain by wasting his money on things he considered unnecessary. He dispensed with Grabiner's services and conducted the appeal himself. But he did no better than his celebrated silk. Mr Sugar turned to me to advise whether, now that the internal FA appeal procedure had been exhausted, there was any chance of a remedy elsewhere. Together with Herbert Smith, I contrived a challenge in the High Court. The FA tried, but failed, to have the action struck out without a merits' hearing on the basis that its internal decisions were in law final.

A compromise was then negotiated. To avoid a hearing in the full blare of publicity of a High Court case, an Arbitration Panel was set up presided over by Roger Parker.[35] The Judge summoned us to his Chambers to give directions. There was a dispute as to the date upon which the hearing should be held. Out of the two dates on offer, the FA's silk could only manage one day, and I could only manage another. It seemed like deadlock. But I had a sudden inspiration. As I had walked down Chancery Lane to the meeting, I had noticed the banner headline in the *Evening Standard* – 'Ossie Ardiles sacked'. I said to the Judge that it might be thought particularly harsh on Spurs if it lost in the course of a single day both its manager *and* its QC. This heartfelt plea softened the Judge's heart; and the date was fixed for my convenience; Peter Goldsmith was then briefed for the FA.

The Panel decided that the penalty imposed on Spurs was disproportionate because the current owners and manager had nothing to do with the irregularities perpetrated under the ancien regime. It substituted a substantial fine. Spurs remained in the Premier League. For this achievement I earned a profile in *Sports Mail*[36] headlined 'The real hero behind Spurs incredible comeback' and an

---

[34] The ambit of the duty of care owed by sports governing bodies to sportsmen has achieved new salience in 2021 now that memory loss is said to be linked to concussion in contact sports.

[35] By now a former Lord Justice of Appeal.

[36] 26 March 1995 by Simon Greenberg. See also Alan Sugar *What You see is What you get* (Sugar, 2010) pp 451–452. It is not crystal clear whether his reference to the '"bee's knees of barristers", one of the most respected in the country' is to me or to Peter Goldsmith. The context cuts both ways.

invitation to lunch in the Directors Box at White Hart Lane. Alan Sugar had sent a car for me. As I was being driven away, I noted a group of fans pointing in my direction and cheering loudly. For a nanosecond (maybe more) I thought I had been transformed into a transient Tottenham celebrity before realising that they had confused me with Alan Sugar himself. We share, if little else, a certain bearded facial resemblance.

Other club clients included Chelsea, Manchester United, Preston North End, Leeds, Swindon, Middlesborough, Sheffield Wednesday, Watford, Portsmouth and Barnet, success in whose disputes was sometimes followed by lavish hospitality. I was invited to lunch and a match at Stamford Bridge by Ken Bates, then Chelsea's owner. With the female guests all segregated at one arm of the table the lunch started at 12:15 pm and had barely finished three hours later just before kick-off. When Tom (later Lord) Pendry, shadow Minister for Sport, arrived a little late he was greeted with a verbal volley by our host accusing him of freeloading. Later at a pre-match repast when Roman Abramovich owned the Club, the atmosphere was a trifle more civilized and a good deal more lavish. It reminded me of Michael Heseltine's quip about John Smith's prawn cocktail city offensive, 'Never have so many crustaceans died in vain'.

At Old Trafford I sat next to Bobby Charlton in the Directors' box. He asked which team I supported and when I said it was Spurs, replied soothingly that it takes all sorts to make a world. Swindon, demoted two divisions for financial irregularities of which I salvaged one, hosted a celebratory dinner, which I could not attend. Maybe that was just as well. It lasted so long that my junior Edward Grayson could only return to London by taxi, which cost him a sizeable chunk of his brief fee. I also was involved in various cases concerning the 'fit and proper person' test to be passed by oligarchs and others before they could be permitted to play a leading role in English premier league clubs, the new hobby of the wealthy.[37]

One of the different hobbies of Kerry Packer, the Australian media magnate, was polo. He owned a team, Ellerston White. Unlike other rich men who own teams in various sports, he carried his enthusiasm to the point of playing himself. For that reason it was particularly important for him to ensure that all his professionals were available for the sport's Cup Final. However, the team's star Pedro Gonzales, said to be the best player in the world, was under suspension for a rule infringement; Mr Packer appealed the damaging decision.

I was summoned to the suite in the Savoy overlooking the Thames which served as Mr Packer's London home. There he gave voice to a prolonged rant about how he had been deprived of the services of Bob Alexander QC, his usual counsel[38] who had since left the Bar to become Chairman of the NatWest Bank. We then trooped (or rather taxied) off to the Hurlingham Club for the hearing. Mr Gonzales's defence was that he had not been guilty of deliberately colliding with an opponent. After a brief opening I left it to the rider himself to explain,

---

[37] One concerned 'Red and White Holdings', an Arsenal shareholder.
[38] Victorious in the famous case upholding the rights of English cricketers to take part in his rebel tour.

with a voluble comment on a video recording of the incident, precisely why he was innocent of the charge. It came better from the rider's, if not the horse's, mouth. Our joint advocacy partially carried the day; the suspension was lifted and a fine of £10,000 imposed in its place.

We returned for some celebratory champagne to the Savoy Suite where Mr Packer said to me with a lupine grin 'I wound you up good and proper didn't I?' As indeed he had. He then turned to Mr Gonzales and said that the rider would have the fine subtracted from his wages. Mr Packer was clearly a man who knew many methods to get his way. The Polo Association itself later sought my advice on how far the free movement provisions of EU law entitled overseas players to exploit their skill on British soil.

Sports bodies themselves have to battle with public authorities. I advised the Boat Race organisers that the Metropolitan Police were wrong to suggest that they had to keep the peace not only on the river, but on the riverbank. For a few weeks the very fate of the venerable competition hung in the balance because of the potential costs involved if the Met had been right. The Met accepted my opinion that public order on the towpath was a matter for the police. Oddly the same issue arose in respect of the Henley Regatta. My advice was the same; and once again the local police backed down.[39]

As a boat race bonus I was offered a privileged place in one of the armada of following launches. Alas, eve-of-race, I was marooned in Trinidad (flight cancelled) where I had been in Court and spent the time when I should have been on the Thames in the over-optimistically named International Hotel in the vicinity of Port of Spain airport. Luckily next year the invitation was renewed, and I had a duck's eye view of the proceedings or would have, if my fellow passengers, including David Steel, a High Court Judge and an Old Etonian rowing blue, acclimatised to somewhat Jollier Weather, had not, contrary to the pleas of the launch's proprietors worried about their Health and Safety responsibilities, stood up to cheer the rare Oxford victory.

Boat race crews are increasingly manned by mature graduates engaged in a single year, sometimes contrived, course of study, more honoured in the breach than in the observance. In 2007 Cambridge were stroked to victory by the 6ft 5in German rower, Thorsten Engelmann, the heaviest oarsman ever to compete in the race, who abandoned his economics degree course a few days later and returned home to Germany to vie for a place in the national Olympic crew. Oxford claimed that this was in breach of a joint agreement introduced to prevent the universities fielding internationals who were not genuine students. There were CAS precedents that a team which fielded an ineligible player might forfeit the match[40] but in the

---

[39] The police are, explicably, anxious to pass the costs of policing sporting events on to the organisers and I was in two cases which finally (at any rate so far) resolved the issue in favour of the football clubs, Leeds and Ipswich [2014] QB 168 and [2017] 4 WLR 195.

[40] The law was in fact not wholly cut and dried. The IAAF and the USATAF had been at loggerheads over the extent of an IAAF member's duty to report positive drug tests. The former contended that

end Cambridge refused to agree for the race to be voided and Oxford thought it ungentlemanly to litigate. The result stands in the record books. Mr Engelmann is unique in that he was nonetheless denied his Blue.

Rowing is not the only water-based sport. The Hampstead Swimming Club sought against the City of London for a declaration that its members be allowed to swim in the open air ponds on the Heath even in the absence of lifeguards. I had the advantage of multiple notes of advice from Lord Phillips, then Lord Chief Justice, himself an enthusiastic dawn icebreaker, and Lord Hoffmann, the second most senior Law Lord, who was Chairman of the local Heath Society. No more illustrious pair of ad hoc juniors could have propelled me to victory after I had stigmatised my opponent, adapting the name of the Labour MP turned TV celebrity, as 'the Killjoy silk'. Chuckles in Court.[41]

Summer sports; winter sports; four legs and two. In racing I advised the Horse Race Owners Association,[42] the National Association of Bookmakers, the Race Course Association Limited and The Tote.[43] The Aga Khan wanted a judicial review of the Jockey Club's decision to disqualify his Oaks winning filly for doping. My pessimistic advice as to the likely outcome led to me being jocked off in favour of Sydney Kentridge QC, the Lester Piggott of advocates; but he too could not persuade them that judicial review could be applied to private bodies.[44] Later I advised John Gosden, the well-known trainer, on a similar issue. His wife, Rachel Hood, was one of the first generation of women to attend a former all-male college in Cambridge, and a former pupil in my chambers. I also paid a visit to the Somerset countryside when instructed to challenge the decision by the local authority to ban stag hunting over its property, where I saw stag, hounds and huntsmen during the day, but never in the same place at the same time. But at least I won the case.[45]

I was briefed in the case of Alain Baxter, the Scottish skier, whose Olympic slalom bronze medal was removed because he had used a Vick's inhaler (US style).

---

an American Olympic gold medallist should not have been allowed to be part of the US 4x400m men's relay team in Sydney. Although the runner in question did not compete in the final, the IAAF argued that the US should nonetheless have been disqualified. The parties compromised on an arbitration before a CAS panel, comprising a former Canadian Ambassador to the United Nations, a former Australian Attorney-General and the head of Freshfields Paris office – a true 'A' team. Briefed for the IAAF, I found myself cross-examining Craig Masback, CEO for the Americans, himself a Trinity graduate, and once third-fastest miler in the world (first were Coe and Ovett) – not the best way, I thought ruefully, of maintaining alumni relations. Even with the support of Francois Carrard, the wily advocate for the IOC, an insider's insider, the claim failed because of a lacuna in the rules, subsequently filled. And justice was eventually done in 2008 when one of the finalists was found to have been ineligible in consequence of a doping offence and the team were retrospectively stripped of their medals.

[41] [2005] 1 WLR 2930.

[42] By the grace of my solicitor I held the consultation in a box at Lord's awaiting the World Cup final of 2003 and was able to stay for the match.

[43] Sarah Curtis (ed), *The Journals of Woodrow Wyatt Vol. 3: From Major to Blair* (Curtis, 2000) p 534, where after saying he had been told I was very left wing (an early example of fake news) he observed 'He can be a communist if he likes as long as he is a good counsel'.

[44] I wrote about the case in *Leading Cases in Sports Law* edited by Jack Anderson (Anderson, 2015) Ch 8.

[45] [1995] 1 WLR 1037.

The *Daily Mail* headline the day after the event ran 'British skier wins Olympic Alpine Medal', but after the adverse lab rests results came in two days later the headline was 'Scottish skier tests positive'.

The IOC's written submissions start unpromisingly by describing Alain as a 'cross-country skier'. Baxter's main point was that the methamphetamine in the US inhaler was not the same as the amphetamine in the UK inhaler, and was not, on a fair construction of the rules, a banned substance at all. In the end Baxter did not get his medal back, but CAS did acquit him of being a drug cheat – so it wasn't quite downhill all the way.[46] Alain autographed an inhaler for my personal museum of legal-sporting memorabilia along with my Versapak,[47] the standard container for urine samples in athletics, whose screw top was under scrutiny in the Michelle de Bruin case, of which more later. Not to worry, mine is empty.

Four legs but four wheels too. I advised David Coulthard (he won his first Grand Prix the next weekend, for which even I cannot claim credit), Jenson Button, the FIA in the wake of the chaos of 2004's Indianapolis Grand Prix, as well as a cohort of Formula One teams who considered the regulations for Grands Prix to be anti-competitive, being stacked against them and in favour of such traditional giants as Ferrari. Oxfordshire counterbalances Oxford city's reputation for concentration on things intellectual by being home to a number of Formula One headquarters. I had a consultation with Flavio Briatore, then in charge of Benneton at their racing car factory, but declined his offer of a lift back to London in his private helicopter, a form of travel for which I am not an enthusiast.[48]

Sometimes I carried out functions *for* an SGB. My first instructions from the RFU involved Tim Rodber, the England flank forward sent off for fighting during England's tour of South Africa in 1995 and punished by those in charge of the tour but in my view immune, because of the rule against double jeopardy, from further sanction by the RFU itself. This was but an hors d'oeuvre to a more substantial meal.

On New Year's Eve of 2001 Gloucester played and beat the Newcastle Falcons, in Rugby Union's Premier League. Rob Andrew, the former England fly half and Newcastle's CEO, asserted that the fiery French Gloucester flanker, Mr Azam, had uttered racist abuse against Newcastle's Mr Taione supported by a chorus from the crowd. The two players were disciplined by the RFU Tribunal for fighting. I was then appointed by the RFU to preside over an inquiry into the allegations of racism with Budge Rodgers, ex British captain, and Gordon Skelton, an ex-cop, in the spartan surroundings of the Holiday Inn, Coventry. Evidence was taken from team owners Tom Walkinshaw (about to jet off to the Melbourne Grand Prix to watch his Arrows team) and David Thompson. In Rugby Union – like

---

[46] There is a lengthy discussion of the case in chapter nine of Andrew Ross's authorised biography of Baxter, *Unfinished Business* (Ross, 2005), where it is said that 'It was a huge bonus to have Beloff present Baxter's case' and refers to 'my polished presentation'. Not quite polished enough it seems.

[47] Borrowing from the film title *Sex, Lies and Videotape* I once wrote an article entitled 'Drugs Laws and Versapaks'.

[48] When I went to Monte Carlo to prosecute drugs offences for the IAAF, it was my solicitor's preferred option from Nice Airport. I concede that it did save time.

Association Football – clubs are the fashionable accessories of the macho male super-rich; more prestigious even than trophy wives or Porsches. One key question was would Mr Azam have sworn in English or French? We concluded that he was more likely to have used his native tongue, but were less impressed by the argument that he would not have known what the words 'black bastard' meant. We ruled that Rob Andrew had gone over the top but did so in good faith, a more yellow than red card offence. Later Rob was one of my Treasurer's guests at Grand Day in Gray's Inn; he had clearly forgotten our earlier contact but I refrained from agitating his memory.

Abuse of minors in sport by those responsible for their welfare was another issue which increasingly came to the fore. Taking over from Keir Starmer, who had become Director of Public Prosecutions, I authored a report on the subject for the Lawn Tennis Association (LTA) as well as others for the FA and English Cricket Board (ECB). There is a balance to be struck between due process for the alleged perpetrator and proper protection for the alleged victim. Recent revelations from football and gymnastics in particular suggest that it has tilted too far away from the second of these desiderata.

I next took up a role in deciding cases, not simply arguing them. I acquired over the last quarter of a century a large portfolio of appointments: as a member CAS, Chairman of the International Cricket Council's (ICC) Code of Conduct Commission (CCC) and its Dispute Resolution Committee (DRC), first Chairman of the IAAF[49] Ethics Board and first Chairman of the IAAF Disciplinary Tribunal, a Steward of the Royal Automobile Club (RAC) (on the recommendation of Lord Rawlinson), a member of the FIA International Appeal Tribunal; a member of the Ironman Appeal Tribunal of the Ultimate Fighting Championship (UFC) Tribunal, and of the European Golf Tour Doping Appeal Panel. I also was for a brief period, as part of a trio with Seb Coe and Michael Grade, responsible for recommending which major sporting events should be ringfenced to be available on terrestrial television. Because of these plural roles I was a two-term President of the British Association of Sport and Law (BASL), once mistakenly addressed in correspondence as the President of Basildon which, if it exists, is clearly a superior office!

Not all these posts generated much work. The Golfing tribunal never sat at all; the substance has not been concocted that can guarantee a hole in one. The two motoring appointments, neither of which were remunerated,[50] led to only two cases over two decades. The RAC gave its Stewards (which included the likes of Jackie Stewart, a triple world champion, and Gordon Murray, engineer supreme) honorary membership, as well as an annual lunch attended by its President Prince Michael. When the well of potential cases had run completely dry, the RAC conveniently promoted all of us to the rank of Vice President.

---

[49] Since 2019 rebranded as World Athletics.
[50] Expenses were paid.

The FIA's meetings were held in its Paris office off the Place de la Concorde. There was always afterwards an excellent dinner usually in some Michelin starred restaurant. The FIA hosted the last one which I attended in the Hall of Mirrors in the Palace of Versailles. Sitting in the Eurostar lounge (business class, natch) on my return journey I spied at a discreetly located table the diminutive figure of Nicholas Sarkozy with Carla Bruni in tow (it may have been the other way around). I noted that the waiter had a photograph taken with the illustrious pair and congratulated him on my way out to the train. 'Oh', he said, 'It was Mr Sarkozy who invited me to have the photograph taken. I wasn't bothered one way or the other. I suppose I can give it to my mother'. I marvelled at his indifference.

For the years of my membership I had a heavy gold coloured badge allowing me free access to any Grand Prix anywhere in the world. I realised in my last year in post that it was now or never. I went to the British Grand Prix at Silverstone where I lunched and watched Lewis Hamilton's inevitable victory in the company of Ken Clarke, who was bemoaning the fact that the organisers had inconsiderately decided to stage it at the same time as a Test Match. What they had done, however, was to provide in the lounge a screen to show the men's final at Wimbledon – it was the peak weekend of a British sporting summer – so I could watch Federer's last victory far from the madding crowd fighting their way to the exit.

The first and most important of these posts, which opened the door to the others, was my membership of CAS founded in 1983 on the initiative of the aristocratic Marquis de Samaranch, then President of the IOC, to provide a mechanism 'to secure the settlement of sports related disputes' away from the national courts. CAS's jurisdiction is based on contract. It is located in Lausanne, the Olympic city, deemed to be the legal site, wherever taken in fact, of its decisions, which are only reviewable by the Swiss Federal Tribunal (SFT) on extremely limited grounds akin to those of judicial review. Most major international, especially Olympic, sports now provide for appeals to it in their constitutions; exceptions include motor racing, baseball and American football. Since 1996 it has provided select ad hoc panels at, amongst other events, summer and winter Olympic Games as well as, recently, at the more ornamental Asian Beach Games.

When David Dixon, a senior partner of Withers, a former international hurdler in charge of the Commonwealth Games Federation, another client, suggested that I might wish to become a member, it was not a body of which I had even heard. My appointment in 1996 coincided with my selection for the 12-person ad hoc Panel at Atlanta. It was a little like being appointed to the Cabinet just after one's first election as an MP.[51]

---

[51] Meeting one of my co-arbitrators on the bus from the airport I sought to engage him in polite conversation. The following dialogue Q & A ensued: Q 'Were you an active sportsman?'; A 'Yes – an equestrian'; Q 'Did you compete internationally?'; A 'Yes'; Q 'At the Olympics?'; A 'Yes'; Q 'Did you win any medals'; A 'Yes'; Q 'More than one?'; A 'Yes – six'; Q 'What colour?'; A 'Gold'. Collapse of stout Beloff. My colleague was Reiner Klimke, one of the standout post-war riders. I suffered a similar embarrassment when, at a reception for the Australian cricketers at Australia House, I equally politely asked another guest why he was there, to which he responded 'I'm Michael Clarke – the team captain'. My only excuse is that his features were well concealed on pitch by the baggy green cap.

My love affair with the Olympics dates back far earlier. On my vacation between school and college I attended, as first stop off point on an Italian trip, the Rome Olympics of 1960, sharing a room in a suburb with two raucous Glaswegians. They seemed more interested in chatting up the landlady with their two Italian words 'Bella' and 'Signorina' than in the Games themselves. Those were the days. No oppressive security, indeed no obvious security at all. One could wander freely between the stadia. Tickets could be bought on the spot, though my Latin did not help me to realise when ticket touts sold me a ticket for a heat not a final. But I attended every track and field event. My neighbour, a voluble and partisan American, greeted each appearance of a US athlete with the cry 'You can win this', Art, Dave or Wilma, as the case might be. When the great Australian middle distance runner Herb Elliott[52] took the bell in the 1500 metres final already almost out of sight and certainly out of reach of his rivals I could not resist shouting loudly but with greater confidence 'You can win this Herb'. I watched two competitors whose friendship I later enjoyed, Dick Pound swimming for Canada, a future Vice President of the IOC and member of the CAS governing body whom I regularly met at Olympic and Commonwealth Games from the nineties onwards, and Peter Radford, sprinting for Britain, a future chief executive of UK Athletics.

I next went to the Munich Olympics of 1972 with Jeffrey.[53] I marveled at his ability to purchase multifarious pins at one end of the main platz and sell them for a mark-up at the other. Jeffrey, whose features vaguely resembled those of the Soviet sprinter Valery Borzov (double champion at the Games) if his speed was somewhat less, satisfied a curious by-passer by posing for a photograph under his assumed personality. We stayed late into the night to cheer Mary Peters on in the high jump and win UK's only athletic gold in the Pentathlon.[54]

So absorbed were we in reflecting on the games, memorable not only for the high standard of the athletics but, more poignantly for the murder of seven Israeli athletes, while sitting in the airport lounge awaiting our flight back to London that we had to be summoned by tannoy and driven – shamefacedly in my case – to the aircraft itself to ironic cheers from the passengers waiting on board.

Though Jeffrey is ordinarily a stickler for punctuality, on our next Olympic trip – Barcelona 92 – he was so late to pick me up from my house in Holland Park that I was in near meltdown. Jeffrey ambitiously (but unsuccessfully) tried from his car to ring Lord King, then chairman of British Airways, to ask him to hold the plane. Once we had – but just – caught it, Jeffrey assured me that we would be met at the other end by the British Ambassador. My silent scepticism was vindicated,

---

[52] Elliot was never defeated in his career over mile or 1500m, for both of which he held the world record. I was by chance present at the only time he nearly lost when running for Cambridge in the blues match.

[53] A couple of rows behind us sat Eddie Kulukundis, the husband of Susan Hampshire. His substantial bulk belied his keen interests in the sport. He was a considerable benefactor of British athletes and athletics.

[54] Mary and I also met at several Olympic Games when she was the British team manager. More than half a century later I gave the keynote speech at a sports law conference in Belfast held in her honour.

though some junior staff member was indeed there to hustle us through the immigration control. Jeffrey had insisted that I and my son join him in a designated floor in a five star hotel, where other guests included Jarvis Astaire, the boxing promoter, as well as a cohort of wealthy tickets touts who could afford the expense rather better than I.

Encountering a Chinese delegation outside the main stadium – Beijing were mounting an early bid to host the Olympics – Jeffrey berated them for flaws in their marketing approach and predicted correctly that they would lose out to Sydney.

We visited the British team's HQ in the Olympic village and came upon the 400 metre star Roger Black having a massage. 'Who is he?', Jeffrey whispered to me, and, after I told him, strode forth and shook the recumbent athlete by the hand with a 'very good luck Roger' as if they were the oldest of friends. Some years later when we encountered him – by then an Olympic silver medallist – at a party, Jeffrey by now confident of his identity and at the start of his own (aborted) campaign for the London mayoralty greeted him, 'Roger I want you on my team' – an invitation which he somewhat indiscriminately extended those days to people, at any rate those of a certain cachet, after the very briefest of encounters. On both occasions I appreciated his characteristic aplomb.

In Barcelona John Major came to press the flesh. Jeffrey was a close ally of the then Prime Minister[55] and organised a dinner party for him in a private room at a local restaurant, compelling me somewhat reluctantly to invest in a pair of trousers appropriate – if barely so – for the occasion. There was much excitement as Jeffrey kept in telephonic touch with the security men escorting 'the Boss' (as he called him) so as to be primed for his arrival. After the main course John Major came to sit next to me. I recognized in our conversation, what others have noted, how bright he shone in a one to one, but how that light became diffused and dimmed whenever he was addressing a larger audience. Years later when I was invited as one of two selected members of the Bar to a reception in Downing Street, Sarah Hogg[56] purported to introduce me to our host who said 'Of course I know who Michael is'. I had long since learned that politicians have a rolodex memory for anyone who is actually enfranchised.

At that Barcelona dinner I clumsily spilled a glass of red wine over Andrew Lloyd Webber sitting on my other side, some of which soaked into the famous composer's suit. I was faced with a protocol dilemma. Would it be more offensive to offer to pay the multi-millionaire for the dry cleaning than to do nothing other than to offer profuse apologies? My parsimony won the day.

Jeffrey's interest in what was going on inside the stadium was beginning to dwindle. By the time we came to the next games in Atlanta, our relationship had undergone a role reversal. As a member of the CAS panel I was housed in the main

---

[55] It was John Major who said at the opening of the folly constructed in the gardens at Grantchester where Jeffrey could pen his best sellers (think Shakespeare and Ann Hathaway's cottage) that 'it was Jeffrey's first folly but Mary's second'.

[56] Baroness Hogg – his chief of staff.

Olympic family hotel in the city centre to which access was restricted. Jeffrey had been able only to obtain board and lodging in a location barely within Georgia's state boundaries. We were still able to meet sporadically in the stadium itself. When I was celebrating over exuberantly Carl Lewis's unique fourth gold medal in the long jump, Jeffrey chastised me 'Don't be so silly Michael'.

Jeffrey was always adept in seeking out old contacts wherever he found himself. At Atlanta we had a dinner with Pierre Salinger.[57] Later to mark my election as President of Trinity – a post I would take up on my return from the Games – he (Jeffrey, not Pierre) hosted a dinner in my honour. In a short speech he prophesied that I would one day be Lord Chief Justice. This provoked a hearty guffaw from one well lubricated guest, earning him an instant rebuke from Jeffrey. The guest was the better prophet.

One of the benefits of travelling with Jeffrey is that one never lacked for transport. In Barcelona he boarded a bus booked for the Korean weightlifting team (I and my son following sheepishly in his wake). Though his presence prompted much pointing and incomprehensible (to us) comment, no one actually forced us to disembark. In Athens at the world championships in 1999, absent any available taxis at the stadium, Jeffrey simply tapped a stranger's car on the bonnet and asked its astonished driver to take us to our hotel. By the end of the journey he had made a new – if transient – friend.

Jeffrey was prevented from attending the Sydney Olympics for force majeure reasons. Nonetheless, from his open prison he drafted an article for *The Times* urging the case for a London Olympics in which he recalled that the UK had produced so many great Olympic champions such as – there followed a blank space which he asked me to fill in, as I dutifully did, before he sent the piece on to the newspaper. In due time the Games did take place in London. Jeffrey had had aspirations to be in charge of the volunteers – a role for which he was admirably suited – but the call never came.

In Sydney I found myself at the swimming sitting next to Gough Whitlam, the former Australian Prime Minister. Since he was an Oxford alumnus I introduced myself venturesomely as Max Beloff's son. He then explained to me how his canvassing of the African votes had won the games for the city. This he did at some length until his wife, Betty, said 'Do stop talking Gough, the young man wants to watch the swimming'. In Beijing I watched Becky Adlington win the first of her two gold medals in the VIP section along with Bill Gates and Henry Kissinger[58] but could think of no plausible reason to engage them in conversation long or short.

Returning from poolside spectating I was told by the hotel receptionist that there was a parcel waiting for me. Opening it I found that it was the first edition of my book *Sports Law* translated – I hope accurately, I have no way of knowing – into Chinese by a Professor from Shanghai. I had not given permission for the translation

---

[57] President Kennedy's press secretary.
[58] Actually, Kissinger did know Max but my nerve was less than it had been in Sydney.

and have never received a single renmimbi for the Chinese edition, but I felt flattered by the fact that my book had even been thought worth translating. Many years later, I gave a lecture at a sports law conference in Xiamen and was assured that I was well known to sports lawyers in the PRC so someone must have read it.

Every two years, book-ending the Olympics, there were the World Athletic Championships, which sorted out my summer holiday. It was something of a lucky dip. The excellence of the sport was guaranteed, the interest of the host city less so. Gold medals to Beijing, Moscow, Paris, Berlin and Seville. Silver to Athens, Osaka, Gothenburg.[59] Bronze to Doha, Daegu and Edmonton, the last of these cruelly named by the British press Deadmonton. Out of friendship with Jack Agrios[60] who had secured its hosting rights, I wrote to the local rag saying I would rather call it 'Friendmonton'. This ungainly compliment earned me, if nothing else, his gratitude and a kiss from the local mayoress. At most of the stadia I used to sit with the President of British Athletics, gold medallists both, Lynn Davies, followed by Jason Gardener. Lynn and I coxed and boxed at mealtimes, one keeping the seat, the other foraging at the buffet (Michelin starred at Paris, edible at Athens only for those with sweet teeth).[61]

What true sports lover wouldn't dream of being able to go to the Olympics for free as could the CAS ad hoc panels? Throw in business class travel, accommodation in an IAAF designated hotel, a *passe partout* including access to the VIP (if not the *VVIP* areas) in any stadium including the hospitality suites, freedom of the Olympic lanes with personally allotted drivers, a generous per diem allowance. Other nominations to serve on Panels for the FIFA World Cup, initially for 2002 under the auspices of the International Chamber for Football Arbitration, thereafter for CAS, were less enticing since the small print promised a trip to the games only if an arbitrator's presence was required, which it never was.

I served on five ad hoc Panels, the last at Rio[62] – I refer to myself as the Steve Redgrave and not just the Matt Pinsent of Olympic arbitration.[63] Together with three Commonwealth Games (Kuala Lumpur, Manchester, Melbourne) my number of appointments may remain a record.

The summer Olympic ad hoc panels are made up of 12 persons whose diverse nationalities are designed to ensure that any tribunal of three cannot be accused of conflict of interest vis à vis the appeal before it. The chosen threesome has to resolve any dispute within 24 hours of its initiation. The adjudication process bears as little similarity to ordinary arbitration as does 20/20 to Test Match cricket.

---

[59] Where I encountered on a staircase in the IAAF hotel the indigenous Cathy Freeman who attained national heroine status at the Sydney Olympics but was at this stage in the foothills of her career. When I asked for her autograph prior to signature, she replied in all innocence 'Do people collect these things?'.

[60] A leading local lawyer.

[61] As Honorary Legal Adviser for London 2017 I had in right of status my own seat and, on a tip from transport guru Jeffrey, a trip back to the city centre de facto, if not de jure, in one of the athletes' buses...

[62] Strictly speaking a specialist anti-doping panel.

[63] The former had five rowing gold medals, the latter four. You probably knew that already.

The mantra coined by a German colleague was 'fast, fair and free' though fair should have been the gold medal adjective.

The docket of ad hoc panels consisted, amongst other things, of disputes over eligibility or alleged doping offences. The former, for obvious reasons,[64] often had to be decided prior to the games. The latter for equally obvious but different reasons[65] usually arose also out of prior events. Not all the issues were of major significance.

In Atlanta, two cases concerned a hurdler from the Cape Verde team – the smallest at the Games.[66] He had been expelled from the Olympic village for having seized the national flag from the chef de mission as the team entered the stadium for the opening ceremony, so depriving the latter of his moment of televised celebrity. We decided that he had been denied natural justice and should be removed from the ranks of the temporarily homeless. Seated next to Archbishop Tutu, both of us on hotel gymnasium bikes, I watched on screen the hurdler, carrying an obvious leg injury, literally falling out of his blocks but presumably fulfilling his contractual sponsorship duty to compete. Sometimes all's well even if it ends badly.

In Sydney, a Samoan weightlifter had been suspended by his national federation because of allegations that, during an away match, he had had sex with a minor.[67] The High Court of Samoa lifted his suspension; but the International Federation was adamant that he could not compete. We decided that comity – the principle of respect that one judicial body must have for another – required us to reinstate him but felt obliged to add, primly, that our ruling was not to be taken as an endorsement of the participation in the Olympic Games of persons convicted of serious sexual offences.

In Athens, a dispute arose as to whether French gymnasts had breached the rules restricting the size of advertising logos on clothing during the medal ceremony. The essence of the problem was that a combination of modern elastic textiles and size of chest (or breast) meant that whereas the logo on the vest as sold was compliant with the rules, as worn it was not. Two principles of construction were pitted against each other: the principle of legal certainty which favoured measuring the logo on the former; and the principle of teleological interpretation which favoured measuring it on the latter. We decided that a literal construction trumped a purposive one.

Some arbitral awards affected the destination of major medals. We upheld the award of the gold medal in the Athens men's all-round gymnastics competition to an American, even though the Korean had admittedly been undermarked in the penultimate round. We applied the so-called field of play rule which seeks to immunise from scrutiny the decisions of umpires or referees, other than in cases of

---

[64] The need to know who the competitors would be.
[65] The time taken to process urine samples A and B.
[66] Gabrielle Kaufmann-Kohler, *Arbitration at the Olympics* (Kaufmann-Kohler, 2001) pp 112–13.
[67] I was reminded of Margaret Mead's anthropological classic 'Coming of Age in Samoa'.

bias or bad faith. 'Finality in this area', we said, 'is all important. Rough justice may be all that sport can tolerate'. I observed to my flanker colleagues that we would no doubt be feted in Seattle, but would need to take care if walking unguarded in Seoul.

To combine duty (as an arbitrator) with pleasure (as a spectator) requires a nice sense of timing as well as a large measure of adrenalin. At the Manchester Commonwealth Games the President, Judge Pathak, former Chief Justice of India, appointed me to chair the appeal hearing brought by a Canadian triathlete alleged to have taken a prohibited substance. The matter had to be decided by that night so that he could, if successful, fly in from Canada. At 20:59 the winning teams in the 4 x 400 men's relay – the last track race of the Games – crossed the metaphorical tape simultaneously. At 21:00 three elderly gentlemen, myself, a South African judge Deon Van Zyl, and a New Zealand attorney were seen dashing (not the *mot juste*) out of the stadium into waiting cars. At 21:30 the hearing commenced. We sat until 03:00 and delivered judgment at 06:00 on the Thursday morning. Who talks about the law's delays? The triathlete at least saved on his flight ticket.

The fringe benefits of being at the eye of the Games are considerable. In Sydney I wrote a lengthy diary from a CAS perspective for the *Daily Telegraph*[68] of which the only censored sentence was my comment 'No expenses spared' about a four-hour lunch we hacks (including Seb Coe) enjoyed at a beachside restaurant. In rainy Manchester, after I had recently advised the BBC on their interactive sports service, I was given a tour of the media centre by Brendan Foster[69] and Sue Barker.[70] I saw a familiar figure hastening with upright stride to the BBC commentary box. Beloff: 'Aren't you Michael Johnson?' Michael Johnson (for it was he):[71] 'No'.

In sunny Athens I sat between Seb Coe and Michael Johnson himself at the *Sports Telegraph* eve of games dinner. I refrained from reminding Michael of our transient convergence in Manchester. I was also entertained on the yacht of Keith Mills, Seb's deputy, lobbying for the Games.[72] In smoggy Beijing I bumped into Lionel Messi and Carl Lewis, enjoyed an evening drink with Nadia Comaneci[73] and her American husband, Brett Connor, also a gymnastic gold medallist, and watched boxing *cote a cote* with Evander Holyfield.[74] While at the Men's Triple Jump Final I spied both Teresa Jowell, Minister for the Olympics, and Boris Johnson, then newly elected Mayor of London. I persuaded them to pose with me for a photograph, which I suggested would illustrate that the staging of the

---

[68] For several years I wrote an annual piece for the same newspaper on the subject of sport and law to fill the journalistically awkward gap between Christmas and New Year as well as delivering what purported to be a witty grace at the sports teams' annual dinner. Both roles were abruptly terminated upon a change of editor.

[69] Much medalled athlete; founder of the Great North Run.

[70] Grand slam tennis champion and broadcaster.

[71] 400m much-medalled superstar.

[72] The BCC had put a spoke in the wheel of London's bid by publicising alleged corruption of the IOC's Bulgarian member, and I spent some time explaining to anyone who would listen that the BBC was not an organ of the Government.

[73] The first gymnast ever to score a 10.

[74] World boxing champion; had his ear bitten by Mike Tyson.

Olympics was not a matter which divided the main parties. Boris, who had only just arrived, was concerned that he might miss the next jump of Philips Idowu, the British hope, so I had to explain to him that with 12 finalists the gap between jumps was measured in more than mere seconds.

For Rio, which I attended for the IAAF in my capacity as Chairman of its Ethics Board as well as for CAS, I flew out in the same cabin as Princess Anne (two seats in front) and Andy Murray (two seats behind). I spoke only to one of that illustrious pair (no names no packdrill other than to say that my good luck wish bore fruit).[75]

I was not, however, a member of the ad hoc panel in London, despite being the ante post favourite as the most experienced Anglo arbitrator. The selectors had perceived some potential conflict of interest because of my ties to LOCOG[76] dating back to the time in 2004 when I had been invited by Barbara Cassani, former chief executive of Go Fly, then in charge of London's bid to stage the 2012 Olympics, to take up the bespoke post of Ethics Commissioner. In that role I had to assist in navigating the shoals of the bidding cities' International Olympic Rule book, whose size and complexity was a physical reaction to the Salt Lake City Scandals. Barbara announced my appointment in grandiloquent terms which owed much to her script writer.

> Mr Beloff is an internationally respected lawyer, who has held a number of significant judicial, tribunal and arbitral posts. I am therefore delighted that he has agreed to fill this important role and to chair our advisory group. This is a key element in our approach to good corporate governance and will help us maintain and ensure integrity and transparency throughout the bid process.

The Advisory Group included Lord Paul, Sir Stephen Redgrave, and Charles Flint. But I was Chair of a group that never met and Barbara herself soon recognised that she was an alien in the world of international sport. She yielded her place to her deputy Seb Coe who had in it an unsurpassed profile. In fact my contribution to the successful bid was limited to a single brief memorandum for Seb, the gist of which was that London should monitor and mimic the efforts of Paris, London's perceived main rival, but with a soupcon less by way of offer of benefits so that if either were vulnerable to an accusation of breach of the Code, Paris would be the prime suspect. On the day of the announcement I was in a room overlooking Trafalgar Square where the bid's B team were being entertained and was able to

---

[75] I had been in Rio a few months earlier as a CAS flanker on a domestic football case to which I had been nominated by one of the parties. The cost to CAS was only lessened by sending me via Lisbon on TAP, Portugal's national airline. On the way back after a day's stopover I found myself on the airport bus filled with British female rowers returning from their training camp. I chatted to their team leader who looked vaguely familiar and it was only as we all disembarked that I said, as I had belatedly worked out, 'You must be Katherine Grainger' (Dame, lawyer and Olympian). I had a similar moment of uncertainty in spotting an equally familiar face on the plane to Beijing in 2015, who turned out to be Mike Powell, the world record holder for the long jump. Katherine has since been made an honorary bencher of Gray's Inn, Mike not (so far).

[76] The London Organising Committee for the Olympic Games.

witness the unrestrained enthusiasm of the crowds when Jacque Rogge, President of the IOC, announced the unexpected result.

Seb asked me to stay in post, although its original functions had been fulfilled once London had been chosen, My peculiar role was to be the designated recipient of any approach by someone who wished to blow the whistle on some perceived impropriety in the behaviour of LOCOG[77] or any counterparty. Not a whistle blew in the run-up to the Games and my annual trek to Canary Wharf, LOCOG's HQ, would, in the taxonomy of aircraft landing cards, be ticked with the box Visitor rather than Business.

As a consolation prize for my non-selection for the ad hoc Panel in 2012, I was asked to be CAS's vicar on the terra firma of the capital city. There was the customary concern that disaffected participants in the Games might take their complaints to the local courts. I had a discrete informal discussion with the Lord Chief Justice, Igor Judge. There could, of course, be no direction from on high that judges must decline to hear any case which could properly be heard by the ad hoc panel, but I was assured that as long as the judiciary were informed of the presence of CAS and the width of its jurisdiction, it was odds on that any hard-pressed vacation judge would prefer to render unto CAS the things that were CAS's.

I was also asked as a kind of CAS social secretary to introduce the two judges who were in charge of the ad hoc panel to Igor, and the President of the Queen's Bench Division, John Thomas.[78] One of the judges hailed from Puerto Rico, the other from Boston. We met in the Chief's chambers behind his Courtroom, the largest and most impressive in the Royal Court in the Strand. So seemingly overwhelmed were the two transatlantic lawyers by the architecture and the company that it was left to the English hosts to keep the conversation if not exactly flowing, at least not entirely static. Otherwise, I had my choice of tickets. Had I been in fact on the London panel I would have been ineligible for Rio, maxed out on the basis of the number of my nominations. Fortune favours the fortunate.

I was also free to accept instructions in a trio of cases concerned with selection for the Olympics of Tonia Couch, the diver, who wanted to be chosen for the solo as well as the synchro event; and of Aaron Cook, ranked number one in the world at the 80kg Taekwondo event but passed over in favour of the world ranked number eight, which made many speculate that the work at the cross roads had not been entirely clean.[79]

The two failures in these cases had to be balanced out by my success in the third which procured for the British Rhythmic Gymnastic team selection for the Games. Graham Mew, the arbitrator, found the selection criteria to be 'repetitive, using inconsistent language and having a certain cut and paste appearance' and, key to

---

[77] The Games' organising committee.

[78] Later Igor's successor in the senior post.

[79] He later changed citizenship to compete for Moldova. Many years on I was a CAS panellist in an intermittent dispute between Moldova's taekwondo federation and its national Olympic committee. I do not know if Mr Cook thought that he had jumped out of the frying pan into the fire.

his ruling, misapplied to the team. What on its face appeared to be a dispute of marginal significance in a minor sport achieved its salience because one member of the team came from Gibraltar, its only potential Olympian, and the interest that the territory took in the team fate resulted in my meeting with its Prime Minister in Gibraltar House.[80]

CAS's main work takes place outside these quadrennial occasions. It now decides 600 cases a year arising from a variety of sports, some better known than others (Wushu? American sambo?) and across the spectrum of issues from commercial to disciplinary, from elections to athletic sporting office to sexual shenanigans in Afghan football.

A first tranche involves anti-doping rule violations (ADRVs as they are known in the trade) rarely admitted. I ruefully observed in an award in a sentence which I and others regularly repeated 'The currency of such denial is devalued by the fact that it is the common coin of the guilty as well as of the innocent'.[81] The Scottish cycling star David Millar in an appeal designed to procure his reinstatement in the Tour de France told the Panel 'There is no one who can compete at the top of our spot without taking drugs'. David who, like Dwain later, 'fessed up', became a prominent anti-drugs campaigner on the side of the angels and was on the platform with me at a seminar organised by the British Association of Sport and Law (BASL). He remembered his devastating indictment, but not that I had been on the Panel which heard it first.

A second tranche concerned the other major scourge of modern sport – corruption. I presided over the first case in which UEFA charged a referee with taking bribes to assist a match-fixing scam in the interests of a gambling syndicate. I wrote 'Match officials are an obvious target for those who wish to make illicit profit through gambling on match results. They must be reinforced in their resistance to such criminal approaches'.[82] I was later told that had the case not been found proved Michel Platini, then President of UEFA, would have thrown in the towel on the whole corruption issue.

The perception of possible corruption is almost as worrying as its actual occurrence. In 2011 I was sitting in the Daegu stadium in the company of Sir Craig Reedie, a Vice President of the International Olympic Committee and WADA's chairman, eagerly anticipating the final of the men's 100 metres, the blue riband event, from which Usain Bolt was disqualified for a false start. Immediately after this dramatic incident Craig turned to me and said 'Michael, I would be very interested tomorrow to see the trends in the Asian betting markets'. There is not the slightest evidence that Mr Bolt's false start was deliberate or designed to assist a sophisticated gambling conspiracy. It was most likely an unfortunate error by an over-enthusiastic athlete determined to give not the slightest advantage to his competitors. But, that so worldly-wise and experienced a sports administrator as

---

[80] The grateful girls gave me a signed photograph of the whole team.
[81] 98/148 para 40
[82] 2010/A/1272.

Sir Craig could even suggest that the false start might be other than accidental shows how deep run the concerns about whether sports fans are being constantly deceived by what they see on track, pitch, road or across country, in stadium, velodrome or pool.

A third tranche relates to compensation to be paid by one football club to another for player transfers, player training or breach of a player's contract in jumping club.

A fourth tranche springs from internal governance issues, often, if not always, arising from the risks inherent (in my view) of the absence of time limits for the head honcho, whether Chair, President or CEO, and the development in some cases of authoritarian tendencies when the leader has the ability to purchase votes by the judicious deployment of the federation's funds, benefitting from the concept of one member, one vote which gives disproportionate weight to the vote of the smallest.

Some cases which have come before a panel on which I served reflect, in fact if not in form, historic political disputes concealed beneath a carapace of construction of the sport governing bodies' rules. I instance three examples.

Fiji was denied entry to the Delhi Commonwealth Games when it had been suspended from the Commonwealth as a result of the refusal of its military rulers to commit to democratic elections. We held that there was no discrimination; any Commonwealth country which abrogated democracy would be treated the same way.[83]

A Taiwanese female taekwondo competitor was disqualified from the first round of the Asian Games, by an official from the People's Republic of China, for allegedly wearing improper clothing. It was widely reported that the Taiwanese government was at risk of falling, so high did emotions run. Mercifully, shortly before the hearing before us the athlete withdrew her complaint.

A footballer with dual British and Irish nationality was controversially allowed to play for the Irish Republic although he had already played for a Northern Ireland junior team. In our award[84] we noted that we were only concerned with the application of the relevant FIFA rules to the facts, 'not with any wider implications which others might perceive to flow from our ruling in the context of football or otherwise'.

And yet others without any such political dimension trigger equally strong emotions. On the eve of the 2018 FIFA World Cup I chaired a panel which had to rule on the appropriate period of ineligibility for the Peruvian star striker and skipper Paolo Guerrero, guilty of an ADRV. Albeit accepting his case that his ingestion was inadvertent – he had imbibed a traditional local tea which contained cocaine – we held that his degree of fault was such that he would have to sit out the Cup.[85] Cue a national protest, the President of Peru himself publicly describing our decision as an injustice, and the Peruvian equivalent of *The Sun* calling us, loosely

---

[83] 2010/A/2039.
[84] 2010/A/2071.
[85] 2018/A/5546.

interpreted but grammatically dubious, 'Bastards of shit'. The dispute played out in this way. Pending an appeal the SFT stayed our decision as a holding measure. Mr Guerrero played in the World Cup. Neither he nor the Peruvian team had any success. When the SFT decided the substantive appeal it upheld our verdict. Netflix have now made a film of Mr Guerrero's travails. I never received a call from Brad Pitt's agent asking if he could play me.

Some cases raised issues of general law. In *Mecca-Medina and Madjen v FINA* two long-distance swimmers claimed that the steroid found in their urine was the result of eating a Brazilian delicacy, Sarapatel, a stew made of boars' testicles. We found no evidence that they had even eaten the stew.[86] Nonetheless, the case proceeded to the ECJ which ruled controversially that in principle even anti-doping rules could engage EU competition law.[87] (In one of the most celebrated of common law cases *Donoghue v Stevenson*, the modern law of negligence was similarly established on assumed facts – in that instance that there was a snail in the plaintiff's ginger beer bottle.)

Other cases have involved the development of a free-standing *lex sportiva* or (for classical purists) *ludica*, said by a CAS panel to consist of 'general principles of law drawn from a comparative or common denominator reading of various domestic legal systems and, in particular, the prohibition of arbitrary or unreasonable rules and measures' – in echo of the old lex mercatoria fashioned for trade disputes. In that case I was the advocate unsuccessfully seeking to persuade the panel that it was lawful for someone to own two football clubs both participating in the same European competition.[88] But it provided a potential tool for decision making when I graduated to the rank of arbitrator.

Most CAS hearings take place within a day, even if a day for that purpose may last 12 hours. In civilian jurisdictions more attention is paid to the written record than to oral evidence and far less importance than at common law is attached to cross-examination as a means of ascertaining the truth. But sometimes even an elongated day is not enough. In 2014 the CAS Secretary-General telephoned to ask me whether I would be prepared to fly to Australia and chair a Panel for a week's hearing. The issue was whether members of the Essendon Australian rules football team had been fuelled by a prohibited substance, Thymosin beta 4, during the whole of the 2012 season. An AFL Tribunal hearing in the 2014/15 offseason acquitted the players. That decision was appealed by WADA to CAS. Knowing nothing about the sport in question I asked an Australian colleague why the case was so important. He invited me to consider a hypothetical situation in which the same allegation had been made against Chelsea or Manchester United. Point taken.

Essendon was based in Melbourne; so the hearing had to take place in Sydney. One of my Panel was Jim Spigelman, only recently denied the Chief Justiceship

---

[86] 2000/A/270.
[87] [2006] ECR 1-699.
[88] 98/200 Digest of CAS Awards II p 38 at p 44.

of Australia for which he had been a deserved favourite. We returned a guilty verdict which was unsuccessfully appealed in the SFT.[89] The 34 players were suspended for two years, affecting 17 still-active AFL players who missed the 2016 season as a result of the findings. Our decision provoked endless discussion, much of it critical, in the Australian media and twittersphere as well as questions in Parliament. The legislature itself was lobbied by one Bruce French who claimed to have spent 10,500 hours researching the case, calling it with antipodean understatement 'The greatest injustice and acts of bastardry in Australian sporting history'. Even in 2020 I received a vituperative letter suggesting that so perverse a decision could only be the result of corruption of the Panel.

It used to be the case that CAS arbitrators could also be advocates before CAS, but as the precept that justice must not only be done but be seen to be done came to be ever more strictly applied to dispute resolution, CAS changed the rule. I opted to remain an arbitrator (to the disappointment of my senior clerk and bank manager). The lower (and how) fees were trumped by the interest of being able to work with lawyers, initially colleagues, now friends, from so many different jurisdictions and learning the different roads to the common destination of justice.

I had several years before the rule change been instructed by the Gibraltar Football Association in connection with their simultaneous applications to become members of both UEFA and FIFA, and after no less than three separate hearings spread over eight years succeeded in the first of that two-pronged initiative.[90] I had to give up my brief for the second, and act as a surreptitious back seat driver.

CAS does not allow full dissenting judgments. More discreetly, where there has been such dissent, awards are described succinctly as majority judgments. They are extremely rare and I have only twice found myself unable to concur with my colleagues. In one early case, in which members of the Chinese swimming team attending the world championships in Perth were found guilty of ADRVs,[91] the arbitrator from the PRC intervened so frequently on the Chinese side that the hearing had to be briefly adjourned so that he could be reminded that an arbitrator is not meant to be an advocate. When the verdict went against the Chinese he provided a statement to the SFT in support of the appeal accusing me and my other colleague, an eminent lawyer and senior member of the IOC, of racial bias. The SFT dismissed the appeal. The Chinese arbitrator's term was not renewed. This was an all but unique example, in my experience, of an arbitrator not acting impartially.

I was party during almost quarter of a century[92] to between 150–200 decisions and was one of a fortunate inner circle recurrently selected as a panel President.[93]

---

[89] 2015/A/4059.

[90] Starting with 2002/O/410.

[91] 98/208.

[92] A survey of published awards in Lindholm 'The Court of Arbitration for Sport and its Jurisprudence' ranks me sixth of all serving CAS arbitrators in quantitative terms.

[93] The other arbitrators are nominated by the parties, and have a right of veto over the putative President selected by a member of ICAS, CAS's governing body.

I have even survived all but two of the challenges now in double figures to my sitting on grounds of apparent (not actual) lack of impartiality. One challenge[94] which succeeded was brought against me by Sepp Blatter – not perhaps my strongest claim to merit as a dispenser of justice (or maybe, on second thoughts, it is). Curiously I was not only part of a Panel which dismissed appeals by Jerome Valcke,[95] Mr Blatter's right-hand man as FIFA's General Secretary, but had been asked in advance by his lawyers whether I would accept his nomination. As Mr Valcke left the hearing he was promptly arrested by the Swiss police; but for me yet more memorable was his answer to a question posed to him about how he could justify the lavish expenses he drew from FIFA funds: 'Mr Beloff you have to understand, there are two worlds. There is the real world and there is the FIFA world'. That may explain, if it does not excuse, the irregularities which occurred under FIFA's ancien regime.[96]

I voluntarily recused myself from the Panel which eventually found the Chinese swimmer, Sun Yang, the PRC's pre-eminent sporting star, guilty of an ADRV after facing a second challenge on all but the same grounds to the first which had been dismissed. For me to have held fast risked an unacceptable delay in the proceedings which had to be concluded before what were then the 2020 Tokyo Olympics.[97]

It is never clear to me why such challenges on grounds of apparent bias, a tedious but ever more prevalent feature of modern arbitration, are made, in the absence of concern about actual bias. I suspect that some arbitrators are perceived as more friendly to athletes, others more friendly to regulatory bodies. On the basis of such perception, it is thought that a successful challenge may lead to the revised constitution of more sympathetic tribunal. But the Sun Yang decision in my favour by the ICAS challenge commission at least emphasised that the mere fact that an arbitrator may have regularly decided in favour of the party which nominated him is no proof at all of bias, especially if in those decisions the arbitrator has been party to a unanimous or majority decision, the more so if he has occasionally ruled against the party which appointed him.

In 2020 I was appointed as Chair of a panel, in an ad hoc arbitration between Newcastle United and the Premier League arising out of the latter's refusal to approve a takeover of the Club by a Saudi entity, by Lord Neuberger and

---

[94] The other was when I had failed to notice that Tom Coates, a talented junior Blackstone colleague, was part of the Appellant's team.

[95] 2017/A/4003.

[96] I was one of a trio of lawyers asked to advise the Prime Minister of Trinidad and Tobago whether Jack Warner, the controversial politician, could remain a Cabinet Minister while serving as Vice President of FIFA. All three, unaware of the others' involvement, as was widely reported in the local press, advised that there was no constitutional objection to his dual role. Given his subsequent – not to speak of his earlier – history it may be thought that neither body profited by his involvement.

[97] The case was ill fated. After handing down a guilty verdict the President of the Panel was found by the SFT to have been tainted by apparent bias when some remarks of his, said to show an anti-Chinese bias, were unearthed from the twittersphere. Eventually Sun Yang was barred from the postponed games by an entirely fresh Panel.

Lord Dyson, as dynamic and well qualified a legal duo as could be imagined. My appointment was challenged (not, I stress superfluously, because of their identity) in what the *Newcastle Chronicle* loosely characterised as a *mano a mano* between Mike Ashley, the Club's owner, and Mike Beloff. The challenge failed with the peculiar consequence that my last ever appearance in a law report is one where I am defendant.[98]

Sun Yang's case was the first ever broadcast in the wake of the famous Pechstein decision which had ruled that Article 6 of the ECHR presumptively required an open hearing at the request of the Appellant in disciplinary cases so my recusal was at the expense of my reputation (or maybe not). I had by coincidence been party to the first ever CAS hearing made open to the public, because of the consent of both parties – that of Michelle de Bruin,[99] the much medalled (at Atlanta) Irish swimmer who, in a later out-of-competition test, we found to have ingeniously, some might say wastefully too, adulterated her urine sample with Irish whisky. The public, however, unlike in the Sun Yang case chose not to exploit their opportunity to witness the proceedings.

I was next appointed Chairman of the ICC CCC, by Lord MacLaurin of Tesco fame, succeeding Lord Griffiths, the only man to have been President of the MCC, President of the Royal and Ancient, and a Law Lord, whose boots I was therefore unable to fill on at least three counts. I was briefed by Lord Condon, formerly of the Met and the executive arm of the CCC. Corruption threatens cricket much as drugs threaten track and field[100] and is the main, but not the only issue for the CCC.

Almost at once in 2001 I had to chair an inquiry into the decision of Mike Denness, ex England skipper. As Match Referee in a test match between India and South Africa he had charged six Indian players with offences against the ICC Code of Conduct, which attracted accusations of racism and put at risk not only the remainder of that series but the forthcoming Indian tour to England. In order to resolve the controversy a compromise was reached and our mandate was limited to consideration of whether Denness had followed the proper and fair procedures. Denness, however, had to undergo unexpected heart surgery; the heat went out of the affair and the Indians decided not to press on with it on humanitarian grounds.[101] A few years later I met one of my co-adjudicators, the former fast

[98] 2021 EWHC 3239 Comm. The Chronicle in its issue of 22 June 2021 did its own research into my pedigree and elicited a comment from Albie Sachs that I was 'top of the game … in the field of sports law'; from Jeff Benz, a CAS colleague and former ice dance champion that 'I was widely regarded to be the Dean of the International Sports law bar'; and from Marie Demetriou QC, 'He just knows what fairness requires and he is very principled in that way'. Whether true or false, these dicta were at least unsolicited. A controversial settlement relieved us of a duty to make an award.

[99] 98/211. Ms de Bruin has since become a successful lawyer.

[100] Mainly east of Suez. Again I had some part in feminising what was, when I joined it, an all-male body. It was in this forum that I encountered a single but serious challenge to my role by an arbitrator who claimed that I had tried to muzzle him, urged my removal from the Chair and proposed himself as my successor. The ICC declined to take his advice.

[101] *Sticky Wicket* by Malcolm Speed, Ch 10 esp p 144.

bowler Wes Hall,[102] at a dinner in the Long Room at Lord's. 'You seem smaller than I remember you in the 60s', I observed. 'That's what they all say', he replied.

By chance I was a guest in the ICC box at Lord's in a test match between England and Pakistan on the day after news broke of the biggest scandal in cricketing history – involving three Pakistani players, Messrs Butt, Asif and Amir. They had agreed at the instigation of their agent that three no balls should be bowled at selected times during an innings (so called spot fixing) in aid of an apparent betting coup.[103] Unfortunately for them the agent himself had been deceived by an undercover journalist, the so-called Fake Sheikh with a track record of beguiling his unwitting targets into self-incrimination, captured on tape or video or, on this occasion, on both, until his career was terminated in a case in which he actually fabricated the evidence.

The first ball of the day prompted – inevitably – a cry of 'no ball' from someone in the stands who must have fancied himself, with little justification, as a wit. For me, given my role, the matter was far more serious. The ICC duly brought charges against all three players for breaches of the Code by which they, though not the agent, were bound.

A preliminary hearing was held before me in Dubai where counsel for the players sought to have the proceedings struck out on the basis that there was insufficient evidence in respect of the charges to justify a trial. I was unpersuaded and directed that there should be a full hearing.

A challenge was then made to my involvement in the full hearing. It was argued that in directing that the case should go ahead I had forfeited any claim to be perceived as impartial. I was unpersuaded of this too. It would in arbitration as in litigation put huge obstacles in the path of the effective administration of justice if someone who had made a ruling that expressly or impliedly accepted that a charge or claim was fit to be heard (but without any forceful indication as to his or her view of the likely outcome of such hearing) should play no further part in it.

My next task was to select two fellow arbitrators out of a pool of 12. One choice was of Albie Sachs.[104] His impeccable reputation for fairness and high international profile would, I reasoned, give enhanced credibility to our verdict, whatever it was. My other choice was of Sharad Rao, a former Director of Public Prosecutions in Kenya, and a senior member of CAS.

The hearing itself took place over nine days in Qatar. (Mr Asif had a conviction for drug use, and as a result, would not under its immigration law be admitted to Dubai, the usual seat of ICC arbitration.) Serendipitously the newly formed Commercial Court of Qatar had a courtroom which had not yet been used and the Court's secretary allowed our Tribunal to give it a test run. The case was prosecuted

---

[102] The Reverend and a Jamaican MP, also knighted.

[103] Nick Greenslade, *The Thin White Line: The Inside Story of Cricket's Greatest Scandal* (Greenslade, 2020) pp 153–70 where I'm described as 'one of the most esteemed lawyers in London … a popular figure at the Bar as well liked socially as he is regarded professionally'.

[104] Celebrated as an anti-apartheid activist and as one of the first judges of the South African constitutional court set up during the Presidency of Nelson Mandela.

by Jonathan Taylor[105] of the firm of Bird and Bird; the players were represented by counsel, one from Lahore, and two from England, Ali Bajwa[106] and Alex Cameron QC, the brother of the then Prime Minister.

One matter on which we had to take a decision was whether at lunch to segregate ourselves from the others (as always happens in Court proceedings) or whether to share lunch in the same room (as often happens in Arbitration proceedings). We decided that we would prefer the less formal course and spent the mid-day breaks in conversation with counsel and players, not, of course, on matters to do with the case itself, but, especially with the players, about tennis. Later that summer when I was interviewed in the usual slot in Test Match Special in the space station like media room at the opposite end to the pavilion at Lord's by Jonathan Agnew ('Jonners') he expressed surprise. But informality is the hallmark of arbitration even if the day is unlikely ever to come when judges (or juries) lunch with the persons in the dock. After lunch the Tribunal did return to its own break-out room to enable Albie to take a swift cat nap.

The hearing itself proceeded smoothly enough until, on the eve of the last day, it was announced that the Attorney-General had authorised the institution of proceedings for corruption in the English criminal courts – why exactly then must be a matter for speculation. Inevitably we were invited to adjourn the hearing and suspend the delivery of any verdict until after the conclusion of the criminal proceedings, so as to avoid any prejudice to the players' defence against the criminal charges. A similar submission had been made to me in Qatar when the making of such charges was merely a possibility. Now it was a reality. Nonetheless we reached the same conclusion – the show must go on. We reasoned that the world of cricket had its own interest in the enforcement of its own rules. In any event we doubted that any jury, properly directed by a judge to consider only the evidence before it, would be influenced by knowledge that our Tribunal, many months before in a faraway place of which they knew little, had reached a verdict adverse to any of the players on the evidence which was unlikely to be identical to that before them. In that we were proved right.

On the last day itself during final submissions I asked the Pakistani advocate for Amir whether he could provide us with any explanation as to how the agent was able to tell the Fake Sheikh precisely when all three no balls would be bowled unless he had inside information. A statistician had given evidence that the odds against this being pure coincidence were of the order of several thousand to one. 'That, Members of the Tribunal' replied the advocate with consummate charm 'is the issue with which all of us in this room have been wrestling for the last nine days' and without any further elaboration moved smoothly on. Charm is an enviable quality for an advocate but by itself it is sometimes not enough. We decided that the charges were made out and imposed bans of 10 years upon Messr Butt and

---

[105] QC and renowned sports lawyer, regularly instructed by many SGBs.
[106] QC.

Asif, and five years upon Mr Amir, for whom, led astray as we thought by elders who should have known better, we had considerable sympathy.[107] (Incidentally although this played no part in our reasoning, he missed the chance of a hat trick at Lord's by his second no ball.)

But if the hearing itself had run smoothly, the same could not be said of its aftermath. Albie needed to catch a flight to India to collect another honorary degree; and I, as Chairman, had to fine tune the writing of the reasons for the judgment we had all reached (the basic facts of which I had provisionally pre-drafted on an ancient typewriter left in my suite in our ultra-modern hotel as a kind of display antique rather than an operational machine) and whose result we had announced, so I remained in the court for some hours to proofread and correct the text.

In the event it passed muster with my colleagues, albeit Albie, who had proposed that we gave an incentive to the players to accelerate the end of their period of ineligibility by imposing a condition that they act, under a programme to be devised by the Pakistani cricket authority, as proselytisers for a clean sport, objected to my soundbite explanation, 'Sinners who repent are often the best educators'. I had in fact in my original draft used the word 'crusaders' (potentially highly offensive to the Muslim players) in place of educators. By some providential subconscious instinct I had removed it in time.

The penalties imposed did not pass muster with some members of the media who had remained in the vicinity of the court building. I was ambushed as I tried to get into the car that the ICC had provided for me, and had questions hurled at me as to why the Tribunal hadn't imposed life bans for all the players. This was a criticism made by several others in the press later, including Freddie Flintoff, perhaps more distinguished as a cricketing all-rounder than as a jurist – though I received a congratulatory note from Tariq Ali.

When I arrived back at the hotel, I found the English advocates together enjoying a convivial drink in the bar. They invited me to join them for dinner. I could see no objection. The case was over; the verdict delivered; there was no possibility of influence being wrongly exerted; and in any event both sides' representatives were present. Such a benign view was not taken by some journalists, staying in the same hotel, who thought they spotted a story with some legs given the involvement of the PM's brother. Wielding the heavy artillery which passes as the modern camera, they erupted into the dining room, and started interrogating us as to the propriety of our behaviour (they used somewhat different phrases), while snapping away. It took all the skills of the ICC media manager to dissuade them (or their editors) from recording this incident. The case itself occupied several pages in *Wisden*, an annual in which I had never appeared before and in which I am unlikely, to put it at its lowest, ever to appear again.

---

[107] The decision of 5 February 2011 can be found, suitably redacted, on the ICC website. It contains, unusually for an award, photographs of the no balls. The same website can be sourced for all the other decisions in which I was involved.

Over a year later the three players appeared in the dock at Southwark Crown Court and were duly convicted. Two then appealed to a Court presided over by the then Chief Justice Lord Judge, a cricket enthusiast. He dismissed the appeals and in the course of his judgment mentioned our award as part of the history of the case.[108] In 2016 Mr Amir returned to the international arena but decided to retire from it when he was only 28.[109]

As for the three arbitrators, we were reunited in a quite different context when Sharad was appointed by the Kenyan government as Chair of the Judges and Magistrates Vetting Board to vet serving judges for integrity and brought Albie in to assist him. Unsurprisingly potential victims of a cull went to court to claim that the whole enterprise was unconstitutional and a threat to the independence of the judiciary. The response was that the new Constitution contained an exclusion clause which ruled out any such challenge – the issue on which I was asked to advise. The Attorney General, Judicial Service Commission and Law Society of Kenya were all of the view that allowing sacked judges to challenge the board's decision would itself be unconstitutional. The challenge ultimately failed.

Tampered balls made a change from no balls. In 2016 the South African captain Francois Du Plessis was charged with altering the condition of the match ball, in a Test Match against Australia, with saliva mixed with the residue of a mint sweet. I found him guilty but added by way of postscript

> No doubt there are two possible views on this issue as to where the line should be drawn. Some might say that since shining with natural substances is permissible, there is no reason to prohibit shining with artificial substances. (In the same way that some argue that since good food is performance enhancing, there is no reason – health considerations apart – to prohibit performance enhancing drugs.) But where the line is drawn and what conduct is or is not considered to be offensive to the sport of cricket is a matter for the custodians of the game (the MCC and ICC) and the rule-makers. It is emphatically not a matter for the Commissioner, or anyone else, on or off pitch, who have to apply the rules as they stand.

In 2018 the Sri Lankan captain Dinesh Chandimal committed a similar offence using saliva mixed with either a Strepsil (said to be for a sore throat) or an almond (said to be for energy). The main issue was as to the penalty for his team who, in solidarity with their skipper, quit the pitch for several hours.

Other disciplinary matters on which I had to adjudicate included the temporary decommissioning of a designated test match pitch at Kotla in India on health and safety grounds[110] and a governance dispute in USA Cricket (a lesser known cricketing jurisdiction) which pitched those whose origins were from the Caribbean

---

[108] [2012] 2 Cr App R(S)17.

[109] This was not the only corruption case with which I had to deal. With Richie Benaud, the former Australian Captain and esteemed commentator, we exercised leniency in the case of a senior Indian player who wanted to eke out his remaining years as a coach.

[110] Not a sanction meted out either in respect of the new Wembley or the London Olympic stadium in both of whose constructions I was qua lawyer involved and raised issues of contract, not discipline.

against those whose origins were from Asia. In the wake of my ruling a new body was set up to administer the sport across the pond. USA Cricket's chief executive has said 'It is widely recognized at the ICC and around the world of cricket that the single biggest non traditional cricket market that could be developed in the short to medium terms is in the USA'.[111] As Michael Caine might have put it, 'I bet you didn't know that'.

But my role extended beyond discipline to dispute resolution. In 2018 after several years of fruitless negotiation and mediation, the Pakistan Cricket Board (PCB) brought a multi-million dollar claim for damages against the Indian equivalent (BCCI) for alleged breach of a contract to play a series in Pakistan. I with my colleagues Justice Annabelle Bennett from Australia and Jan Paulsson, the doyen of international commercial arbitrators and the Vizier of the Emir of Bahrain, dismissed the claim. In a coda[112] we expressed the pious hope that political tensions would not forever bedevil the possibility of a resumption of cricketing rivalry between these two nations, so prominent in the history of the game.

I was not disqualified from acting as an advocate for the ICC[113] and was instructed when Darrell Hair, the experienced Australian umpire, brought a claim against the ICC for racial discrimination after he was stood down from umpiring in Test Matches after the controversy caused by his award of a Match to England when a Pakistan team had walked off the field in protest against his imposition of a penalty of five runs for ball tampering. Hair wrote that the ICC 'would surely enlist the best lawyers to prepare their case and it would be gloves off from the start. I expected to be under attack and I was not disappointed'.[114] I cross-examined Mr Hair, a robust personality, 'brutally',[115] according to Mike Atherton[116] (which I choose to treat as a compliment), accusing him of being a blackmailer and a mudslinger and putting to him that he had 'run himself out'.

A decision had been taken that in order to ensure that the claim failed it would be necessary for all Council members who had participated in Hair's demotion to give evidence. Suffice it to say that, placed in an unfamiliar setting, not all of them scored freely off the bowling of Robert Griffiths QC, an MCC council member, so it was something of a relief as well as a surprise when after seven days Mr Hair withdrew his claim against a promise to review his position after a 'rehabilitation programme', which sounded more Orwellian than it was. After leaving Victory House, the central London Employment Tribunal, the ICC team celebrated with an excellent lunch at the Connaught. It was in the eyes of some unclear

---

[111] *The Sunday Times* 3 January 2021 p 17.

[112] One of India's witnesses was a previous Foreign Minister and a Trinity alumnus but that played no part in our ruling.

[113] Though I accepted that I should not act against it.

[114] Darell Hair, *In the Best Interest of the Game* (Hair, 2012) p 179.

[115] Mike Atherton, *Glorious Summers and Discontents* (Atherton, 2011) p 166–72. For another perspective see also Speed, Chapter 19, p 279, 'The ICC was represented by the brilliant ebullient Michael Beloff, Hair by the dogged Robert Griffiths QC'.

[116] Former England cricket captain and award winning sports journalist.

to whom the forensic laurels of victory should be awarded and it was the dogged Robert who was named *Times* Lawyer of the week.

I was also free to provide advice to the ICC, once in conjunction with Judge Pathak, about the eligibility rules for its Chairman and once solo as to whether the ICC could be restructured so as to give enhanced influence to the Big Three, India, Australia and England, to reflect their financial clout – a controversial and short lived revision which sparked a critical documentary *Death of a Gentleman*.

In 2014 I was appointed first Chairman of the newly created IAAF Ethics Commission, renamed Board, by the then President, Lamine Diack, whom I had encountered on many occasions as an IAAF guest at the World Championships and who offered me the post over lunch in Monte Carlo. He happily laboured under the misconception that I had once represented the Federation in a challenge brought by the South African governing body of track and field to resume its membership, earlier removed from it as a by-product of apartheid. I had in fact represented the South African body. Mr Diack himself was, during the remainder of his time in post, ostensibly very supportive of the Board's activities. He and his son, Papa Massata Diack (PMD),[117] were subsequently convicted in France of various criminal charges associated with his role, which he had to quit in disgrace.

The Board was initially constituted by eight members, all from different regions, all well equipped to perform its functions.[118] Unfortunately, it was also an all-male body – a defect which I had remedied as soon as possible. The rules which the Board inherited were not entirely fit for purpose and on their face created more elaborate hurdles in the path of a prosecution than were warranted by considerations of fairness. Most problematic of all were the obligations of confidentiality which prohibited the Board from disclosing any aspect of its activities, even to the IAAF, unless and until a defendant, subject to its jurisdiction, was found guilty of charges. Inevitably this meant that the media accused the Board of being immobile even when it was paddling away furiously below the surface. The first major case highlighted the problems.

Dave Bedford telephoned me in chambers and told me to expect a submission from a Sean Wallis-Jones alleging what was in effect a conspiracy involving Valentin Balachnikev, President of the All Russia Athletic Federation (ARAF), and the IAAF Treasurer, Alexei Melnikov, former ARAF coach for long-distance runners, Gabriel Dollé, Director of the IAAF anti-doping department, and PMD. An investigation was carried out at my behest by Sir Anthony Hooper.[119] It emerged that the central issue in this case was whether each of the Defendants

---

[117] With whom I once shared a taxi from the airport in Daegu to the IAAF Hotel, not a matter which I would have felt obliged to disclose when his case came before the Board had I even then remembered it.

[118] It had a series of excellent legal secretaries all appointed by me from Blackstone, Tristan Jones, Tom Mountford, Jana Sadler-Foster, Natasha Simonsen.

[119] A retired judge of the Court of Appeal in England and Wales and a criminal law specialist.

was in breach of various provisions of the IAAF's Code of Ethics (the 'Code') by their involvement in the suppression of findings of ADRVs by the female Russian marathon runner, Lilya Shobukhova ('LS'), and the exaction of monies as the price to pay for enabling her, though a proven doper, still to compete. This case was in point of fact and timing the first which cast light on the problems, now widely recognised, of Russia's pervasive non-compliance with anti-doping regulations. It was less publicised than the comprehensive reports authored by Dick Pound and Richard McLaren[120] who dealt with the LS episode as part of a wider picture – a fresco compared with the Board's miniature. But because of the rules then in force what the Board was doing had to be kept in the shadows.

One part of the factual jigsaw was a memorandum of a meeting that Craig Reedie had in Moscow with senior Russian officials including the Deputy Prime Minister. I bumped into Craig in the IAAF hotel at the Beijing World Championships where we conducted a peculiar dialogue in which Craig intimated to me that he had information at his disposal which might assist the Board in its inquiries, whose very existence I was inhibited from confirming. Later when I was in Monte Carlo for the Board's annual meeting, I was advised by a contact within the anti-doping department that there was someone who also had information of potential relevance and wished to see me. This turned out to be none other than Paula Radcliffe,[121] who came surreptitiously up to my hotel bedroom. In the end, the finding of the Board's Panel, which I chaired, that the charges were made out was upheld by the CAS[122] and I was able to procure a rule change which enabled the Board in future to waive confidentiality if such waiver was required to assist in the better performance of its disciplinary functions.

The Board encountered other hazards. The vice-chair, Carlos Nuzman, was himself indicted for corruption in connection with Rio's successful Olympic bid which he had masterminded. Several members of the IAAF Council fell foul of the adjudications of the Board, and its successor the IAAF Disciplinary Tribunal, as did Nick Davies, the chief of staff of Seb Coe, Diack's successor.

At the time of Seb Coe's great rivalry with Steve Ovett, which divided track fans the length and breadth of the country, I was in the cavalier Ovett camp. It was odd that whereas Seb became a friend, I only encountered Steve on a single occasion. Making a pilgrimage to Preston Park in Brighton (where the Council had unveiled a statue to him more Turner prize than Michelangelo) in order to take a photograph of this objet d'art, I saw two runners approaching. It was Steve and his training companion who, spotting what I was doing, shouted 'It's the real thing'. In my hurry to record on film man and monument in juxtaposition I omitted to remove my finger from the camera lens. The moment will nonetheless remain in my memory.

---

[120] Two good friends, the former a prominent IOC member, the latter a long-serving CAS arbitrator.

[121] Long-distance runner and multiple medallist at various international games and for many years holder of the women's world record for the marathon.

[122] PMD from his safe haven in Senegal accused the Panel as being part of an Anglo conspiracy.

Years later, at a lunch at Radley College where I had been giving a talk to the sixth form, one of the masters launched on a tale of how in his youth he had raced against Ovett. His story had just reached the end of the third lap when I interrupted to ask the boys how many had heard of Steve; and answer came there none. How swiftly time erases the traces of even sporting legends.

But I digress. (Indeed you do – Ed). To return to my theme, the Board's greatest challenge came when the LS affair reared its head again. It brought into the spotlight Seb Coe himself who was always scrupulous in his dealings with and support for the Board.[123]

Coe had told the Digital Culture Media and Sport Committee, who were enquiring into doping in sport, that he had been unaware of 'specific allegations' related to the Russian doping scandal prior to it becoming public. However, Bedford testified in front of the same committee that he had emailed Coe about the LS's affair. Coe's response was that he had not read the Bedford email but had forwarded it to me as being on its face a matter within the independent Board's remit. The Committee wrote in its report: 'It stretches credibility to believe that he was not aware ... of the main allegations that the ethics commission had been asked to investigate'. It added that it was 'certainly disappointing that Lord Coe did not take the opportunity, given to him by David Bedford, to make sure he was fully informed of the serious issues at stake in the Shobukhova case and their wider implications'.

The Board then opened an investigation to determine whether Coe had intentionally misled Parliament. I appointed Sir David Calvert-Smith, former DPP and High Court judge (and no mean athlete himself at Eton), to carry it out, but since it appeared that I might myself be a witness in any proceedings, I abstained from any further involvement in the matter. Sir David concluded 'there is insufficient evidence to proceed to lay disciplinary charges'. His report was next reviewed and validated by two members of the Board, Thomas Murray, a scholar of ethics, and Kate O'Regan, my Vice Chair, and a former member of the South African Constitutional Court. The Board's own report concluded: 'Lord Coe's evidence is that his PA forwarded the email with its attachments to the Chairperson of the Ethics Board and that he (Lord Coe) did not read the attachments. The investigation did not find any evidence inconsistent with that position'. As to the Dave/Seb disagreement it best calls to mind what the Royal Household said in its Official statement about Meghan Markle's allegations of racism in her Oprah Winfrey interview 'Some recollections can vary'.

Despite strenuous efforts by one journalist to identify that the outcome demonstrated some lack of independence in the Board, to the contrary I regard the episode as reinforcing what I said in my inaugural speech to the IAAF Congress,

---

[123] Seb had also been the subject of a ruling about whether his commercial activities were compatible with his Presidency of the Federation. Colin Moynihan proposed in a debate in the House of Lords on 19 November 2019 that my advice on the matter should be placed in the House of Lords library. I do not know if it in fact enjoyed such an august destination.

that it would carry out its functions, echoing the judicial oath 'without fear or favour'. Because, absent any other source of income, the Board was funded by the IAAF,[124] it could never be seen to be wholly independent;[125] it was, not in my experience, ever inhibited from taking action for that reason.

A controversial issue which came before the Board was whether the unexpected success of Doha in being selected to host the 2019 World Athletics Championships resulted from more than the IAAF's ambition to spread the gospel of track and field into pastures new. Ed Warner reported to us[126] rumours of brown envelopes being handed out to voters, but 'the matter was shelved pending the emergence of any corroborating evidence'.[127]

As part of his reform package Seb created two new institutions: an Athletics Integrity Unit (which investigated and prosecuted) and a Disciplinary Tribunal (which decided on whether charges were or were not made out). All members of the Board bar one continued to serve on the Tribunal with 30 plus reinforcements recruited on a global basis. As its first Chair I chose the Panels of three for particular cases, and, like Lord Denning when Master of the Rolls, appointed myself chair in the most interesting ones. The exercise was in fact dispiriting as the evidence compelled the finding of ADRVs by a series of Olympic and World Champions and medallists such as: Asbel Kiprop, Jemima Sumgong, Ruth Jebet and Valentin Bakulin[128] – all of whom I had watched in their moment of sporting triumph.[129]

Although under the rules the primary location for a hearing was in Monte Carlo, in fact all except the last of those cases were heard for convenience in London. In that one exceptional case the doping expert for the IAAF had to participate by Skype from a cruise ship off the Galapagos and my Kenyan colleague on the Panel added a new concept to jurisprudence by pronouncing the defendant '*very* guilty'.

After five years plus of hard pounding and involvement in ethical issues which ranged from electoral malpractice to racism, I declined to put myself forward for a second term on the Tribunal. My successor as Chair was Charles Hollander. But no more than 72 hours before I was due to hand the reins over in Doha, I was roused from my jet-lagged slumbers at midnight to be told that the IAAF was to seek an injunction restraining a candidate from standing in the Council elections, due to take place that same day at 11am for breach of the rules against canvassing. After an interrupted night receiving sundry emails from Sport Resolutions, who administered the Tribunal's operations from London, and document deliveries at

---

[124] This relationship is common to the disciplinary arms of many sports governing bodies – hence one value of the appeal to CAS.

[125] A feature of the ICC CCC and other global sporting bodies.

[126] 'specifically to that doughty commercial silk Michael Beloff QC'. Ed Warner *Sport inc.* p 229.

[127] Ibid.

[128] All decisions can be sourced on the World Athletics website.

[129] Likewise the world women's 400m champion Salwa Eid Naser who was prevented by a CAS panel on which I sat from running in the Tokyo Olympics for failure to be available for three out of competition tests in a single year 2020/CAS/7056 and 7059.

dawn from the IAAF legal team, I granted the injunction at 9am. As envois go this was some envoi.

In my valedictory address to Congress I uttered in my peroration some cautionary words

> While world athletics, like other sports bodies, lacks the powers of public authorities which deal with breaches of the criminal law it has its own distinct interest in policing its own code, which is, for good reason, wider in scope than the law of the land. That is why I have proposed that serious consideration should be given for measures, to protect honest whistleblowers whose disclosures are vital to the gathering of information about breaches of the code but who, as I know, are vulnerable to a variety of pressures which may deter them from acting in what is (objectively) in the interest of the sport.

> In my respectful view, world athletics' reputation would suffer a grievous blow if the time were ever reached when it had to declare itself unwilling or unable to ensure that its code could be enforced or alleged breaches of the code not adjudicated upon because of lack of funds.

> This is, as some of you will know, my valedictory address to Congress. I have been chair of the Ethics Board and of the Disciplinary Tribunal since their creation and for a period of almost six years. I will now pass the baton to someone else.

> It has been for me a huge privilege to have been able to put my professional experience as a lawyer to the service of a sport that I have followed with so much pleasure for more than seven decades.

> I step down with confidence that those who have been selected to serve on the tribunal over the next four years will dedicate themselves with expertise and integrity to seek to ensure that athletics, the queen of sports, has an untarnished crown.

I meant each and every word.

On the domestic front for several years I sat on Panels which handled athletes' appeals against their non-selection for major international games or the refusal of funding so vital to their progress. I had once been invited by Dave Collins, then the British coach, to become a selector myself for the 2008 Olympics – would that I'd had the time to spend my summer trackside! For that Panel's purposes I had to rid myself of the preconceptions of an athletics aficionado and to concentrate on the limited appeal grounds. The Panel was not permitted simply to second guess the experts who made the initial choice and the best we could usually offer were warm words. Sometimes later results showed that the selectors had misjudged; but then hindsight is always a wonderful thing.

My IAAF role brought me into contact with some of the greatest athletes of the century who had become Council members and I took a delight, whether childish or not, in being on first name terms with the likes of the Russian Sergei Bubka,[130] the Cuban Alberto Juantorena,[131] the Pole Irene Szewinska and the

---

[130] Six times World Champion in the pole vault in which he also won Olympic gold and held the world record.

[131] Double gold medallist in the 400m and 800m at the Montreal Olympics.

Algerian Nawab Al Moutawakel,[132] as might a cineaste who could say 'Hi there' to Leonardo, Sylvester, Sharon or Keira and expect a friendly greeting in reply. Not that I was necessarily inhibited by lack of prior acquaintance to fatten my autograph collection. After the annual night of stars hosted by the IAAF in Monte Carlo in 2018 I stumbled upon the female winner, the Ethiopian Ayana, who had smashed the world record for the 10,000m (prior to the advent of the super shoe), crouched outside her room for which she had clearly mislaid the plastic key. To my shame I first solicited by gesture her signature before indicating how she should seek assistance at Reception. Not the sense of priorities of a *preux chevalier*.

In the inaugural proceeding before the UFC Arbitration Panel which I chaired in Malibu the issue was as to the appropriate sanction under the UFC ADP rules for an admitted ADRV by Jon Jones, a mixed martial art (MMA) fighter, described as the best pound-for-pound fighter in the world in multiple publications. Jones's case was that he had taken a Cialis tablet (what he called graphically a 'Dick Pill') but which unbeknown, indeed unknowable, to him was contaminated. Cialis is itself not a prohibited substance but a legitimate erectile dysfunction medication; its purpose, as I said in the award, 'is to enhance sexual not sporting performance'.

I had a degree of apprehension about sitting at a table in close proximity to someone who was probably the most dangerous man in the world at unarmed combat, but for whom millions of dollars were at stake depending on the period of ineligibility imposed. I consoled myself with the thought that he would be unwise to assault an arbitrator when the verdict was still to be delivered. I had a similar fear when in a break during a CAS hearing I encountered Alexander Lovchev, the heavyweight wresting champion, in the confined space of the gentlemen's lavatory in the Chateau de Bethusy.[133] In the event Mr Jones behaved in a becoming manner throughout the proceedings; and candidly bemoaned the fact that on the night in question, to add insult to injury, he had no opportunity to test the efficacy of what he had taken; or, as he put it mournfully, 'I didn't even score'.

Sports Law calls upon many discrete disciplines: contract, administrative, employment and intellectual property law; but it is my contention that we are witnessing the development of a *lex sportiva* drawing on all of them but with its own distinctive elements, peculiar to the sporting context.[134] To promulgate that message I co-authored one of the first books on Sports Law; contributed to the *New Oxford Companion to Law* and still edit the Sweet and Maxwell *International Sports Law Review*.

Such law is informed by one overriding objective – to ensure that competition is fair, and that it is not deformed by corruption, drugs, violence or racism.[135]

---

[132] 400m hurdler and the first woman from Africa to win an Olympic gold medal.

[133] CAS's headquarters.

[134] I gave a lecture to the Max Planck Institute in Hamburg with the title 'Is there a lex sportiva?' at the invitation of the celebrated comparative lawyer Reinhard Zimmerman and touched on the issue again in my Edward Grayson lecture for BASL.

[135] The subject of my High Sheriff's Lecture in 2019, 'Good at Games'.

In the summer of 2004 I was in Athens as a member of the CAS ad hoc panel. Seeking to return to my hotel I found the entrance temporarily blocked. Along with other guests I waited patiently to ascertain the cause of the hold up. After a few moments all was revealed. Tony Blair, then in his political pomp and only a year away from a third successive election victory, strode up at the apex of a flotilla of advisers and security men, on a mission to lobby members of the IOC in support of London's successful bid to stage the quadrennial event in 2012. Catching sight of me among the crowd, he called out 'Michael, what are you doing here?', to which I vaingloriously replied, 'I'm here to try to bring justice to the Games'. That is indeed what CAS seeks to do generally for sport, no longer simply a recreation but the twentieth-largest industry in the world.

The coincidence of my profession and my passion[136] has not only enabled me to travel the world,[137] but to meet with many heroes and heroines of my childhood and (I confess) of my more mature years,[138] both from home and abroad,[139] and although sports law was for most of my career only a fraction of my practice,[140] it has given me more pure delight (as well as free tickets)[141] than the rest of it put together.

---

[136] As I put it in my inaugural address to the IAAF Council in 2014.

[137] In addition to CAS cases in Lausanne and at various Olympic and Commonwealth Games, I have arbitrated for CAS in New York, Los Angeles, Montreal and Malibu; for the IAAF in Monte Carlo and New York; for the ICC in Doha and Dubai and have given talks on sports law in New Orleans, Atlanta, Charlottesville, Amherst, Singapore, Seoul, Xianmen, St Petersburg, Potsdam, Paris, Brussels, The Hague, Florence, Prague, Hamburg, Nuremberg, Medelin, Monaco, Aberdeen, St Peters Port and St Helier as well as at various places in England.

[138] Not that I ranked as high in their eyes as they did in mine, see Brian Folley, *A Time to Jump: Jonathan Edwards: The Authorised Biography of an Olympic Champion* (Folley, 2001) in which the triple jumper described a breakfast in a Gothenburg hotel the day after he shattered the world record, 'present in the breakfast room were Jeffrey Archer ... and Sir Michael Belloff QC, Principal of Trinity College, Oxford' p 163. Three errors in nine words – another world record for Jonathan?

[139] And have had as clients including, as well as those whose names are scattered throughout this chapter, a stellar rugby trio: George Smith, Tana Umaga and Jerry Collins, and multiple tennis grand slam winner Stefan Edberg.

[140] In Ian Hewitt's *Sporting Justice: 101 Sporting Encounters with the Law* (Hewitt, 2008) I was involved in one capacity or another with seven of them.

[141] Three times in the Royal Box at Wimbledon, twice courtesy of my old Trinity pupil, Ian Ritchie, then its Chief Executive, and once after my advice had persuaded the Inland Revenue that the courtesy cars laid on for the players was not a taxable benefit.

11

Judge Not Lest Ye Be Judged

There's an old saying that there are four ages of the Bar – three less than Shakespeare's seven ages of man: 'Pupil, Junior, QC and I haven't seen him around much anymore'. For a select cohort the fourth age is a full-time judicial career. Because I never travelled that path my own career as – in that fashionable phrase – a resolver of disputes, in a variety of different settings, is uneven, arguably broad, certainly not deep.

My experience as a judge actually preceded my experience as an advocate. The Oxford Union often produced elections for office in which, as Henry Kissinger once said about academic controversies, the degree of bitterness has an inverse relationship to the importance of the issue. Losing parties from time to time challenged their successful opponents for some perceived infringement of the unduly complex rules which prohibited any form of canvassing – a bizarre bar since those prematurely ambitious undergraduates who aspired to a political career would certainly need to learn the dos and don'ts of drumming up support.

Such challenge was described in an awkward word, 'tribunalising'. I sat on one such tribunal, as a still-resident Union ex-President. The candidate challenged, Robert Jackson,[1] had, in our view, broken the rules but so had his opponent: by age-old tradition the rules were honoured by all candidates more in the breach than in the observance. We decided that rather than nip his then glittering prospects as a politician in the bud we would, as we put it pompously among ourselves (though not publicly), save him for the nation. In the event his career on the national stage ended in no higher office than that of Parliamentary Under Secretary – the most junior of governmental posts. Later, with impeccably poor timing, he crossed the benches from Tory to Labour just as the latter party was waning under Gordon Brown and the former waxing under David Cameron. No life peerage came his way; and he remains no more than a miniscule footnote in political history, or an answer to a question in a quiz game modelled on Trivial Pursuits.

My intermittent career as a judge in her Majesty's Courts started as an Assistant Recorder, a post for which I had been encouraged to apply by Harry Woolf. I attended judicial away days, along with others without forensic pedigree in the

---

[1] Prize Fellow of All Souls, writer, MP and singer. The conclusion of enjoyable dinners at his home would be signified by an operatic serenade by the host.

field of crime and punishment, elongated by an overnight stay at places of uneven standards of comfort – more Travelodge (if that) than Ritz. We tyros were first given hypothetical cases for which we haltingly proposed appropriate sentences. It was then demonstrated by an experienced circuit judge in charge of the seminar that we generally displayed troublesome signs of leniency. The solitary Admiralty lawyer was, however, rumoured to be disappointed that keel hauling, favoured by Captain Bligh of the Bounty, was not a statutory option.

My first case as an Assistant Recorder was memorable, only because I had first to decide which of two advocates, both of whom claimed to be briefed, was to represent the defendant. Pure Henry Cecil. No other case, criminal or civil, which came before me in that lowly status was a fraction as interesting.

The rank of Assistant Recorder became extinct when the Lord Chancellor's department (LCD) decided that such part-time judges might be perceived as avid for the possibility of preferment to the no less part-time but visibly superior rank of Recorder, and, if so, might be held to lack the quality of perceived independence mandated by Article 6 of the ECHR. To avoid the risk of reversal of their judgments on that somewhat far-fetched basis, the Lord Chancellor promoted the entire group.

I duly (and therefore effortlessly) climbed the next, actually by now the bottom, rung of the greasy judicial pole. As a Recorder I once had a verdict of a case, over which I presided, set aside by the Court of Appeal on the ground – I suspect unique, and not merely unusual – that I had, even with the aid of the standard form helpfully provided by the Judicial Studies Board (JSB), somehow managed in my summing up to misdirect the jury on the criminal standard of proof. I was chastened by the formal notification of the Appellate judgment, not least because the accused had, as a result of my error, been let loose. Oh lucky man.

The stipulated sitting requirement was 20 days a year; the demands of my Bar practice were such that I used to infill on the odd days off, sentencing more often than presiding over actual trials. Successful criminal advocacy at any rate, in trials at these lower levels of the Crown Court, seemed to me to depend upon distracting the jury from what were the key issues by a series of flanking sorties into the periphery of the case, indeed sometimes far beyond it. Counsel must as a matter of professional ethics never deliberately mislead a court; but short of deceit anything seemed to me to go. I was at least consoled by the fact that only once did a jury find guilty someone whom I thought was innocent – a nightmare scenario. But I fear that many whom I – rightly or wrongly – thought guilty walked free. I was not entirely influenced by my personal access to the list of previous convictions (often for identical offences) hitherto scrupulously kept from a jury until the moment when sentence fell to be passed. I could, if called upon, explain my (private) conclusions; juries do not have to explain theirs. As to sentencing and the appropriate tariff in the locality, I found that the Court ushers were often a source of valuable insight if I missed the chance to speak to the resident judge.

On the civil side my diary records that I was gainfully despatched as a bird of passage with no fixed nest to a variety of county courts in and around the suburbs of the metropolis. There too I handled the kinds of apparently humdrum case that the regular judges were only too happy to release. To the parties cases are rarely humdrum. I was touched that when I made an adoption order the new parents asked for a commemorative photograph with me in my borrowed judge's chambers.

My next step up was appointment as a deputy High Court judge. I had a special ticket to sit in the Crown Office list (as the Administrative Court used to be called) but only in housing cases. The docket of that Court is now so much fuller than it was 30 years ago, that the complement of full-time judges has for some while been afforced by QC deputies without any such restriction as to the public law subject matters assigned to them.

When I became President of Trinity, I decided that I should retire as a Recorder before I was pushed. My letter of resignation was met by a courteous response from Lord Mackay, the Lord Chancellor, thanking me for my years of loyal service of which the adjective was less than wholly deserved. But I lingered on for a few more years as a non-playing deputy High Court judge[2] until Richard Scott, the Vice Chancellor,[3] had his attention drawn by some eagle-eyed civil servant to my prolonged inactivity. In rather more peremptory language than Lord Mackay's he promptly stood me down.

There is a melancholy footnote to that sad story of sporadic public service. A retired Recorder (and University contemporary) Dermod O'Brien took a case to the European Court of Justice which established that part-time judges were entitled pro rata to a judicial pension. I had overlooked this potential boost to my bank balance, so in 2015 I wrote to the Ministry of Justice (MoJ) asking what I was owed. Speedy is not the epithet with which to do full justice to their e-mailed reply. It came within minutes of my own message. The MoJ pointed out with ill-concealed relish that my claim was 20 years out of time. My Blackstone colleagues, who submitted valid claims before the expiry of the limitation period, found unsurprisingly that it could take weeks to receive even an acknowledgement, let alone actual money, from the same quarter.

In 1992 Tom Bingham, then Master of the Rolls, inquired whether I wished to upgrade. I had always wanted to be asked to become a High Court Judge as a validation of my standing in the eyes of the profession. When the moment of truth arrived, I realised that I did not actually want to take that irreversible step. I sensed that Tom's approach, in which he noted with scrupulous sensitivity that the appointment was not in his gift, was not random. My impression was fortified when several senior judges, in particular Harry Woolf, expressed the hope that I might change my mind. In the event John Dyson was the next appointment to the better benefit of the English legal system.[4]

---

[2] With my scope extended to sitting in the Chancery Division which, had it ever come to pass, would have been in the nature of a hazardous experiment.

[3] Later a Law Lord.

[4] Dyson *A Judge's Journey* (Dyson, 2019) pp 87–88.

A few years later I was summoned to tea by Sir Thomas Legg, Permanent Secretary to the Lord Chancellor. His function in sounding out potential judges was then an informal constitutional convention. To him I reiterated my reluctance. Finally at the Blairs' first dinner party at Chequers,[5] in the gallery at that historic location Derry, by then Lord Chancellor, asked me once more to reconsider.[6] Even with the circumstantial pressures of place and person, I was not for turning.

It was for a pot pourri of reasons that I rejected these offers. I knew I enjoyed advocacy more than I thought I would enjoy judging. The prospect of presiding over lengthy trials, either civil, or, more so, criminal (six week affray in Sunderland?) did not fill me with joy – not least because in those pre-Livenote days the odds against my making a legible record of the evidence would have been long indeed. I would have been happier with an immediate appointment as an appellate judge. Though Charlie Falconer, then Solicitor General, idly canvassed that possibility with me at a feast in Trinity, it would have been a step without modern precedent (even if less revolutionary than Jonathan S's appointment straight from the Bar to the Supreme Court). Many of my ambitious lawyer acquaintances were no sooner appointed to one office than they were looking to promotion to a higher one.[7] I had no wish to risk succumbing to a similar state of perpetual anxiety.

More respectably, I appreciated that once on the judicial ladder there would be no turning back to the Bar. I preferred the possibility of travel down a series of roads not closed to me in silk rather than down a one-way street. If those other avenues never opened up, I had at least the solace of a QC's income far in excess of the judicial salary with which to support my family. The conventional knighthood I could live without (after all in the mysterious terms of formal precedence a peer's son outranks a knight, even if that only becomes apparent, as far as I can tell, when the list of those attending some memorial service is published in the *Times*).

When Igor Judge was so overwhelming a favourite to become Lord Chief Justice in 2006 as to deter any potential rivals, I was tempted to put my hat in the ring just so that I could register another *proxime accessit* and revel in it, like the mythical Indian student in John Huston's film of the Kipling story *The Man who would be King* who described his qualifications as BA Calcutta (failed). I would not, however, overreach myself still further by applying for a place on the new Supreme Court.[8]

I did yield to another of Derry's solicitations. He set up a new tribunal to deal with national security issues in data protection and asked me to become a member.

[5] Read more about it in chapter 13, 'Life at the Bar'.

[6] Joshua Rozenberg, *Daily Telegraph* 26 January 2006.

[7] The classic example was of my mentor, Gordon Slynn, who held an all but unrivalled portfolio of posts but still resented that he was passed over for the office of Senior Law Lord.

[8] Though Professor Robert Stevens, in *The English Judges*, wrote 'One could for instance, think of leading public law silks like Michael Beloff and David Pannick who would obviously be strong candidates for a Final Appeal Court' (Stevens, 2002) p 153.

We discussed the amount of work required. He speculated that there would be a maximum of 40 days sitting per year. I said I could not in conscience commit to more than 10. So it was on a somewhat inconsistent understanding that I accepted the offer.

The first case under the new legislation was brought by Norman Baker, an assiduous Liberal Democrat MP. It gave the Tribunal, chaired by Sir Anthony Evans,[9] the opportunity to state a position on many of the issues of construction which arose under it, even though only a few were actually necessary to resolve the case before us.[10] As a result of this pre-emptive strike a bare handful of claims were brought later. My first was almost my last case in that forum. I had to sit on only two more cases in 15 years of my service – during which the Tribunal changed its name twice so that I was finally converted into a Judge of the Upper Tribunal. Just before my seventieth birthday I was reminded by a letter from the MoJ as clear as it was brisk – even brusque – that I was about to reach my sell-by date.

A by-product of my Trinity post was my appointment to the Courts of Appeal of Jersey and Guernsey – again at the suggestion of Alan Milner who edited the first set of law reports in the larger of the two jurisdictions. My fellow appointees in this round were two more old Etonians, Jonathan S and Sir John (Johnnie) Nutting Bart. All three were Royal appointments mediated through the Home Office, then under the stewardship of Michael Howard. We were not subjected to any form of open competition or even interview; the posts indeed were not even advertised. The swearing-in ceremonies in both Royal Courts with their impressive architecture and portraiture and receipt of letters patent were memorable occasions but I am still perplexed as to why there had been left on the bench in front of me, as I waited to take the oath in Guernsey, a solitary pamphlet – the text of *La Loi de Sodomie 1929*.

I was sworn in in Jersey before my two OE colleagues – a matter of pure chance – and ended up as the Senior Ordinary Appellate judge[11] (the adjective 'ordinary' is used to signify that the Bailiff of each Channel Island was in point of law the senior judge – though in my case the adjective may well have had its usual meaning as well).[12]

The Courts consisted of 12 judges. The Bailiff in each bailiwick almost always served in the other's appellate court as well as its own, the balance being made up by English lawyers, with two senior Counsel from Scotland and, during my time, one from Northern Ireland. At the dinner held in London on the fiftieth anniversary of

---

[9] Lord Justice, Treasurer of Gray's Inn.

[10] 2003 NSA2.

[11] Johnnie Nutting was by that token senior to me in Guernsey, a point he made with charm and without rancour, at a farewell dinner organised for both of us in London. But it was administratively convenient to have a single holder of that informal post and Jersey was the busier of the two courts–at any rate that's my story.

[12] Though Charlie Falconer, by then an ex-Lord Chancellor, with whom, amongst others, I spoke at a constitutional conference in Jersey, said ex tempore (ie without time for reflection) 'There's nothing ordinary about Michael Beloff'; see *Jersey Law Review* (2012).

the foundation of the Courts I described them in my speech as broadly falling into three categories: the refuseniks (those who had declined domestic appointment), the birds of passage (those on their way up from Bar to Bench) and the comeback kids (ex-senior English judges).

The law of both bailiwicks was Norman French in origin. The encroachment of statute in so many areas limited the impact of those origins, but the maintenance of respect for them was a driving force among many local lawyers; as evidenced – most conspicuously – by the recurrent debate over whether to construe contracts subjectively or objectively. The need to familiarise oneself with legal concepts and rules in which one had not been educated added flavour to the exercise for us part-time judicial immigrants as well as testing our skills in a new way. We were furnished with contentions, not submissions. We had to learn on the job about such exotic concepts as *voisinage*, a variant of private nuisance, the *clamor de haro*, a form of summary self-help, *desastre*, an apt synonym for insolvency and to immerse ourselves in the writings of such as Pothier and Terrien. We had to appreciate the difference, quantitative, not qualitative, despite the deceptive language, between the Superior Number and the Inferior Number.

In terms of sentencing, English precedent guided but did not dictate. For example, the Islands being particularly vulnerable to those who traded in drugs, the sentences for supply were markedly and designedly higher than on the mainland. Crown Advocates proposed sentences and did not simply remind judges of their options.

The Courts sat in panels of three;[13] for, usually, two weeks in Jersey and one in Guernsey. Overall, the squad had expertise in most areas of law, but it was not always easy to ensure that the experience of the members was neatly aligned to the cases in the docket for any particular session. Sometimes to pick the horse for the course presented no problem. Johnnie, and later Claire Montgomery,[14] would lead on crime. But there was no one with a specialist background in family law, until Hugh Bennett[15] joined the Court, and the growing number of such cases were often put previously in the hands of Heather Steel,[16] for no better reason than the fact that she was a woman. Once, I had to give the lead judgment in a case about conflict of laws and probate, in neither of which separate areas, still less when they were in combination, was I an expert; but neither were my brethren.[17] During my near

---

[13] Though in one case in Jersey we sat in a court of five to decline to follow a judgment of Jonathan S's in Guernsey which had caused some public anxiety as to the leniency of its sentence on a defendant who had accessed recordings of child sexual abuse. Even a polymath can be forgiven unfamiliarity with pornography.

[14] QC, reported in the media to be part of Prince Andrew's legal team.

[15] A retired High Court Judge.

[16] Another retired High Court Judge.

[17] Johnnie Nutting did confess to having been one of the executors of Princess Margaret's will, but this, impressive in itself, did not persuade me in good conscience to hand the possibly poisoned chalice to him.

two decades on the Courts I was party to decisions in over a hundred cases, with a range no different from that which engaged the English Appeal Courts. My particular interest in public law led to my presiding in a case which introduced judicial review to Jersey,[18] and I was appointed a commissioner to decide a case involving the issue of whether disciplinary action taken against a Senator of the States, the Jersey legislature, as a result of comments made by him about the Bailiff in the states was immune from challenge because of parliamentary privilege. Derry promised me that my judgment might find its way into a footnote in *Erskine May* but I cannot confirm, several editions on, that his promise, binding at most in honour only, was ever fulfilled.

One memorable case had lasted before the Commissioner at first instance for more than three months and pitted two Gulf sheikhs against each other. Each before us on appeal alleged sundry procedural misconduct by the other. We held that the case had, in consequence, become all but untriable. The next day we were told that it had settled to the Commissioner's palpable relief. Some time later I was sitting in the airport in the BVI next to a young English barrister. I asked him what he had been doing in the island, and discovered that the sheikhs had resumed the same battle in a different forum. The litigation, which had started in the Emirates, might yet win the *Bleak House* award for longevity.

The different rituals of the two Channel island courts were fascinating. In Jersey the trio would process into the court room and proceedings would open with the Presider intoning 'On va assoir la cour' at which point we would actually stand for the prayers in French. In Guernsey we would come in with our toques (the ceremonial headgear). In order to recollect the sequence of the next steps, we invented a silent acronym in part tribute to our Irish colleague 'BHPS', in full Benny Hill,[19] Peter Smith – bow, hats off, pray, sit – going into reverse at the close of proceedings. This device worked only as long as we could remember the acronym. On the last time I sat in Jersey I had a classic senior moment and forgot, until prompted, the phrase I had uttered dozens of times, 'la séance est levée'. Maybe my amnesia stemmed from a subconscious reluctance to quit.

In both jurisdictions we were royally treated. We were chauffeured from airport to hotel (L'Horizon in Jersey, the Frégate, later Old Government House, in Guernsey) and hotel to court and back. We were given a free choice of where to dine in the evening with the bills sent straight to the administrative Greffe. Because Oxford term times were dedicated to my college duties, I opted for summer months sittings so I could swim in Jersey off a sandy beach like those in nostalgic 1950s travel advertisements, in Guernsey off the enclosed Victorian enclaves in the sea, in the company, when we sat together, of the ever-glamorous Liz Gloster.[20] The Annual meeting of the Judges Association in Jersey went through its agenda at Bolt-like pace with those present able to recover from the ordeal with pre-dinner oversized goblets of champagne filled to the brim.

---

[18] [1996] JLT 77.
[19] Not a member of the Court but the louche comedian.
[20] Lady Justice.

My senior judge status also made me a de facto consultee on new appointments to the Court. I had some influence, with my personal knowledge of the candidates, on who was, and, more importantly, who was not appointed, and to that extent was able to ensure that we were a truly collegiate and industrious cohort.[21]

We judges appear to have given satisfaction. In his installation speech in February 2009 the Bailiff, Sir Michael Birt, said

> As Deputy Bailiff most of my time has been spent in judicial work. I am delighted therefore to welcome the senior judge of the Court of Appeal, Mr Michael Beloff QC. When I was an advocate, I remember telling a QC at the English Bar that I was shortly to appear before the Jersey Court of Appeal consisting of Sir Godfray Le Quesne (whom I am delighted to say is also able to be here), Mr Leonard (later Lord) Hoffmann and Sir Patrick (later Lord) Neill. The QC then replied he thought that it was at least as strong if not a stronger court than could be put out at the time in the English Court of Appeal. The quality of those appointed to the Jersey and Guernsey Court of Appeal is just as high today as it was then and we are fortunate that lawyers of the calibre of Mr Beloff and his colleagues are willing to contribute to the administration of justice in Jersey in this way. Knowing that one's judgments are going to be picked over by lawyers of the stature to be found in our Court of Appeal is a salutary experience.

I take vicarious, if unmerited, pride in the fact that of my junior colleagues in those Courts some went on to what most, though not all, would think of as higher things. Patrick Hodge (a Trinity parent to boot) became Vice President of the Supreme Court, Jonathan S, a member of the same Court for seven years, and Geoffrey Vos, Master of the Rolls.

I served on the Courts for 19 years, second only in terms of judicial longevity to the unrivalled Sir Godfrey Le Quesne, until required to retire on my seventy-second birthday: the Bailiffs had procured an exception and extension in my case from the conventional terminus for a judge who had reached three score years and 10 on the intelligible basis that three intermittent sessions per annum in the islands were less demanding than the annual stint of a full time English appellate judge. The exception has, as is the habit of such things, hardened into a presumption benefiting all my successors.

Just before I was stood down from the Court I was appointed a Commissioner – a first instance judge in the Royal Court. My beginnings in my new relegated role were not wholly auspicious. In my very first case I was asked to recuse myself. The ground for the application was that a complaint of professional misconduct had been made to the Law Society by three members of the Court of Appeal. It was argued that for me to preside over the appeal from the Society's disciplinary body would be improper because, given my previous professional relationship with the complainants, I could not be an independent and impartial tribunal.

---

[21] In both bailiwicks I also chaired bodies which provided an appeal mechanism against various forms of electronic surveillance and was given a free hand to nominate the other members. This gave me the chance to bring aboard a number of lawyers, barristers and solicitors with whom I had enjoyed cordial relations, both personal and professional. These tribunals were ships which sailed but twice during my periods of office.

I declined the invitation. I observed in my judgment, which was not appealed, that the idea that I could be, in any way, institutionally predisposed to accept the views of three previous colleagues who had determined that there was a case to answer, betrayed an ignorance of the ways in which judges operate. Far from it, I might be, if anything, instinctively prone to approach their complaint with the highest degree of scepticism – as they might indeed approach any ruling of mine. I was indeed once reversed, albeit with extreme politeness, by colleagues who had previously sat with me.

My second case lay at the other end of the spectrum. It involved the convicted drug baron Curtis Warren. The hearing took place for security reasons in the Magistrates' Court. It is the only occasion in which I have had to come into Court through a door outside which stood an officer toting a fearsome piece of weaponry – not to prevent my authorised entry but Mr Warren's unauthorised exit. It made me appreciate the potential threats to limb or life faced on a recurrent basis by judges in control of terrorist trials.

I enjoyed that role of Commissioner for three years until William Bailhache, the then Bailiff, decided that I had reached the age of judicial senility at 75, so depriving me of the chance to emulate Sir Richard Tucker[22] who was dragged kicking and screaming from his perch (not literally of course) just after his eightieth birthday.

Once free of all judicial duties in the Channel Islands I was able to appear in a fascinating case in the Supreme Court on the respective roles of Her Majesty's Government and Courts of the Bailiwicks in vetting bailiwick legislation for compatibility with the ECHR. The Supreme Court needed an amicus because the Respondents, the Barclay Brothers, had declined to appear – not in their case because they were the victims of the recent cuts in legal aid. (I had many years before given advice to the Barclay Brothers but that hardly differentiated me from many senior English public lawyers.) The President, Lord Neuberger, and Vice-President, Baroness Hale, expressly asked the Treasury Solicitor to appoint me because of my Channel Island experience.

The Bailiffs had rightly observed that, as a sitting judge, I could not as an amicus fulfil my function of impartially setting out the arguments on each side of the case since one of those arguments would necessarily be contrary to the position that the Bailiwicks (which had their own representation) would advance. My retirement removed that obstacle and I opened my address to the Justices by saying that as amicus I would at least be freed from the usual sense of forensic failure attendant upon the rejection of my submissions for a client who actually had a partisan interest in the outcome of the case.[23]

My decade at Trinity as a senior member of the University exposed me to further adjudicative activity. One of the provisions of the 1994 Education Act

---

[22] High Court Judge.
[23] [2014] UKSC 54.

entitled students to a complaints procedure, if dissatisfied in their dealings with their student unions. I was appointed to hold a hearing into two such complaints – at neither of which the complainant troubled to show up. However since neither had formally withdrawn the appeal I was left to pronounce judgments which were of no practical importance or interest to anyone at all.

Professions usually require its aspirant members to satisfy certain ethical standards as well as to pass exams. At Oxford I had to chair a panel to determine whether a potential doctor with excellent academic results was fit to practise when he had overlooked the medical needs of a three-year-old child injured by its mother, with whom he was in an intimate relationship. As Vice-Treasurer of Gray's Inn, I and a Panel of fellow Benchers, had to decide whether to admit to the Inn a student with first class honours in his law degree who had misrepresented GCSE grades in his application to the Inn for a scholarship, a deceit for which he had, the Panel found, no consistent or convincing explanation. These two cases in both of which someone had jeopardised his entire career ambitions by a single aberration did bring home to me forcibly the responsibilities born daily by the regular judiciary, as well as how difficult it often is to balance the public interest in these cases – the integrity of two ancient professions – with sympathy for the private interests of a talented youth.

Lastly, I was appointed along with Robin Butler, an old Harrovian, to the Provost's Panel at Eton, established to hear appeals by any pupils who have been expelled. Since, I suspect, cases of expulsion are likely to be thought a fair cop the Panel has never in my time been wheeled into active service.

Advocacy and judging demand different skills. The first lesson for someone who crosses the bridge between these two areas of legal practice is to purge both the inherited instinct to re-enter the arena as well as the temptation not only to think, but to show that one thinks one could do a far better job than the advocate. Patience is a primary judicial virtue and impatience a secondary judicial vice. Respect for, if not necessarily concurrence with, the views of one's colleagues in a multi-person court or Tribunal is no less important.

I would agree with Jonathan S when he said in a five-minute broadcast that resolving issues of fact can pose problems at least as challenging as resolving issues of law.[24] In part because of my experience in working with civilian judges in CAS I have become sceptical of placing undue reliance on a witness's demeanour – the advantage that first instance judges certainly have over appellate one. Rogues can be plausible, honest people hesitant witnesses. My only self-imposed rule is that unless all the pieces of the evidential jigsaw fit together, the conclusion must be wrong. Go back to square one.

---

[24] He also said in that broadcast that he had never encountered a legal issue which caused him the slightest difficulty. I wish I could say the same.

Judging is, whether of law or fact, a serious business. I was once a guest at the regular Friday luncheon at the Old Bailey to which outsiders are invited to break bread with the sitting judges. By tradition the Lord Mayor or another senior City figure leads the judges back into court after what is by any standards a luxurious, even Lucullan meal. I did not stay long to observe its impact, if any, on the quality of postprandial justice. I can only assume that the hosts must have been more abstemious than the invitees. But speaking for myself I would add to the admonition 'Don't drink and drive', 'Don't drink and judge'. Be Pret a manger but not Pret a boire (though FE Smith the subject of my Birkenhead Lecture at Gray's was famously both).

Not all great advocates make great judges; and many great judges have been indifferent advocates. Not all who choose the bench find themselves content with their choice: the same dissatisfaction can be found in some heads of house. Yet the opportunity, where available, to dip a toe into the water part-time before striking out into the sea of full-time judicial experience ought to enable a rational choice to be made by persons who are, at least, good judges of themselves. The choice I personally made was to frolic in the shallows rather than to swim, in the main.[25]

---

[25] I was once standing at Charing Cross station more than three decades ago and chatting with Jonathan Mance and Mary Arden, all three of us en route to see our daughters at the King's School Canterbury. They were clear that they wished to become judges, and both had preeminent careers ending up in the Supreme Court, Jonathan as Vice-President. I expressed ambivalence about the possibility. They obviously made the right choice. I think that I did too.

12

Odds and Sods

Life at the Bar is monochrome, if vivid. Life as a Head of House is polychromatic, if in pastel shades. There was not only the office itself. There were the spin-offs. I became a fixture on the media Rolodex and an acceptable invitee for broadcasts. I was duly Humphried, Paxoed, Starkeyed, Stourtoned and Naughtied. When the first-named shared an after dinner double-billing with me, at the annual away weekend conference of a mega international law firm in Barcelona, he sprinkled his own speech with polite references to our earlier conversation, as if I had gravitated to the role of a minor public figure. But the last-named on the *Today* programme referred to me as David throughout. Maybe, if you've heard one barrister you've heard them all.

Through the good offices of Peter Stothard,[1] who had become editor of the *Times Literary Supplement* (TLS), I rejoined the carousel of book reviewers from which I had dismounted when my practice at the Bar required complete focus on the day job. I was classified as a writer on sport or law, but occasionally ventured into pastures novel, not always to good effect. I twice had reviews spiked; one of a biography of Warden Sparrow by Erica Wagner at *The Times* – I alleviated my upset by speculating that she may have invited me in the belief that I was my father; one of a book on privacy by Joshua Rozenberg by Miriam Gross at the *Sunday Telegraph* where I had no such possible excuse. I did send my rejected draft to Peter Stothard who pointed out, with a candour which only a friend can deploy, that the purpose of a review, which I seemed to have overlooked, is to focus on the subject, not on the reviewer. Only a trio of old Colleger Etonians, David Horspool of the *TLS*, Sam Leith of the *Spectator* and Harry Mount of the *Oldie*, rescued once more my journalistic career.

I was in 1996 appointed an associate editor for the *DNB*, when I had the function of proposing, if not deciding, which deceased lawyers were worthy of posthumous celebration in this prestigious book of record by placing them in the upper two rankings of a table which stretched from A–E, the unforgettable downwards to the unmemorable. I was also allowed to choose one a year to write myself. As with a sonnet there were certain rules which dictated both the form and

---

[1] A journalist telephoned me to ask for my reaction to the rumour that Peter might be my successor at Trinity. My comment that this would be a novelty was treated as an expression of disdain, which was neither what I intended nor what my words could reasonably have meant. In my experience it is generally safer not to speak to the Press unless off the record.

content of the resulting essay. The opening line summarised in a sentence the role that the subject had played in national life. The conclusion was designed to be a bang, not a whimper. In between, the recitation of a distinguished career had to be illuminated where possible by some unusual detail, such as, in my contributions, the common ancestry of Peter Taylor, Judge and Gwyneth Paltrow, actress and GOOP guru, or the chaste first marriage of Lord Shawcross.

There were posts offered, posts accepted, in right of my office, not my person – magnified far beyond my natural proportions by the Presidency. As Peter Quince said it in Twelfth Night 'Why Bottom thou art translated'.

In 1997 the Prime Minister, John Major, offered me membership of the Senior Salaries Review Body (SSRB). After discussing the proposal with Robin Butler in Whitehall I responded formally, if somewhat archly, that if the invitation had the support not only of the Prime Minister and Cabinet Secretary, but also of the Chancellor of the Exchequer, and the Lord Chancellor, it fell firmly into the category of an offer one couldn't refuse.

The work was unpaid and required the return of a brief when the several meetings conflicted with court hearing dates. So, it was public service not only for no profit but at an actual loss. Simon Brown told me later that had I asked for a case to be adjourned I could have prayed in aid my public duty. Still, there's no use crying over spilt briefs either. My colleagues were all template models of the great and the good, high-powered and diverse, in gender if not ethnic terms. The Chairman, Michael Perry, then Chairman of Unilever, exercised the calm authority to be expected of a tycoon of industry. I was hugely impressed by the quality of the civil servants assigned to assist us, even if I chafed at the pruning of some of the florid prose in the drafts of my own section of the annual reports. And the biscuits were uncharacteristically edible.

The SSRB's remit included the pay of permanent secretaries, and other high ranked administrators, and their equivalents in the armed forces and the judiciary who had, for reasons either of constitutional propriety or amour propre, their own sub-committee. The last-mentioned had originally insisted on this as the non-negotiable price for their participation in the process. I ended up by chairing the sub-committee with George Staple[2] and David Williams as my flankers.

Job evaluation was previously a mystery to me; the notion of reading across from one remit group to another seemed as intrinsically as imprecise as comparing not so much apples with pears, but bananas with carrots. What was right and what was acceptable tended to diverge. Once, as something between a trial exercise and a parlour game, we made a calculation of what the Prime Minister's job was worth per annum and came up with a figure between four and five hundred thousand pounds, substantially more than was politically possible, though a good deal less than the pay of a senior clerk in a premier league set of chambers, let alone a Premier League footballer of indifferent quality.

---

[2] Senior Partner of Clifford Chance and Head of the Serious Fraud Office.

The customary processes of consultation to calculate what judges should be paid were well established. An advance guard of senior civil servants, from what was then the LCD, would come and explain to the sub-committee the Government's view which characteristically favoured the lean over the lavish. At a later plenary meeting the Lord Chancellor would arrive in all his glory accompanied by his Permanent Secretary. Either between or after, depending on the respective parties' schedules, the Lord Chief Justice would have audience as spokesman for the Judiciary, accompanied by one other Judge, usually Sir Andrew Morritt,[3] in a double role as shop steward and shepherd. Following exchange of the usual courtesies, more elaborate in the last two meetings than in the first, carriage of the debate was left largely to the Sub Committee.

A problem that we already noted at the turn of the century was the impact of the growing gulf between the fees of top earners at the Bar (still the pool from which the senior judiciary was overwhelmingly recruited) and the salaries enjoyed (not necessarily the fitting verb) by the judges, compounded by the lure of other potential roles for them on campus or in the city. Since the Lord Chancellor and the Lord Chief Justice were well aware that I was a refusenik, there was an ironic, but unspoken, undercurrent to our discussions.

In 2002 we had to produce a fundamental review and for the purpose processed, like the court of a mediaeval monarch, around the kingdom, to Belfast, Edinburgh, Cardiff and Birmingham, receiving Oliver Twist-like petitions for more. In our report we duly sounded a warning about the alarming increase in the numbers of those known to have refused appointments to the High Court.[4]

Nolanisation prevented me from serving for more than seven years. At the end of mine and others' service a party was held attended by again the Lord Chancellor and Lord Chief Justice. We were presented with leather-bound copies of our reports and formal photographs of the party itself. Our wives were given generous bouquets, whose costs must have survived the eagle gaze of the National Audit Office.

I was complimented by several judges as having done a good job (that is, protected them against damage to their standard of living). The circuit judges hosted a dinner for me in Lincoln's Inn. However, the sense that justice was not done, or at least seen to be done, if lawyers were being looked after by their own resulted, after my departure, in an immediate purge of practising lawyers from the sub-committee.

When I gave a lecture in Chennai in 1999 some lawyers in the audience expressed astonishment that no objection was taken by my opponents in Court on the ground that my SSRB role gave me a perceptible advantage in arguing before a tribunal whose income I could influence. Such advantage, however, never progressed from the theoretical to the actual. My role did however have

---

[3] Chancellor of the High Court.
[4] Cmnd 5389-II para 4.30.

several by-products; instructions from the Trinidad judiciary who considered that an alteration in their benefits constituted a breach of the constitutional principle against any diminution in judicial pay during the judges' term of office; a theme for my Neill lecture at All Souls in 2006, and to cap it all, a brief for the High Court judges in their pensions dispute with the Department of Constitutional Affairs (DCA), my last ever case.[5]

I waded a few further feet into the waters of public service. I was on the appointment panels of two Treasury Solicitors, the Lord Chancellor's Permanent Secretary and the first Chair of the Competition Tribunal. I also assisted the aptly named David Staff, a career civil servant, in picking the list of aspirant Recorders. His last question, enhanced by his distinctive accent, was always 'Is there anything in your past which, if it came to light, would cause the Lord Chancellor embarrassment?', except on the occasion when he never had to reach it with a candidate whose opening remark 'I do not understand why someone like me has to go through this process at all'. Did he really want the appointment? He certainly didn't get it.

I did, however, miss out on another chance of playing a role in the public sphere. While arbitrating at the Beijing Olympics I received an email from headhunters for a new Chair for the Committee of Standards in Public Life, mentioning that my name had arisen on several occasions during their initial scoping work and asking me to contact them. Interpreting this to mean that I was merely being invited to give my views on possible candidates for the post, I decided that the request did not warrant interruption of my duty or even my pleasure at the Games, not least because of the time differences between Beijing and London. It was only when I returned that I discovered that they had wished to canvass my own interest in the post itself.

There were other posts offered which I rejected, some with more enthusiasm than others. This was certainly to the advantage of the body which had approached me since the person chosen was certainly better qualified than I, sometimes overwhelmingly so. The Chair of the Prisoners' Advice Service was filled by Douglas Hurd; the Chair of an inquiry into British Athletics by Chris Chataway; the Presidency of the AAA by Seb Coe.

William Pepper, a renowned radical lawyer, whom I had met while working for the Church of Scientology, invited me to join an International Commission to review and report on the attempted coup d'état in Venezuela in April 2002 and wrote 'I confirm that President Chavez would be grateful for your participation'. Further turbulence in Venezuela made my participation, even if desirable, given my college duties, impractical. In 2003 Theresa May invited me to join a think tank, to be run by Francis Maude and Michael Portillo. To preserve my ostensible political virginity I politely declined.[6]

---

[5] Discussed in the Epilogue.

[6] I did, however, briefly serve on a panel set up by You-Gov, the brainchild of two of Jeffrey's former aides, Stephan Shakespeare and Nadhim Zahawi, now Secretary of State for Education, given the name 'Lemon Curd' by Jeffrey. It was chaired by John Humphreys and intended to act as a sounding board on contemporary political issues. I remember only that the Chairman insisted that deliberations were fuelled by bacon butties.

My Presidency of Trinity did lead directly to my Chairmanship of the Jardine Matheson Scholarship Foundation, set up by that famous firm,[7] in the hope that its scholars, all sourced from Asian countries with whom Jardine's did business, would eventually come to work for it. There were four Cambridge and three Oxford Colleges (of which Trinity was one) to whom the scholars could go. The explanation for the selection of that septet was that they were the colleges at which had studied the members of the Board who set up the scheme. The Chairman, to avoid unnecessary wrangling which would have accompanied the choice of only one College in one University (and more importantly would have involved a delay to lunch), suggested that they specify all seven, so every new year during my Presidency I and Judith spent in Hong Kong, enjoying the firing of the Jardine's gun at midnight (and the accompanying dinner and dance) and a visit to the races at Happy Valley or Sha Tin through the good offices of Bobby Kwok, a member of the Jockey Club.

On one occasion the film magnate Run Run Shaw, now on the verge of his century, was in attendance and, as befitted his age and status, was given the prime pickings of the lavish buffet before the rest of us. It was not, however, to compensate for any shortfall in what was left that Judith and I took tea with Anson Chan, the Chief Secretary, at her house on the Peak in which, in a happy melding of two cultures, we were served both cucumber sandwiches and dim sum.

The interviews of prospective scholars took place the next day. Most wanted to do STEM degrees so Trinity (Oxford) very rarely had an applicant, but Trinity (Cambridge) a multitude. The personal statements generally had the naiveté of those of candidates for Miss World; but the successful applicants had a better degree ratio overall at Oxbridge than Rhodes or Marshall Scholars.

My time as Chairman of the Foundation ended abruptly when I left Trinity, but it – and indeed my time on earth – might have ended earlier had I not declined instructions to go to the Maldives en route to Hong Kong to make representations on behalf of a detained politician. It turned out to be the unhappy time when those low-lying islands were inundated by the tsunami. I acquit my Senior clerk of any malice aforethought and disclaim for myself any prophetic gifts. I was simply fortunate.

An appointment which was not even indirectly the consequence of my Presidency was the Chairmanship of the UK Advisory Committee for All Nippon Airways (ANA). The Committee had a constant component of both former Japanese ambassadors to the UK[8] and, reciprocally, of former UK ambassadors to Japan and of persons with expertise in the aviation or travel industry. I was myself asked to suggest for consideration potential appointees from outside that field.

---

[7] Which, together with Mary Arden, I had once advised on the move of their official headquarters from Hong Kong to Bermuda.

[8] The serving one also attended but without a speaking role.

Those approached who accepted included: Nigel Lawson, Peter Mandelson, Brian Griffiths (sometime head of Mrs Thatcher's policy unit), Anji Hunter (Tony Blair's diary secretary), Lord Paul, Gerard Lyons (economic adviser to Boris Johnson during his mayoralty of London), Vittorio Radice (chief executive of Selfridges), Bill Emmott (former editor of the Economist) and Rachel Billington (the novelist). Their tenure and their contribution varied. Michael Portillo, however, declined the invitation; he was, it turned out, more a great railway than a great airborne journeys man.

The demands of this post were by no means exorbitant. Once a year the Chairman and CEO of ANA, accompanied by senior staff, would fly in to stay at Claridge's. I would make a short speech of welcome, the text of which I had given to the excellent interpreter. (She was clearly not used to check the letter that I received from the Chairman after I congratulated him on his receipt of the Grand Cordon of the Rising Sun which stated 'I would like to appreciate your warm hearted massage'.) After that we would be taken through the annual report sometimes accompanied by a brief video. The Committee were then invited to explain how ANA could expand its business in the United Kingdom. The most testing part of my Chairmanship was organising the discussion in the limited time – barely an hour or so – available. The excellent dinners apart (at the Reform Club, Nobu or Claridges itself) the reward of membership was two first-class return tickets to Japan in one of the prestigious ANA fleet. Since every Committee member wanted to guarantee the extension of membership by display of his or her worth, all had to be given their moment to shine. Unfortunately, all good things must come to an end and ANA switched their attentions from London to Frankfurt. Sayonara …

ANA's bounty funded my travel to speak at the International Bar Association (IBA) conference in Tokyo when the company, in a display of characteristic Japanese hospitality, also provided a chauffeur to drive me to and from the airport, as well taking me on a trip to Hokaido where we fed the brown bears and stayed in the hotel which had hosted the G7. But lecturing, as well as litigation, gave me many opportunities to voyage. To borrow Keats's line, 'Much have I travelled in the realms of gold and many goodly states and kingdoms seen' – at other people's expense.

In 1988 I spoke at a colloquy in Salzburg, alongside members of the European Commission on Human Rights, on Judicial Safeguards for Administrative Procedure.[9] We all stayed at the Goldener Hirsch, a five* hotel which bears scant resemblance to a Premier Inn.

In 1990 the IAAF held a conference in Monte Carlo, where I first learned from a fellow speaker, Sydney Kentridge, the meaning of the word 'boondoggle'. There I was introduced to Prince Albert, the merrie monarch of Monaco, whose sense of duty compelled him to stay at least for the first lecture which happened to be mine. I next encountered him at the Beijing Olympics, where my fellow arbitrator, Deon Van Zyl, engineered an ad hoc conversation on the still more slender pretext

---

[9] Printed in Franz Matscher (ed), *Verfahrensgranatien im Bereich des offentkichen Rechts* (N.P. Engel Verlag, 1989) at 39–63.

that the royal spouse was herself, like Deon, South African. The Prince bore this uncovenanted interruption with good humour.

In 1997 I was invited, along with Tom Bingham and David Williams, to deliver a paper at a conference in Auckland in honour of Robin Cooke.[10] In his closing remarks the organiser revealed that, since the other English representatives were bankers, he had been prepared to take a gamble on me which had – unlike most gambles – paid off. Phew …

Later in 1997 the European Commission funded a group of English lawyers, led by the former British Foreign Secretary, to participate in a series of joint seminars with Chinese counterparts in an effort to resume contacts broken off after Tiananmen Square. I co-chaired the session on administrative law. As a souvenir I took home with me the hard plastic tablet on which my name was supposed to be inscribed in Chinese script, When I showed it to a Chinese speaking Malaysian friend he burst into laughter. When I inquired the reason for his reaction, he explained that what it actually said was 'Geoffrey Howe'.

Helen Mountfield, the rapporteur for our session, felicitously summarised it as a meeting of Peking duck and duck à l'orange. However, the divergence between the two nations' approach to the rule of law was made manifest without metaphor when I later met the Chinese Minister of Justice at a lunch party hosted by Jessica Rawson.[11] I asked him what would happen in a Chinese Court or Tribunal if a foreign company made a claim for breach of contract against its Chinese counterparty which, if successful, might cause significant financial damage to the latter. He responded that it would be bound to take those consequences into account. After a hurried interchange with his vigilant interpreter he promptly changed the subject.

In 1999 through the good offices of a Trinity graduate, highly ranked in the Japanese foreign service, I was also offered a government-sponsored tour of Japan. My assigned male guide apologised for the fact that he was a late replacement for a designated female, a substitution to which I was indifferent. Indeed, it saved me embarrassment when, staying in a traditional inn in Nara, Japan's ancient capital, I found that I was to share, as part of the overall experience, a hot tub with my guide. At the outset of my tour I gave a lecture to the Kedenran, the Japanese equivalent of the CBI, on 'The Rule and Law and the Wealth of Nations'. This ostensibly scholarly treatise, designed to explain the connection between the two limbs of the title, was of no interest to the hard-headed businessmen who made up my audience and whose questions were entirely focussed on whether the United Kingdom was going to join the euro.

My KR Ramamani Memorial lecture in Chennai in 2000 was on 'The Supremacy of Human Rights – Legal Triumph or Legal Tragedy?'[12] I argued that judicial prioritising of human rights, without full appreciation of the consequences, had

---

[10] Law Lord as Lord Cooke of Thorndon.

[11] President of Merton and an expert on Chinese culture.

[12] *Law Weekly* (2000) 2, journal section.

obliterated such hallowed and rational legal doctrines as sovereign immunity or the paramountcy, in common law jurisdictions, of legislation. My audience of Indian judges and advocates applauded enthusiastically under the mistaken impression, as I later learned, that I was making a coded attack on the Anglo-American threats against Iraq. A senior diplomat, who was sent a copy of the lecture, passed it on to Kofi Annan, then Secretary-General of the United Nations, in consequence of which I was invited to his eyrie in the UN building where, to my surprise and pleasure, I encountered none other than Edward Mortimer, his key adviser.

In 2000 I also gave the first Espeland lecture on the subject of Advocacy in Oslo in the auditorium where the Nobel peace prizes are conferred. The lecture was endowed in honour of Rolv Ryssdal, former President of the ECtHR, in front of whom I had appeared on several occasions. The next day, before a private visit to the Edvard Munch collection, Judith and I went to look at the Oslo Court itself. It being a Saturday the Court was not in session. When I encountered a youthful woman informally dressed in jeans and t-shirt I foolishly assumed she must be one of the staff, possibly a cleaner. I was saved from making some shamefully inept remark when she said that she had attended my lecture on the previous night as a member of the senior judiciary, all of whom seemed to have been corralled for the occasion by the Chief Justice.

In 2000 the American Bar Association (ABA) decided to hold its millennial conference in London. The Chairman of the host Bar, Peter Goldsmith, asked me to act in a mock trial, held in the Queen Elizabeth Centre, as the defence counsel of George III in which the king was imagined to have been washed ashore in Massachusetts and tried for treason. To keep the British end up I chose Helen Mountfield as my junior,[13] a gender balanced ticket, and we upheld the royal honour against our American opponents.[14]

At the invitation of Gary Roberts,[15] I twice, in 2001 and 2003, taught a mini-course grandly called International Sports Law at Tulane Law School (New Orleans) where I rejoiced in the title of Visiting Professor of Law. My first class, all graduates, numbered 32, many of whom, as my initial discussion identified, planned a career as sports lawyers, or (more profitably) as agents. My understanding had been that the American law school teaching depends upon the Socratic method, in which the students are quizzed on pre-read cases (ie the students do all the work) rather than the English law department didactic method, in which the professor stands and delivers (ie the teacher does all the work). I fell far short of Socrates in my capacity to provoke and was reduced to orating nine marathon lectures of 75 minutes each.

---

[13] As it turned out for the last time.

[14] Martin Bowley QC, the conference's roving reporter, wrote in advance 'For many years the highlight of the conference has been the Litigation section's Trial of the Century' *New Law Journal* 150 p 1046. Having opened so high – a dangerous exercise for any advocate – he was committed to vindicating his prophecy and duly delivered calling the performances 'as always carefully researched, beautifully staged and argued by top UK and US advocates with style and wit' adding 'the undoubted star was Michael Beloff' ditto p 1156.

[15] Author of the standard American textbook, *Sports and the Law*.

I had, however, a captive audience since their credits depended upon passing an open book exam based on the lecture series for which I had not only to prepare questions, but model answers as well, and was given a fixed framework into which to fit the results, ie at least 20 out of the 32 *had* to score B plus or higher – irrespective of actual quality! At the end of my last lecture, I was to my surprise clapped by my class, though whether on account of the course or of its conclusion I did not enquire.

The whole experience gave me a deep affection for New Orleans, its jazz, Spanish quarter architecture and creole cooking, coupled with a deep phobia of Miami airport. Second time round I insisted on travelling via Chicago.

Among other incidental benefits, I was able to hear visiting speakers, Janet Reno, one of Clinton's attorneys-general, and Anthony Scalia, the originalist member of the Supreme Court. Their different perspectives on contemporary issues of law and society persuaded me that, whereas when I visited the USA in the 1960s there was at most a gap between the politics of centrist wings of the Democratic and Republican parties, it had by the turn of the century become a gulf – a trend which, in the time of Trump, widened still further.

In 2002 I spoke at a conference of Commonwealth judges in Kuala Lumpur chaired by Michael Kirby of the High Court of Australia and attended by two judges from California. (This was not because history was being scrolled back, but because it was American money which provided the funding.) During a discussion on judicial corruption Michael observed that this was a problem common to all nations. I protested that there was no recorded incident of corruption of an English High Court judge for several centuries, only to be visited with a magisterial rebuke 'Don't be so chauvinistic Michael'. I continue to think this owed more to his sense of diplomacy than of reality. The same could be said of his effort to soothe my feelings, by complimenting me, in a polished summary of the colloquy crafted overnight, on my efforts to participate in a Malaysian dance, part of our extra-curricular activities. I was of the John Sergeant/Ann Widdecombe Terpsichorean tendency.

In 2004 I gave a keynote speech on human rights in Gibraltar on the occasion of its tercentenary at the initiative of the wife of its then Chief Justice, Derek Schofield. This gave me the opportunity to visit the Governor, Francis Richards, whose path had crossed with mine when each was at the other end of his time in College at Eton. It was an unforeseen by-product of my lecture that I was briefed to appear for the (by then former) Chief Justice himself before the Privy Council.[16] Simon Brown in the first of his memoirs[17] gave as an example of 'my ever appealing advocacy' my plea 'I come not to praise the Chief Justice but to urge your Lordships not to bury him' – but they did 4-3. I would have sacrificed his tribute to gain his vote.

---

[16] [2009] UKPC 43.
[17] *Playing Off The Roof & Other Stories* (Brown, 2020) p 137.

In 2004 and 2006 I gave a quartet of lectures on board the transatlantic liner the Queen Mary 2, under an arrangement between Oxford University and Cunard in which cruise passengers would be entertained, even edified, by a series of lectures, for which the lecturers (and their partners) would receive on board lodging and subsistence. My first series was called 'Anglo-American law – same roots different branches' and my second 'the Theatre of the Law'. I was impressed by the fact that I ranked second in popularity to PD James in terms of audience numbers until I realised that my attendees were lawyers who, unlike their fellow travellers, could claim their voyage as a tax-deductible expense.

In 2011 under the auspices of the Lord Slynn of Hadley European Law Foundation I visited Kiev to deliver human rights training to judges of the Ukrainian Supreme Court together with Dr Sweeney, a senior lecturer in the Durham Law School. I was much struck by the beauty of the Court (and of old Kiev) but less so by the quality of the Judges whose paramount interest was not so much on how they could enforce such rights to the benefit of the Ukrainian citizenry, but whether, and if so how, their salaries could be protected from diminution by the state.

In 2012, in the depth of Greece's economic doldrums, the Onassis foundation decided that it would seek to improve the popular mood by staging a televised recreation of the trial of Socrates in front of a panel of international judges, chaired by Loretta Preska, later responsible for the early management of the Ghislaine Maxwell case in New York. I was briefed as leading counsel for Socrates. With the invaluable assistance of Gail Trimble, the classics fellow at Trinity (and former star of University Challenge) I concocted a robust defence. I had decided to end on a dramatic note by leaving counsel's bench and striding to the front of the stage to deliver my peroration. This intended climax was marred by the fact that my foot became entangled in the bag in which I had kept my notes and which followed me across the floor like a ball and chain. Still I had a private view of the newly opened Acropolis museum.

In 2016 a quartet of Gray's Inn Benchers accepted a challenge from the American Inns of Court to debate the motion that 'the Declaration of Independence was an illegal act' in no less appropriate place than Independence Hall itself in Boston. Our opponents included the Deans of three prestigious law schools. Recollecting my Short Walk on the Campus and assuming (correctly) that the transatlantic style of debate was likely to have remained a stable feature even in a country that had seen so many changes in the intervening decades, I decided not to meet intellectual fire with fire, but rather to resurrect the Oxford Union style of playing the man (or woman) not the ball. One of the audience actually fell off her chair with convulsive laughter (possibly from astonishment rather than amusement) but that did not save us from a home town decision. On the next day in the great tradition of the busman's holiday we attended hearings in both civil and criminal courts. In the criminal trial a witness was asked by defence counsel whether she was sure that a noise she claimed to have heard was of gunshot. Her answer illustrated the truth of the advice that one should rarely ask a question in cross examination unless one thinks one knows the answer, 'Mister' she said 'if you lived where I live you'd know what a gunshot sounds like'.

Bloodied but unbowed we offered a return match in Gray's Inn Hall itself. The USA team, however, brought a charabanc full of supporters, enjoying the chance of a trip to London in the pre-Christmas season, and were as successful away as at home.

In 2017 I gave lectures (somewhat belatedly given the topic) on the Global Influence of Magna Carta both in Singapore and Malaysia. In Malaysia the excuse was the celebration of a newly created five-star hotel near Ipoh. There may have been no obvious, or indeed concealed, connection between theme and location but it was not for me to worry.

In 2018 I was invited to speak at the annual week-long conference in St Petersburg for lawyers from all over the world, opened by Prime Minister Medvedev, which for the first time had sessions on sports law, a matter of some sensitivity given the claims of state-sponsored doping levelled against Russia. Since I had been party to several decisions both for the IAAF Ethics Board and CAS which touched on the topic, I had to chart a careful course. The event, designed to burnish the host nation's image in the world, was also an opportunity for dedicated card swapping and contact-making. I had no interest in networking; more the reverse, what I termed Nyet working. One afternoon I skipped a session and went to the modern wing of the Hermitage, two floors up, and found it wholly unoccupied apart from the gallery staff. It was an exclusive personal view in fact, if not in name.

In the same year I gave the Oxford High Sheriff's Law lecture in the Examination Schools, 'Good at Games? Does the Law Help or Hinder Sport?' My apprehension was no less than on my previous visits to that venue more than half a century before. It was, if anything, increased, when I noted that the advertisement for my talk had amputated all but the first three words of the title, encouraging members of my audience into a belief that I was going to deliver a coaching manual. However, since the lecture was delivered at a time when a Red Judge was sitting in Oxford, the lecturer was given the traditional white gloves, made in Woodstock, to avoid any perceived discrimination between the academic and the practical.

In 2020 I gave my annual lecture as a Visiting Professor at the University of Buckingham (which, despite the adjective, I have not given every year) by Zoom on the subject of Free Speech on Campus with the subtitle 'Was Gladstone a Villain?' It had recently been reported that the student body at the University of Liverpool had petitioned the University to rename a hall of residence which bore his name because of his family's connection with slavery. I noted that Gladstone was honoured for his accomplishments as the outstanding liberal (and Scouse) statesman of the nineteenth century; and that the retention of his name could not sensibly be taken to indicate an approval of slavery. I spoke in vain, but not too soon.

Several months later the University agreed to the replacement of Gladstone's name with that of Dorothy Kuya, Liverpool's first community relations officer, who ticked the right contemporary boxes, but might, without disrespect to her, be estimated a less durable figure than Gladstone in the annals of history.

It remains my view that it is far more important to tackle contemporary discrimination than to focus on a now universally condemned practice itself abolished more than a century and a half ago by removing artefacts or names which do not themselves celebrate the practice. Explanation yes; eradication no. I see too no obvious virtue in evaluating figures of the past by the standards of the present. As a lawyer, I am troubled by the arbitrary nature of such evaluation. But then I must declare a familial interest. My father held the Gladstone Chair at Oxford; I won the Gladstone scholarship at Eton. I am unpersuaded that I should not continue to remain proud rather than ashamed of even so slender an association with the Grand Old Man. How sleepy is that?

Just as I learned that one can deploy legal skills in many ways without being an advocate, I have equally learned that there are many opportunities for oratorical display other than in argument before courts or tribunals. I twice gave valedictory addresses on behalf of the Bar for two Lords Justices of Appeal in the cavernous Lord Chief Justice's court. The intimidating atmosphere of that environment is multiplied by the risk that, given that such occasions are traditionally attended by a significant proportion of the senior judiciary, one might lose in the space of five minutes any oratorical reputation that one might have built up over decades.

I delivered countless different after-dinner speeches or, more accurately, the same or similar after-dinner speeches to countless different audiences, working on the basis that one could get away with telling the same joke to an audience no more than a third of whom will have heard it before. I spoke at two Magdalen gaudies, the first and fifth for my vintage; I reflected how on the former occasion we were still on the upward slope of our careers, whereas on the latter, the conversation seemed to be devoted to nothing but the three Ds, death, disease, divorce. I had to devise grace at a Rugby League Cup Final lunch (on 40 seconds' notice). The match coincided with the day after Tony Blair's first – and largest – election victory, and John Prescott, the chief guest, Deputy PM designate, was in a fervently amiable mood.

And without the need to utter a single syllable but, as a kind of 'C' List academic celebrity, I enjoyed over the years the best of hospitality at the National Gallery, the Tate, Covent Garden, and the Albert Hall – nothing beats culture with champagne – as well as the multitude of sporting venues I've mentioned before.

Happy days indeed!!

13

Life at the Bar

Kipling famously wrote that, inter alia (as we old fashioned lawyers would say), 'if you can meet with triumph and disaster and treat those two impostors both the same, you'll be a man my son'. Not a bad motto for a barrister, man or woman.

While barristers are in principle independent practitioners, for administrative convenience they congregate in and operate out of sets of chambers. In an unauthorised biography of Derry Irvine, Dominic Egan fairly summarised chambers in my first decade at the bar.

> Chambers to date had not been run like businesses so much as gentlemen's clubs. Barristers came and went as they chose and did whatever work took their interest. They often shared little more than an address, a clerk and a library. Chambers' administration was rudimentary, management systems virtually unknown. Practice development consisted of clerks taking solicitors to the pub for a few drinks on a Friday night.[1]

2 Hare Court conformed to that template. It was a second-ranking commercial set some distance short in achievement, if not in ambition, of the likes of Essex, Brick or Fountain Court. It was Anthony Lester who developed its parallel practice in the fastest growing areas, administrative and employment law – interests that he shared with Derry Irvine then at 2 Crown Office Row.

Anthony and Derry, together with their like-minded protégés, discussed the possibility of a kind of superset, with a more modern and meritocratic organisation, the highest earners no longer subsidising their irredeemably weaker brethren, the senior clerks paid salaries commensurate with their contribution rather than the still conventional percentage. The plan foundered because of absence of agreement as to which candidates for inclusion from either set were sheep and which goats. The bar was set too high – some of those thought unsuitable have had hugely successful careers including on the High Court. Derry chose in lieu to set up his own set at 11 King's Bench Walk. I was left with my regrets, but, as I explained to Dominic, 'The fact is that barristers are prima donnas and it's very difficult to accommodate a lot of prima donnas'.[2] In the years to come I was to be both the beneficiary and the victim of the new fluidity.

---

[1] Dominic Egan, *Irvine: Politically Correct?* (Egan, 1999) pp 65–66.
[2] Egan, pp 66–68.

In the 1980s, already making my way in silk, I had two firm offers to move.[3] The one I rejected was to become Head of Chambers at 2 Garden Court, a set with a growing administrative law practice: two successive Treasury Devils Simon Brown and John Laws were prominent members. But I did not wish to take on a role of Head of Chambers so early. It was John Dyson[4] who accepted the challenge.

The one I accepted was from 4–5 Gray's Inn Square, a set with two distinct wings, the commercial side headed by Richard Yorke QC and the planning and local government side, headed by Konrad Schiemann QC.[5] It was Richard with whom I had worked side by side in the *Zinovia* who persuaded me to take the plunge. I could see no reason why a concern about one's present set (which did not exist in my case) should be a condition precedent to a journey into pastures new; a career move was commonplace in business and by no means unknown among solicitors. My letter to Presiley Baxendale QC[6] characterised my move as made 'neither in sorrow nor in anger, but for adventure'. *The Lawyer*, retrospectively, described it as 'the biggest shock at the Bar in the last thirty years'.[7] In an era when a commitment to chambers was seen as akin to a marriage and the rare moves followed some irretrievable breakdown in the relationship, the very notion of transfer of allegiance itself was novel.

The major attraction for me was that 4–5 Gray's Inn Square did central as well as local government work, so I had a potential client base at that stage lacking at 2 Hare Court. I discussed the matter with respected professional friends. David Neuberger, on a walk up Chancery Lane, said obligingly 'Neither set is quite first rate but you are' and thought I could prosper whether I went or stayed. Tony Grabiner, another consultee, described Richard as 'a decent bloke' and, like the junior judge in the Court of Appeal, had nothing to add.

After Richard's premature retirement Elizabeth Appleby QC[8] took over as senior silk. Stoy Hayward was commissioned to take a dispassionate view at Chambers to see what changes could be made to maximise efficiency, reputation and income. The study identified me as having at that time the highest profile in the set. It was to refresh the image that I, with David Keene QC one year senior to me,[9] became part of a leadership trio which would have been called a triumvirate had Elizabeth been a man.

Elizabeth and I worked well together. She did the heavy lifting; I fronted up the show, concentrating on recruitment both from outside and within chambers.

---

[3] I had a third from Louis Blom-Cooper QC, to succeed him as head of Goldsmith Buildings against the contingency that he was called to public service.

[4] (Dyson, 2019) pp 80–81.

[5] Judge at the ECJ.

[6] By then Joint Head of Blackstone Chambers.

[7] 'Time called on loyalty at Bar as lit boom sets in' Issue of 21 January 2011 (for those who require a glossary lit = litigation).

[8] Treasurer of Lincoln's Inn.

[9] Lord Justice. He shortly afterwards took his rightful place on the bench, David Keene, *Leaving the Arena: A Story of Bar and Bench* (Keene, 2019).

Among the most notable of the outsiders were Alan Moses,[10] David Bean,[11] Andrew Collins,[12] Robert Griffiths,[13] Richard Spearman,[14] Malcolm Grant[15] and Eleanor Sharpston[16] (as well as academics to be termed associate tenants such as Bill Wade, Gunter Treitel, David Williams and Gordon Borrie).[17] I even had a brief discussion in the House of Commons with Michael Howard, a genuine, not a Parliamentary, silk (a now obsolete troop) when he was contemplating the options of a life after leadership. Among the most notable of the insiders, all pupils, were Rabinder Singh,[18] Clive Lewis,[19] David Wolfe,[20] Murray Hunt,[21] Karen Steyn,[22] Helen Mountfield, Martin Chamberlain[23] and Marie Demetriou,[24] an extraordinary talent pool in which I could happily fish for juniors. When Lewis LJ and Steyn J, as they had then become, together dismissed the challenge to the Prime Minister for rejecting the finding of his advisers on Ministerial standards that Priti Patel had broken the Ministerial Code by bullying – the first example of a joint judgment by former 4/5 pupils – I felt a quasi paternal pride in their collaboration. You've come a long way babies.

I also added a small coterie of public international lawyers, John Freeland QC,[25] Henry Darwin[26] and Lady Hazel Fox QC and various overseas lawyers to give Chambers the veneer of a global set. It may or may not have been for that reason that it was chosen to host a visit from the then President of the Federal Republic of Germany.

My enthusiasm may, however, have overreached itself when, after reading in the Draconian that the Dragon's top years star pupil, one Matthew Farrington, all of 13 years old, was thinking in the long term of a career at the bar, I asked him to make contact – a premature endeavour, briefly and satirically picked up by a daily tabloid. *Pas trop de zele s'il vous plait.*

My most celebrated recruit was Cherie Booth, the wife of Tony Blair, who was then rapidly ascending the commanding heights of the Labour party. Cherie had been passed over in favour of Tony for a place in Crown Office Row[27] although academically her first at LSE overshadowed his second at Oxford. She was then made a tenant at 5 Essex Court[28] headed by George Carman, who was something

---

[10] Alan was said somewhat imaginatively to be the model for the television character Judge John Deed.
[11] Lord Justice.
[12] High Court Judge.
[13] QC and MCC committee member.
[14] QC.
[15] Provost of UCL, Chairman of the NHS.
[16] Advocate-General at the ECJ (by now the CJEU).
[17] Former Director of Fair Trading – more a quasi-academic.
[18] Lord Justice.
[19] Lord Justice.
[20] QC.
[21] Head of the Bingham Institute for the Rule of Law.
[22] High Court Judge.
[23] High Court Judge.
[24] QC.
[25] Judge at the ECtHR.
[26] Of the FCO legal team.
[27] (Egan, 1999) pp 57–58.
[28] On Irvine's recommendation, Frederick Reynold QC, *Cheek Chance and Some Heroics* (Reynold, 2018) pp 112–13.

of a lone wolf, and spread lustre, but little else among his colleagues.[29] Upon disintegration of his own set George himself joined us for his last year in practice before his untimely death. Derry telephoned me one day in 1989 and said that he knew this young lady, marooned in a set unsuitable for someone of her interests and talents, and asked me to see her. I was hugely impressed by her.[30] It took a little time to persuade my colleagues of her merits – but she came, they saw and she prospered.

In court her presence attracted press attention unrelated to the case, but before she took silk she was my junior on several occasions. Memorably, in a private arbitration (no press present) before Patrick Elias, we were pitted against Charlie Falconer on behalf of the Sovereign Pension Fund of Pennsylvania which presented us with the state flag as a memento. The solicitors settled the dispute before we could cross swords, leaving us time to spend outside the arbitration venue in well remunerated gossip. Once at a weekend Tony came to collect her from Gray's Inn when we were both working outside office hours and called out to me 'How's the busiest member of the Bar?' I hope I didn't reply – 'and the best' but I am not sure.

In becoming a colleague Cherie also became a friend. Our family lacked the Chateau near Toulouse in which David Keene provided a holiday retreat for the Blairs,[31] until they transferred for security, and possibly other reasons, to the summer resorts of the likes of Silvio Berlusconi and/or Cliff Richard. Judith and I did however invite Cherie and Tony to spend a weekend with us in our Oxford home and planned a small party to introduce them to some of the university great and good. Walking back from court to chambers I saw the ominous Evening Standard headline 'Labour Leader dies'. My immediate reaction doing scant justice to the event was – bang goes the weekend. But I wrote to Tony that everything I had learned from my study of history and politics suggested that he had to seize the chance, which might never be repeated, to make an early run for the leadership, which with more influential encouragement he duly did.

As the time for the next general election grew closer we reprised the invitation. At the rescheduled party Euan Blair, on being introduced to Roger Bannister, said 'I've read about you in history' to Moira Bannister's[32] conspicuous amusement. During the weekend Tony spent some time on the phone with Paddy Ashdown, I infer, in discussion about the possibility of a Lab–Lib pact, the need for which evaporated after his landslide electoral triumph. Cherie took her children to morning service, I went for a walk with Tony. He told me, when crossing a stile along the by-pass, that he had a vison for the country. While I

---

[29] (Reynold, 2018) pp 147–49.
[30] Cherie Blair, *Speaking For Myself: The Autobiography* (Blair, 2009) pp 154–56 where I am described as 'a brilliant man with impossible handwriting'. In an interview with the *Guardian Weekly* magazine in 2007 she described me as one of her two main mentors. See also (MacDougall, 2001) pp 122, 158–159.
[31] (Keene, 2019) pp 112–15.
[32] Artist and Roger's wife.

retain a vivid visual image of the moment, to my regret I cannot actually recall what the vision was. We were invited to share his victory celebrations on election night but, since like Cinderella, I am ill-equipped for activities after midnight, I went to bed instead.

Cherie was an athletics aficionado so we had hosted another pre-election dinner party in an Italian restaurant in Covent Garden for some articulate athletes, past and present. In 2005, during the second Blair administration, I introduced her to Mihir Bose,[33] then the chief sports reporter of the *Daily Telegraph*, which was campaigning for London to bid for the Olympic Games. At a meeting at the Reform Club we discussed the possibility of her actually heading up the bid.[34] In the end she did not take on a formal role, but she was certainly effective in gladhanding the members of the IOC, an elite electorate conscious of their exclusive power and not immune to flattery.[35]

I accompanied Cherie to several athletics meetings, first at Crystal Palace, sometimes together with Alastair Campbell,[36] another athletics buff, and later at the Olympic Stadium itself. Cherie also assisted in procuring a long-overdue honour for Sidney Wooderson, the filiform bespectacled solicitor, British athletics' major star in the pre-Bannister era – something of which Rob Hadgraft, sportswriter, was unaware, but which he has promised to record if ever there is a second edition of his biography *Sydney Wooderson – a Very British Hero*.[37]

Cherie did not at first find the role of spouse to the prospective Prime Minister an easy one, though once in Downing Street she rapidly acclimatised.[38] I added the odd joke to speeches which she had increasingly to give and I collaborated with Fiona Millar, Alastair's wife, then her unofficial adviser, in handling the various adverse images with which the right-wing press sought, in my view unfairly, to fix her. With Peter Goldsmith I wrote a piece in *The Times* defending her right to argue cases at odds with New Labour Government policies. She for her part agreed to be interviewed by my daughter Natasha for the St Andrews student newspaper in what was at the time something of a journalistic coup since she resisted all similar approaches by the national press.

Cherie had in Chambers a room close to mine. I once came upon her lying on the floor with another woman on top of her. Momentarily taken aback by this unusual spectacle I rapidly realised that she was engaged in a fitness routine with Carol Caplin, her wellness adviser. I sat at Cherie's right hand at her fortieth birthday party. On her left sat Peter Mandelson. He offered to give me media training, an offer I never took up.

---

[33] Author, President of the Reform Club.

[34] Mihir Bose, *The Spirit of the Game* (Bose, 2010) pp 520–21.

[35] Ibid, pp 522–23.

[36] Blair's Director of Communications and serial diarist. In Vol 7, p 125 he mentions bringing by bicycle a signed copy of Vol 3 to Chambers for me with the reflection that he pitied those with an office-bound life. My life was less office-bound than he may have thought.

[37] He attributes the honour solely to the lobbying of Chris Brasher.

[38] Susan Crosland, widow of the former foreign secretary, wrote a sympathetic profile after seeking my input at a delicious lunch in her flat.

During the Blair years I went several times to Downing Street and with Judith to Chequers. We were at the country seat for the first famous dinner party attended by amongst others Roy Jenkins, Derry, Jonathan Powell,[39] Robert Harris[40] and their wives. It is true that, as has been reported,[41] Derry did say 'Tell the boy Blair to get me a whisky', a command obeyed by his former pupil. In his more recent role as Prime Minister Tony professed incredulity when Roy Jenkins described to him the length of Cabinet meetings in Harold Wilson's day; the Blair method with Cabinet proved indeed to be more sprint than marathon.

I was by chance having tea with Cherie at Number 10 about a fortnight before Derry's peremptory removal from the Woolsack, saved no longer by his status as an ex-pupilmaster. In the course of the idle chit chat beloved of lawyers (but not only lawyers) she assured me, as it turned out wrongly, that Derry would remain in post until at least the next election. On the actual day of the reshuffle I was passing through security at the Royal Courts of Justice in a queue just behind Marianna, Charlie Falconer's wife.[42] She remarked that she was crossing fingers in hope of Charlie's elevation. Ah these footnotes to footnotes in history!

We also went to a farewell party at Chequers after Tony had announced his intention to step down from the Premiership. At a riveting tour d'horizon speech he gave at a private function a little later at Blenheim Palace I turned to Cherie, my neighbour at table, and said that it seemed a pity that he had quit when still apparently at the peak of his powers. She whispered back 'To satisfy the ambitions of a lesser man'.

I was at one time contemplating a book called *The Last of the Lord Chancellors* – last since to attach the label of Lord Chancellor who was in name and fact a Minister of Justice but bereft of judicial functions seemed to me to be an abuse of language. I had lunch at Brooks's with Haydn Phillips, Derry's permanent secretary, who was still not certain what had led to his master's demise. The received view is that the decision to remove him and to embark upon a consequential programme of radical constitutional reform was taken late in the day for reasons of politics. The full story has yet to be told.

I had mixed feelings about that aspect of the reforms, which I considered compelled by principle but unnecessary in practice,[43] and which has relegated justice to the position of Cinderella of the social services. I also thought it a pity that Derry's formidable abilities were not put to better use afterwards. I imagine that Oxbridge colleges might have been wary of the possible price tag of someone who had become, unfairly, notorious for the price of the new wallpaper in his official residence, and the possible impact on collegiate administration of someone who had compared himself to Wolsey. I was by chance present at the speech he

---

[39] Blair's Chief of Staff.

[40] Best-selling author of *Enigma* and other best sellers.

[41] Peter Oborne, 'Guess Who's Coming to Dinner' *The Spectator* 9 March 2002.

[42] Her Honour Judge Hillyard QC.

[43] See my foreword to *Off with Their Wigs!: Judicial Revolution in Modern Britain* (Banner and Deane, 2003).

gave to the Political Committee of the Reform Club where he first so described himself. It was a speech which I remember chiefly because during it he mentioned me three times by name – a matter of no interest other than to myself but which (I like to think) showed that our relationship was one of affectionate, if wary, mutual respect.

At 4–5 Gray's Inn Square, as well as my role as recruiting officer, I also introduced the concept of an academic panel including such heavy Oxford hitters as Francis Reynolds[44] and Paul Craig[45] – a new development for the bar approvingly commented on by Lord Mackay the then Lord Chancellor in his speech to the new silks in 1991. I set up too a Pro Bono panel and created a special relationship with Liberty.[46] To those who were resistant to the notion I argued, moral considerations apart, that there were tangible rewards to participation in high profile and interesting cases and popularity among the powers that be. Judges are quick to acknowledge the contribution of barristers who appear before them without fee.[47]

When I became President of Trinity things at 4–5 started slowly to fall apart. Some of the innovations proved to be largely cosmetic. The Stoy Hayward report gathered dust. The gap between the planners and the commercial lawyers, which I had been able to bridge to some extent with the increase in commercial judicial review, started again to widen. The centre could not hold. Many of the best commercial lawyers, Stuart Isaacs,[48] Mark Hapgood,[49] Neil Calver,[50] Mark Templeman were seduced, when in silk, into other mainstream commercial sets. Talks of mergers to reinforce one flank foundered because it would bring no perceptible benefit to the other flank. The outstanding and popular Genevra Caws died suddenly on a skiing trip. Because of my collegiate duties I was less and less visible in Chambers itself.

Nonetheless it was a considerable shock, and a cause of deep upset, when, on the eve of my passage to India to deliver a lecture, two of my protégés, Helen Mountfield and Murray Hunt, came to tell me that several members of chambers had decided to set up a set of their own, 'an interdisciplinary set that had human rights at its heart, modern with modern systems'.[51] I could hardly call it a betrayal when I myself had set a precedent earlier for a move designed to better oneself professionally. Fifteen years on I reaped what I had sowed.

---

[44] Editor of *Bowstead on Agency*.

[45] Author of a standard work on Administrative Law.

[46] The renamed NCCL.

[47] In chapter 14, 'The Art of Advocacy' I cite what was said by the Master of the Rolls when I acted without fee for Ian Brady, the Moors murderer in a judicial review ([1997] EMLR 185). See too Potter LJ in Counsel, referencing me as an example at an annual awards ceremony.

[48] QC; later a solicitor.

[49] Banking specialist and triathlete.

[50] High Court Judge.

[51] (Blair, 2009) p 292.

Unable to prevent the exodus I promptly resigned as Head of Chambers. When the news of the planned secession became public I adopted the carefully crafted Heseltinian formula 'My present intention is to join the new set in due course' and was quoted as calling it 'potentially the Silicon valley of human rights law'. I was truly torn by the emigrants' invitation. On the one hand many were persons whose careers I had personally nurtured; I admired all and liked most of them. On the other hand, I had no appetite, now aged almost 60, to embark on a new and possibly perilous venture when I would no longer be in a pole position to influence events.

I realised that I could not stay at 4–5, despite the pleas of the majority of my fellow member remainers; I would be haunted by the ghosts of colleagues past. It would never have been glad confident morning again. Identified as someone who might be on the market, I was approached through a variety of channels by all the major sets at the bar whose practices were aligned with mine – the exception oddly being Fountain Court, where I could have taken up a tenancy three decades earlier. When I returned to Blackstone, as 2 Hare Court had now become, there was a headline in a legal broadsheet suggesting that *it* was *itself* the exception – an inaccuracy which I was persuaded not to have corrected since it would hardly be the most propitious start for the renewed relationship. I had in fact been approached by the two heads of Chambers, Charles Flint and Presiley Baxendale, new brooms who had swept out traces of the old guard still in control when I had left. In short, I opted for the known rather than the novel, a little like a man return-ing to his first wife after divorce from his second wife and rejection of the chance of a third. I record that 4–5 had three times been runner up in Chambers of the Year awards. Whether despite or because of me Blackstone's regularly took top spot.

In the end when the date approached at which I had indicated I might join the new set, now named Matrix, I formally notified Nicholas Blake,[52] head of their management committee (heads of chambers being so last century), that I would not in fact be coming. This sparked some press interest (only because Cherie was a Matrix founder member) with, notably, a news story in *The Times*.[53] I issued for the only time in my life a press statement 'After careful consideration of a variety of attractive offers I have decided to rejoin the outstanding set which gave me my first chance at the bar and where I can practice again in the company of many former colleagues and personal friends'. The *Independent on Sunday* said that Matrix was 'reeling' from my decision; maybe it was an eightsome reel because it has pros-pered without me. Cherie herself speculated that I feared that Matrix would be 'too left wing'.[54] Others somewhat illogically suggested that my chances of a peerage would be improved if my link with her was broken. The actual reason was neither of the above; but I am not minded now to disclose it. It relates to a happening 'in another country'.

---

[52] High Court Judge.
[53] *The Law Society Gazette* (5 April 2001) had a headline 'Beloff Shock'.
[54] (Blair, 2009) p 371.

A durable feature of the Chambers system, ancient or modern, has been the clerks. But for my clerks I would undoubtedly have earned no more than half of my actual income and probably far less than that. I can recall few, if any, instances when my tentative proposal of what price tag a particular piece of work should carry came within striking distance of what the clerks procured. If clerks are usually better at negotiating a fee than recording it I can recall no instance at all in which I considered that I had been underpaid. I must therefore admit to a sense of great gratitude to my Senior clerks, especially to Les Page and Michael Caplan at 4–5 Gray's Inn Square and Gary Oliver and Martin Smith, their equivalents at Blackstone, who played in sequence the role of in-house mentor to my often demanding and sometimes even truculent person.

I never rejected a solicitor's cheque on the basis that I thought it was for an excessive amount, though sometimes I did think the sums simply ridiculous. I was paid a substantial four-figure sum just to be interviewed by some of Mr Deripaska's henchmen who wanted to size me up as a potential team leader for some prospective litigation (I didn't even get the gig) and a similar sum for simply announcing a settlement which the solicitors had already agreed in a high-profile music industry squabble – a bonus still less merited since the brief was a late return from a colleague who was unavailable to reap the fruits of his earlier labours.

I was on any view very well paid. I once joked, when a newspaper speculatively reported that I was earning half a million pounds a year, that it didn't know the half of it. In my best year in 1992 I earned what would in today's currency be over £2 million. Although, unlike some of my contemporaries, I was never offered a brief marked £1 million, I did once turn down a brief for £500,000 (with daily increments of £5,000) for a client facing civil claims in Hong Kong arising out of the Carrian collapse. It was due to last up to a year and I was unwilling to become an exile in that period for all the tea in China, part of which Hong Kong was soon to become. Temporarily mesmerised by the size of the prospective fee, I accepted a brief on the recommendation of a specialist silk in a construction case involving the Great Ormond Street Children's Hospital. But after the initial consultation I realised that not only was a case which involved so much detail and so little principle not my cup of cocoa but rather a goblet of hemlock, and I explained to those instructing me that they would be wise to look elsewhere, advice they prudently accepted.[55] I have never repented either decision (even though the Carrian case settled after seven days) – at any rate not all that much. Anthony Lester coined the titillating acronym 'TOTR' – 'think of the refreshers', but sometimes even that thought cannot carry the day.

Had I not been tempted to Trinity and remained on my upward trajectory, I would, on a conservative estimate, have trousered several million pounds more than I did but ended up a far less happy bunny. Money may not be the root of all evil, but it is not a cast iron guarantee of contentment.

---

[55] As my replacement they briefed Mark Potter and I joked with him that it was my decision which enabled him to earn enough to go on the bench ending up as President of the Family Division.

It is a human tendency when inequalities of income are discussed to locate an acceptable hypothetical maximum marginally above one's own remuneration, but the media interest in the top earners at the bar diverts attention from their abnormality. Sometimes the apparent extravagance provokes a judicial reaction. In a case where in 1992 I acted in the Court of Appeal for Hyundai who complained about an arbitrator's insistence on a non-returnable commitment fee if the case settled,[56] Nicolas Browne-Willkinson VC said in a postscript to his judgment

> Many practitioners in specialist fields now demand and secure fees which to some (including myself) appear to be excessive. For most members of the Bar fees are very much lower and produce annual earnings roughly commensurate with what could be obtained from people of similar skill working in non-legal fields. I hope that the figures mentioned in this case will not be taken as typical of the Bar as a whole.

During the hearing Sir Nicholas unusually left the court for a short time. I only later ascertained that he had done so to avoid letting loose some spontaneous thunderbolts whose force had been diminished after reflection by the time he delivered those still pungent last words.

When Derry, fresh to the Woolsack, launched an attack on fat cat lawyers, I was fingered by the *Daily Mail* as one of the gallery of the greedy, funding a millionaire lifestyle; in my case, said, without any apparent awareness of the incongruity, to be exemplified by my dishevelled appearance, scuffed shoes and second-hand Saab with 100,000 plus miles on the clock. A big spender, other than on my family, I am not; my mother, influenced by her own immigrant childhood, taught me many things, and thrift was certainly among them. Even had I an appetite for luxury goods I lack the taste to make a wise selection. I prefer a little vanity philanthropy, with my endowments carrying my own name.[57]

It was and is increasingly the case that the criminal and family bar struggle to attain a sufficiency, let alone a surfeit of fees. Legal aid is no crock of gold or even of gilt, and claims are scrupulously scrutinised. I once had to take up cudgels on behalf of a fellow bencher who was subject to an investigation for an excessive claim for fees in a publicly funded case in the House of Lords. In another of my cases the issue was whether a solicitor in a criminal case had been entitled to download the case papers for which the firm could charge on a page by page basis when no trial took place after a guilty plea.

There is for all barristers the occasional bad debt – red to set off against the black. A former law officer in Singapore whom I advised on a personal matter simply declined even to acknowledge, let alone pay, the fee notes sent. While a

---

[56] [1992] 1 QB 863. My opponent was Jonathan S who opened his submissions by saying (of me) that some arguments require special talents to advance them. He repented this sardonic remark and wrote me a note of apology the next day.

[57] See examples in chapter six 'Transition to Trinity' as well as the public essay prize at Gray's Inn and a gift to the Oxford Union, recognised in a list of benefactors inscribed at the entrance to the debating chamber. I lack, alas, the humility to make anonymous donations.

solicitor has a professional duty to pay counsel, few barristers would put in jeopardy the prospect of a long-term relationship by triggering it in a single case.

There are some aberrant features of clerkonomics. It is difficult to persuade a clerk that in a competitive world one should ordinarily seek to lower one's charges. There is a belief, sustained, if not consciously, by the teachings of Thorsten Veblen, if few others, that the more one charges the more desirable one becomes. Nor is it always easy to persuade a clerk that if he rejects a solicitor's offer of £5,000 for work that he assesses to be worth £10,000 he has lost his barrister £5,000 rather than somehow won its equivalent, or that desire to accept a brief in a high profile or legally interesting case may outweigh any fee considerations.

I was once offered but did not in the end obtain instructions to act on behalf of the Central Bank of an independent Caribbean state. I happened to be acting in another case in the same jurisdiction and, curious to find out what had happened, asked my solicitor if he could find out through his contacts why the brief had gone elsewhere. He discovered that the bank's solicitors had wanted me to act but since the fee quoted was double that of those tendered by other chambers they could not justify the differential to the bank. When I taxed my clerk with this episode his ingenious explanation was that if word got around among other professional clients that I was prepared to lower my usual rates, they would insist on a similar bargain. Maybe so, maybe not.[58]

Fee assessment has traditionally been an art not a science. The Bar has never been attracted to the idea of quoted hourly rates; indeed, adherence to such a formula favours the slow over the quick. A colleague of mine once explained that he was being paid for 30 years' experience, not for the 30-minute telephone consultation. Nonetheless solicitors have started (reasonably) to have some advance indication of fees, which filters through to the barrister by the clerk's question 'How long do you think this will take you?'. This is a question to which no rational answer can be given before delivery of the papers or indeed until they have already been considered in some depth. Catch 22.

Clients, lay and professional, are much more sensitive to costs than they once were. It is possible that, in the not too distant future, barristers' rates may have to be published which would or could reduce the clerk's role vis à vis fees to one of bare computation. But for the moment, probably forever, the jury is out on whether a fine fee is a reflection of a barrister's talent or the guile of his clerk. Which comes first, the chicken or the egg?

---

[58] On another occasion I was asked to assist a firm which was itself tendering to become legal adviser to a major games event to be staged in England. When their bid failed it declined to pay my fee even though to the best of my – and indeed my clerks' knowledge – I had not accepted instructions on a contingency basis. Years later when a member of the firm took me out to lunch, a few glasses into the excellent meal, he confessed that that had been a try-on, and, if pressed, they would have to have paid up. Even in the best of all possible clerks' worlds, not everything is always perfect. I will add that when my living expenses fell to be taxed after a commercial case in Hong Kong my solicitors relished telling me that the Registrar had described me in his decision as 'a man of considerable modesty' who appeared to be 'virtually teetotal'. Overly greedy I was not.

The current clerking system has survived for so long, because what for me is the first thing, is for many barristers the only thing. Fee is the three-letter word which lies at the core of clerking. As one clerk candidly responded to me when I asked why he had said 'good' after I told him that the other side were appealing a case I had won: 'I was thinking of the added fee'.

There are certain phrases which recur in clerk speak over and above the pervasive 'no probs'. A clerk seeking to sell a less than obviously attractive brief to a reluctant barrister will say 'They specially asked for you', which, actually, means the solicitor is at his wits end because he's tried almost everyone else. A clerk seeking to downplay the decision by a solicitor to send a more attractive brief elsewhere will say 'They will not be instructing you [PAUSE] this time' which consoling words conceal the reality, which is that, for whatever reason, the solicitor will not ever be coming back to you.[59] At the end of a hard day in court the conventional – and well-meant – 'How did it go today?', can be more irritating than soothing, unless one is possessed of the chutzpah of Stanley Brodie who, after a crushing defeat in the High Court, used to retort 'I won the right to open in the Court of Appeal'.

The other main aspect of the clerk's role is to promote the reputation of the barristers in the chambers. Long gone are the days when that role was unique to them. Since a barrister's record and experience is now a matter publicised on a chambers' website for all to see – accompanied, where possible, by laudatory puffs from legal directories or even admiring quotations from unnamed solicitors, there is or should be much less scope for clerical input into the solicitors' selection process. This is especially so when some firms require beauty parades of potential counsel – sometimes, regrettably, a covert means of soliciting a variety of views on an unpaid basis.

Inside the sets new clerks still usually start off as file carriers to court – an exercise in brawn – before being promoted to fixers of fees and arrangers of diaries – an essential role to support a busy barrister – an idiosyncratic version of the career path from shop floor to board room. The internal solidarity of a clerks' room is one of its more attractive features; there are few involuntary departures. One durable character, though a key member of the chambers' five a side football team, was eventually recognised as not making the grade – because directed to deliver an urgent file to the House of Lords where I was appearing, he took it to the famous cricket ground.

As sets of chambers have increased in size, so has the clerks' room with its various annexes. But the salaries paid to clerks would astonish the public even if they pale in comparison with the fees paid to star footballers' agents: justified equally and only by reference to the terms they negotiate for their principals.

---

[59] On occasion of course clerks have to exercise a degree of tact – the truth about what a client has thought about a barrister's performance can sometimes be hurtful. They might not wish to borrow the phrase derived from *Sex and the City* and used by Agony Aunts (as they then were; sex columnists as they now are) explaining to a girl seeking an explanation as to why she has been jilted, 'Maybe X is just not that into you'.

I have a yellowing cutting from Atticus' column in the *Daily Telegraph* in 1973 about clerks entitled 'the Indispensables' recording with a sense of apparent awe 'one clerk in the Temple is rumoured to take home £25,000'. Even taking account of inflation in the intervening half-century Senior Clerks in top sets have long since burst that barrier.

So much has changed upstairs in the profession over the last half century – but far less in the bar's equivalent of downstairs. There is now an Institute of Clerks, yet 'Tempora mutantur nos et mutamur in illis' is not the epigram which most readily springs to mind for the clerks' room, even if two journalists, commenting on the advent of an experimental robot clerk, wrote 'the move is the latest sign of the changing world of the clerk, a role variously described as a pimp or theatrical agent or historically a career for Essex boys who went into the job from school'.[60] Most legal soaps portray sets of chambers and their barrister inmates as if pickled in aspic for several decades. Indeed clerks have altered little at any rate in outward appearance from the days of Rumpole or Kavanagh QC – they are still largely white, largely male, rarely graduate.

That division between the employers and employees is nonetheless far less marked than before. Only the older clerks have not rid themselves of the habit of calling the barristers – at any rate the senior ones – 'sir'. The newcomers happily use first names on first acquaintance. When I travelled to Blackstone from Trinity I would be addressed in the morning by a Fellow as 'President' and in the afternoon by the most junior clerk as 'Michael'.

Assume that whether through good luck or good management a barrister develops a practice, what then? Barristers' main and best-recognised role is to present oral argument. But before a case ever reaches Court and, not infrequently to avoid that outcome, clients want advice sometimes for internal consumption only, but sometimes – and in my case not infrequently – for external circulation to explain the strength of their position on some fraught issue.[61]

My mentor in this secondary exercise was Henry Cecil, nom de plume of a county court judge, but better known as author of such classic comedies as *Brothers in Law*. He wrote that the client's only real interest is in the destination, not the journey, the what rather than the why. So, I would always start my advice by identifying the issue in the first paragraph, and then in the second starting with the familiar formula 'In my view for the reasons hereinafter set out' with what was, for better or for worse, my opinion. Only after that I would set out the facts, the law and how I reached my conclusion. For me this exercise created a quarry from which any forensic submissions could later be excavated. Busy clients might ignore all but the first two paragraphs.

---

[60] *The Times* 15 December 2017 by Jonathan Ames and Francis Gibb.
[61] See, eg, The Report of the Constitutional Affairs Committee on the Consumer Credit Bill, Head of Public Policy and Regulation Lloyds TSB together with the Legal Opinion of the Honourable Michael Beloff QC and Andrew Hunter, Blackstone Chambers, one of many examples.

So, what is a typical day in Court like? High Court hours were presumptively 10:30am to 1pm and 2pm to 4.15 pm – though the timing was always in the hands of the judge or judges. When I started judging myself, I identified this as the key difference between being at the bar or on the bench. Preceded by a clerk and, in most recent times, an admonition to ensure that mobiles are switched off, the judge would enter. Woe betide the latecomer. Stanley Brodie once arrived after the Court had already taken their seats. He apologised with the excuse that his watch said 10.29am. The presiding judge said 'Mr Brodie my watch says 10.31' to which Counsel responded with self-sacrificing sycophancy 'Your lordship's watch is always right'.

The scheduled hours, unlike in arbitration, do not allow for comfort breaks. To gain a brief respite a colleague resorted to the formula 'I am in some personal inconvenience'. Enoch Powell once advised that it was better to speak with a full bladder to give edge to one's eloquence. I must dissent; the first rule for any advocate has always been: enter court with an empty one. There is enough tension from waiting one's turn in the queue. Richard Drabble[62] once turned to me just before the Court of Appeal entered, propelling us to our feet, and asked sotto voce 'why do we do this?' I know exactly how he felt; but if a moment comes when that frisson of fear is extinguished, it is probably time to retire.

Once the case has been called on, the Judge will indicate with a gentle inclination of the head who has the floor. Counsel used to open with the phrase, now obsolescent, 'If your Lordship pleases', to which AP Herbert suggested the addition 'As your Lordship invariably does'. The case will then proceed until what is called the midday adjournment although the metaphorical bell will not sound for another hour when Counsel will politely enquire whether this is 'a convenient moment' – in translation it's time for lunch. Judges will ordinarily take an hour's break, by convention in their Inns, though the tendency towards a rapid sandwich has developed among them as well as among the bar, so that if the morning session has lasted until 1.10 pm they say 'Adjourned until ten past two', unless like some of the keener (usually younger) ones they want to resume as early as possible.

The characteristic atmosphere in court is one of calm and gentility. In the confines of the Court a curt thank you is no substitute for 'I am much obliged to my Learned friend' who may in truth be neither learned, nor a friend. Counsel tend to treat the Judge and each other with sometimes extravagant politeness. 'With respect' means 'I disagree'. 'With great respect' that 'I disagree profoundly' and 'With the greatest respect', 'I simply do not understand how you can adhere to that point' and the insertion of the adjective 'possible' before greatest is a euphemism for 'you seem to have gone off your rocker'.

Not all judges are so clement. Not for nothing was Lord (Sydney) Templeman known at the bar as Syd Vicious. When appearing before him I used to ask my

---

[62] QC Expert in Social Security Law with two famous novelist sisters.

father, once ennobled, to sit in the public seats in the hope that his presence might act as a restraining influence. Lord Justice Lawton was another hard man but wily too. If you said you had four points, he would ask which was your best one; and when you told him he would say 'I don't think much of that one' so discouraging any reference at all to the other three. I was once waiting for my own case to be called on when a portly Midland silk (subsequently a well-regarded High Court Judge) rose ponderously to his feet to open an appeal in a runner (bar speak for a civil claim arising out of a traffic accident). Before he could say anything Lord Justice Lawton said, 'Mr X there's nothing in this is there?', to which the silk replied, 'If your lordship pleases' and sank back equally ponderously onto his seat. Short if not particularly sweet.

At or about teatime another 'convenient moment' will occur, and Counsel will race back to chambers to draft a sketch for the next day's submissions, hold a conference (or, if a silk, a consultation) or write an advice on some wholly different matter. Successful barristers need to be able to keep several balls in the air at once, an aim not always accomplished.

Occasionally proceedings risk a false start when one party or other wishes to challenge the judge on grounds of apparent bias.[63] There was a customary procedure which was used in the good old days on less contentious occasions. The judge would come into court and say that he knew one or other of the parties (if an individual) or owned a part of the shares (if one or other of the parties was a listed company) and ask whether either side had any objection to his continuing to sit. A barely perceptible glance would pass from counsel to solicitor and solicitor to client (if in court) and back, and there would then be an effort by each counsel to be first off the mark to assure his Lordship that they were *entirely* confident that he should continue to preside. On one occasion despite such protestations of confidence the Judge, before whom I was due to appear, decided of his own motion to retire because he had taken communion from a member of the Board of my client (the Broadcasting Standards Commission) on the previous Sunday. What was the actual reason for his disinclination to sit I have to this day have no idea.

Though much of a barrister's time is spent, if not in court then at his desk, occasionally it is necessary to take a look at the locus in quo – or site – simply to get a feel for what might have happened. I say a feel, though in the case of *West Oxfordshire District Council v Beratec*,[64] it was my nose rather than eyes that were engaged, since the issue pivoted around whether or not the Respondents were in breach of an undertaking not to commit a nuisance by smell in their factory used for conversion of chicken offal into chicken feed.

---

[63] Michael Beloff, 'Conflict of Interest – the United Kingdom Dimension' in Cyrus Das and K Chandra (eds), *Judges and Judicial Accountability* (Chandra and Das, 2003). It is a more frequent phenomenon in sports arbitration. See chapter 10, 'My Sporting Life'.

[64] TLR 30 October 1986.

Such visits were of varying degrees of interest. A perennial legal question with implications as wide as the question itself in short is whether someone is an employee or an independent contractor. In 2020 it was resurrected in the Supreme Court in the case of Uber drivers. More than 40 years back in a matter of lesser moment I had to attend a display of mediaeval mummery at Stoneleigh Park to decide into which category women (or wenches as they had to be called) who doubled up as singers and waitresses should be classified. Privately I thought that the real issue was whether they should have been engaged on so hapless an enterprise at all.

Those who were counsel in Lord Scarman's enquiry into the Brixton riots of 1981 went on a walkabout in South London, following in Lord Scarman's wake (rather as the page followed Good King Wenceslas). But inside Lambeth Town Hall, where the hearings took place, there was a display of theatrical oratory – the full Donald Wolfit – by the controversial Rudy Narayan, co-founder of the Society of Black Lawyers. Its volume prompted enthusiastic responses from supporters outside as it was surely designed to do. Lord Scarman wisely refused to rise to the bait.

A discrimination claim was brought by Indian employees of British Steel who refused to employ them because they could not read English safety signs. The parties' lawyers, led by Anthony Lester, whose junior I was, and Derry Irvine trekked out to the company's manufacturing HQ in Suffolk[65] to see whether the refusal was explanation or excuse.

Competition issues were said to arise when my client Sealink decided to launch a catamaran-cum-hovercraft on the Holyhead–Dublin route. I was invited to see the Holyhead harbour and promised a ride in the company executive jet. When I arrived at Gatwick, I was told that our team was too small to justify the expense and offered an alternative trip in a small single-engine propeller plane piloted by someone whose aeronautical career seemed to have peaked during the Korean War. My fear of seeming a coward won out over actual cowardice; we clambered aboard in single file; and the little craft valiantly fought its way through the clouds. We navigated apparently by (occasional) sight of the land below and landed on a runway in Wales otherwise used for military jets performing a series of hair-raising manoeuvres which delayed our departure back.

For the same general purpose I visited the refrigerated bowels of a 'ro-ro' (roll-on roll-off) cargo vessel moored in the Thames estuary (wearing a pink padded overall rather like the Michelin man) and scouted out the site where my client proposed to build riding stables in the vicinity of Lloyd George's grave.[66]

Sometimes, however, it has not been feasible to pay a site visit. In my only murder trial, my client had killed a woman in the public lavatories in St Giles[67] – and

---

[65] I have a fading photograph from the local newspaper, showing us all in our hard hats – very George Osborne.

[66] See chapter 4, 'An Utter Barrister'.

[67] See chapter 5, 'The Silk Road'.

decency as well as squeamishness inhibited me from going down stairs which were firmly marked 'Ladies'. Whether the trans lobby would have called for an alteration in the sign cannot be determined since the facility has been long since decommissioned.

My most bizarre sortie came when I was instructed by Spearmint Rhino, the curiously named international business, which is to lap-dancing what Exxon is to oil production. Its licence to supply alcohol to its customers was under threat because of a complaint made by the Metropolitan Police that 'lewd and indecent' acts were taking place at its various outlets (the club's not the Met's).

According to their American attorney, who instructed me, via a telecon from Los Angeles, the appeal raised high issues of principle focussing on the freedom of expression guarantees in the First Amendment to the American Constitution. In the Highbury Magistrates' Court, the putative location for the hearing, they naturally talk about nothing else. At the end of the consultation the clients' English representatives suggested that I could best appreciate the classy nature of their enterprise by sampling the wares. I suggested that we go at once, insisting only that my solicitor come too, so as to interpose himself between me and the roving lens of any paparazzi. After a cursory glance at the lavish, if ornate furnishings, the well-stocked bar and the naked ladies posturing by the poles, I said that I was satisfied that I had the flavour of the thing.

But my host insisted that I enjoy the Full Monty: I was hustled into an empty booth, guarded by a large bouncer, to be entertained by a striptease performed by a youthful blonde from South Africa, who told me that she had ambitions to be a ballet dancer while I sat, trapped against a wall, with a gaze immovably fixed at a level midway between her belly and her knees. At the end of her Salome-like performance she, noticing my apparent discomfort, said 'Don't worry, my dear, you'll be properly warmed up by the end of the evening' and kissed me lightly on the forehead. I realised then, if not before, that she thought I was a punter, not a lawyer (though the two statuses may not be incompatible). I made, as they say, my excuses and fled. It was, I suppose, all in a day's – or night's – work.

Acting for the Church of Scientology involved visits home and abroad. I went with David Pannick to the Church's English headquarters in East Grinstead where we saw in operation the E-Meter, a device used to locate areas of spiritual distress prior to auditing. David, whose penchant for the appropriate apercu was equalled only by his acute sense of good client relations, murmured 'very interesting, very interesting'. I also went to their blue-fronted headquarters in Hollywood and ventured into the adjacent countryside where, moored in the sand, was the boat whence L Ron Hubbard guided his flock. In one of the cabins was a box into which visitors were invited to 'send a message to Ron'. Impromptu I could think of nothing suitable. There I met with David Miscavige, best described as the Church's CEO and for the believers a kind of John the Baptist figure.

I was asked to attend, as a simple spectator, a hearing in Paris where the Church was represented by the Batonnier, the leader of that city's bar, and to meet in New York Leonard Boudin, the left-wing activist[68] whose other clients included Daniel Ellsberg of Pentagon Papers fame and Dr Benjamin Spock. Neither trip involved me in more arduous activity than to listen and to observe.

During the *Grell Taurel* case[69] I had a Sunday excursion with Helen Mountfield, my Junior, to the island of Tobago, Trinidad's little – and lovelier – sister which was, by coincidence, paying host that very day both to a Caricom conference chaired by Madeleine Albright, the US Secretary of State, and to the inaugural landing of a BA flight. These two huge jets on the tarmac (Airforce 2 and BA Jumbo) flanked and dwarfed the little propeller plane due to take us on the return journey. The stewardess, clipping our return boarding passes, said 'Yours is the one in the middle'. One can never be too careful.

Some of these professional excursions and their spin offs are pleasurable. Others less so. A day's excursion to the Belgian HQ of client Eurocontrol left no time for any refreshment other than a plastic cup of lukewarm coffee. And they speak of the joys of an international practice!…

Potential conflicts of interest are one of the hazards of a barrister's business. At its most basic and obvious level one can only act for one side in a dispute. Once I inadvertently found myself giving advice on a disclosure issue when I had already, some time before, advised the other side on another aspect of the same litigation. (See what I wrote above about balls in the air.) When belatedly a tinkle of recognition sounded in my head I promptly withdrew from the case altogether so no harm was done other than to my income.

Nor can one ordinarily act for two parties even on the same side. I had to turn down a brief for Dame Shirley Porter in the Westminster homes for votes scandal in a case which went all the way to the House of Lords, because I had accepted instructions for a minor player in the same affair, who subsequently, to my excusable irritation, dropped out of the picture.

In the absence of even a perceived conflict of interest, the sensitivities of a potential client can cost a barrister a lucrative set of instructions. I acted on a number of occasions for the Turkish Republic of Northern Cyprus. In one case I had successfully procured a ruling that the decision of Transport for London to ban advertisements for holidays to the northern part of Cyprus was an illegitimate restraint on freedom of commercial free speech.[70] But that had a knock-on effect. The Greek government were looking for representation in a property claim brought in Strasbourg by ex-King Constantine to recover his confiscated royal estate. George Petrochilos, a Greek doctoral student at Trinity, came on a scouting expedition to watch me on my feet in the House of Lords. He told me afterwards that I had passed his quality control test, but that he had concluded

---

[68] Another of the same radical stripe, William Pepper, on a visit to me in Oxford, inscribed 'Orders to Kill' (his analysis of the murder of Martin Luther King) to me with the words 'who with diligence, competence and grace serves two master pursuits – those of justice and truth' – a tribute more eloquent than accurate.

[69] [2002] LLR 655.

[70] [2005] UKHRR 1231.

regretfully that it would be impossible to have me instructed, since the most superficial research by any journalist would uncover that I had already represented their surrogate enemy.

Abdullah Ocalan, the Kurdish leader, needed to evaluate the prospect of an emergency application,[71] also to Strasburg, to restrain his possible execution. In the event the Turkish Government decided instead to imprison him for life. Some while later I was invited to the Turkish embassy and asked if I would be interested in handling their human rights cases before the same Court. This would have meant a constant stream, indeed an overflowing torrent, of work, because Turkey was a record-breaking recipient of claims there for various breaches of the Convention. But once I told them, without revealing any details, I would not be able to act for them in any case involving Mr Ocalan, I heard no more about the possible retainer.

I also accepted – unenthusiastically – the view of my senior clerk to refuse one-off instructions from the Spanish Ambassador to advise on the vires of the referendum proposed by the Gibraltar government on Gibraltar's status which he accurately said would, if accepted, cause grave offence to the Gibraltar government who were then regular clients but would have been unlikely to remain so.

A further self-imposed rule was never to represent a friend. The exercise of advocacy is strenuous enough without distortion by that added responsibility. Jeffrey decided to bring a libel action against the *News of the World* for alleging that he had slept with a call girl, Monica Coughlan, and then tried to buy her silence. He asked me to represent him. I prudently declined. Through the forensic skills of Bob Alexander and the summing up of the judge, Mr Justice Caulfield, smitten with Mary's 'fragrance',[72] Jeffrey won the case, but my reluctance, with the benefit of hindsight, proved wise for it was Jeffrey's own evidence in that case which later led to his perjury charge and conviction.[73]

By coincidence while the criminal case was pending, I had arranged for Jeffrey to come to address the Political Society at Trinity. Forty-eight hours before it was due to start a highly embarrassed Nick Purnell QC, his leading Counsel, telephoned me to say that the trial judge, Potts J, had forbidden Jeffrey to fulfil his commitment. Both Nick and I doubted the Judge's power to make such an exorbitant order, which fanned Jeffrey's belief that the Judge had taken against him (a fear he later confided to me),[74] but we both agreed that it would be counterproductive for Jeffrey to challenge the ruling.

---

[71] Just before the consultation in Trinity I was asked by *The Times* to write a piece about Lord Denning who had died the day before. But I was also due on that day to speak to the sixth form at a girls' school near Abingdon. Less risk-averse and more energetic than I now am, I scribbled some lines before I left, had the typescript faxed to me at the school, and sent it on just in time.

[72] In 2021 use of the adjective was belatedly proscribed in the *Judicial Equalities Handbook*.

[73] Jonathan A never made the same suggestion though he did ask me informally for some general advice. Another outstanding silk, Charles Gray, seemed by all accounts to have persuaded a jury of Jonathan's virtue, until George Carman pulled another winning rabbit out of his bottomless hat. Jonathan later suffered the same fate as Jeffrey.

[74] Jeffrey Archer, *A Prison Diary* (Archer, 2002) vol 1, p 71.

Sarcastically I inquired whether the order also prevented Jeffrey from coming to dine (a matter to which Potts J had not, it seemed, turned the judicial mind). It did not, so Jeffrey at least had his supper but without singing for it. Some enterprising undergraduate wrote over the poster advertising his visit 'Postponed to a later date' and earned the usual £5 from Private Eye for its inclusion in its I-Spy section.

Jeffrey's solicitor asked me to be a character witness at the criminal trial. I was certainly not disposed to abandon an old friend in his hour of need; but, required by my oath to tell the truth the whole truth and nothing but the truth, I feared I might have been in some difficulty if asked whether I thought that Jeffrey had always and absolutely subscribed to the same principle.

As Mary once elegantly put it, he had a 'gift for inaccurate precis' – and his flights of fancy, which surely fuelled his success as a writer of best sellers, were sometimes, if harmlessly, detached from strict reality. When Jeffrey was giving a Robert Kennedy memorial lecture in the Oxford Union library I had crept in after a high table dinner to enjoy the performance. Jeffrey spotted me and started an impromptu riff about how, stunned by the news of RFK's assassination, we had walked round the Radcliffe Camera in a candlelit procession of mourning students. But it was at the time of JFK's not RFK's assassination that we were both up at Oxford together; and any candlelit procession was, I am all but certain, a figment of his novelist's imagination.

Not so another episode which actually *did* happen. Jeffrey and I were walking together through Westminster to collect Mary from some function hosted by Colin Moynihan when a young woman stopped Jeffrey in the street. She told him that, when her boyfriend had been seriously ill in hospital, she had brought him Jeffrey's latest novel to cheer him up, and that he had afterwards swiftly recovered. Whether Jeffrey's fables had the therapeutic qualities attributed to the mediaeval monarchs, *les rois thaumaturges*, may be doubted; but I can vouch for the truth of the tale. To borrow the title of a biography about Jeffrey it was indeed *Stranger than Fiction*, but I was uncertain as to how it might play with a cynical jury.

My witness statement was accordingly carefully prepared. I was able to testify to Jeffrey and Mary's close and mutually supportive relationship, to the popularity that Jeffrey enjoyed among the many people we had met on our overseas trips to sporting events and to Jeffrey's 'capacity to raise one's enthusiasm and one's love of life whenever one comes into contact with him'.[75] With my then senior clerk, Martin Smith, as chaperone, I passed – for the only time in my life[76] – through the doors of the Old Bailey. Potts J, before whom I had appeared as counsel on several occasions, clearly was unenthusiastic about my presence in the witness box but my ordeal was short-lived. Prosecuting Counsel Roy Amlot QC rose to his feet and asked me but a single question, 'Mr Beloff do you consider that someone who aspires to public office should be a person of integrity?'[77] It was what Latinists

---

[75] Margaret Crick, *Mary Archer: For Richer, for Poorer* (Crick, 2005) p 252.
[76] One lunch apart. See chapter 11, 'Judge Not Lest Ye Be Judged'.
[77] Ibid.

called a nonne rather than a num question. Even I could not be troubled by so soft a ball. Grateful for small mercies I sped past the paparazzi on a relieved return to chambers. When the Bailiff of Guernsey expressed some displeasure at one of the Bailiwick's appellate judges giving character evidence on Jeffrey's behalf, David Williams reminded me that Felix Frankfurter had done the same for Alger Hiss. If precedent were needed, that one carried some weight.

As part of my training to become an Assistant Recorder I had been sporadically exposed to prison life. Being a prison visitor for Jeffrey was quite unlike that experience. Far away in the bleak fenland though his open prison was, it was as difficult to make a booking for a visit to see him as for the most popular of West End shows. I went à deux with Gillian Shepherd – and the week after Michael Portillo, not on this occasion on one of his great British Railway Journeys. Jeffrey, ever irrepressible, talked non-stop about his role in the prison library and the characters he had met – many of which featured in his *Prison Diaries*. He has always had a unique capacity to turn even the most unpromising of situations to his advantage.

Once restored to the outside world Jeffrey resumed his previous life as author, auctioneer and host – in mid-summer marquees, where the Archer garden seemed somehow miraculously immune to the ambient cloudbursts, and at the classic Krug and Shepherd's pie – the sublime to wash down the ridiculous – pre-Christmas parties in his Embankment penthouse with a fairly fixed cast list of ever decreasing remnants of the Thatcher-Major cabinets and a few newer Tory faces (Priti Patel, Kwasi Kwarteng, Adam Afriye), hacks, luvvies and other celebs. Jeffrey lost only few friends as a result of his incarceration; and rightly so. He had paid his dues.[78]

At one of our quarterly dinners pre his sequestration Jeffrey announced with a flourish that I had been chosen to propose the health of the happy couple on their fortieth wedding anniversary. He reminded me that my predecessor at the thirtieth had been the sometime contender for the Democratic presidential nomination in 1988, Senator Bill Bradley. I count this among my most challenging extra-curricular oratorical assignments, matched only by the occasion when I had to address (impromptu) a thousand or so supporters of the Chinese secondary school movement in Malaysia with reliance on a young interpreter to make what sense she could of my emollient English phrases.

Margaret Thatcher congratulated me on 'a very fine speech' before the climax of the evening – a musical parade of the band of the Grenadier Guards in perfect step and harmony turning and turning about out of the artificially created mist, a classic Archer spectacular. A year and a half later at the annual Christmas party I reminded George Carey, former Archbishop of Canterbury and Jeffrey's favourite grace sayer, that we had met at the anniversary. He reminisced that the master of ceremonies had proposed an excellent toast. I was uncertain as to whether to be

---

[78] It was, nonetheless, suggested to me that to bring him to lunch at the Bencher's table in Gray's Inn might be a step too far.

offended by the fact that he could not recall my face but decided I was more flattered that he could recall my speech.

Ten years on Jeffrey, again a free man, invited me to make a comeback. Like George Carey, but with more excuse given the passage of time, he had forgotten that I had performed the same role before. When I reminded him, he said 'Don't worry. No one will remember a word you said'. Despite that ambiguous encouragement and overcoming the temporary silencing of the microphone – a device I hate using since it suggests an inability to be heard without it – I took my motto from Frank Sinatra 'let me try again'. If sixtieth anniversary there were to be I shall be (if still alive) in the audience not at the rostrum. The Cab Rank principle is inoperative outside the bar.

It is often said that a barrister is only as good as his last case. I always operated on the basis that my next case might be my last case. At the Bar, as in most walks of life, there are good moments and bad ones, snakes (usually temporary) and ladders (usually more permanent).

One snake is being replaced by another Counsel for reasons other than a collision of dates. It used to be the convention that the successor Counsel would write to the one succeeded as a matter of professional courtesy, a practice which, while intended to sweeten the pill, tended to rub salt in the wound. The reasons are various and can be bizarre: one lay client, against the solicitor's strong advice, relied on Chinese metaphysics to replace me. Sometimes, like a football club hoping that a change of manager will improve the record of a losing team (often rightly), the lay client opts to roll the dice. Sometimes it is because Counsel is at odds as to strategy or merits with the solicitor, who may already have committed himself. Sometimes it is the Attorney-General exercising a legal droit de seigneur. I gave original advice in the famous Belmarsh case where the House of Lords held that detention of foreigners suspected of terrorism violated their human rights. Sometimes it is both simply and rightly because the barrister has fallen below a desired standard (I confess that I gave inadequate original advice in the *Tin Council* case) or given, through misunderstanding, advice other than the advice wholly on the topic desired (with on at least one occasion the client refusing to allow me a second chance to get it right or even to pay for what I had so far provided). In these scenarios, all of which I have experienced, the common factor is a sense of hurt.

Another snake is when one has overlooked a material fact buried in the instructions or a relevant point of law. In a case in the Supreme Court, arising out of the now defunct *News of the World*'s telephone tapping designed to enrich its sources, the issue was whether the alleged hacker could resist giving evidence on the basis of the privilege against self-incrimination including of the offence of conspiracy.[79] I argued that the language of the relevant provision of the relevant

---

[79] [2012] UKSC 28.

statute encompassed the infringement 'from conception to death' and that any agreement which amounted to a criminal conspiracy to intercept messages is sufficiently 'wrapped up with' the interception to come within it. Lord Walker said this 'Neither the respondents' written case nor Mr Beloff's oral submissions cited any authority in support of these metaphorical propositions. But there is authority which provides such support'. Ouch.[80]

I can only remind myself of the last line in the film *Some Like it Hot*, 'nobody's perfect'. The only lesson to be learned from these mistakes, whether spotted by one's client, lay or professional, or publicised in observations by judges or jurists, is that one *should* learn from one's mistakes.

On the ladder's side of the board is the scenario when one attracts clients who have been on the losing side of one's advocacy. After the Dr Gee case I was instructed to defend Esther Rantzen's *That's Life* in another libel action (which settled). The City of London, whose efforts to prevent adult swimmers from enjoying the facilities of Hampstead Ponds without the presence of a life guard I had defeated,[81] instructed me to defend a plan which put at risk the very future of the Ponds.[82] And two high profile businessmen decided that it would be better to have me as an ally than an enemy – Ernest Saunders – whom I had first encountered when I represented most of the upmarket print and broadcasting media to resist an ambitious application that the trial of the Guinness four be held in private[83] – which had it succeeded would have been a loss to journalism as much as to justice – and Willie Stern who had me briefed to defend him against a director's disqualification application,[84] having watched me on my feet in a somewhat arcane (to me) agency case in which he was the defendant to my client's claim.[85]

I have frankly often found it odd that such switches are not more common but, especially in my early junior years, I concluded, uncharitably, that some solicitors were bound to their regular barrister in a relationship of shared incompetence, or a mutuality of mediocrity. Even later on in my career I faced an opposing QC who was sacked in mid-case by his client who reasoned, correctly on my view, that he could make a better fist of his case than could the experienced counsel who was representing him so poorly. Maybe the market explains the phenomenon; not everyone could

---

[80] In the *Morgan Grenfell* case about whether legal professional privilege applied to documents in the taxpayers' hands which the Revenue wished to see. I had advised the Bank that it would win in the House of Lords; but two successive defeats in the Courts below led to my replacement before this final staging point. Lord Hoffmann said of one argument for the Revenue which was on the opposite side that 'it had difficulties which were not fully addressed either in the Court of Appeal or in the Taylor case'. That is to say, to put it bluntly, that I had overlooked a significant argument in the Court below. It was small consolation to me that my prediction was vindicated when my advocacy was not, or even that the reference to the Taylor case involved a similar criticism of none other than Tom Bingham. Ouch encore. Academics can also exercise hindsight after the event. See AW Bradley [2000] PL 518 suggesting a point I could have made in [2000] 1 AC 395.

[81] See chapter 11, 'My Sporting Life'.

[82] I had to return the brief because of a clash of dates.

[83] [1990] TLR 2 Feb.

[84] [2001] 1 All ER 633.

[85] [1994] 2 All ER 864.

afford, say David Pannick, even were he to be available. But once when I was acting for Lloyd's defending one of the many claims brought by the names, I was astonished that my opponent did no more than read out the skeleton argument, drafted by his junior, with intermittent comments which gave the impression, true or false, that he was previously unacquainted with that document.[86] I had to deploy no greater skills than did Mohammad Ali when, in his second fight against Sonny Liston, the latter obligingly for reasons never fully explained lay down in the first round on receipt of what appeared to be a featherweight punch.

Success in a case which has been identified as unwinnable by other Counsel (and indeed may have been lost by them) is another ladder. The Indian Oil Corporation had been the object of an award of $18 million damages. Unusually one of the arbitrators, Gordon Pollock QC, added a postscript saying in effect that the IOC's legal team had a stronger case than had been advanced on its behalf. The award was made under the Arbitration Act 1979 and by agreement was unappeal-able. There appeared to be no remedy; two QCs successively so advised. Sarosh Zaiwalla,[87] newly instructed and no stranger to ingenious arguments, drafted an application on a ground described by yet a third QC as 'illusory', which was that the award was not based on a true analysis of the evidence so that its enforcement would be contrary to public policy. He passed it to me to present it. Since nothing ventured is nothing won, I decided to give it a whirl. Lord Justice Evans accepted the argument borrowing a classic dictum of Lord Atkin's 'finality is a good thing, but justice is better'.[88]

A third, and in my view, the highest, ladder scaled is the receipt of instructions on behalf of another barrister whose career is at stake because of some alleged misconduct or serious breach of the Bar's Code of Conduct. Such acts speak louder than words.[89]

One such client wrote to my Senior Clerk

> for what it is worth, in one capacity or another, over the last 30 years I have had the pleasure of watching many well-known members of the Bar give outstanding displays of advocacy, both on paper and in court. Among them, I would mention especially Lenny Hoffmann, Tom Bingham, Sidney Kentridge and Michael Briggs. I am not sure that any of them over-topped what we got from Michael during the last month. As my wife whispered to me in court 'talk about age cannot wither him'. The man is a marvel and whereas most of us are supposed to have dimmed by the time we get to his decade he seems to be one of the very lucky ones who loses none of his intellectual force or powers of advocacy, not to mention stamina (as my father would have said: 'lucky dab'). He was, quite simply, magnificent … It was an awesome performance.[90]

---

[86] On the prudent advice of my son I shall avoid referencing the law report to prevent identification of the Counsel.

[87] Whose admission to the United Kingdom I had procured as an immigration junior many moons before.

[88] S Zaiwalla, *Honour Bound* (Zaiwalla, 2020) p 55.

[89] For further examples than those given below see chapter 14, 'The Art of Advocacy'.

[90] I have struggled but failed to resist recalling that when I met the Judge in the street he added his halfpennyworth by saying 'You were wonderful'.

Along with Philip Sales,[91] then Treasury Devil, I was asked to advise Peter Goldsmith as to whether the Bar Council had any disciplinary jurisdiction over him in relation to the advice he gave as Attorney-General to Tony Blair as to the legality of the proposed invasion of Iraq. We decided that it did not, an advice which coincided with that of David Williams, separately instructed on the same issue.[92]

The Bar proclaims itself as an honourable profession; a feature, as I have mentioned, drawn to the attention of the newly called by every Treasurer of an Inn of Court. One has to trust one's opponents; and be trusted by the Court. But that trust can be illustrated in less obvious ways.

In one of my last cases as a junior I had been led by Stephen Sedley, himself still a junior, and instructed by Harriet Harman on behalf of a Mr Williams, suing for his treatment when detained in a so-called controversial and short-lived Control Unit, introduced by the then Home Secretary as another step of the endless search to cut crime.[93] Stephen had been unsuccessful in his own application for silk in 1980 so in the Court of Appeal there was a role reversal, unusual, if not unique in which I then led him.

In a speech in the House of Commons Peter Rawlinson suggested that Stephen had, during the hearing at first instance, read out in open court extracts from an 800-page dossier of home office documents for the sole purpose of hitting the headlines. I wrote to Sir Peter (whom I had never then met) a letter in which I explained that Mr Williams' team had indeed discussed whether or not reading out these documents would better his case in the eyes of the Judge but not whether it would do so in the eyes of the press. In his reply Sir Peter said that he naturally accepted an explanation from a fellow member of the Bar. The interchange provided an insight, very much I suspect of its time, into the assumption that the Bar was a profession for gentlemen. The next year Stephen got silk and the injustice of his earlier failure was properly corrected.[94]

---

[91] JSC.

[92] I referred to this advisory overlap in the introductory passage of my Williams lecture: *Denning Law Journal* (2010).

[93] [1981] 1 All ER 1411.

[94] The story did not end there. Harriet was found guilty of contempt of court for disclosing Home Office documents released for the purpose of the litigation only to a newspaper reporter – the *Guardian*'s David Leigh. While most of the information had been read out in court, Leigh used the documents in depth to write a story criticising the setting-up of the units. The Appeal Court and House of Lords upheld the finding of contempt against Harriet. But the case forced the government to liberalise the contempt laws after she won a case in Strasbourg that the finding infringed her right to freedom of expression.

But that was not the only consequence of the case from my perspective. In 1980 Lord Hailsham, the Lord Chancellor, had invited me to become a member of a committee chaired by Tom Bingham, to make recommendations on what steps could be taken in response to the Strasbourg decision. Nicholas Lyell, the Solicitor-General, was interviewed by the Committee. He must have sensed the way that the wind was blowing in favour of liberalisation because shortly after the Committee was stood down.

In an article for *Verdict*, the Oxford Law Society magazine,[95] I wrote

> It isn't necessary to be a little mad to be a barrister, but it helps. Every case is (you think) your last one. If you have too little work, you fret; if you have too much work, you fret more. The Greek notion of the golden mean is utterly alien to the practising advocate; practice is like a shower with a defective fitting – either too hot or too cold. and with no means of controlling it to the right degree of amenable warmth.

True, if not the whole truth.

And in a speech 'A Career at the Bar' which, as I've mentioned I hawked round school after school sixth form in the hope of recruiting the best and brightest to Trinity, my final answer to the question 'Why become a barrister?' was

> Most of all though, because it is a drug which once swallowed makes you an addict for life. It has given me many sleepless nights, lost weekends, sacrificed holidays but there is nothing quite like the excitement of untying the red tape which surrounds new briefs and identifying the problem, new or old, which you are invited to solve; nothing quite like that anxious moment when you rise to your feet, grasp the lectern, and say, with the butterflies still flapping in your stomach, 'My Lord, in this matter I appear with my Learned Friend', nothing quite like the exhilaration of fencing with the wise judge, or jousting with the clever opponent, while knowing that, however hard the contest inside the Court, the warm relationships outside it will remain undamaged, nothing quite like the adrenalin surge of the successful submission, or the satisfaction of snatching victory from the jaws of defeat.

In the electronic era the tape around instructions has disappeared into the dustbin of ages past; but my sentiments remain the same.

---

[95] 40th anniversary edition, Hilary 2004.

14

The Art of Advocacy

It is a truth generally acknowledged that if a judge praises your presentation in his judgment – the standard formula being 'Mr X has said everything that could possibly be said on his client's behalf' – you have lost the case. Criticism of your presentation is, alas, no prelude to victory. In *R v Horsham Justices ex parte Farquharson*,[1] Lord Justice Shaw said that a submission of mine was 'with all respect to Mr Beloff's forensic prowess, talking in the air'. In *The Raphael*,[2] Lord Justice Donaldson said 'Finally Mr Beloff put forward a new submission. Initially I thought that I was being obtuse in not understanding it, but I was relieved to find that My Lords appeared to suffer from a similar disability'. This was not all. After identifying the content of the submission, he continued 'Mr Beloff frankly admitted that this was an argument of last resort. Not only is it an argument of last resort, it is also plainly wrong …'. In that case my Junior Charles Hollander moved stealthily along the bench behind to make it appear that he was on the other side supporting a Brick Court silk; indeed, shortly afterwards he did switch to those specialist commercial chambers. In *Saunders v Richmond Upon Thames LBC*,[3] I was accused of making 'numerous submissions, mainly of a trifling nature'.

Christine Hamilton in a textbook example of spousal loyalty fired two successive shots at me when I represented Mr Al Fayed against her husband Neil, the former MP, in his various cases arising out of the cash-for-questions saga.[4] She described me as 'droning on at interminable length' in the House of Lords on a preliminary issue about parliamentary privilege. She elaborated her critique when I appeared in the Court of Appeal to rebut the allegation that Mr Al Fayed's victory in the subsequent libel action had been unfairly achieved because the Al Fayed team had advance notice of the Hamilton cross-examination strategy gleaned from documents retrieved from chambers' dustbins by the scavenger known as Benjy the Binman.[5] Not only did I remain 'interminable' but

---

[1] [1982] QB 762 at p 796.
[2] [1982] 2 LLR 42.
[3] [1978] ICR 82.
[4] Christine Hamilton, *For Better for Worse* (Hamilton, 2005) pp 213, 246.
[5] In Lady Hale's *Spiderwoman: A Life – by the former President of the Supreme Court* (Hale, 2021), a member of the Court discusses the case with an illustration of Mr Al Fayed's Boycott like defensive strokes to his cross-examination, p161. I would have quoted this myself, but she got there first!!

'I never used one word where fifteen would do. A Beloff performance exhausts time and begins to trespass upon eternity' (a line originally attributed apocryphally to Lord Denning). Not to be outdone Neil described me as 'a fungus-faced geriatric Teletubby. Much of the time he is buried in his notes. When he does look up at the judges, he flutters his eyelids, squints and speaks with his eyes shut'.

While I admire Christine's decision to stand by her man it is just possible that her, and his, judgement was affected by the fact that Neil lost the case. Lord Phillips MR, presiding, described it as 'being about a load of rubbish' (a little laughter in Court) – a summary to which she also took objection. *Private Eye* rechristened me Michael Ballsoff QC in one of their recurrent series of law reports before that all-purpose judge Mr Justice Cocklecarrot.

Obstinately undaunted by these dicta, I lectured and wrote about advocacy,[6] reasoning that this exercise might create the impression, false or not, that I knew something about the subject.[7]

My starting point used to be that advocates are born, not made. In my Howard lecture I drew a crude analogy with the difference between sprinting and distance running, claiming that it is necessary for success as a sprinter to have fast twitch muscles while distance runners have to train hard to compensate for lack of such genetic advantage. Unfortunately, my audience included Sir Roger Bannister who took mild umbrage at my premise. But watching advocacy trainers on Gray's Inn awaydays working their magic on the young I appreciated, albeit belatedly, that advocacy can indeed be taught; and I myself by the same token have learned that it can be learned – at any rate up to a point.

So, what are the lessons I have gleaned from experience, bitter or sweet? There are many. The object of the exercise is not to show the judge how clever one is but to show the judge how clever he is. The only audience to keep in mind is the court, not the client. The client may relish grandstanding at the time, but not if, when judgment has been delivered, he has lost the case. Still less is it the press. In order that the judge should be led up the right rather than the garden path consider use of the hallowed precept that a submission should be in three parts 'say what you are going to say, say it and say what you've said'[8] (even if the modern judicial habit of clock watching demands removal of the third section). An initial route map is at least as helpful to the judge as it is to the advocate.

Submissions should be structured like a downhill ski race, where the racer seeks the best line down the slope to arrive at the finishing line, and not like a slalom where he veers from side to side. If one's first point should be one's best

---

[6] 'The Art of Advocacy', Margaret Howard Lecture, Oxford 2000. 'Advocacy a Craft under Threat', First Espeland lecture, Oslo 2002. 'Advocacy the End of the Affair', *New Statesman*, January 2004.

[7] I also chaired a panel of High Court Judges at the Bar Conference for the young bar entitled 'Master Class' and another panel of a quartet of Gray's Inn stars for Inn students called 'Tricks of the Trade'.

[8] Mr Justice Fordham at the launch of the seventh edition of his innovative *Judicial Review Handbook*, which dissects administrative law into a series of propositions, claimed to have been influenced by my 'goldmine reported submissions'. The seam may have been too swiftly exhausted. Anyhow all that glisters is not necessarily gold.

point one's last point should certainly be one's last point. It should not be followed up by an interminable sequence of 'in conclusion', 'finally' and 'to end' (and worse still 'for completeness' which is simply a synonym for superfluous). There are few, if any, tribunals that nowadays allow an advocate unrestricted opportunity to make submissions.

I once appeared in the High Court in Singapore in a complex commercial dispute[9] against a venerable silk from Lincoln's Inn whose appeal it was. The Chief Justice asked him for an estimate of the length of his opening and he replied: 'about five days'. The judge then leaned forward somewhat threateningly and said 'Mr ...' – I'll charitably omit the silk's name – 'Singapore does not have five days available for your opening'. So disconcerted was my opponent by this observation that he actually stepped backward and was only stopped from falling by the prompt action to prop him up of his Lilliputian local junior. While he shortly recovered his balance, he never recovered his stride.

'Horses for courses' is another useful guideline. It is futile to address the disciplinary tribunal of the British Board of Boxing Control as if it were the Supreme Court, and even more futile, were that conceivable, to address the Supreme Court as if it were the British Board of Boxing Control. Advocacy is usually easier for a senior silk appearing before a domestic tribunal because of the disproportionate respect sometimes paid to one's status. But for that very reason it is necessary to avoid becoming tagged as a 'cow pasture' barrister (the metaphor is taken from shot putting) in top form only in low-level events. As with mountaineering, the higher one climbs, the more difficult, but also more rewarding the activity. I found, counterintuitively, a much more relaxed and conversational atmosphere in the House of Lords and Supreme Court than in other courts[10] partly because the judges were and are unrobed, partly because they sit at eye level so that counsel is only metaphorically looking up to them.

In the European courts there is an added dimension of difficulty. Submissions made in English have to be translated for the benefit of the non-Anglophone judges. The key is to make sentences short – and, if possible, to speak to the interpreters in advance giving them a provisional text. Rhetorical flourishes should be avoided. I once ended a speech in Strasbourg with the words 'It is of the essence of the rule of law that legislation should be fair, rational and should always be observed'. The interpreter misheard and mistranslated the last adjective as 'absurd'.

Nowadays younger members of my Chambers appearing for the first time before a particular judge prudently circulate emails asking for any useful information about the judge's perceived likes or dislikes, better to equip themselves for the task to come. Some judges are interventionist – the less so the further removed they are from their initial appointment from the Bar – for old habits die hard. Robin Jacob, an intellectual property specialist, always enjoyed a chatty

---

[9] [1993] Sing LR 114.
[10] My take is quoted in *Final Judgment* (Paterson, 2013) p 33.

dialogue. Others prefer a monastic silence. David Eady, a libel specialist, made the sphinx appear garrulous.

As to style I am a fan of Aesop's fable, in which the Wind and the Sun were disputing which could cause a traveller to take off his cloak more quickly. The Wind blew hard but the traveller only wrapped his cloak more closely around him. The Sun shone hard and the traveller doffed his cloak. Final Score Sun 1: Wind 0. Aesop's motto was 'Kindness effects more than severity'. Likewise, for an advocate, charm works better than bluster.[11] I was never one to challenge my opponent to make my day being by temperament, unlike my father, more diplomat than warrior.[12]

But with some judges neither is effective. Jeremiah Harman, who died aged 90 in 2020, was known as Harman the Horrible. When I appeared before him in a case where my client was responsible for aspects of the career of Madonna, the uninhibited chanteuse, he snarled 'Mr Beloff, Madonna was the mother of the Christ'. And what was I to say next? Neville Faulks suffered from a troublesome skin complaint, and to ease the itch would sometimes walk about the Courtroom dais – and on one occasion right out of the Courtroom – as if the script said exit stage left. I thought it wiser to pause my submissions rather than to continue to address them to the royal coat of arms behind the judge's chair.

Always, always, always, in the scout's motto, be prepared. When I was a very, very junior I found myself in the robing room putting on my milk-white wig next to Robert Johnson,[13] accompanied, as senior silk were in those days, by a clerk who had physical custody of his brief. Turning to this prototype Sancho Panza, Robert asked 'Remind me which side I'm on' before sweeping courtwards. I was stunned by this seemingly genuine throwaway line.

Still, it is unwise to trust that it will all come right on the night. In one insurance case in which I was against Gordon Pollock the signs were that it would settle; and I gambled that it would. Come the morning and there was still no confirmatory call. Only when I came at break of dawn into chambers to do as much last-minute swotting up as time allowed, did our early bird fees clerk say that there was a message on the answerphone that settlement had indeed been achieved. If I were religious, I would have given a silent prayer to a merciful deity. I still wonder what I would have done if the case had fought. Gordon was in court the forensic equivalent of the great white shark – though out of it a good companion. A split personality not unique to but not uncommon at the Bar.

---

[11] I have to say that, since in Chambers Directory 2019, an anonymous referee said 'He could charm the birds out of the trees', the tribute being only slightly devalued by the cliché and the fact that it brought me no benefit since by then I had retired from advocacy.

[12] Stephen Sedley in a flight of fancy at a post seminar speech in Lincoln's Inn compared a clutch of leading advocates to composers. He chose Wagner as my musical counterpart (not, as far as I could tell, because the length of my submissions exceeded *The Ring*). I would have preferred a dulcet Italian analogy.

[13] Chairman of the Bar and High Court Judge.

There was one silk with whom I worked who was famous for his elaborate submissions made without a single note. But his performance reminded me of Dr Johnson's comparison of a woman's preaching and a dog's walking on its hind legs. 'It is not done well; but you are surprised to find it done at all'. Another made no distinction between advocacy and recitation. Even after being diverted by some judicial question, he would give himself stage directions 'I must now return to my script'. The best technique must be located somewhere between these two extremes but precisely where, that is the question.[14]

Out of a mild respect for the fourth estate, not to speak of a desire to see my name in print, I would try, at the outset of a case that might attract some attention, to incorporate into the opening paragraph of my submission some phrase, whatever its intrinsic merit or lack thereof, that was easily transferable into a news story. I always felt sorry for the reporter who was reduced to writing uninformatively 'The Council acted unlawfully says QC'. In seeking to preserve the right of stag hunters to cross National Trust Territory[15] I spoke of the 'obliteration of an immemorial tradition after the briefest of debate'. When applying for an injunction against a Mr Boddington who continued to smoke on trains run by Connex I said that he was 'publicly, persistently and even proudly' flouting my client's regulations: the alliteration hit the bull's eye on the press bench. Still more succinctly, when representing the Kent brewery Shepherd Neame, who claimed that the proposed one pence-a-pint increase in duty was in breach of European harmonisation rules, I called it 'a threat to British beer' which again satisfied the media's desire for a snappy headline. There was one occasion when oddly I did not fail to manipulate or even anticipate the coverage. Persuading the Court that a jury should be empanelled for the Princess Diana Inquest because of the lessons which might be learned from it, I riffed, on the spur of the moment, about the intrusive press coverage to which the then Kate Middleton was being made subject.[16]

Cross examination in witness actions requires different skills to submission, but in both aspects, it is best to start low and end high: in submission because one's own witnesses may, for whatever reason, depart from proof, in cross-examination of the other party's witnesses because it is better to start with questions which are unlikely to provoke dissent. Not all witnesses roll over like Prince Andrew, albeit apparently without awareness on Newsnight. Cross-examination is easiest when the witness has committed himself in print to a point of view different to that which he advances from the witness box. I would echo Job 'oh that mine adversary had written a book' – but an article can do the trick. In an insurance case where the issue was whether a nationalist uprising against the Portuguese colonial power fell within the war risks exclusion clause, the other side's expert had committed himself in a journal, not only to a different analysis to the one which he had been engaged to support at trial, but the exact opposite.[17] Even I could scarcely miss

---

[14] Alan Moses said pithily, but privately, that one must find the judicial G spot.
[15] [1995] 1 WLR 1037.
[16] Inquest Law Reports 198.
[17] [1991] 2 LLR 281.

such an open goal. I took the expert sentence by sentence through his article to the dismay of my opponent Bernard Rix and the barely suppressed mirth of the judge Mr Justice Saville.[18] Had there been any wind in St Dunstan's, then the home of the commercial court, the expert would surely have twisted in it.

(By contrast where the case is of the common or garden 'he said she said' variety, one has to trust to luck and make use of that unavailing phrase beloved of the youngest barrister confronting the obdurate policeman 'I put it to you ...', preferably not followed up, still more feebly, with a variant of the classic cliché 'Don't fence with me officer'. The recurrent reality is that it may be the other parties' witnesses who are telling the truth and obstinately sticking with it – the bxtrstxrds!)

I have become, not only because of that singular incident, sceptical about experts. I have never encountered a situation, which ought to be the norm, in which an expert to whom my solicitors had made approaches rejected the approach on the simple basis that he did not accept the argument he was being asked to support. And on occasion an expert who in consultation seemed like a typhoon would be reduced to a zephyr in court by some not particularly pungent questions from my opponent. It is advisable to use a consultation to quiz the expert in advance of the trial. The pugilist who succumbs to blows in the gym is unlikely to remain upright when it comes to the fight itself.

I have to issue a health warning about these precepts, few of which are anyway applicable to jury trials. The *Daily Mail* once described me as 'one of the Bar's more eccentric performers, exuding an air of indifference which lures his opponents into a false sense of security'.[19] The lure, if any, was accidental not designed.

I was always an admirer of the contribution made by academics to the law. Indeed, my first port of call, when confronted by a new set of instructions, was to see whether anyone had written anything about any point of law in issue, whether in textbook, treatise, practitioners' handbook or journal. I was always too conscious of this apparent anomaly. I could for a substantial fee address a legal issue explored in greater depth and at greater length by some legal scholar who was paid far less for the research, if indeed paid at all. But an academic will enjoy complexity, while the advocate must strive for simplicity: To adapt Isaiah Berlin's analogy, the academic will be the hedgehog, the advocate must be the fox.

The twentieth century may be seen not only as the golden, but as the last, true age of advocacy. Those born with silver tongues in their mouths could once achieve a celebrity status nowadays accorded to a singer's sibling, a footballer's partner in one-night stand, or anyone, male or female, who combines the maximum of physical charms with the minimum of designer clothing. Silks could save men from the gallows, destroy reputations or, as in the Archer Shee case, the real-life version of Rattigan's *The Winslow Boy*, stand up for justice

---

[18] Later Lord Saville of the Bloody Sunday enquiry fame.
[19] Issue of 16 February 1997.

against the power of the establishment. FE Smith, Edward Carson, Rufus Isaacs, Marshall Hall, Norman Birkett and Patrick Hastings were household names. A Pollock, a Perry or a Pannick of the twenty-first-century bar might emulate their talents, but who, apart from George Carman or Mike Mansfield, has had in recent times a public profile higher than that of an average Premier League footballer, let alone an annual income greater than a fraction of the latter's weekly salary.

One reason for sure is that murder most foul is no longer committed under the shadow of the noose; but other more prosaic reasons include Europe and economics. The indirect effect of the Europeanisation of English procedure has been profound and Brexit will not reverse it. In the ECJ written submissions are almost all that count. Oral submissions are treated as a kind of pre-prandial apéritif.[20] In the ECtHR the Convention right of freedom of expression is given greater respect; but even in that forum a hearing will be measured in hours rather than days. A case which has migrated from the Strand to Strasbourg will undergo a process of forensic miniaturisation: honey they've shrunk my speech. Nonetheless judges in both these Courts (as well as arbitrators in CAS) have told me privately that they rank English advocates as the best.

Not only the European example but economic reality spurred the switch from oral to written advocacy in the late 1980s, a trend which has continued to develop. Lord Donaldson MR was as enthusiastic for case management as for law-making. It was through his initiative that skeleton arguments developed from an optional extra to a *sine qua non*, originally intended to be mere heads of written submission – a platform for oral presentation; instead they have developed obese proportions. Oh, for a Lord Atkin's diet!

Such skeletons, intended to be a support, became, at any rate in their early days, a snare. With some judges, fidelity to the skeleton prompts the retort, 'I've already read this'; with others, any departure from it, the testy question 'Where is this in your skeleton?'. And the problem is compounded by the bizarre insistence of the listing office that skeletons be submitted often far in advance of the hearing and well before any judge could conceivably have time or wish to read them. Another hazard is that they appear all too often to be mislaid en route – when a chambers' clerk telephones the judge's clerk to confirm receipt, the answer sometimes confuses what ought to have happened with what actually hasn't.

I was pleased by Lord Donaldson's comment, that mine was the best skeleton he had ever read,[21] which owed everything to the fact that the phenomenon was in its infancy. The batsman who tops the averages in the season's pipe opener in April will be well down the list by season's end in September. It was only when I started to hand down judgments myself that I appreciated that the best skeleton is one drafted in such a way as to enable the judge to incorporate it in his own judgment with minimal adaptation.

---

[20] Mr Justice Richards and MJBQC. 'View from the Bar', Mr Justice Richards and MJBQC *European Practitioners' Handbook* pp 11–28.

[21] [1986] Imm AR 382.

There is pressure from on high and pressure from below to curtail oratory. In a series of trenchant observations in the 1990s the then Senior Law Lord, Lord Templeman, excoriated 'torrents of words' and proclaimed that it was not 'the duty of counsel to advance a multitude of ingenious arguments in the hope that out of 10 bad points the judge will be capable of fashioning a winner'. From that time on it became normal for a message to be received from the House of Lords or the Supreme Court in advance of a hearing asking Counsel to estimate the proposed length of submissions; the response 'it all depends upon how many times I'm interrupted' was discouraged. In the Greek myth the bandit Procrustes used either to elongate his guests or lop off their limbs to fit the size of his bed. Only the second of those options was favoured by the Judge when confronted with a time estimate for Counsels' addresses.

Down at the Old Bailey it is no longer just a case of His Honour Judge Bullingham (aka the Mad Bull) asking Rumpole whether he actually wished to put any questions to that fine officer, whom the jury would no doubt admire for the dutiful way he had recorded the admissions of the accused. Modern managerial judges are keen to prevent the elaborate becoming the endless. Counsels' legal aid fees may be cut on post-trial taxation (the process by which barristers' fees are assessed by officers of the court) as a sanction against uncontrolled advocacy. Wasted costs orders are another deterrent to the over voluble barrister.

How far down the written track can we go? After all, in the Supreme Court of the United States, Counsel is allowed only 30 minutes for his oral submissions with no added injury time for interruptions. I once sat in the row reserved for Justices' guests, through the good offices of my Magdalen college contemporaries, Justices Souter and Breyer.[22] From that vantage point I observed Chief Justice Rehnquist, who had mysteriously disappeared behind the black curtain which is the backcloth to the bench, while the advocate was in full flow, returning only to cut him off in mid-sentence as his half-hour had expired.

Lord Woolf's *Civil Justice Review*, the foundation of the new Civil Procedure Rules (CPR), effective from the fin de siècle, emphasised the virtues of speed, economy and judicial control. Judges increasingly see their role as persuading parties not to litigate rather than as deciding litigants' disputes. Alternative Dispute Resolution (ADR) spanning arbitration, conciliation and mediation is the flavour of the first two decades of the millennium, settlement rather than adjudication the name of the modern game. A party who resists mediation may be mulcted in costs. Even in public law cases, where judgments often have implications for a far wider constituency than the particular litigants. Lord Woolf himself stressed 'the paramount importance of avoiding litigation wherever this is possible'.[23]

---

[22] En route from the Breyer chambers, a veritable hive of industry, I almost collided with Souter who was making his own way to the Court. His gasp of astonishment on seeing this bearded apparent stranger in these private quarters suggested to me, until I disabused him of the notion, that he thought I was some kind of terrorist.

[23] His was no solitary voice.

Lady Hale was a particular enthusiast for ADR. In one speech she said 'We should beware of equating access to justice with access to litigation'; while in another, she noted sardonically, if not entirely originally, that asking the Bar to support such moves was like 'urging turkeys to vote for Christmas'.

Yet something is lost on the route to reform. Where written supplants oral advocacy, an assumption has to be made, sometimes unjustified, not only that the judge has read the argument, but also that he (or she) has understood it. And even if both those assumptions are correct, the true advocate wishes to engage with a judge who disagrees with it. Twice in a single year I lost a case at the highest level by 3–2, once in the Privy Council over the issue of the constitutionality of all-male juries in Gibraltar,[24] once in the House of Lords about whether a feature of the rating of public utilities offended the principle against double taxation,[25] when the decisive point had barely, if at all, featured in the debate. The risk of this happening inevitably increases the more the proceedings are conducted in writing rather than orally.

The development of the common law, like the English language, one of England's major contributions to civilisation, has been the product of a constant dialogue between bar and bench. No experienced advocate doubts that cases can change shape, sometimes dramatically, when what seemed an impeccably logical submission is tested sometimes to destruction, sometimes not, by the judge. As Lord Justice Laws said 'That judges in fact change their mind under the influence of oral argument is not an arcane feature of the system; it is central to it'. Or as Mr Justice Megarry put it still more succinctly 'Argued law is tough law'.

The Hutton Inquiry into the death of government scientist David Kelly provided evidence of the enduring values of the advocate's art. It showed that it was not only a Paxman or a Humphrys with capacity to extract the truth from ministers and mandarins, who would prefer to be economical with that rare commodity. By the same token the Chilcott inquiry into the Iraq War suffered from the non-involvement of lawyers in the questioning of key witnesses. While my colleagues on CAS from civilian jurisdictions would beg to differ, in my view cross examination, compatible with the Bar's Code of Conduct, is still the best method of ascertaining fact.

As Lord Justice Sedley, no Conservative he, once declared, to let the oral tradition die 'would be a tragedy for a skill in which this country had for generations been a world leader'. Mind you he also said in a judgment on another episode of the long running Beloff-Pannick road show, 'that this court has spent two days hearing from leading counsel on the meaning of the words "is" and "where" might be thought to be an indictment or a vindication of our system of

---

[24] [2004] 1 WLR 201.
[25] [2003] 4 All ER 209.

oral advocacy'.[26] But I for one should regret it if the trend became unstoppable, and not just through a sentimental attachment to an ancient craft, like thatching or Morris dancing.[27]

What then are the qualities required of the successful advocate? Fluency obviously, stamina preferably, but above all the ability to separate the wheat from the chaff – and hope that there is some wheat.[28] But advocacy is never a form of art for art's sake. It serves a purpose best epitomised by Tom Bingham, who, amplifying his much-quoted Williams Lecture on the rule of law into a slim volume, wrote in his chapter on a Fair Trial, 'scarcely less important than an independent judiciary is an independent legal profession, fearless in its representation of those who cannot represent themselves, however unpopular or distasteful their case may be'. In that single sentence are identified three elements crucial to the Bar's ethos: availability, fearlessness and independence – but the greatest of these is independence.[29]

It is the availability as much as the quality of representation which is the guarantee provided by the Bar. Under the so-called cab rank rule any barrister not otherwise engaged or conflicted out and competent in the relevant area of law must appear for any client willing and able to pay an appropriate fee, even if he disapproves of the client's character or cause.[30] It is to barristers what the Hippocratic oath is to doctors.

In 2021 the reach of the rule came under scrutiny in three cases. The first was that of David Perry, instructed by the Government of Hong Kong to prosecute protesters charged under the new Beijing inspired National Security law. In response to a wave of protest led by the Foreign Secretary, Mr Perry withdrew from the case which did *not* actually engage the cab rank rule, since it involved foreign work as defined by the Bar's Code of Conduct. The second was that of Dinah Rose QC, President of Magdalen, who encountered flak for representing the Cayman Government in the Privy Council to defend its position that it could constitutionally deny marriage to same sex couples. She, with typical courage, persuaded her student body that she was fulfilling her professional duty[31] which, not being foreign work, *did* engage the cab rank rule.[32] The third was that of the quartet of members of Essex Court Chambers who co-authored an opinion, widely publicised (but not by them), about the treatment of the Uyghurs, resulting in the Chambers being listed by the PRC as an entity subject to International Sanctions

---

[26] [2007] All ER D 220.

[27] In Alex Wade's book *Wrecking Machine* (Wade, 2006) where he drew an interesting analogy between advocacy and boxing I am quoted as saying 'Traditional oral advocacy is a plant to be cherished, not pruned', pp 200–01.

[28] For further pointers see the answers to the standard question asked of me in *The Times* Lawyer of the Week, 2 November 1999.

[29] Much of what follows is a distillation of my own Williams Lecture 'A View from the Bar' at Cambridge in 2008 and my McDermott Lecture 'Virtuous Voices; Advocacy and the Rule of Law' at Queen's University Belfast in 2013.

[30] See now the Courts and Legal Services Act 1990 (CLSA) Section 17(3)(a).

[31] Though not all her fellow lawyer heads of house agreed.

[32] The LGBTQ plus Society have since asked her to give her fee to charity.

because it 'maliciously spread lies and disinformation [about] the so-called human rights issues in Xinjiang'.

In vain did their statement state (correctly) that the Chambers had no legal or collective identity and (equally correctly) that the writers were providing independent, legal advice in accordance with the Bar's ethical code. The damage was done. Some members skipped the set; and major firms of solicitors proclaimed that they would not in future use the set as the source of advice or representation of behalf of Chinese clients. Whether or not the authors had to accept instructions it was certainly proper for them to do so. The price they paid is a badge of honour.

I have myself never found it difficult to be faithful to the cab rank rule. My clients have included the Government of Iraq – at that time in reality Saddam Hussein himself[33] – Ian Brady, the Moors Murderer, and many others who would not be candidates for secular canonisation. I would concede that my fidelity is a little tarnished by the appreciation that it may increase and certainly not decrease the number of potential instructions as well as the perverse pleasure that I gain from representing clients with whose views and actions I may be in fundamental disagreement.

Indeed, as long as I was instructed only to argue or advise on a case without pronouncing on the underlying cause, I have been prepared to act in circumstances beyond the dictates of the Code, advising another Caribbean Government on the same issue as confronted Dinah Rose, and yet another Commonwealth Government on the other side of the globe as to how it might defend continued criminalisation of homosexual acts without violating its Constitution. As long as he is not acting in breach of the Code, an advocate must surely be free to accept any instructions. Now, all passion spent, I sometimes ponder on how far I would be prepared to push that proposition and whether I may have from to time unduly prioritised the argument over its destination. Freedom to do something does not entail a duty to do it.

Not everyone, certainly outside the legal profession, subscribes to the virtues of the cab rank rule itself. When I appeared within the Committee of Privileges in a vain effort to postpone the ejection of the hereditary peers from the House of Lords,[34] Margaret Jay, then Leader of the House, came up to me in the Moses Room shortly before the hearing and expressed her surprise at my appearance, as she phrased it, 'on *that* side'. But when some years later in an article in *The Spectator* I suggested that *retired* members of the University who lived in Oxford had no more obvious right to vote on the University affairs than had hereditary peers to participate in the deliberations of the Upper House, Lord Trefgarne, one of my sometime clients, wrote a letter complaining that my views seemed inconsistent with my representation of the hereditary interests in the earlier litigation.

---

[33] [1995] 3 All ER 694. Our instructing Solicitor, Jo Kosky, sent me a bonus cheque which he said came from the great dictator. For the sake of good order I forwarded it to a Jewish charity. It is noteworthy that all the Iraqi legal team were Jewish. Pragmatism can sometimes be more powerful than prejudice.

[34] [2002] 1 AC 109. See Lord Hope's diaries *House of Lords 1996–2009* (Hope, 2018) pp 95–96. See also chapter eight, 'Politics and the Law'.

Regular clients too are not always happy. When I sought to uphold the Home Office ban on the Reverend Moon's entry to the United Kingdom, in which my Junior was Ian Burnett,[35] the Church of Scientology wrote to me to complain about my having accepted the instruction in the first place. I was indeed assailed for losing the case[36] as well as for taking it on. An aggrieved Michael Howard, then Home Secretary, rang me (bypassing of the usual convention that lay clients only speak to counsel in the presence or with the consent of the instructing solicitor) to protest against Mr Justice Sedley's decision. (The whole affair was something of a charade because the Rev Moon, though certainly alive, had no intention of actually coming to the United Kingdom at all.) Richard Scudamore, the brains behind the rise and rise of the Premier League, put an embargo (later lifted) on my being briefed in one case because, my solicitor told me, he had been aggrieved by my acting against the League's interests in a sports arbitration.

Mohamed Al Fayed was concerned when I represented Lonrho in the House of Lords, when the *Observer* was charged with contempt in publishing a diatribe by Tiny Rowland, Lonrho's head honcho, at the moment the House of Lords was to decide on an aspect of Lonrho's takeover bid for Harrods.[37] Despite that concern, he let me know via Royston Webb, one of his inner circle, that he recognised that I was acting in accordance with the Bar's Code. The IAAF were also uneasy when I acted for Dwain Chambers. In neither case was a long-term relationship fractured but I had no choice but to run the risk that it might have been.

Some have suggested that the rule is more mantra than mandate, too easily by-passed by barristers or their clerks taking advantage of a recognised exception by insisting on a fee which the proposed client will not or cannot pay, or simply ignored on ideological grounds. Rumpole would decline to prosecute – but then he was never asked to do so.

But even in sets which house the alternative bar or those of avowedly left of centre persuasion, there is no substantial evidence to support the claim that their members could, or indeed would, purge from themselves the so-called DNA of the Bar.[38] It is not for the barrister to confuse his role with that of a judge in a client's case whether in criminal or civil litigation. The only constraint, prudence apart, on the way he advances is his paramount duty to the Court – at its core a duty not to mislead. In my view that duty, deeply embedded in the English common law tradition, no more acts as an undesirable restraint on the barrister's freedom of action than do the Queensberry rules on professional pugilists. If politicians were (unthinkably) made subject to a similar duty, democracy's air might be purer.

---

[35] Lord Chief Justice of England and Wales.

[36] [1996] 8 Admin LR 427.

[37] (Trelford, 2017) p 286. See my description of the case in chapter five, 'The Silk Road'.

[38] When a review of its utility was carried out, I co-authored with Pushpinder (now Mr Justice Saini) Gray's Inn's response opposing its abrogation.

How far then should the barrister himself fortify the structures of independence? Should a barrister be a cause lawyer or a case lawyer? I have always thought that a barrister's views should better be kept as private as his vote for reasons both of actuality and of appearance,[39] even if I both respect and admire others who choose to campaign and wear their views on their sleeves.

The function of the advocate is to give advice and then to conduct a case with detachment, his only ardour being for success on behalf of his client. Ideological or emotional involvement in an outcome seems to me to risk infection of analysis and presentation. I was very conscious that when I was by conviction on the side of the case I was advancing, I had to guard against an excess of the adrenalin – not an exogenous prohibited substance – essential to the most effective advocacy. In 1976 I appeared in an unsuccessful effort to preserve St Marylebone Grammar School, the last of its kind in London. Lord Denning in one of his most elegiac passages was able to indicate how he would have wished to decide the case. 'Many will grieve' he said 'when that which was great is passed away. But so it must be'.[40] I grieved too, but necessarily in silence. Every time I now pass by its premises when embussed on the Oxford Tube I give a rueful smile.

My dislike of the Strasbourg-inspired rule that the United Kingdom cannot deport individuals proven to be a threat to its own national security to their country of origin because of concerns about risk of the treatment they would there receive may, despite my best endeavours, have percolated into my submissions before House of Lords[41] as a sub-text if not in the text itself. Lord Hope felt constrained to address full frontally the argument 'surely the sooner they are got rid of the better. On their own heads be it if their extremist views expose them to the risk of ill-treatment when they got home' and administered what Touchstone in *As You Like It* called the 'reproof valiant'. 'That, however, is not the way the rule of law works. The lesson of history is that, by depriving people of its protection, because of their beliefs and behaviour, however obnoxious, leads to the disintegration of society'.[42]

Clients, be they prisoners, parents or public authorities, may welcome the barrister's sympathy as well as his skill, but they are best served if they enjoy, without any sacrifice of courtesy on the barrister's part, only the latter. The case he advances is after all his client's not his own: that is why the advocate formally abstains from any expression of belief and deploys the neutral concept of submission. But how he advances it must be the product of his own dispassionate judgement.

I once had myself to tell my instructing solicitor that Mr Al Fayed could promote his case for British citizenship with Max Clifford (the public relations guru) or with Michael Beloff, but not with both. After, in the language of *Wednesbury*, taking all

---

[39] 'I fight cases not causes'. My interview by Alex Wade, *Independent* on Sunday, 4 November 2003.
[40] [1978] 1 All ER 411 at p 418.
[41] [2009] 2 AC 512.
[42] At pp 209–10.

material considerations into account, the barrister must, as Frank Sinatra would have recommended, do it <u>his</u> way.

It is the development of *public* law and its supplanting of private law as the most important element in appellate adjudication, and the concurrent migration of political issues from the legislature to the courts, which expose the advocate more readily to the temptations of partisanship and more importantly to the perception of it.

In the highly sensitive and increasingly complex field of immigration law in which, in my far-off days as a junior, I used regularly to practise, I noted the significant attachment of clients to lawyers of their own ethnic background, not always to the advantage of their claim, sometimes because their chosen champion had inadequate command of the language in which the Court had to be addressed.[43] I am uncomfortable too with the converse position when women advocates are instructed to defend men on trial for rape – not on account of their forensic abilities (which may often be considerable) but on the crude calculation that juries will be beguiled into thinking that no woman would defend someone who had committed an act of violence against members of their own sex.

I do *not* believe that barristers of known left wing sympathies are necessarily best placed to defend striking Trade Unionists or those of publicised Europhobic tendencies to represent UKIP or its derivatives. A barrister who can appear at *different* times for the BNP and the Socialist Workers League, is not the forensic equivalent of the Vicar of Bray, but an adherent to the true professional faith. It is dangerous to adopt a mindset that virtue can only repose on the claimants' side (or vice-versa). For it is not only the advocates for claimants but those for respondents too who are responsible for assisting in the construction or clarification of the law. Barristers, after all, do not make law, they supply from *either* side of the Court the materials from which the judges can fulfil their own distinctive role. A barrister's arguments, whether mediated through advice or advocacy, will be given greater weight and respect if he is recognised by any test to be truly independent.

I was once asked by a former employee of the World Bank, who had lost a claim before its tribunal from which there was no appeal, to provide an opinion to 'shame' the Bank into granting him compensation. I replied in a letter

> As a matter of principle and practice I have to distinguish between my roles as an advocate professional instructed in a particular matter and as a person carrying out a lobbying activity on behalf of a group or an individual and have tended to abstain from the latter in order not to impair my role in the former.

There are institutional as well as ideological pressures on the independence of the Bar. Sir Gavin Lightman in a much-discussed lecture 'The Civil Justice System and Legal Profession – The Challenges Ahead',[44] somewhat like a former cabinet

---

[43] See chapter four, 'An Utter Barrister'.
[44] (2003) 22 *Civil Justice Quarterly (CJQ)* p 235.

minister, freed from the burdens of collective responsibility, rediscovered the path of true principle for the profession he had left a decade before. He excoriated 'the metamorphosis of the legal professions into legal business'[45] and the consequent impact on the internal organisation of the Bar.

> The dominant philosophy today amongst many chambers', he wrote 'is to place the highest premium on keeping all available work for clients 'in house'. Indeed chambers have increasingly in all but name and law become partnerships between the members committed to the pursuit of the best interest of members. Chambers have for practical purposes a corporate existence.

Without questioning pedantically the proposition that a partnership can at the same time be a company I find much force in the analysis. But it was not just for convenience that personally, when I had the choice, I worked when in silk with juniors in my own chambers. I could not conceive of any better allies.

There is a moral issue created by the art of advocacy itself.[46] The fact that advocates do make a difference itself causes a problem. A court or tribunal may be deflected from reaching the right result – let alone a just result – by the superior advocacy skills enjoyed by one side. To that problem, inherent in any adversarial system, there is no obvious solution – in particular when legal costs compel an ever-increasing number of people in civil cases to appear on their own behalf – as litigants in person – and when cutbacks in criminal legal aid mean that legal representation is often provided at a lower level than the gravity of the case may deserve. With the odd exception of a Tony Benn, arguing his case to be relieved of his hereditary claim to membership of the House of Lords, the advocacy of the non-professional tends to fall short of that of even the tyro pupil. When the clerk to Lord Justice Staughton, not the easiest of judges, just before the start of the afternoons session, said that his master had asked him to give me a pamphlet entitled 'A user guide for the litigant in person' I opted optimistically to treat it as a tease, not an implied criticism; the judge was after all Head of the old Eton Collegers' Association.

The principle of equality of arms does not mandate parity of representation QC for QC. 'The importance' said Lord Woolf 'is to have an advocate, whether he be a barrister or solicitor, who can ensure that a defendant's defence is properly and adequately placed before the Court'. Up to a point Lord Woolf, for there are only two possibilities. Either the relative quality of representation has no impact on the outcome or it does. The first possibility is at odds with everyday experience in the Courts.[47] Mr Justice Megarry wisely said 'As everybody who has had anything to

---

[45] At p 243.

[46] [1994] Ch 204, 'Advocacy is more an art than a science. It cannot be conducted according to formulae. Individuals differ in their style and approach'. Sir Thomas Bingham MR at p 236.

[47] See from my own casebook [1996] AC 1996 where in the Court of Appeal I won a commercial case before a Court presided over by Tom Bingham, rarely wrong, only to lose it in the House of Lords when the other side switched Counsel to the leader of the pack of commercial silks to overturn Tom's decision.

do with the law well knows, the path of the law is strewn with examples of open and shut cases which, somehow, were not'.[48]

Claims in civil cases should not reach the stage of requiring adjudication by judge or arbitrator unless there was at least *some* scope for more than one outcome. Prosecutions would, at any rate should, not be brought or pleas of not guilty entered unless there is a measure of uncertainty, however small, about the verdict. It is precisely to alter the odds that particular advocates are selected. A senior silk at the top of his game is worth as much to a legal team, as a Ronaldo, a Messi or a Harry Kane is to a football team.

As Gavin Lightman also said 'Cases are won and lost by reason of the quality of representation at the trial: hence the extravagant fees paid to litigation lawyers. ... The scales of justice favour those who can afford to buy it.[49] And to quote, inevitably, myself 'We would all give up if we thought we were merely there to make up numbers. Who would pay us if that were so?'[50]

All barristers are equal, but some are more equal than others. Geoffrey Robertson coined the phrase 'The Justice Game'. Contests between unevenly matched contestants may be acceptable in a game, but not when justice is the intended trophy. There are indeed some barristers who are seen to fall below acceptable standards of competence. The Quality Assurance Scheme for Advocates (QASA) – an accreditation scheme for criminal advocates wishing to exercise rights of audience in the higher courts and potentially extendable to civil practitioners – was abandoned in 2017 after four years of controversy. The abandonment of the cure does not mean the extinction of the malady.

The growing commitment of both branches of the profession to pro bono work provides some solace. My own services were usually provided free of charge to institutions to which I owed allegiance, Trinity, Gray's Inn or the Bar Council, for whom I wrote a multitude of advices; ranging from the suspension of the award of silk and the procedures of its disciplinary tribunal to QASA itself, often bringing in promising juniors not just to do the basic research – though naturally for that too – but to publicise their names to the powers that be.

Sometimes I would work for nothing simply because the case had an intrinsic interest whether legal or factual. Renee Calder was a junior barrister who had been disciplined by the Visitors of the Inns of Court, for allegedly forging a receipt in a small dispute over a car. The issue was whether there was any remedy available in law against that decision which threatened her very career. To resolve it required analysis of the Visitatorial jurisdiction (now defunct) which dated back many centuries as well as of the dimensions of the modern jurisdiction of judicial review. Fortunately, not only did our team establish that the Visitors were amenable to

---

[48] [1970] Ch 345 at p 402.
[49] (2003) 22 *CJQ* p 238.
[50] (Paterson, 2013) p 49.

judicial review, but also that there was no basis for finding Ms Calder guilty of forgery.[51]

I acted, pro bono, for Geoffrey Shaw QC, one of my juniors in the Dr Gee case, when it was claimed that he had been guilty of misleading the Court in a libel action involving the wife of the Yorkshire Ripper. The Bar Council, the prosecuting authority, was represented by Anthony Hooper who many years later became my star inquisitor for the IAAF Ethics Board. Playing the trump card of Sydney Kentridge QC as my expert witness on the ethical issues involved, I procured Geoffrey's acquittal.

The mother of Lawrence Dallaglio whose daughter had tragically perished in the Marchioness disaster was another pro bono client. Lawrence himself was a close friend of Gary, my senior clerk, and promised me a signed photograph of the British Lions team shortly to take on the All Blacks. Unfortunately for me (as well as for the Lions) he suffered an injury in a warm-up game and was flown home before he could fulfil his promise.

In my representation of Ian Brady I combined both my fidelity to the cab rank rule and my willingness to act pro bono. For this I earned at any rate some bonus brownie points, Lord Woolf saying

> I would like to express particular appreciation to Mr Beloff and those who instruct him on this matter. I note from correspondence put before the court that they are both acting on a pro bono basis, without charge, in relation to the application to this court. It is a matter of some importance, especially where issues of this nature arise, that where legal aid is not available members of the Bar and experienced firms of solicitors should enable the matter to be properly presented before the court. The court is very appreciative of the course that has been adopted in this case.

I agreed, at the request of Tristan Jones, an up-and-coming junior member in Blackstone, my Chambers, and first legal secretary of the IAAF Ethics Board, to represent Owen Holland. He was a Cambridge graduate who was sent down from the University for six terms for having orchestrated a variation of no platforming by the shouting down of David Willett, then Minister for Universities in the Cameron Government.

Although I had little sympathy with this apparently somewhat Dave Spart-like figure (though, as is so often the case, much more agreeable when met in person) in his attitude to free speech, I found the prospect of appearing before the *Septem Viri* (*anglice* Seven Men), the University's apex domestic court, an intriguing one. It was certainly an august body. Derry Irvine presided, with the assistance of, amongst others, three heads of house, including Sir Richard Dearlove, Master of Pembroke and previously head of MI6. I noted, however, that both Latin and mathematics seemed to have been ignored in setting up this particular panel, since it was constituted by six, not seven persons, one of whom was a woman. And we did save Mr Holland's academic career.

---

[51] [1994] QB 1.

I also succumbed to the blandishments of another Blackstone colleague, Tim Otty QC, a human rights specialist – and to me yet more impressively, a sub three-hour marathon runner – to argue that the Human Dignity Trust, a body which campaigns on a global basis for the decriminalisation of homosexual acts, was entitled to be registered as a charity. I persuaded the Tribunal that to seek to implement human rights was law enforcement, not law reform, and therefore not a political activity.[52]

But for all the efforts to improve access to legal services whether by provision of free advice or representation, crowd funding or insurance, there remains a moral hollow in the crown of the adversarial system. What is paid for is what is got. How the hollow is to be filled, in the real, as distinct from the ideal world, I confess I do not know.

---

[52] See the Report in the *Guardian* dated 6 June 2014: 'Michael Beloff QC, acting for the trust, spoke for three hours without stopping, had a sandwich, and spoke for an hour more. The powers of concentration of lawyers are frankly awe-inspiring'.

15

Change or Decay?

Act I. The Past: The Way We Were

A la recherche du temps perdu. Decked out in white tie and tails I was called to the Bar of England and Wales by Gray's Inn in November 1967. I had eaten the mandatory 36 dinners, where we sat along benches in the elegant hall, cheek by jowl with each other, but if only notionally, in messes of four, toasting each other in mediocre house wine. With the tables cleared the hall resounded with the cry 'Up Junior' and the addressee who happened by mischance to be at the end of the last row had to rise to his feet and ask the Senior in Hall (no bencher he) for permission to smoke. Permission, once given, was generally exploited. To echo one of the songs in *Fiddler on the Roof*, attendance at these dinners was Tradition, Tradition, enjoyed by some, endured by others. The call ceremony itself at the rainbow's end of the qualifying period was, by contrast, formal; with the fledgling barrister only bursting into unmelodious song when the benchers had retired.

In order to qualify, eating apart, I had, in addition to subjects covered in my Law degree,[1] to study a few additional subjects. This I was able to do, in my own time, from nutshell Gibson and Weldon notes given to me – free of charge – by Maurice Mendelson[2] who had just done exactly that. The practical training consisted of watching my pupil-master, to whom I was apprenticed for the next year, and learning from his triumphs and disasters in equal measure. For this facility I had to pay him the princely sum of £100.

Barristers still conventionally wore cutaway black jackets and striped trousers; and a small cohort continued to affect bowler hats. A barrister in less than prescribed clothing – wig, gown, bands – though perfectly audible, might be greeted from the bench with the sonorous phrase 'I cannot hear you'. Wigs, the archaic symbol of the profession, were worn at all times in open court unless the judge permitted their removal in equatorial conditions. The only form of alternative dispute resolution, after the demise, long since, of the duel, was arbitration.

---

[1] But not all barristers were then graduates. Mary Hogg, who became in the fullness of time a much-admired High Court judge in the Family Division, was a degreeless pupil at 2 Hare Court in the year after me, at the same time as Judith my wife to be.

[2] Public International Law Professor and barrister at Blackstone.

Barristers' clerks arranged one's diary, negotiated one's fees, and took 10 per cent of them – the so-called shilling in the guinea – although, according to my calculation, a shilling is not 10 per cent of a guinea. All but omnipotent they acted as one's agent to the outside world, being the sole means of legitimate communication with solicitors, the hands that fed the Bar. Clerks could make or break careers.

Clerks (but not only clerks) conventionally objected to women being admitted to chambers on the basis that – as they saw it – the women would inevitably soon depart to pursue their proper role of child-bearing and rearing. The coup de grace was that there were no separate toilet facilities. There were accordingly few women in the profession – in the year of my Call approximately 7 per cent of the newly called. There were fewer, if any, female clerks. More than two decades later a client of mine claimed sex discrimination when her application to join a clerking team was rejected because she might have to enter a robing room with partially dressed male barristers. A frantic Bar Council prompted a settlement.

Ethnic minority counsel were still rarer. While the Inns of Court had a significant proportion of overseas students from the new Commonwealth, and the old Empire, they were expected to return to their country and exploit the title of barrister-at-law to immediate advantage, accelerating to positions such as Attorney General or Chief Justice with a velocity which their English equivalents could only envy when awake or hope for in their dreams. In consequence the Bench was, to use that convenient transatlantic acronym, largely WASP – White, Anglo-Saxon, Protestant, Male – and inevitably so since, three decades on, it was the mirror image of the Bar of the pre-war years.

Chambers were generally small – my own set, 2 Hare Court, had, when I arrived, 12 members and no QCs – supported by a skeletal staff of two clerks and two typists. Membership was for life. The Head of Chambers alone, himself selected on the basis of Buggins' turn, selected pupils and tenants; unaffected by considerations of democracy or diversity. Whom you knew could be as important as what you knew. Departure from the set to which one had been admitted on his solitary say so was as rare, and as disagreeable, as divorce.

Chambers' names were their addresses too. In London they were all located within the confines of the Inns of Court, although there were provincial sets in major city centres feeding the circuits.

Solicitors' firms, even in the City of London, could still put all their partners' names on their letterheads – a legacy of the recent statutory cap on partnership numbers. As those letterheads disclosed, women were rarely to be found as partners in major firms.

The relationship between barrister and solicitor was a vertical, not a horizontal one, even though it was upon solicitors that barristers depended for their livelihood. It was a breach of the Bar's professional etiquette to fraternise with solicitors; just as it was to advertise a barrister's own expertise (such as it was) however discreetly.

Under the legal aid system inaugurated in 1949, in broad terms anyone who satisfied both a means test and a merits test could walk through the door of any solicitor who was entitled, regardless of expertise, to take the case through from beginning to end at public expense – a bonus for the Bar.

Barristers could not sue for unpaid fees from private clients but – an implicit quid pro quo? – could not be sued for negligence. They enjoyed a significant monopoly since solicitors enjoyed no rights of audience in the higher courts.

Control of the barristers' profession still rested substantially with the Inns. The Bar Council was more a representative than a regulatory body.

The Lord Chancellor by means of the usual – but archaic – processes of consultation, himself determined who should become a Queen's Counsel or a Judge. It was clear that some who aspired to such status had a black mark against them; but who had put it there was obscure; and there was no formal means by which it could be exposed, still less eradicated. Judicial appointments were made entirely from the ranks of Bar.

It was assumed that most barristers *did* aspire to such status: the High Court Bench was seen as the natural culmination of a successful silk's career. A QC, if tapped on the shoulder, was expected to accept the offer of appointment; one Judge, Harry Fisher, who foreswore the bench, first in favour of City and then of College life, after brief exposure to the monotony of personal injury litigation in Bristol, punctuated by the occasional trial of an affray in Birmingham (a fictional but realistic schedule) was regarded to have done that which a gentleman should not do.

The judicial power to end someone's life, to the extent it survived, gave the judiciary a certain awesome stature, enhanced by the paraphernalia – the religious service, the Rolls Royce, high living in the Lodgings (chefs, butlers and all)[3] – which attended them as they processed around the ancient assize towns.

Judges were not expected to be user friendly and rarely were. High Court and Appellate Judges could sit beyond 75. Lord Denning was well into his eighties when he stood down, and there were not a few grumpy old men (of which he was certainly not one). Under the Kilmuir rules, named after the eponymous Lord Chancellor, they were under a vow of silence where the media were concerned.

In civil Courts the tradition of oral advocacy and oral evidence was unchecked: cases in the law reports would not infrequently be recited in full. Judges conventionally declined to read any papers before coming into court in case it prejudiced their otherwise open minds. They acted as referees, determining who won or lost, penalising foul play, but otherwise uninvolved. Cases proceeded at a leisurely pace and could be stood out of the list for 'counsels' convenience', and sometimes because the judge had 'a public duty to perform', occasionally a synonym for attendance at a Buckingham Palace garden party.

---

[3] I do not complain, having been later entertained by sundry judicial pals when they were billeted in Oxford or even Reading (reciprocating, where possible at High Table). When one of my dearest mates, Alan Moses, was sitting at Oxford the butler sonorously informed the guests 'Sir Moses is on his way'. I had hardly stopped laughing when his lordship appeared. The Oxford lodgings (before they were switched to the more convenient Rhodes House) were at Shotover, where inside the entrance stood a huge stuffed grizzly bear, and on the table perched a visitors' book with signatures from the Queen downwards.

Judges recorded evidence and argument in slow-moving manuscript. Even in the late 1970s written submissions drafted by Anthony Lester and me in an equal pay case[4] were simply rejected out of hand; Tony Grabiner on the other side had more shrewdly eschewed such novelty. The works of academic authors were, by a convention whose rationale lacked something in reasonableness, cited in Court if the authors were deceased but not otherwise – in short read only if dead. Latin phrases were not outlawed. Classical quips ('piling piller on mareva'[5]) could be appreciated by at least a few of those to whom they were directed.

The technology to support litigation, indeed legal services overall, was immature. Typewriters were (at best) electric not electronic. Communication was often by telex; the fax machine had not yet arrived on the scene; the word processor was unheard of. Copying was a laborious process. Documents arrived in Chambers in bundles,[6] with red tape around them, unless for government work when the tape was white. Conferences for juniors and consultations for silks took place with lay and professional clients face to face in barristers' chambers. Research was done in libraries.

Precedent ruled. Even though the law was manifestly developed by judges, they adhered to the fiction that they were merely discovering and declaring it, as archaeologists not architects.

In the domestic sphere the common law itself was still regarded as the true law. A significant number of judges still regarded the interpretation of statutes, already a major part of their judicial functions, as an exercise for nit-picking and hole finding, sometimes expressing weary contempt at infelicities of draftsmanship. When Lord Denning said in the Court of Appeal 'We do not sit here to pull the language of Parliament and ministers to pieces and make nonsense of it', his approach was rejected by the House of Lords. Interpretation of contracts also suffered from a narrow technical approach.

The laws of evidence, even in civil litigation, were complex, reflecting in particular their original purpose to avoid allowing juries, perceived as incapable of distinguishing between the weight to be given to different types of evidence, to consider material whose probative force might be submerged by their prejudicial impact.

Administrative law was only just emerging from its long winter.[7] There was no such thing as judicial review, indeed there was no such thing as public law so-called; *droit administratif* was seen, due to Dicey's persistent influence, as utterly alien. Lord Devlin lamented that judges appeared to have abdicated entirely to Parliament their historic role of controlling misuse or abuse of power by the executive.

---

[4] [1978] QB 11.

[5] Two novel forms of interlocutory orders.

[6] Noel Ings, a Balliol graduate, in house lawyer for the Monopolies and Mergers Commission must have been one of the last and was certainly the best who wrote my instructions, enlivened by his scholarly wit, in manuscript.

[7] See chapter 8, 'Politics and the Law'.

Tort law, concerned essentially with responsibility to avoid harm to others, had only just recognised that negligent words as well as negligent acts should give rise to redress.

Libel law was enmeshed in a procedural maze in which parties' pleadings – their formal statements of case – seemed designed to obscure every fact except that one party was suing the other and that the other was defending the claim.

Individual employment law was in its infancy; still essentially a matter of contract – which the boss could impose upon the worker (to use the vocabulary of that era) – notwithstanding the inequality of bargaining power between them. The statute providing for redundancy payment was in its infancy. The statute providing for compensation for unfair dismissal was as yet unborn. There was no anti-discrimination law in the fields of sex, race or disability.

The diet of the family law practitioner was the undefended divorce, and ancillary arguments about custody of or access to children. Marriages were for men and women. The nuclear was the normal family.

In the field of criminal law, the police were responsible for the triple process of arrest, charge and prosecution. Their practices in connection with these activities were only modestly constrained by the so-called Judges' rules, sporadic provisions of statute and the principles of common law. The criminal courts still bore their ancient names – assizes, quarter sessions.

Juries were still selected, until the Juries Act 1974, by reference to a property qualification; and were therefore also predominantly male and middle class. They found the facts under the guidance of judges, a few of whom could not resist garnishing the formula 'it's entirely a matter for you' with sighs or even winks which would not feed into any transcript.

The lay bench also shared the same, if not more elevated, social background, although there was a far larger representation of women, given that it was difficult for persons in full-time employment, still mainly men, to be able to satisfy the demands to sit on a weekly basis.

At the start of the decade male homosexual activity, prostitution and abortion were all criminal offences as was blasphemy. The common law crime of 'conspiracy to corrupt public morals' had yet to pass into history. Literature and drama were still subject to different forms of censorship. It was only at the end of the decade that the liberal spirit of John Stuart Mill, mediated through the political skill of Roy Jenkins, redefined the boundary between law and morality.

The sentencing options for crimes were limited – essentially, if not exclusively, prison or fines. Capital punishment for murder still survived, although itself under sentence of death.

In 1967 England was truly an off-shore island, although QCs could still travel to exotic off-shoots of the old Empire, Singapore, Hong Kong, the Caribbean islands, to appear in full fig and with white wig in courtrooms cooled only by revolving fans. The common law was uninfluenced by the Common Market, or by the Convention. European law, sardonically caricatured by Anthony Lester in private as 'filthy foreign muck', was something they did on the other side of the

English Channel. It was only in 1967, the year of my call, that the right of individual petition was granted to British citizens to enable them to plead a case for violation of their human rights in Strasbourg before the international organs, the ECtHR and the ECommHR which policed and enforced the Convention. It was only in 1971 that the European Communities Act was passed after the United Kingdom belatedly subscribed to the Treaty of Rome and brought euro law into the domestic law bloodstream.

Act II. The Now: There's No Time Like the Present[8]

Fast forward the clock to 2022, more than four decades later. The picture is painted in quite different colours. Bar school is compulsory with private providers vying for students – all of whom will be graduates. Dinners as a qualifying necessity are being phased out. *Hinc illae lacrimae* if of the crocodile variety. The law of the land proscribes the giving of permission to smoke. At call night business attire suffices. The halls are filled with family and friends, encouraged to clap. The Treasurer's speech will not only acknowledge but applaud their presence. Post-call continuing education is mandatory leading until recently to the New Year's Eve rush to complete online – in some cases to commence – the prescribed number of hours or now to furnish other proof of compliance.

Pupillage (now sometimes called supervision) is still a necessary part of the aspirant barrister's education; but it is preceded by a year's specific training in such matters as advocacy, negotiation, client relations and other matters which previously he or she had been expected to acquire out of the air. There is a choice of institutions which provide such education. The Council of the Inns of Court (COIC) in collaboration with the Inns of Court College of Advocacy (ICCA) has complemented the teaching by other private authorised providers with a two-cycle course, said to be not only 'flexible and accessible' but also 'compelling and interactive', part one partly delivered online, although the Bar Aptitude test itself is under review.

Sets of Chambers publish handbooks to encourage applications. Pupils no longer pay for the privilege of pupillage; on the contrary the major sets of chambers fall over themselves to offer substantial scholarships, £50,000 and more, to attract the best and brightest of their generation, who could otherwise parlay their promise into the six-figure sums offered by major international firms, usually with headquarters in the USA but with colonial outposts in London and dotted around the globe.

Heads of Chambers no longer reign supreme but are elected. Their authority is diluted by and shared with the creation of numerous committees. Tenants, and indeed pupils, are chosen by a rigorous process conforming to modern best practice, informed by democratic principles, anti-discrimination legislation and

---

[8] This section should be treated as if an impressionist painting, not a photograph.

the HRA. It is now conventional for upwardly mobile barristers to trade up in sets, causing (usually) regret but no offence. Transfers are even solicited just as they are between Premier League Football Clubs: 'tapping up' is not forbidden, indeed is barely frowned upon.

The barristers' formal attire of yesteryear gathers mothballs in the attic. Dark suits are still obligatory – although the concept of darkness appears somewhat variable. Bob Alexander QC opened for the government in the Crown Agents Inquiry in a suit whose colour had some affinity to the leisure wear of a Latin-American dictator; lesser barristers would have feared to emulate such a grandee. Wigs are still worn in criminal courts but ever less frequently in civil ones and are optional in the Supreme Court. Peter Taylor's tentative efforts to procure their removal encountered resistance from a bizarre combination of counsel and criminals who saw the wig as a validation in itself of the competence of their representative: Rumpole and the Timsons were in an alliance as bizarre as the Molotov-Ribbentrop pact.

Women, who now constitute 50 per cent of those admitted to the profession, usually wear the trousers. They have made considerable strides both as heads of chambers, and senior or managing partners in solicitors' firms. Ethnic minority counsel are on the rise.[9] These are now the offspring of first-generation immigrants rather than first-generation immigrants themselves. On behalf of the Bar, at the invitation of Richard Scott, I drafted legislation to outlaw race discrimination in choice by chambers of pupils and tenants and indeed choice of counsel by clients. The Bar's and Solicitors' codes of conduct go, if anything, further than the law of the land in inhibiting discrimination on *any* arbitrary ground. Both branches of the profession now fall over themselves to enhance the diversity of their intake in terms not just of BAME but, sometimes, of LGBTQ+ too.

The market-wide percentages of female trainees, associates and partners have all increased in the past five years albeit that white, male, heterosexual(cis) lawyers populate the profession in a greater proportion than the population at large. Progress is still pyramid-shaped.[10] But the Law Society has elected its first black President; and female senior partners in city firms are becoming as fashionable and frequent as heads of house in Oxbridge where now the Masters in title are often Mistresses in gender.

[9] The BSB Report for 2021 shows an increase in the percentages of both woman and minority ethnic barristers at both junior and silk level but at pupil level – the pointer to the future – there was male/female equality and the highest proportion ever of minority ethnic backgrounds and the largest year on year increase since the first Diversity at the Bar Report in 2015.

[10] Recent data from the Solicitors Regulation Authority show that Law firms with more than 50 partners have the lowest proportion of partners from BAME backgrounds – 8 per cent compared with 26 per cent at firms with two to five partners. Three per cent of partners in law firms are black but only one per cent in large firms. RARE, a company which specialises in contextual recruitment – framing candidates' grades in the context of their backgrounds – has developed software used by all the magic circle firms; but the same company has identified that the rate of attrition in the top firms is far higher among BAME lawyers, especially female, because of the tension between the majority and minority cultures; regional and niche firms are in the forefront of recruitment of ethnic minority trainees; and there are greater numbers of LGBTQ+ and disabled members of the profession.

Barristers, whatever their background, can now be sued for negligence for work done in chambers or court (with consequent impact of their insurance premia) and can be made, in extreme cases, subject to wasted costs orders. But they can now sue for their fees.

Chambers are larger. The former relocated 2 Hare Court numbers at the time of writing almost six score barristers, of whom almost half are QCs, but pales into insignificance in terms of size with the two mega-sets in Birmingham. It has been rechristened Blackstone in the modern style where no significant figure in English legal history from Bracton and Erskine, to Denning and Wilberforce has *not* been pillaged to add borrowed lustre to a chamber's name.

Some sets, reluctant to sacrifice the good will perceived to attach to their name, retain it even when it is no longer concurrent with its address; Essex Court chambers are in Lincoln's Inn Fields; 39 Essex Street in Chichester rentals. Doughty Street, whose name is geographically correct, can enjoy its accidental, if appropriate overtones of audacity. Yet other sets call themselves by names like Enterprise Chambers thought to represent their zeitgeist. But the Inns of Court no longer define the boundary within which chambers can be located. When I had a substantial practice in immigration law I was a guest at the opening of a set as far afield from the heart of legal London as Brick Lane. Outside London there are sets in towns and cities where in 1967 there were none. There is devolution as well as evolution at the Bar.

Discreet advertising is allowed. Chambers have gaudy websites and solicit commendations from solicitors to gild their members' CVs. There are proliferating directories or encyclopaedias in which lawyers' specialities can be recorded. If told by some publisher that one has been identified as a leading expert in a particular field, one will then be invited to pay several hundred pounds to ensure that such piece of intelligence may be broadcast to the outside world. More through vanity than meanness I only once succumbed to this quasi-blackmail. These perennials have their own ranking lists, which are treated by barristers with reverence or contempt depending on how they are personally assessed – in the same way as politicians treat opinion polls.

Despite the supplementation of clerks by persons with titles such as Chief Executives, Practice Directors or Office Managers, the battle for power between the old and the new is a familiar theme in legal soaps. Clerks, who hold the purse strings, still rule the roost. Money always talks loudest. Clerks' rooms are still largely male but there are some female, some minority ethnic and even some graduate clerks. The atmosphere is less laddish, more focussed. Senior Clerks now pay regular visits abroad. If Chambers already have professional links in those jurisdictions the rationale is 'client relations', if they do not, the rationale becomes 'business development'.[11] The increase in the number of barristers is reflected in an increase in staff performing the multifarious services chambers are nowadays

---

[11] Cynical barristers privately and sotto voce describe these global jaunts as 'jollies'. It remains, however, imprudent openly to diss one's clerks.

expected to provide both internally and externally,[12] with functions not conceived of when I started, ranging from taking orders for lunch to be eaten al desko, through marketing and party planning to IT. Only typists are all but redundant. We are all word processors now.

Solicitors too have concluded that big is beautiful: and what the Bar has done in tens, have done in hundreds: the largest London-based firm, Dentons, is the largest law firm in the world. They too are in the merger game, linking up formally or informally with overseas law firms, and maintaining outposts in every area where local law permits and fees can be earned. After the liberalisation of the Legal Services Act 2007 seven law firms have converted to companies listed on the London Stock Exchange.

The gulf between the professions has narrowed. Large parts of their education are common. Transfer between them has become easier. From 2010 barristers could become partners with other barristers. Few have done so because they forfeit the benefit of having members of chambers representing different parties in the same case – a practice to which clients, especially from overseas, find it difficult to adjust. Barristers could also own shares in Legal Disciplinary Practices (LDPs) so becoming equity partners in a solicitor-led practice. Few have done so for similar reasons.

Lord Falconer, when Lord Chancellor, now an ex-shadow Attorney-General[13] (oh what a fall was there my countrymen?), in his former incarnation envisaged the breaking down of all such intra- and inter-professional barriers, creating a Tesco-type service shopping centre (but without, sceptics would say, the ability to obtain legal services of a Harrods' level of quality). But while Alternative Business Structures (ABSs) have been permitted for more than a decade[14] such new world, brave or not, has yet to come to full fruition, even if the odd silk has joined the odd blue-chip firm preferring a single guaranteed source of litigation opportunities to the unpredictable advantages of several such sources.

The balance of power between the professions has shifted too. Solicitors are no longer prohibited guests; but encouraged to attend chambers parties, where they are wooed, some say excessively, with champagne and canapés, golfing days or bowling nights. All these new beginnings are designed to cultivate cosier relationships with favoured firms – and are activities in which the ever-sociable clerks come into their own.

---

[12] Blackstone Chambers has a Director and a Deputy Director (with a Personal Assistant), 11 clerks (plus junior clerks who fetch and carry while being trained for higher things), an Events and Marketing executive, a Marketing and Communications executive, a Graduate Recruitment and Pupillage administrator, a Finance Manager, two fees clerks, several IT specialists on call at all hours, three receptionists and a lady who delivers pre-ordered sandwich lunches and provides tea and coffee.

[13] Somewhat slightingly, though not deliberately so, referred to by Lord Woolf, when he attained the office, as a 'cheerful chappie'. In 2021 he was removed from the position of a shadow Attorney-General, allowing him to concentrate on his impressive practice as a partner in a prestigious US law firm like his old Fountain Court colleague and rival Peter Goldsmith.

[14] Introduced by the Legal Services Act 2007.

Conferences frequently take place in solicitors' offices rather than barristers' chambers. Video and Skype and other forms of video conferencing are used ever more frequently: Covid-19 boosted the popularity of Zoom.

Since the Courts and Legal Services Act 1990, solicitors have rights of audience up to the highest court, if fulfilling certain criteria in terms of experience and training. The removal of further roadblocks by the Access to Justice Act 1999 increased the number who did so. They can wear wigs and take silk. Rights of audience have also been granted to the increasing cohort of employed lawyers, including barristers employed by solicitors.

To counter this encroachment of their territory Bar Direct opened up access to the Bar for institutions ranging from Trades Unions, through insurers and banks, to not-for-profit agencies, enabling them to instruct barristers unassisted (or unimpeded by a solicitor), in areas where the institutions have appropriate experience. Public Access,[15] a mark 2 version, widened the range of persons able to instruct barristers, but, notably, not for criminal trials. This was a facility which, with my plate already full, I eschewed.

Since the publication of the Clementi report in 2003, both professions have seen an increasing erosion of their autonomy. The Legal Services Act 2007 introduced the concept of 'reserved legal services ranging from litigation to probate' to be undertaken only by professionally qualified lawyers or authorised members of the professions. But it also transformed the oversight of the legal professions with the establishment of the Legal Services Board (LSB) and Office for Legal Complaints, which in turn spawned the Legal Ombudsman. 'Regulation, regulation, regulation' is the modern mantra.

The legal aid gravy train once denounced by Tony Blair has long since collided with the buffers. There is a ceiling on overall expenditure and fixed, even frozen, fees. The criminal and family law bars have been particularly hit. Barristers have even resorted to strike action eroding further the boundary between a profession and a trade. Successive statutes – the Access to Justice Act 1999, LASPO 2012 have different names, but the same result – less cash. There is no longer public funding for cases involving housing, welfare, negligence, employment, debt, immigration and for most private family law cases, other than of domestic abuse.

The historic impediments to third party involvement in litigation, Maintenance and Champerty, have gone with the wind; Conditional Fees,[16] Contingency Fees,[17] third party funding and Crowd Funding provide a patchwork panacea. Litigants in person without access to any such cash can make use of McKenzie friends, to supply advice, preferably, sotto voce. To seek to deal with the increased cost of litigation Briggs[18] has been sandwiched between Jackson[19] – Briggs dealing with structural changes, Jackson with procedural mechanisms.

---

[15] Now called Direct Access Portal.
[16] No win no fee, Courts and Legal Services Act 1990.
[17] A cut of the damages as fee, Legal Aid, Sentencing and Punishment of Offenders Act 2012.
[18] 2016 Report.
[19] 2010 and 2017 Reports.

The major change in the structure of the Courts has been the replacement in 2008 of the Appellate Committee of the House of Lords as the Apex Court, with a Supreme Court whose members do not, as did the Law Lords, concurrently serve as members of the legislature. The notion that Law Lords could adjudicate on the meaning of legislation in whose enactment they may have been involved as members of the Upper House sat ill with the principle that justice must not only be done, but be seen to be done.[20] Powers are truly separate. Constitutional principle has triumphed over history.

The Justices no longer sit within the precincts of the Palace of Westminster. They have their own premises sprung phoenix-like from the old Middlesex Guildhall. The creation of a Supreme Court – adequately staffed, sufficiently funded, properly accommodated, beautified by Lady Hale's chosen décor – has been a valuable asset. There is more space for the public to watch cases live, with the option of use of the Courts' own dedicated TV channel. But it is not clear that the Justices handle matters of substantive law in a manner different to that of the Law Lords.[21] Individuals count for more than institutions.

The Lord Chancellor's position was still more suspect than that of the Law Lords. He was not so much the embodiment of the notion of separation of powers as its antithesis. The ECtHR in 2000 had ominously ruled that the Bailiff of Guernsey, who enjoyed both legislative and judicial powers, ought to have disqualified himself from sitting in a planning case on the grounds of conflict of interest.[22] Thenceforth the writing was on the wall; if Westminster did not act, Strasbourg would surely have done so. The Lord Chancellor was stripped of judicial powers by the Constitution Reform Act 2005. He[23] is no longer a judge and need no longer be a lawyer. The title retained as an adjunct to that of the Secretary of State for Justice, a Europa rather than Champions League career politician, has no more reality than the smile on the face of the Cheshire cat. The Lord Chief Justice has become the voice of the judiciary.

Changes have taken place at different times on the slopes below the summit. The Crown Court was born of the Courts Act 1971, another brainchild of Dr Beeching, though not resulting in the drastic surgery he administered to the railway network, but more a matter of name change and nips and tucks. The Family Court is new too; that ungainly hotchpotch of Probate, Divorce and Admiralty is only a footnote in a book on legal history. New too are the Administrative Court and Commercial Court; whose specialist business was once conducted under the umbrella of the Queen's Bench Division. The Rolls Building, which houses the Business and Property Courts of England and Wales, is, architecturally, far removed from the extended Victorian Courts in the Strand. With better facilities

---

[20] Article 6 makes an 'independent and impartial tribunal' a cornerstone of a fair trial.

[21] In a seminar to celebrate Freddie Reynolds' (surely interim) book on the Court in 2019 I was on a panel with Lady Hale and Lord Simon-Brown, and Jeffrey Jowell, all shared this perception.

[22] When I teased out the consequences of this in an article in the *Observer*, which described the Bailiff as a lesser potentate than the Lord Chancellor, the then incumbent took umbrage.

[23] Here including she – ie (so far) Liz Truss.

but less charisma it continues to attract international litigants to replace the EU ones. The quality and reputation of the English Judiciary is unaffected by such physical moves.

When the Lord Chancellor ceased to be a judge, the office of Vice Chancellor lost his Vice and became the Chancellor pure and simple. The holder has full responsibility for the Chancery lists of the Business and Property Courts, which includes the Business List, the Insolvency and Companies List, the Intellectual Property List (including IPEC), the Property Trusts and Probate List, the Competition List, the Financial List (jointly with the Commercial Court) and the Revenue List. He selects as well who sits on which cases. The Official Referee, a title impenetrable by the uninitiated, has been replaced by the Technology and Construction Court. The District Judge is a new animal in the judicial bestiary.

Judges are now colour coded, their rank was identified by the colour tabs worn at the neck of the black gown, Court of Appeal Gold, High Court Red, Circuit Judges purple, District Judges blue – an innovation pioneered by Lord Phillips as Chief Justice, not always to universal applause; some said it made the judges look like gospel singers. They are no longer thrown in at the deep end to learn on the job but now are subject to regular training under the auspices of the Judicial College,[24] with a focus on the triple elements of substantive and procedural law, judicial skills, and the social context of judging. Part-time Recorders are no longer associated with particular towns but pass through selection hoops and are at least semi-trained. Appointment as such is a necessary, if not sufficient, condition of elevation to full-time judicial status.

A time limit has been imposed on a judicial career.[25] An octogenarian like Lord Denning is as obsolete as any dinosaur or dodo. Given that so many senior judges upon compulsory retirement find new scope for exercise of their talents as arbitrators, this reform is, curate's egg-like, good in parts only. Youth, a relative concept in this context, must be given its head; but wisdom does not repose exclusively in the young. Lord Bridge is his last case bemoaned the 'statutory presumption of judicial incompetence at the age of 75'.

In the appointments system overall there is light where before there was at best dusk. Advertisements for applications for appointment to the High Court Bench featured before the turn of the century. An independent Commissioner for Judicial Appointments revealed that the 'secret soundings' carried out by the Lord Chancellor's Department elicited observations from consultees such as 'She's off-puttingly headmistressy' and 'smug and self-satisfied and pompous'. (If these observations were well-merited, I am not myself entirely clear why they should be thought to be irrelevant.) He concluded that a picture emerges of 'wider systematic bias in the way that the judiciary and the legal profession operate that affects the position of women, ethnic minority candidates and solicitors vis à vis judicial

---

[24] Previously the Judicial Studies Board.
[25] Judicial Pensions and Retirement Age Act 1993.

appointments'. Like appears, unsurprisingly, to recommend like, and to exhibit dislike of unlike.[26]

With the coming into effect of the CRA 2005, the power of appointment of judges was removed altogether from the Lord Chancellor and assigned to a Judicial Appointments Commission.[27] Since 2005 silks have also been appointed by a Commission. In both, an improvement in openness had to be balanced against an increase in complexity. Candidates at both stages need to set aside several days to complete the forms' box-ticking and those who apply for silk having to pay a substantial financial fee not returnable on failure.

Following the Tribunals, Courts and Enforcement Act 2007 legal executives were eligible for appointment to County and Magistrates' Courts and Tribunals. Government lawyers have become eligible to sit as civil recorders, deputy district judges in magistrates' courts and tribunal judges; the Crimes and Courts Act 2013 allows for part-time appointments. Diversity has become a tie break at all levels where candidates are assessed as of equal merit.

While women – a majority – and ethnic groups – a minority – are still under-represented, in relation to their numbers in the population at large,[28] they are at least more highly represented than before and fortified by Master McCloud, the solitary transgender judge. Women have become heads of one of the divisions, initially (predictably) the Family Division, but later of the Queen's Bench Division too. In 2017 Baroness Hale became the first female President of the Supreme Court with two more of her gender by her side. Women constitute almost a third of the High Court[29] and a quarter of the Court of Appeal. Lord Judge, then Lord Chief Justice, said in 2012 'we are turning a tanker around and it takes time'. The time has speeded up and has been well spent.

Solicitors can also become judges, not only indirectly by promotion from the lower ranks, but straight onto the High Court Bench – a path taken by Lawrence Collins, a distinguished expert in private international law[30] who ended up as JSC. Patrick Elias and Jack Beatson, better known as professors than practitioners, took the Queen's shilling and ended up as senior members of the Court of Appeal, swapping a don's gown and mortarboard for a judge's wig and robes. In 2020 the final frontier was reached when Andrew Burrows, an Oxford scholar in the law of restitution, was made a JSC.

The Kilmuir rules have been abolished and there are media judges just as there are media dons – although *Murmuring Judges*, the title of David Hare's play, carried

---

[26] The process of appointment of QCs, vested exclusively in the Lord Chancellor, was suspended between 2003–05 after the Commissioner pointed out that the system was also the opposite of transparent.

[27] As I had proposed in my Atkin lecture in 1999. See Chapter 8 'Politics and the Law'.

[28] In 2020 32 per cent of the judiciary of England and Wales were women; that contrasts with 51 per cent of the overall population. Seven per cent of the judiciary are BAME compared with 12 per cent of the population.

[29] But BAME only 3 per cent with Rabinder Singh an outlier and trail blazer in the Court of Appeal.

[30] A partner in Herbert Smith.

a somewhat different connotation. In 1992 Peter Taylor, the first Judge to appear on Desert Island Discs, gave the Dimbleby lecture. In 2019 Lord Sumption gave the Reith lectures. Judges now regularly speak out in Court and outside it on issues directly or indirectly concerned with the provision of judicial services. Much of the panoply and privilege of circuit life has disappeared. The traditional Lodgings may soon be replaced by hotels, even motels. It is no longer necessary for judges to dress for dinner. Crown Courts are located in places reflecting the size of the catchment area rather than their historic resonance.

There is a qualified right to trial by jury in civil cases only in the areas of malicious prosecution, false imprisonment and fraud.[31] Otherwise a right to a jury trial is at the discretion of the Court including in defamation cases.[32]

Juries too, since abolition of the property qualification,[33] have become more diverse – some say dumbed down. While the age range has expanded from 21–60 to 18–70, the increase in the length of the trials of the most complex cases has meant that those in full-time employment can be excused from service leaving a residue of the retired or unemployed. The abolition of the peremptory challenge in 1988 – by which objection could be made to someone called into the jury box with no reason given, has made obsolete the traditional trick of provoking such objection by the wearing of a three-piece suit and the carrying of a copy of the *Daily Telegraph*. The recommendations of Sir Robin Auld in his 2000 review of the Criminal Justice System led to the removal of exceptions which allowed persons, such as lawyers, to escape jury service.[34] Judges have since sat as jurors, even at risk to equality of authority *within* the jury room and the removal, albeit temporary, of the judge-juror from the day job.

Lay magistrates, more diverse and better trained (and appraised) than they once were, are complemented by the paid District Judges (Magistrates' Court) and will ordinarily sit alone rather than in a bench of three. There is a greater use in major cities of professionally qualified stipendiary magistrates, or district judges (criminal) as they now inexplicably prefer to be called. In the fullness of time another of the Auld proposals for the new may result in lay magistrates being no more than flankers to a legally qualified chairman – in the same pattern as occurs in Employment Tribunals or the Employment Appeal Tribunal. There is constant closure of rural magistrates' courts, so that the umbilical link between the magistracy and the community they serve is more and more attenuated. Indeed, it is sometimes suggested that a defendant on a charge of burglary needs to steal again to be able to afford the bus fare to the court where he is to be tried.

There has been a rationalisation in the wake of the Leggatt report[35] of the Tribunal system which has more custom than the Courts of Law. Its status is best

---

[31] Senior Courts Act 1981.
[32] Defamation Act 2013.
[33] Juries Act 1974.
[34] Criminal Justice Act 2003.
[35] The Tribunals, Courts and Enforcement Act 2007.

reflected by the fact that its Senior president sits alongside the other heads of Division on such formal occasions as the swearing in of new superior judges[36] and the valedictories (at their option) on the occasion of their departure.

In the early part of the century the Lord Chancellor, wearing his Minister of Justice hat, and the Lord Chief Justice, wearing *his* hat as shop steward of the judiciary, continued to debate the extent to which persons approached to serve on the High Court decline to do so. It became clear to me, from my vantage point on the SSRB, that the charms of the city, the college or even the cash mountains enjoyed by a QC of the calibre eligible for appointment, which dwarfed the fixed salary of the appointee, were dissuading a significant number from accepting judicial preferment.

There has been a sea change in attitude towards the prospect of a judicial appointment. It was once said that every private soldier carried a field marshal's baton in his knapsack. The thought, secreted in this vivid pronouncement, was that every soldier both could, would and even should, aspire to the highest rank. But it is no longer the case, to adapt the proposition to a legal context, that every barrister sees the bench as the natural culmination of a legal career. I know of only one case in recent times where a QC appointed to the High Court actually increased his annual income; there are real concerns as to whether High Court vacancies can be satisfactorily filled without adulterating the gold with baser metal.[37]

Judges have become interventionist in the sense of controlling the pace and length of litigation; and have assumed case management powers under the CPR devised by Lord Woolf. So-called skeleton arguments are now all but mandatory in advance of a hearing. Woe betide the barrister whose skeleton argument is late. Witness statements are exchanged in advance too. Judges are expected to pre-read, and often do so. They certainly have negotiated for reading days with the Lord Chancellor's department. Even in the Supreme Court pre-estimates of time spent in terms of hours are solicited (in the benign and unrealistic assumption that no questions come from the Justices). Documents are now emailed to judges in preference to delivery as hard copies. It is not unusual for written submissions to be produced at the conclusion of anything but the shortest of hearings.

Far from spurning the writings of academics, judges now compete to display their familiarity with the periodical literature from home or abroad. And as for evidence, in the words of the Cole Porter song, *Anything Goes*.

There is a severe restriction on the role and scope of expert witnesses, expected to assist the Courts and not to act as surrogate advocates. The Code of the Patent Court, where science and the law collide, makes provision for trials on paper, dispensing with disclosure of documents, cross-examination of witnesses and oral presentations.

---

[36] So-called because of the unlimited nature of their jurisdiction and not because they are necessarily of higher quality than inferior judges whose jurisdiction is limited by statute – though in reality they usually will be.

[37] See my article 'Judge not …' in the *Spectator* (24 January 2019).

Courts are encouraged to make summary orders for payment of costs and summary assessments of costs. There are specialist procedures for trial of small claims.

Latin has now been expelled from the Court. This is not an unalloyed blessing. For some Latin phrases an appropriate English equivalent is available. 'The thing speaks for itself' is as easy to say as *res ipsa loquitur*. But is 'having changed all those things that have to be changed' any improvement on the deliciously succinct *mutatis mutandis* (my personal favourite)? All lawyers know that *de bene esse* means let the evidence in whether admissible or not on a provisional basis, although no-one seems to know (a few classical scholars apart) quite *why* it means that. I could challenge Lord Woolf to produce a phrase with as few words, indeed letters, as that to convey the same meaning. Many English neologisms can be as arcane as the Latin they replace. Is a 'statement of truth' any better than an *affidavit*? How many people, in the ordinary course of their daily lives, say 'I am about to make a statement of truth'? A true statement maybe. And is permission really a better word than leave? Newspeak can be cumbersome, and not just unfamiliar.

Technology has transformed the operation of the law. The developing world of e-commerce has provided legal practitioners with new opportunities for providing services, as well as new problems to solve. Legal advice can be provided over the Internet. The courts can provide for simultaneous display of evidence on the screen. Submissions are handed up and judgments handed down on disk. More and more research is done through the electronic database and the world-wide web.

Most significantly of all procedural rules and guidelines encourage the use of mediation. In the language of the pre-action protocol, 'litigation should be a last resort'.

As to substantive law, once again the picture has been significantly transformed. Judges have become much less hostile to legislation, and try to work with, and not against, its grain. In a tax case Lord Steyn referred to the view once held by judges that 'Parliament generally changes the law for the worse, and that the business of the judges is to keep the mischief of its interference within the narrowest possible bounds' but added 'During the last 30 years there has been a shift away from literalist to purposive methods of construction. Where there is no obvious meaning of a statutory provision the modern emphasis is on a contextual approach designed to identify the purpose of a statute and give effect to it'. New sources of interpretation arrived; reports which identified the mischief which subsequent statute was designed to cure; explanatory notes from 1999 and, controversially, the statements of Ministers introducing particular provisions in Parliament, *Pepper v Hart* (1993).[38] In 2000 the House of Lords

---

[38] Objection has been raised on constitutional grounds that it is not for the Executive to decide on the meaning of legislation and on practical grounds that it has encouraged the Bar in long, expensive and ultimately fruitless trawls through Hansard.

held that words could actually be added to a statute by way of rectification to give effect to Parliament's intention where their omission was the product of obvious error. Under the HRA the Courts are mandated to adopt linguistically strained constructions to give effect to convention rights. As Lord Nicholls has said[39] 'it is a little ironical that a provision in the Human Rights Act should in this respect fit uneasily beside the principle of legal certainty which is one of the principles underlying the Convention'.

There has been an equivalent development in judicial techniques of interpretation of contracts. Surveying the case law of the last 30 years, Lord Hoffmann said 'The result has been subject to one important exception – to assimilate the way in which (contractual) documents are interpreted by judges to the common sense principles by which any serious utterances would be interpreted in ordinary life'. However, the balance between text and context still causes problems. Even at the highest level the judges have constantly reviewed the precise location of the boundary between them.

There has been modest relaxation of the doctrine of precedent, where justice requires it. Judges are not only conscious but self-conscious of their law-*making* and not only law-*finding* role, especially in the area of Judicial Review of administrative action. The lack of effective Parliamentary scrutiny of the mushrooming delegated legislation has created a vacuum for the judges to fill. In an era when party machines and substantial government majorities have made the backbench MPs increasingly impotent,[40] at any rate in the political sense, the judges have taken up the cudgels in their place. Challenges to alleged misuse of public power which used to occupy the Lord Chief Justice and two colleagues a morning or two a week have come to occupy a number of judges in the Administrative Court list all the time. The triple test of administrative law – lawfulness, fairness, rationality – has been applied to strike down decisions ranging from the provision of funds by the Government to build a dam in Malaysia to a local authority's ban on stag hunting over common land, as well as less unusual but no less important cases in fields of immigration, town and county planning, welfare, housing, utilities regulation, the closure of schools and the opening of sex shops.

Judges are alert to the fact that whereas it is a fundamental principle of English law that a private person may do anything which is not forbidden, a public authority must be able to justify its activities by reference to particular powers. They have resuscitated the all-but-obsolete tort of misfeasance in public office so that officials who abuse their powers consciously or maliciously can be held accountable to compensate the aggrieved citizen.

The judges' function in this area remains nonetheless one of review not appeal. They are concerned with legality in the broad sense, not with merits. But this is not how it always seems to the victims of their rulings. Their exercise of control over the executive has been such as to provoke the wrath of many politicians, most notably successive Secretaries of State for the Home Department of different

---

[39] 'My Kingdom for a Horse. The Meaning of Words' (2005) *LQR* 591.

[40] Though they appear to have rediscovered their mojo during BoJo's premiership towards the end of 2021.

parties – whose decisions are taken in such acutely sensitive fields as immigration and prisons. Joshua Rozenberg, doyen of legal commentators, aptly entitled one of his books, published in 1996, *Trial of Strength*, with the sub-title *The Battle between Ministers and Judges over Who Makes the Law*. But a sequel *Enemies of the People* published in 2020 notes the continued debate as to whether the rule of law has been replaced by rule by lawyers, or whether justice has been superseded by jurisprudence. So-called lefty lawyers who conduct the cases find themselves co-defendants with the judges in the notional dock, of public, or populist opinion.

While closing time appeared likely in the gardens of the East, where local Bars are declaring independence, the Courts at Luxembourg[41] and at Strasbourg opened up to the enthusiastic Euro-advocate.

At home as distinct from away there has been a growing impact of supranational law. The European Communities Act 1972 (ECA) meant that, for the first time since Sir Edward Coke in the early seventeenth century proclaimed the existence of a natural law superior to the law of Parliament, another form of law has also acquired paramount status and superior force, dispersed as it is through various provisions of treaties, directives and regulations.

The implications of this seminal change were slow to be digested by the legal profession, and even more slowly by the public at large. Who could have foreseen that one of the consequences of Britain joining the Common Market was that much time would be spent by my clients the Ministry of Defence fighting off sex discrimination claims by female soldiers who had either been dismissed for pregnancy, or had decided to have abortions in order to keep their jobs?[42] It was as late as 1995 that *The Times* in an editorial wrote of the case where the House of Lords[43] held, despite my contrary argument, that the legislative period of grace preceding employers' liability to pay for redundancy or unfair dismissal fell foul of Community law, that for the first time the United Kingdom had a constitutional court. But sovereignty had been lost many years before even if Brexit may recapture it.

The Lisbon Treaty for a European constitution which created a legal entity of the European Union, makes the Charter of Fundamental Rights part of the constitution itself and gave the constitution and the laws adopted by the EU's institutions, 'primacy over the law of the member states'. The UK opt-out did not dissuade English judges from paying attention to the Charter.

Then on 2 October 2000 the Convention was finally domesticated when the Human Rights Act 1998 (HRA) came into force so that the courts of England and Wales themselves could take account of, and give effect to, the Convention which had already been given a trial run in Scotland,[44] and to the Strasbourg jurisprudence too.

---

[41] But not since 1 January 2021.

[42] [1997] ICR 294, [1997] ICR 306, [1997] 1CR 590.

[43] See chapter 5, 'The Silk Road'.

[44] It was indeed a senior Scottish judge, Lord McCluskey, who described the Human Rights Act as 'a field day for crackpots, a pain in the neck for judges and legislators and a goldmine for lawyers'.

As well as direct there has been indirect impact of Euro-law from Luxembourg and Strasbourg through the introduction into English law of such essentially civil law concepts as legitimate expectation, proportionality and legal certainty.

In a parallel development more attention is paid to international treaties, even where, under the British dualist system, they do not become part of the domestic law, justiciable by domestic courts, until incorporated by legislation. Notably the House of Lords held that domestic legislation should be interpreted to make it compliant with treaties into which the United Kingdom has entered.

The early decisions under the HRA were relatively conservative. The Judges detected a balance inherent in the whole Convention, even where the basic right, such as the right to a fair trial, was *not* expressly qualified by a series of exceptions. It was not easy to identify many of those first decisions which could reasonably have inflamed the temper of that legendary figure alleged to haunt the letters page of the *Daily Telegraph*, 'disgusted of Tunbridge Wells'. But human rights points, once characterised as point of last resort, are now more often front runners, and familiarity bred extent. During the peak of the third lockdown the Court of Appeal had to wrestle with the question whether the right to privacy entitled a refugee to have his birth date officially altered to what he claimed without evidence to be the correct date.[45]

There is a greater exposure to, acceptance of, reference to and reliance by judges on comparative law: the decisions not only of Strasbourg (which our courts are required, under the HRA, to take into account) but those of other countries (especially where multinational treaties, such as the 1951 Geneva Refugees Convention, have generated a jurisprudence in overseas courts) – no doubt partly because of the availability of foreign decisions through internet and electronic databases.

Inspired by their novel power under the ECA to override legislation or under the HRA to make a declaration of incompatibility between domestic and convention law, some Appellate judges even flirted with the notion that, without such aids, they could disregard legislation which they considered offensive to fundamental principle. They argued subversively that since the effect of a statute depended upon its judicial recognition, that recognition could be withdrawn as well as granted. Flirtation has not yet matured into consummation.

The swiftly developing law of negligence now casts a lengthening shadow over the professions in particular. Although in this area there was ebb – in particular when the late Lord Keith was senior Law Lord – as well as flow, the underlying movement has been forward. More and more persons have been found to owe greater and greater duties of care in more and more circumstances but how the

---

When Lord McCluskey presided over a criminal trial of alleged drug traffickers in which the defence case depended on an alleged violation of their human rights, an appeal court decided that Lord McCluskey himself did not constitute an impartial tribunal and remitted the trial to another court. History does not record whether *he* thought that this proved the very point he was making in such forceful language.

[45] But the Supreme Court only a little later on rejected the notion of a transgender passport.

existence of a duty is to be recognised was still being revisited by the Supreme Court in 2021. Nervous shock as well as physical damage must be guarded against. Local authorities are liable for failure to detect dyslexia in school children. Employers must pay damages for carelessly written references. The removal of the hallowed immunity of barristers for their conduct of cases in court not only generated temporary terror in the Temple, but the permanent prospect of ever-increasing insurance premiums which looms ever larger on this side of the Atlantic.

Where a young man broke his neck diving into a shallow lake, despite warnings placed around it by the local authority who owned it, the House of Lords took the opportunity to re-emphasise the importance of personal responsibility and the balance that had to be struck in a negligence claim (unrelated to professional duties). Lord Hobhouse said trenchantly 'The pursuit of an unrestrained culture of blame and compensation has many evil consequences and one is certainly the interference with the liberty of the citizen'. Later legislation sought to reinforce the point,[46] but restraint has not been noticeable. The compensation culture is alive and kicking.

Libel law has been modernised: cards have to be placed on the table and not kept close to the chest. A plaintiff must say what meaning he attributes to the words complained of – and a defendant must respond in kind. The Defamation Act 2013 also fortified the defences available to the injuring party. In doing so it represented the next stage on a journey plotted by the judges, who proudly, if not wholly convincingly, claimed that the common law had always been as zealous a guardian of freedom of expression as the Convention. It was the Convention which prompted them to try to ensure that the damages for defamation were not out of line with the damages for physical damage. Now that the 2013 Act has made juries the exception rather than the norm for such cases – even for such high-profile claimants as Johnny Depp or Meghan Markle – the change matters less than it might. There's no longer the prospect of a pot of gold at the end of even a successful libel action – although, despite the reform, libel tourism has not been stifled. Foreign billionaires, like their British equivalent, continue to use the courts, not to enhance their wealth but to deter inquiry into their business or personal affairs.[47]

The judges reacted to concerns about the absence of a statutory or indeed common law of privacy by developing the law of confidentiality and trespass. For example, in a case involving the taking of unauthorised photographs at the wedding of two celebrated film stars – and unconvincing shrinking violets – Michael Douglas and Catherine Zeta Jones. But the HRA has all but created a privacy right if not in so many words.

In the field of employment law, Westminster and Brussels vied with each other to enhance employees' rights, from maternity leave to the minimum wage, so that the contract of employment is now the starting point, and not the terminus of that critical relationship.

---

[46] Compensation Act 2006.
[47] Sean O'Neill, 'Abuse of British Courts is killing free speech', *The Times* (June 2015).

Planning law has developed a valuable mutation in the form of environmental law.[48]

In the criminal field the police no longer prosecute – there is now a much-maligned Crown Prosecution Service. Police powers are regulated by PACE – the Police and Criminal Evidence Act 1984. The so-called verbals attributed to the defendant 'It's a fair cop' no longer play a role since interviews with suspects are tape-recorded.

The Access to Justice Act established a Community Legal Service and a Criminal Defence Service – a system of state defenders. A new array of current sentencing choices has developed curfews, cautions, community service orders and the like. Yet the reflex action of governments to fight, fight and fight again the rising tide of crime by successive statutes, has been criticised by the judiciary. Lord Bingham, when Lord Chief Justice, said 'I venture to wonder if the solution to our problems really lies in the succession of massive criminal justice bills', of which there have been many. Those who believe that this will necessarily cut the crime rate are influenced more by hope than expectation.

The substantive criminal legislation has changed. Unorthodox or minority sexual practices,[49] paedophilia or pornography apart, are no longer proscribed. Terrorism and its adjuncts are newer targets. Immigration has attracted the increased attention of both criminal and civil, especially administrative, law. There have been experiments in new ways of tackling anti-social behaviour falling short of crime and dealing with the increasing scourge of drugs. Controversially the right to silence has been abolished.[50] Failure to speak out can give rise to adverse inferences in four specified situations. The plural purposes of sentencing have been embodied in legislation[51] which simultaneously established a single community order. The victims of crimes, direct and indirect, now have a speaking role in the sentencing process.

In the 1970s, a series of convictions, all said to be IRA-related, were set aside. They featured a mixture of false confessions, police misconduct, non-disclosure and unreliable expert forensic testimony. In response the Criminal Cases Review Commission (CCRC) was established to investigate alleged miscarriages of justice in England, Wales and Northern Ireland.[52]

International criminal law which was seen as newly inspired by the Nuremburg trials then hibernated for almost half a century until 1993 when the United Nations created the ad hoc International Criminal Tribunal for the prosecution of serious crimes committed during the wars attendant on the break-up of Yugoslavia. In 1998 the Rome Statute created a permanent body, the International Criminal Court at the Hague, a hunting ground well colonised by English lawyers.

---

[48] See my David Hall memorial lecture for the Environmental Law Foundation 'How Green is Judicial Review'.

[49] In 1967 the Sexual Offences Act decriminalised homosexuality. Apart from Mrs Thatcher's transient Clause 28 effort to prevent the 'promotion' of homosexuality by local authorities, the trend for equality both in law and respect for same sex unions was not for turning.

[50] Criminal Justice and Public Order Act 1994.

[51] Criminal Justice Act 2003.

[52] Established by the Criminal Appeal Act of 1995.

Divorce has become bureaucratised. Children and money assumed much greater importance than proving a matrimonial offence, but the rights of the sexes have been rebalanced. Equality of assets is the norm where pairs split.[53] Prenups are recognised. Conception has ceased to be the normal consequence of sex;[54] sex is no longer a pre-requisite to conception. Same-sex relationships have been given legal recognition in statute first in civil partnerships (2004) then in marriages (2013) (though marriage itself is fast losing favour);[55] but the judges have used the Human Rights Act to seek to ensure that the consequences of such status are not inferior to those of the traditional relationship.[56] Increasingly the curtains are lifted on family law proceedings where justice is more frequently actually seen to be done.

Women, the second sex in Simone de Beauvoir's phrase, have benefitted from a series of legislative and judge-led changes on the road to elimination of the numerical adjective. Of the former the most significant was the Equal Pay Act 1970;[57] of the latter the removal of the husband's immunity from prosecution for rape.[58] The House of Lords in 1991 overruled the view of the eighteenth-century jurist Sir Matthew Hale, that by marriage a woman consented to sex.

The Divorce Bar became the Family Bar as wider family law became transformed by science, giving the judges novel powers both as to when life starts and when it should end.[59] Not only political, but moral issues have migrated to the Courts.[60] I once was urgently briefed on behalf of a parent who wished to enjoin a hospital from switching off a machine keeping a severely disabled child alive. I was by chance enjoying the ICC's hospitality at Lord's. Returning at once to chambers I spent the night hours seeking for a loophole in the hospital's reasoning only to be informed, come dawn, that the child had sadly died.

It is important not to exaggerate the scope or significance of the changes of the last three and a half decades which I have sought, somewhat selectively,

---

[53] [2001] 1 AC 596.

[54] In 1967 there were two significant statutes: the National Health Service (Family Planning) Act and the Abortion Act.

[55] The Adoption and Children Act 2002 enabled same-sex couples to adopt.

[56] The interests of transgender persons have also been the subject of legislation.

[57] And legislation to secure a deserted wife's right to remain in the matrimonial home, 1967, the reform of divorce law 1969 and of ancillary relief in 1970 and the Equality Act 2010 which, among a raft of more obviously equalising measures, abolished the common law rule that a husband must maintain his wife.

[58] And the endorsement of the common law offence of kidnapping a wife, 1973, the explosion of the doctrine of the unity of husband and wife, 1982, the elimination of the husband's immunity in relation to the transmission of sexual diseases, 2004.

[59] I addressed some of these issues in the Alexander Howard Lecture at the Royal College of Physicians in 2003 'Life, Death and the Law'. Its most obvious feature is how swiftly its content has become obsolete given the velocity of the ever changing law.

[60] In what circumstances can research on embryos be permitted? Is it proper for doctors to give the pill to girls with whom sexual intercourse would be a criminal offence? When is it appropriate to switch off a life support machine? Who has parental rights and responsibilities for test-tube babies or those brought to birth by surrogate mothers? Is it lawful to operate on Siamese twins when to save the life of one would inevitably lead to the death of the other?

to summarise.[61] When I am asked what differences in the law I have perceived during the course of my legal career, I respond 'Everything has changed but nothing has changed'. It all depends upon how keen one's focus is. If one looks closely there have been some shifts in the landscape; but if one stands back, its broad contours remain the same.

The salient features of the system are, after all, still in place. Justice is administered through an adversarial, not an inquisitorial, system. The professional judiciary are still selected from the ranks of the practising professions – and predominantly from one. Unlike in civilian systems there is no judicial career path to choose at the start of one's working life. To become a judge in England is to switch jobs.

The lay element in our systems – the jury and the magistracy – remain in place, exercising a democratising influence over the legal system even if at the expense of expertise in adjudication.

Barristers are still called to the Bar by the Inns of Court. Their training, like Caesar's Gaul, is still divided into three parts, academic, vocational and pupillage, even if in the process of reorganization into four approved pathways.

The Bar and Solicitors are still, despite more commonality in their education, and greater ease of transfer between them, separate professions.

The common law, developed by the judges, is still developed by reference to specific disputes: the technique is more empirical than theoretical. Domestic law, although increasingly governed by statute, is not, unlike in civilian countries, derived from a systematic code. If judges still go out on circuit, to dispense justice, the headquarters of the judicial exercise still remains located in London.

Oral may be complemented by written advocacy in the Courts, wherever they are; but not replaced by it.

Mr Justice Lightman wrote 'English civil procedure has always reflected the values and traditions of the English sport of cricket, most markedly in the adversary system of justice and not only in the sense of being "slow and boring"'.

So, it is only in that limited sense that fings ain't what they used to be. In my first appearance in our highest court, the presider was Lord Reid. In my last it was Lord Reed. As one might say, *plus ca change* …

Act III. The Future: Que Sera, Sera

What's next in the law? I now don the mantle of Mystic Mike but with no special prophetic powers. By 2020 technology had developed far enough to enable the

---

[61] In the area of family law – which I barely explored as a barrister – I owe much to the talk given at the Michael Beloff Law Society dinner in 2019 by Sir James Munby, former President of the Family Division, 'Fifty Years of Change-For the Better'.

legal system to survive Covid-19 if in lower not top gear. But methods outside and inside court have altered. More home, less away work. Less Pret, more Deliveroo. But there can surely be no turning back to five day(plus) in chambers or office.

Video hearing days will become, force majeure, more flexible if lawyers in London have to accommodate parties, witnesses and other lawyers in different times zones dispersed across the globe – an experience familiar to CAS arbitrators for whom that is often the standard, not the exception. In civil courts remote hearings will continue to increase at the expense of actual hearings. HM Courts and Tribunals Service aims to have most civil claims brought online by the end of 2023 with most family and tribunal claims following thereafter. Actual hearings themselves may be held in Nightingale Courts, or even in Lady Hale's caravan courts designed to revive local justice.

Criminal litigation has suffered from long-term,[62] not just lockdown, factors, but in criminal courts[63] there may be a resistance to voluntary perpetuation of a practice compelled by Covid-specific circumstances. Direct sight and sound of witnesses will still tends to play a significant part of the assessment of evidence at a trial. A fair hearing must be complemented by open justice.

Civil litigation may itself be on the wane. There will be more resolution, less dispute. Mediation will everywhere become compulsory not voluntary. Where litigation survives written will continue to increase at the expense of oral advocacy. Wigs will ultimately disappear entirely, but not in the immediate future in the criminal courts. Robes, the more obvious emblem of a learned profession, will remain. But the sartorial traditions of both professions are under attack, wigs in particular being criticised as indirectly racially discriminatory.

Professor Susskind, the apostle of technology to improve the legal product, has prophesied that 'the ad hoc Covid systems will be superseded this decade by asynchronous procedures, court connected online dispute resolution, telepresence, virtual reality, blockchain and artificial intelligence, terms as unfamiliar to most lawyers now as Zoom and Teams were twelve months ago.'[64] He has called the lawyers of the future 'legal information engineers'.

Artificial Intelligence (AI) will assist in the harvesting or processing of data and make many lawyers redundant.[65] It is adieu, not only au revoir, to paper documents and the photocopier. But even if AI can prophesy cases' outcome, at all

---

[62] Of the 320 Magistrates' Courts operating in England and Wales in 2010, a decade later 164 courts had been sold to developers. The costs saved have been at the expenses of justice, not least because of the knock-on effect on jury trials. There has been a decline in court reporting because of the financial pressures on local newspapers and not merely because there was less to report. Open justice is something of a charade if what is done in an open court is witnessed only by a few interested onlookers and not transmitted to a wider readership. Without scrutiny of what happens in court the chance of wrongful convictions or aberrant sentences, whether too high or too low, may pass unobserved. The problem is compounded by the cut in the budget of the CCRC with an increased workload on a decreasing staff.

[63] The Scottish High Court was able to restart Criminal trials by beaming live court action directly onto a cinema screen so that juries can watch and hear evidence with social distancing maintained.

[64] *The Times* 1 April 2016 – not, I surmise an April fool's joke.

[65] A Law Society report in 2020 prophesied a halving by mid-century.

levels of the legal profession powers of persuasion and exercise of judgment will surely continue to count. The future cannot be all robot and no Rumpole. Sir James Munby spoke of 'moving, whether we like it or not, to the digital court of the future'.[66] Me no like, but since me retired, me no care too much.

The solicitors' profession faces challenges above, below and in between. At the top a new challenge to the legal elite's supremacy has emerged over the last few years ever since the Legal Services Act 2007 liberated the market in the big four accountancy firms, PwC, EY, KPMG, Deloitte's, who employ lawyers on a global basis in numbers exceeding those of even the biggest law firms, albeit lacking the specialist legal expertise of the latter required for the most complex tasks. In the middle, Alternative Legal Services Providers like Axiom can compete in terms of cost efficiency on basic, if not refined, legal tasks. At the bottom in the wake of the so-called 'uberisation' of legal services from November 2019 solicitors have been able to give legal advice on a freelance basis whether to individuals or to small- and medium-size business enterprises (SMEs) without being registered as a sole practitioner, or in practice as part of a wider firm or as in-house counsel. They are allowed to generate their own work and be subject to less rigorous regulation than conventional solicitors. The Law Society has critically described the idea of freelance solicitors as a 'Wild West' model.

Challenges come not only from within but from outside. In response to the standards set by transatlantic behemoths city firms have had to enhance the six-figure salaries for the newly qualified, promise flexible working hours to associates and provide, among other benefits, fertility treatment as well as a knitting allowance. The new breed of Lawfluencers aim to nudge applicants towards one firm rather than another. There will be further links made with firms in other jurisdictions, especially the USA. Even Slaughter and May, which alone of the magic circle firms has maintained a national identity, may not hold out for much longer. If you can't beat them, join with them. There will be further IPOs.

The proposed introduction of the Solicitors Qualifying Exam will free an aspirant solicitor from the need to travel through the LPC (and GDL if a non-law graduate) before undergoing a two-year training contract. In future, s/he can pass two tests and after 24 months of legal work experience, qualify. The SRA argues that the plans will help speed up the diversification of the legal profession. Some firms have countered that candidates may satisfy the formalities without acquisition of the necessary skills.

The Bar has always been an insecure profession; Lord Judge, when Treasurer of the Middle Temple in 2014, mused

> Just as one can see the attractions of the CPS to the Criminal Bar,[67] one should recognise the attractions of senior practitioners entering large firms of solicitors which would

---

[66] See n 61.

[67] The Jeffrey report proposed that all advocates should, after a common education, start as solicitors or in the CPS before moving into the bar. I suspect that in such circumstances, a significant number would remain where they were, deeming the sacrifice of security for adventure too high a price to pay.

brief their own in house advocates, and they will attract them into partnership with wonderful packages. There will, of course, always remain a few, but a significantly reduced number of shining stars. But the number of barristers in independent practice would diminish, and there will be less work for them.

There are, despite all that, still too few places in Chambers for those who seek them,[68] whether at pupillage or tenancy level, a deterrent to aspirant barristers given the substantial sums to be invested in qualification. Chambers themselves devote substantial sums by way of scholarships for pupils in the hope, not always fulfilled, of harvesting a crop of tenants but then, by and large, allow them to sink or swim on their own talents. Possibly Chambers will devote, as a collective, sums to support fledgling tenants in their early years as was once the practice in the middle of the last century. More probably, the Inns will switch their funds from the awards made before Call to those who have become tenants.

This is one way in which the Inns, founded in the Middle Ages, have to adjust to modern times. All four (Gray's, Lincoln's, Middle and Inner Temples) have still an umbilical connection with their roots in a way which Livery companies, such as Fishmongers or Tallow Chandlers, do not. All provide as part of their historic function the training and education of aspirant barristers, and, as already emphasised, retain the unique right to calling people to the Bar. But does it make sense in an age of still more austerity for the Inns so proudly to maintain their separate identities and duplicate each other's functions, for example, by provision of separate libraries, especially as traditional libraries confront the abattoir? As in the case of Oxford colleges, there may have to be some modest redistribution of their collective wealth. Inns may even have to throw their membership open to solicitor advocates.

A still more ambitious agenda has been sketched out by Ali Malek QC, Treasurer of Gray's in 2021, saying that the Inns should in a mission statement expressly promote broader moral values and a public interest which he name checked as 'the Rule of law, diversity and inclusion, access to justice and the international reach of *English* law'. The angel will be in the detail.

Publicly funded barristers, in particular, have been adversely affected by criminal court closures putting at risk their very future, already under pressure from legal aid cuts. For them crime doesn't pay. Hearkening to the dire warnings from those who know the score, fewer and fewer graduates will opt to proceed down this perilous path. But criminal, especially criminal defence, work is on any calculus at least as and probably more important, given that liberty and reputation are at stake, than any other of the services provided by the Bar. Indeed, in 2021 more prosperous sets of commercial chambers or their members dispensed money to alleviate the difficulties faced by their criminal brethren, but this act of professional charity provides no longer term solution. As a result of the pandemic some

---

[68] In 2021, 3,301 candidates applied for 246 places through the pupillage gateway.

sets will go to the wall unless they merge with or, less euphemistically, are taken over by others. So the sets, which survive, will become larger still.

In the mid-1990s I wrote in a blueprint 'Chambers – the next step', an exercise in blue skies thinking

> It is possible to envisage a set of Chambers without any clerks: in fused professions the advocates, of course, have none; but even in Hong Kong, where the professions are not fused, clerks have long since quit the scene. Each member of the Bar fixes his or her own fees: and has a personal secretary to deal with the diary. Interestingly the result has been an upward curve in fees; contrary to popular belief, barristers are not inherently prone to sell themselves short.[69]

But the skies were more cloudy than cerulean. I still do not envisage a clerk-less world in my lifetime. Clerking ought indeed to be an attractive option for law graduates who do not wish to be called to the Bar, but wish still to enjoy the special environment of the Inns or provincial legal life. On the credit side they might gain a better understanding of the law in which their principals practise and have a more sophisticated dialogue with graduate solicitors. On the debit side, they might lack the kind of street smarts which is the key quality of the successful clerk when it comes to talking fees, not fine points of law. The ever increasing supplementary Chambers staff will be afforced by wellness advisers and unconscious bias trainers.

The two professions, Bar and solicitors, will continue to have a patently closer connection as well as latent competition. There will be further moves towards a common education; and further fluidity with moves in both directions from one branch to another, but I do not anticipate that fusion will occur.

One certainty is that the face of the legal professions will change. The death of George Floyd led directly to the Black Lives Matter movement but, indirectly (and with less obvious causal connection), to an emphasis of the need for diversity across a whole range of national institutions and activities, the law among them. Its conscious promotion at all levels by implementation of such initiatives as the Charter for Black Talent in Finance and the Professions or the pilot reverse mentoring schemes promoted by the BSB is an unstoppable trend. It is perceived as a good in itself as well as a driver to enrich the qualities of the profession. Diversity, including of gender, will not only be done but be seen to be done.

But, the past will continue to haunt both professions; female lawyers will reveal incidents of sexual misconduct perpetrated by unreconstructed males of an earlier generation. The Bar Council conceded in 2021 that silks could also be sex pests. MeToo came to the legal world. There may be further memoirs of Black or Asian, less secret than outspoken, barristers, chronicling the prejudice they encountered on their rise to the room at the top. Racism and bullying on the bench too will require investigation and, where established, eradication. At all levels of the legal system there will be a fresh focus on lawyers' wellbeing reflecting the contemporary emphasis on mental health.

---

[69] I added in that unimplemented agenda 'There is from my perspective no appetite at the Bar for any fundamental change in the system'. Nor is there today.

Lawyers cannot insulate themselves from the trends of the times and the collision of money and morality. New questions are posed. Should law firms act for fossil fuel companies or Russian oligarchs? How should the Bar react to Chinese sanctions against sets of chambers whose members had authorised a legal opinion on alleged human rights abuses against the Uyghurs?[70] Should English judges continue to sit in the Final Appeal Court of Hong Kong?

From the consumers' perspective the cut in legal aid has caused the demise of half of all not-for-profit legal advice services and law centres in Wales and England since 2013. Pro bono work provided by top city firms as well as members of the Bar, either on a chambers' or an individual basis, is but a partial solution. However, virtue brings its own reward. Involvement in such work provides a ready defence to those who criticise lawyers for having no interest in anything other than the size of their fees. There will soon come a time when a commitment to pro bono work will become mandatory for aspirant members of the professions (and according to David Lammy, when shadow Justice Minister, actual members may become obliged to offer a certain amount of hours for free). For millennials such obligation will be welcomed as an opportunity going with the grain of the times. But legal fees themselves are inexorably rising. Sitting as an arbitrator with sight of lawyers' bills I am astonished at and even – shall I confess it? – envious, at the increase in level since my retirement.

Turning to adjudication there will be few changes in the overall structure of the national courts. It is unlikely that the next decade is the time when two tiers of appeal become one or that the High Court and County Court will be integrated. The Supreme Court will not abruptly be decommissioned. Its justices will continue to sit in the Privy Council, whose role as the final appellate court of the Commonwealth will continue to be eroded as more nations, infused by a spirit of independence, opt out of its jurisdiction. The Court of Appeal and the various divisions of the High Court, already renamed to reflect more accurately their role, will remain as they are. There will be further devolution of litigation from London to other centres. While Scotland will remain, independent or not, a jurisdiction with its own identifiable law, it is unlikely that Wales will ever achieve the same status.

Television having already breached the ramparts of the Courts here will intrude ever further, under pressure from a media as avid for good stories as for the exposure of error. In camera will be challenged by on camera. The family courts may be immune to this development but there will be a move towards what its President has called 'openness and transparency' in reporting of their proceedings. Particularly sensitive are cases in which children have been removed from their parents because of fear for their welfare. I led for the Government in Strasbourg with, as my junior, James Holman[71] in challenges successfully brought by three such parents.[72] Indeed in 2021 there were two notorious cases where children

---

[70] See Chapter 14 'The Art of Advocacy'.

[71] Brother of Christine Hamilton and appointed to the High Court at such early age that he had almost three decades of service.

[72] (1988) 10 EHRR 29, 97.95.

had been killed because the social services had acted too slowly to protect them from abuse in their family home. There is no happy mean. The law cannot always provide a clear cut solution to every problem.

The significant change that will certainly take place will be in the composition of the judiciary. Notably they will be older. In a reverse ferret, prompted by pandemic problem, in February 2021 the Lord Chancellor announced that judges, magistrates and coroners will be allowed under legislation in train to continue to serve until they are 75.

Because of the recent acceleration in the appointment of women judges to the High Court and Court of Appeal, the few have become the many, if not the majority. As a result unless and until there is a Lord (Lady?) Chief Justice, and female Master (Mistress?) of the Rolls or a successor as President of the Supreme Court to Lady Hale who was an outlier, it will only be the appointment to senior judicial positions of ethnic minorities (excluding from that category well-represented Jews) which will retain a residual novelty factor. During his speech of welcome to the high court bench of Rabinder Singh, Lord Judge commented (in addition to a suite of mischievous comparisons between Rabinder's and my successes as an advocate before him) that no-one should misconceive his appointment to be other than on grounds of merit. In Rabinder's case the comment was superfluous,[73] but that Lord Judge made it at all was telling.

Lord Falconer had said that the establishment of the Judicial Appointments Commission 'promotes opening up appointments to some of those groups of lawyers which are under-represented in the judiciary at the moment, including women, ethnic minorities and, at the higher levels, solicitors'. This benign observation raised with some the spectre that the new body, nominally designed to ensure judicial independence, would in fact be subordinate to the fashions of social engineering, appointing not on merit, but solely on grounds of race or gender. It has not proved to be so. Indeed the Judicial Support Network founded by Kaly Kaul QC, a Circuit Judge has branded the JAC itself as being 'institutionally discriminatory' – a modern legal term of art – as well as 'rotten to the core' which is not and invited the Equality and Human Rights Commission (EHRC) to expose 'serious serial and systemic failings' in the way judges are appointed and promoted 'with too much reliance on secret sounding and too much weight given to the views of senior judges'.

Is diversity in the judiciary a legitimate end in itself, rather than a means to improve the objective quality of the judiciary? The case for diversity can be made good on either ground. In a multicultural society confidence in the system amongst minorities will be increased if the judiciary reflects that variety; different perspectives can inform the perception and assessment of fact. They can also influence the development of substantive law, as Lady Hale's judgments illustrate. But, as Holmes was wont to say to Watson 'these are deep waters' and I tread carefully so as to avoid submersion.

[73] In his book *The Unity of the Law* (Singh, 2022) he refers to me as being 'immensely kind and supportive' from his Cambridge days onwards, and reciprocates by calling me 'one of the greatest advocates at the Bar', p 127.

Against the backcloth of increasing judicial review, powerful voices continue to be raised in favour of the scrutiny of senior judicial nominees by Members of Parliament. This would, in my view, inevitably politicise the judiciary; a consummation devoutly not to be wished. Supreme Court Justices in the USA are women and men of great distinction, but their appointment owes as much to their views (if also their ethnicity) as to their qualities. The fate of Robert Bork, who was *not* appointed because of his conservatism and of Clarence Thomas who *was* appointed because of his colour provide dissuasive precedents.

The more imminent challenge to the quality of the senior judiciary lies neither in an over-emphasis on diversity nor in interference by politicians but by the à la carte menu of alternative career choices to successful silks and the diminishing attractions of the office to those for whom the chance of public service may not be sufficient in itself. Judges in post with a pedigree in commercial and associated work, their promotion no longer a prospect but pension secured, will find it harder to resist early retirement to exploit the profitable possibilities of international arbitration; not least because of the risk that work that would have naturally flowed through the Rolls building may become diverted to the newly created specialist commercial courts in Singapore, Dubai, Doha, Abu Dhabi and even in Kazakhstan.

There are constant efforts by Governments of different political stripe – traditionally resisted by oppositions, whatever different position they would have taken, or would in future take in Government – modestly to adapt the boundaries that divide the jurisdictions of magistrates and Crown Courts and to limit the availability of the jury trial. Economics and efficiency provide the inspiration for these efforts; the resistance to them flies under the flag of justice. Since Magna Carta it has been recognised that justice delayed is justice denied but neither King John nor the barons could have foreseen the impact of the pandemic. The growing backlog of criminal cases caused by it prompted demands for an entire suspension of the use of juries (or their temporary reduction from 12 to seven) and for judges to determine not only the law but the facts too, as happened in Northern Ireland during the time of troubles with the Diplock Courts. Failure to diminish the backlog will not only affect those charged with offences, but those who might be charged in the future under potentially perilous plans to improve prosecution rates for rape.[74]

I confess that I have never been an unalloyed fan of juries. My experience as a judge in criminal courts and as an advocate in defamation actions in the civil courts has never eradicated my first and firm impression that the purpose of jury advocacy – certainly of defence criminal advocacy[75] – is to distract the jury from the relevant matters and to obscure rather than to clarify. I believe that the present inhibitions on research into what actually takes place in the jury room[76] stems

---

[74] Only 1.6% of reported rapes result in charges, let alone trials.
[75] See chapter 11, 'Judge Not Lest Ye Be Judged'.
[76] Described by Sir Robin Auld as indefensible and capable of causing serious injustice and apparently due for review.

from the fear that to shine a light on the emperor would only emphasise his entire lack of clothing.

It is better that 10 guilty men should go free than that one innocent person should be convicted – better but not good. Statistically the rate of conviction is lower before juries than before magistrates. Unless this means that magistrates are regularly or even sometimes convicting the wrong defendants I do not see the principled objection to their greater use at least when, in imitation of the Scottish practice, defendants are permitted to choose between juries and magistrates. Each potential magistrate is, after all, subject to a process of assessment, and undergoes, while on the Bench, a process of continuing education. Their qualifications for rational assessment of the cases brought before them should be superior to those of untrained juries, especially if more and more use is made of legally qualified district judges. The need for lay involvement in the justice system is already catered for. Diversity can be respected by the appointment of more magistrates from minority backgrounds. Lord Devlin once said that the jury was the lamp which shows that freedom lives. I fear that the lamp's light is dim and dusty. Whether the right of a jury to decline to accept a judicial direction is a necessary safety valve and shield or opens too wide the door to a verdict which elevates perceived justice above actual law is debatable. The acquittal of Extinction Rebellion activists on charges of criminal damage for their role in (indisputably) defacing the buildings of Shell International and of the quartet of protesters who gave the Bristol statue of Edward Colston, both slave trader and philanthropist, a temporary watery grave, is an ominous precedent for those, like I, who believe that laws should democratically be altered where appropriate, but not ignored because thought inadequate or offensive by some section of the public.[77] Facts should be found on the basis of evidence of witnesses, loyal to their oath to tell the truth, the whole truth and nothing but the truth rather than an Oprah Winfrey styled perceived truth.

But whatever the pros and cons of the system I do not think that the jury will disappear, although it is possible that its use in fraud trials may be curtailed. Even the ECtHR has held that their use does not offend against Article 6, notwithstanding their most obviously controversially characteristic – the absence of a need to give reasons. As Thomas Grant put it in his Gresham Lectures in 2021 'I do not believe that it exists because it is the best mechanism yet devised for the ascertainment of truth. It exists because in order for a justice system to work it has to command the confidence and respect of the populace'. Juries are us not them – and by some measure the most diverse element in the legal system.

The same appreciation of a community element in the justice system may guarantee the survival of the lay magistrate,[78] especially with moves to increase

---

[77] Custodial sentences handed down to the road blocking activists of Insulate Britain shows that judges are predictably less prone to emotion than juries.

[78] Although alarmingly the number of magistrates has fallen from more than 30,000 in 2006 to less than 13,500 now. Since 2015 a single magistrate sitting with a legal adviser can deal behind closed doors with non-imprisonable offences which are administrative in nature, such as minor road traffic offences to which defendants can enter a plea by post – a shortcut which may lead to a miscarriage of justice.

its diversity, rather than its entire supersession by professional judges. Beyond the perimeter of the Court system specialist Tribunals will continue to multiply in new fields such as environmental law.

Law in the time of Covid has undergone its own, potentially enduring, mutations in terms of lawyers' work. There has been a new emphasis on insolvency and restructuring, furlough and employment cover. Companies have needed advice on their obligations regarding contingency plans and disclosures to shareholders, the reach of 'force majeure' clauses in their insurance cover. The regulations spawned by the Coronavirus Act 2020 have sparked civil liberties issues.

Clinical negligence claims may have to adjust to the reality that while the duty of care remains unchanged, its standard may be affected by the decisions taken at a macro level as to the deployment of resources. The most difficult case I encountered in a Channel Islands Court of Appeal was about liability for a severe personal injury whose cause was the direct result of the limited availability of a particular form of specialist medical service in the small island. The case was destined for the Privy Council but never reached it. The parties, recognising that the odds were evenly balanced, decided to settle.

As to substantive law, a sea of legislation will continue to erode the cliffs of the common law. Familiarity with the principles of statutory interpretation will become even more important for the lawyer than familiarity with the principles of judge-made law. It is probable that any parts of an Act's text which have previously been considered to be beyond the pale may become formally admitted into the chamber of formal interpretative aids and the influence of international conventions, if not themselves incorporated as part of domestic law, will exercise influence on the way domestic statutes are construed. Nonetheless important sectors of the common law (and equity) will remain in practice, if not in principle, free from legislative intervention (though the recommendations of the Law Commission will continue to be influential as and when (or if and when) parliamentary time can be found for their enactment).

Contract will remain contract; a mixture of common law on which statute will be superimposed animated, for the most part, by the desire for increased consumer protection. There will be no move towards a comprehensive civil code which would fossilise rather than clarify the law. Even where Parliament has intervened in the past, for example by Mackenzie Chalmer's[79] Sale of Goods Act, its sections have been polished and refined by judicial analysis. The law will adapt to a world of online transaction and cryptocoins. It is to be hoped, if not with entire confidence, that the Supreme Court will abstain from further attempts to reinvent, if not the entire wheel, at any rate a spoke or two of contractual construction. The suggestions of Lord Nicholls, a quarter of a century ago,[80] that the exclusion of pre-contract negotiations and post-contract interpretation by the parties should

---

[79] A graduate of Trinity College, Oxford, whose law library bears his name.
[80] 'My Kingdom for a Horse – the meaning of words' LQR 2005, p 577.

no longer be excluded from consideration, which he described as a plea for flexible rationalisation, remain unripened fruit.

In tort the essential triggers of a duty of care have been resolved after a period of some judicial instability. It is unlikely, though not impossible, that liability in tort will be abolished in favour of a no-fault scheme with direct insurance of accident victims against losses, if not generally then for those damaged by medical negligence. Such a move would be a matter for the legislature, not the judiciary, which has neither the power nor the expertise to create such a scheme.

Privacy and data protection will continue to overtake defamation as a source of litigation, though the Sussexes bid fair to invigorate both kinds of action. In particular the extent to which celebrities have undermined their own expectation of privacy by courting publicity will be a subject of legal debate. The perennial question as to where the boundary lies between a publication in the interest of the public and one merely of interest to the public will find no final solution. Can SLAPP be stopped?

There will be new efforts to guarantee to creators the fair fruits of their labours subject to potential exploitation in a universe or metaverse driven by the new technology. There will be new streams of work as some measure of legislative control is established over dot-com companies, treating them as publishers and not merely platforms, and as those companies in turn seek to control those who use their facilities, as Twitter did with Trump. In an era when dogs are not only not allowed one bite, but not even a single bark, and persons are disciplined or dismissed for words, (mis)spoken or written, perceived as offensive by some group or another, the subjects of such retribution may counter with free speech as a sword or shield, not as a war on but as a defence against Woke. As someone who advised the Home Office on the drafting of the relevant Section 12 of the HRA I have a vested interest in the paramount value of free expression. Expression limited to what is inoffensive may be given many descriptions but free is not one of them.[81]

Divorce itself will become an all but obsolete legal subject now that a party's wish rather than grounds for it will suffice to obtain a decree, though the law on financial provision remains in the words of Baroness Deech 'as uncertain and confrontational as ever'.[82] One matter on which I once had to advise and on which the judiciary have expressed divided views is whether wives who discover the full extent of their husbands' assets by unlawful means should be able to rely in litigation upon the fruits of their illegality – it is an issue apt for an apex court. Foreign oligarchs will find that their spouses with the assistance of expert lawyers, sometimes as famous as their clients, will continue to engage, where it is available, the jurisdiction of English courts, whose reputation for probity is rivalled by their perceived sympathy for the weaker party. Forum shopping has become familiar in family law, as it once was in the field of libel law. The extension of family relationships beyond the conventional mould, accompanied by the scientific means to achieve it, will provide new and

---

[81] But an enhanced vision of on line safety may properly require restrictions. See the Online Safety Bill.

[82] Letter to *The Times* (11 June 2021).

welcome work for the family law bar. The reconciliation of the rights of biological women with trans women will require legal creativity.[83]

There will be new crimes designed to combat an indigenous terrorist threat, scrutinised with suspicion by civil liberties lawyers, or acts (or inaction) which damage the environment. The Law Commission's recommendation for the introduction of a sentencing code to simplify the current complex provisions and remove at one fell swoop the need to refer to historic legislation may founder for lack of Parliamentary consensus and time. The treatment of young offenders, itself a distinct part of the criminal justice system, is more likely to gain attention because of its disparate impact on children of different social and ethnic backgrounds. The boundary between youth and adulthood may itself be redefined.

There will be continued pressure to enlarge the concept of an unsafe jury verdict – before the Court of Appeal and an extension of the remit of CCRC. The Appeal Court's strictness and the CCRC's timidity interact. The CCRC is deterred from referring cases back to the Court of Appeal when so few succeed.

The four horsemen of penal sanctions – retribution, deterrence personal, deterrence general and rehabilitation – will continue to be ridden at uneven pace. Politicians' response to the social evil of crime has been fitful and fretful, caught as they are between their desire to satisfy the public thirst for more and longer sentences and their own uncertainty as to the efficacy of such sentences on the prisoners, coupled with their certainty as to the adverse impact they have on overcrowded prisons. The Police, Crime, Sentencing and Courts Bill 2021 is the latest, but will not be the last effort to square the circle. Nor will the Nationality and Borders Bill of the same vintage be the last word on an equally divisive subject.

EU law will necessarily be a diminishing subject once Brexit is brought to final fruition, though some far-sighted specialist barristers have hedged their bets by call to the Irish Bar. The European Commission can still bring infringement proceedings against the UK for earlier breaches up to 2025. From 1 January 2021 the EU law doctrines of supremacy, direct effect and the duty of sincere cooperation no longer apply. Nor do the EU principles of effectiveness and proportionality. Preliminary references to the CJEU from courts in the 27 (no longer 28) member states will continue to be made where clarity is sought on the interpretation of EU law and the concepts embedded it in, but those rulings will not be binding on the UK courts even where under the UK-EU Treaty and Co-operation Agreement (TCA) EU law has been retained. The extent to which UK Courts will have 'regard' to future rulings of the CJEU is unknown and will only be clarified by test cases. The greater emphasis on comparative and international law will prevent those rulings becoming of academic interest only.

Economic policy will inform legislative activity; whether the consequence is more or less regulation in the general commercial sphere, and of taxation in particular, lawyers will be needed to advise clients how to comply with, or (as the case may be) avoid, but not evade, any new restrictions.

---

[83] As will the issue of whether, and where, a line should be drawn in the participation of trans women in women's sports. See Chapter 10 'My Sporting Life'.

As a reaction to global warming there will be less conventional oil and gas work, and more work on sustainable energy resources. Post-Brexit international environmental law will take on an enhanced significance as being a unique supra-national legal constraint. The lobby to create a crime of ecocide will become louder. Domestic legislation will create a surge in planning litigation. One man's house is another man's eyesore.

The volcano of public law is not exhausted. Judicial review faces new challenges where decisions are taken on the basis of models or equations – what has been called government by algorithm.[84] Governments may continue to rail against the use of judicial review as an impediment to implementation of their chosen poli-cies. Boris Johnson in the wake of his defeat in the Supreme Court in 2019 that he had unlawfully prorogued Parliament used the vehicle of the Queen's Speech to express a wish 'to restore the balance of power between the executive, legislature and the Courts'. Lord Faulks QC headed a review. But, as Horace put it, 'Parturient montes nascetur ridiculus mus'. His recommendation was for two trivial tweaks only. The Lord Chancellor described them as an 'important starting point' but they may well prove to be the finishing point too. Although Governments can place obstacles in the path of judicial review, such as greater court fees, they cannot abolish it without subverting the rule of law itself. The Judges have, in the spirit of Willie John McBride's legendary British Lions side of 1974 'got their retaliation in first'. They have already made by interpretative techniques judge-proofing clauses all but impotent. They have even threatened in the extreme hypothetical situation where Parliament sought the abolition of judicial review to pray in aid the rule of law to annul the legislation. Would a leaked plan for legislation enabling an annual cull of decisions to which the Government objected, even survive? *La lutta continua.*

At a less controversial level there will be the embedding of a general duty to give reasons; the administration of the final burial rites to Wednesbury and the substitution of its controlling test of irrationality by the principle of proportional-ity; a growing willingness to examine whether an executive action is substantively, as well as procedurally, fair; flexibility in remedies to allow the Executive time to adjust to an adverse ruling, and conceivably, praying in aid the spirit of justice itself, the award of compensation for an ultra vires act, even where it fell short of a breach of a private law obligation. What were previously classified as mere constitutional conventions may mature into legal rules. To reinforce the statutory prohibitions on discrimination and to promote the diversity agenda, there will be resort to a free-standing principle of equality. Target rights may by creative juris-prudence be upgraded to legal rights in such areas as education, healthcare or a safe environment. It depends on who the Justices are.

Macro constitutional changes – the abolition of the Monarchy, the Scottish inde-pendence, the absorption of Northern Ireland into the Irish Republic, the supplanting

---

[84] complicated by the concern that mechanisms for identifying or treating illness eg the pulse oxime-ter have, it is claimed, a built-in white bias.

of the HRA by a British Bill of Rights[85] – have different degrees of probability which would tax the foresight of a soothsayer. It is beyond reasonable doubt that any or all of them would have profound implications for law and the legal system.

Envoi

The essential structure of our legal system and the values it protects are founded in, as they are fundamental to, our living concept of a democratic society. Democracy must reconcile two competing principles; the majority rule in choice of government which exists after all only to promote and protect the welfare of the citizens as a whole; and the human rights of each and every citizen as an individual. The judiciary of necessity plays a key role in deciding where the balance is to be struck. The values which it upholds – as it has always upheld – are the safeguarding of life without which other values would not exist; the protection of liberty without which life itself is diminished; freedom of expression so that by transmission of information and ideas, and debate and discussion on them, citizens may make well-informed choices and governments well-instructed decisions; equality before the law, applied, in the words of the judicial oath 'without fear or favour, affection or ill will', without now discrimination on any arbitrary ground such as race or gender, and with proper regard for due process or natural justice; and, underlying all, the rule of law, requiring first that *any*one who purports to exercise public power has a legal basis for so doing, second that *no* one should be above the law, and third that the law itself should be accessible and certain.

In order for these vital interests to be safeguarded, there must not only be an independent and impartial judiciary but one served by an independent and fearless legal profession. The former appears a given. As to the latter a constant refrain throughout my half-century in practice was that the Bar, especially the criminal or family law practitioner, is imperilled by solicitors' advocacy rights, the loss of legal aid, the increase of court fees and the growth of novel forms of dispute resolution. But reports of the Bar's demise, like of Mark Twain's death, have been greatly exaggerated. In the novel *The Leopard* the Prince of Lampedusa said: 'If we want things to stay as they are, things will have to change'. The Bar by continuous reforms has ensured a future for the virtuous voices of independent advocates. Sometimes when, especially when imprisoned during the period of plague, I wonder whether a barrister's functions fall too far short on a scale of value in comparison with those who create or those who care for others I remind myself that they also serve who only stand and speak. And there will always be scope for the buccaneer as well as for the backroom boy.

---

[85] Though a review conducted by Sir Peter, formerly Lord Justice, Gross in 2021 reminded judges that they were never bound by the rulings of the ECtHR but only to take them into account. Dominic Raab, the Lord Chancellor, has proclaimed an intent to free British judges from the need to be subservient to Strasbourg, something, in my view, easier said than done, since it would require withdrawal from the Convention itself.

Epilogue

On 21 November 2017, 50 years exactly since my call, I wrote a piece in the *Times* called 'The Bar and the Way We Were', anachronistically illustrated with a photograph of me sitting in the Old Library at Trinity some 20 years earlier. Gray's Inn presented me (and other oldies of the same vintage) with the traditional silver gryphon.[1] Magdalen made me guest of honour at their annual QCs' dinner.

These appreciated tokens made me think seriously as to whether the time had come for me to quit the stage before the market dictated that roles which might have been mine many moons ago were irretrievably passed to former understudies. Once a frisky young colt I had become a grizzled old warhorse. I had witnessed other examples of contemporaries who, like aging sportsmen, had lingered too long past their personal sell-by date. Lee Child handed over the valuable Jack Reacher franchise to his brother with the words 'I did not want to be the embarrassing guy who sticks around for a season too long'. Better to go before the world said that I was not the advocate I had once been, whatever that was.[2] Solicitors, whose names or faces I increasingly failed to place, would say on meeting me 'I instructed you once'. Whether that was compliment or criticism depended on the emphasis given to the last word.

Prompted by such sombre reflections, in a theatrical gesture on the anniversary date itself, I wrote to my Senior Clerk and Heads of Chambers that I would not accept any new instructions. I could not, of course, properly bow out of cases to which I was already committed so I was for the next few months in run off. But with the same meretricious taste for drama I wanted to choreograph my exit to take place on a high rather than on a low note.

I had been instructed by Bindmans, by happy chance one of the first firms ever to instruct me, on behalf of a sextet of younger high court judges,[3] who had put their head above the parapet to complain of age discrimination in the new arrangements for judicial pension provision. Introduced against a background of an altered tax regime, it had made them victims of an intentional 'double whammy'.

---

[1] To complement in intrinsic, if not economic, value the small effigy in metal of a donkey – the symbol of resistance to the Nazis – that I was given on my retirement from the Guernsey Court of Appeal.

[2] I had done most of what I wanted to do, except that I was never counsel to (rather than at) an inquiry. I did express an interest in such a role in the Litvinenko inquiry into the death of a Russian dissident, but the solicitors in search of an appropriate QC told my senior clerk that he was looking for someone 'less grand'. He was letting me down lightly.

[3] One of whom, Rabinder Singh was, during the course of the litigation, elevated to the Court of Appeal.

I could hardly have more esteemed clients or a more significant cause for my Last Hurrah; not least because behind the six claimants were a far larger cohort, from the Lord Chief Justice downwards, who would stand to gain from their victory. In an associated case the lead litigant was Master McCloud, the first transgender judge, who was rightly unembarrassed by the masculine judicial title[4] and was an assiduous attender at the hearing, supporting Andrew Short QC. Clerkly collaboration with the listing office ensured that the case[5] was brought in front of the three-judge Court of Appeal, carefully selected for their freedom from any conflict of interest, at a time when I was otherwise unbooked.

To my genuine surprise, when my submissions were concluded, the following interchange took place, recorded verbatim in *The Times*, under the heading 'Lap of Honour':

> Michael Beloff, QC, one of the great ornaments of the Bar, left the stage of the London courts last week with a characteristically gentle bow. Having appeared before Lord Justice Longmore in the McCloud appeal, he asked to be excused as his work was done. 'We can excuse you Mr Beloff,' replied the Lord Justice, adding, 'if I may say, it has been not merely an honour, but also a pleasure to be addressed by you in your last case.' John Cavanagh, QC, appearing opposite Beloff, then remarked: 'May I just add, on behalf of the Bar, that Mr Beloff is one of the very most highly regarded members of our profession, and not only for his erudition, but also for his charm and his kindness, and if this is his last time in this court, I thought it might be appropriate, on behalf of the Bar, to mention that.' All of which prompted Beloff to reply: 'I'm so moved, my Lord, I better retreat before I burst into tears.'
>
> However, it is scarcely curtains for the man who is probably the world's most renowned sports lawyer. His international career with the Court of Arbitration for Sport will continue. Finished? I suspect that he has hardly begun.

It was another six months until the Supreme Court dismissed the Government's application for permission to appeal against their defeat.[6] It was estimated that because of its knock-on effect the decision cost the Exchequer seventeen billion pounds.[7] I was only disappointed that no court had engaged with the constitutional convention which lay at its core, namely the impact on judicial independence in allowing the executive to lower a judge's (deferred) pay during that postholder's term of office – a principle dating back to the Act of Settlement.[8]

---

[4] Which had nothing to do with gender – or for the avoidance of any conceivable doubt – with slavery.

[5] Which had already been before an employment judge and a retired high court judge (both also sensibly chosen on the basis that they had no possible financial interest of their own in the outcome).

[6] [2018] EWCA Civ 2844. Lady Hale explained that permission to the government to appeal to the Supreme Court was refused because the decision of the Court of Appeal was 'so obviously right' (Hale, 2021) p 219. I wish that we Counsel had been so confident and free from anxiety!...

[7] Paul Johnson. '£17bn pensions blunder illustrates the cost of political incompetence' *The Times* (20 July 2020).

[8] My argument had at least the support of the doyen of male legal commentators, Joshua Rozenberg. *Enemies of the People?: How Judges Shape Society* describing me, ingeniously and indirectly to add credibility to his opinion, as 'a distinguished member of the Bar' (Rozenberg, 2020) p158. He deals with the case in context, both before and after, at p157–160.

It was a last act more fitting than my Plan B which was to solicit a brief to make a plea in mitigation pro bono for some minor traffic offence in a far-flung Magistrates' court; in my beginning would have been my end. I stuck to my vow never to don my wig again in an English court; but I did accept for a short time an eclectic set of instructions as long as they had some special feature of legal interest or were received at the request of personal friends. In the former category was the constitutional implication of the crossing of the floor of the House by members elected on the ticket of the governing party of Malaysia (for which I delved back into my history for the Churchill precedent of a double cross). In the latter category was a member of the Lee Kwan Yew family – Singaporean royalty – and Debbie Jevans,[9] the interim director of the Football League with whom I had worked on the London 2012 Olympics bid.

In the process of detoxification[10] I gradually persuaded my clerks that no really meant no. For a while I felt twinges of reluctance in my resistance to such offers but gradually even those nostalgic sentiments evaporated. The urges to descend yet again into the arena weren't what they used to be. Eventually I not only ceased to want to make that journey but positively wanted not to.

Apart from such dwindling appetite for the forensic fray I was out of kilter with the times. When I first started in practice I was one of the few barristers who could type. When I finished I had fewer word processing skills than the most junior of junior clerks. I became hugely dependent on the patience of chambers' IT team and the generosity of juniors and staff to clean up my imperfectly crafted documents, or indeed to access for me, at the press of a button, a cornucopia of jurisprudence and journals. It was indicative of the changing legal scene that I was barely able to dispose, even free of charge, of my full set of law reports, bought from Sir John Foster QC. I had thought them at the time of their purchase destined to be an ever-appreciating asset and my offspring's patrimony. Only after a prolonged search did I identify Royal Holloway College, which had just inaugurated a law school, as their final resting place. I was an analogue barrister in a digital age.

---

[9] Former Whiteman cup tennis player.

[10] I declined a brief for the Prime Minster of Trinidad and Tobago; my senior clerk, aware of the tendency of some Caribbean governments to refuse to pay for legal work carried out for the previous administration of a different party (a money-saving strategy which raises interesting constitutional issues), had prudently insisted but, without success, on fees up front. I was approached to join the legal team of a hyper rich Uzbek who wished to intervene in the Russian appeal to CAS over Russia's potential exclusion from the Tokyo Olympics (an invitation I could not realistically accept given my frequent appearances as arbitrator on cases decided adverse to Russian interests). I also declined to advise the governing body of World Amateur Boxing threatened with expulsion from the same Olympics even though I laboured under no such inhibition and still later refused an offer to be a candidate to chair an inquiry for the same body into past misconduct in and out of the ring and to make recommendations for a better future. I resisted an approach, on behalf of a group of banks in a middle eastern state, to represent them in a multi-million dollar negligence claim against a leading firm of accountants, I declined to provide legal assistance to two Tory MPs threatened by different scandals (you – possibly, spoiled for choice? – will have to guess which two). Even the repeated pleas of a valued solicitor friend in Bermuda to make myself available for a constitutional case destined for the Privy Council had to be resisted.

The Covid 19 pandemic confirmed for me, if retrospectively, that I had chosen to quit at the right time. Zoom advocacy is no substitute for direct advocacy at any rate for someone like I who wants to be able to appeal face to face to my tribunal and to interpret its reaction, without anxiety as to whether I had inadvertently pressed 'Mute' or disappeared altogether from its sight. Just as a Parliamentary speech lacks resonance when it has to be delivered to an empty chamber so does a barrister's submission if delivered to a flat screen.

So, what sticks in the memory now that the last chapter in my case book has been penned? It is not easy to know where to start let alone finish. The issues which have crossed my desk have engaged both the stomach and the spirit, from food (Mozzarella, Parma Ham, Ferrero Rocher) to art (Henry Moore Maquettes, Canova's Three Graces, Raphael's Madonna of the Pinks, the Baron Thyssen collection).

My institutional clients have ranged from corporate commercial concerns and public authorities of varied hues, via media and Trades Unions, to pressure groups such as the Maternity Alliance, Amnesty, Liberty,[11] Justice, the Public Law Project and Greenpeace. My natural, as distinct from legal clients (in ordinary language individuals not institutions), have embraced the good, the bad and the ugly, as well as the bold and the beautiful; the last group was, alas, the smallest but certainly included the actress Diane Cilento, the Duchess of Rutland, who diverted herself by knitting during the consultation, and Gazza's wife. His Highness Tengku Muhammad Fakhry Petra ibni Sultan Ismail Petra,[12] His Serene Highness Prince Has-Adam II Von Und Zu Liechtenstein,[13] and Pengiran Digadong Sahibul Mal Pengiran Muda Jefri Bolkiah ibni Al-Marhum Sultan Haji Omar Ali Saifuddien Sa'adul Khairi Waddien, better known as Prince Jeffri, younger brother of the Sultan of Brunei,[14] all jostle for their proper place on the eccentric podium reserved for those with elongated or elaborate names.

The Palme d'Or for my most productive client must go to Mohamed Al Fayed. The work he supplied was wide-ranging spanning representation in challenges to the refusal of the Home Secretary to grant him citizenship;[15] and by his club, Fulham FC, to the Premier League decision not to dock points from West Ham United for playing the peripatetic Argentinian star Carlos Tevez; in a claim for the subterranean trespass by Star Energy on land owned by Bocardo, his company;[16] in various offshoots of the libel actions brought against him by Neil

---

[11] In 1988 Cherie nominated me for Liberty's annual human rights award though, even with her august support, I did not make the shortlist.

[12] Aspirant heir to a throne in one of the states in Malaysia.

[13] His case concerned export licences for art treasures.

[14] And, vicariously, a relation of Mir Osman Ali Khan, Asaf Jah VII, Nizam of Hyderabad seeking to breathe fresh life into an ancient claim for a sum of just over one million pounds held by a London bank in the name of the High Commissioner for Pakistan.

[15] [1998] 1 WLR 763.

[16] [2011] AC 380. Discussed in Lord Hope's diaries, *House of Lords 1996–2009* (Hope, 2018) p48 which reveals he was outvoted on the damages to be awarded to the company.

Hamilton and, in pride of place, several judicial reviews arising out of the inquest into the deaths of his son Dodi and Princess Diana, in which Mike Mansfield did the heavy lifting in the inquest itself leaving me, on one occasion, to seek – unsuccessfully – to have the Queen herself impleaded in her own courts. I was part of different teams giving advice when 'MeToo' allegedly came to Harrods and on an unconnected technical tax matter.[17] He even acted as an ad hoc clerk procuring for me clients such as Mohamed Taranissi who ran a female fertility clinic and Charles Wardle MP, exiled from the Tory party.

Mr Al Fayed would not attend consultations with his lawyers in Chambers or offices. The mouthpiece had to go to Mohamed in his eyrie above his emporium. Once he brought me an autographed copy of the memoir of Monica Lewinsky and then, with a showman's flourish, a cigar. Point taken. On other occasions he gave me a pill box which he told me contained Viagra and a metal bracelet said to cure wrist pain. I never tested either to see if they were efficacious.[18]

When he sold Harrods Mr Al Fayed held a farewell party in which various international celebrities, possibly more English Football than Premier League quality, beamed tributes to him. The party's centrepiece was a vast cake made in the shape of a sphinx. At a crucial moment its head became detached from its body; which somehow seemed symbolic. He was, as a client, never less than accommodating as well as generous and has, in my view, not attracted the sympathy he deserved for the death of his son.

But at another end of the cast of characters I also enjoyed acting for the NUM and, in particular, meetings with the highly intelligent Arthur Scargill who was as restrained in private as he was pugnacious in public. My major case for the Union pitted it against British Coal in an equal pay dispute. Both bodies were by then all but defunct, but the ghostly contest, matching a sepulchral King Kong against a no less sepulchral Godzilla, proceeded all the way up to the House of Lords.[19]

I acted on various occasions for the Maxwells (*père et fils* – Kevin).[20] My first meeting with Robert was at a dinner party at my parents' home in 1964. The newly elected MP for Buckingham, he optimistically predicted that Harold Wilson would make him Chancellor of the Exchequer. By the time of our second meeting he had quit politics for business. Wishing to challenge a block to his bid to purchase a national newspaper he came to Chambers with his solicitor

---

[17] Attending a consultation with his specialist QC in the latter's Chambers, I marvelled at the framed cheque for £50,000 which adorned his wall, an expensive form of decoration, if it was indeed an original and not a mere facsimile.

[18] I was invited by Mr Al Fayed to the Royal Windsor Horse Show which he sponsored. I initially declined after colleagues suggested that I should be prudent to maintain social distancing of more than two metres. He then sent me a photograph of the Queen. The message was hardly hidden – what's good enough for the Queen is more than good enough for a mere Queen's counsel. I was relieved to see that among the other guests was a High Court Judge. When I introduced Judith as my wife he said 'that's what he called the lady he brought last time'. His charm was generally more conspicuous than his wit.

[19] [1996] ICR 515. He also gave me an NUM tie which I wear on inappropriate occasions. I have several ties given to me by clients to be worn without such reservation.

[20] *TLR* 9.10.1992.

Victor (Lord) Mishcon. I thought Maxwell's chances in the proposed judicial review were nugatory but since he insisted on fighting the good (or bad) fight, I left the room briefly to ask my clerks about possible dates for a hearing. By the time I returned Lord Mishcon had argued him out of pursuit of such an unpropitious claim.

Mishcon was one of an elite group of senior solicitors whose numbers were diminished as firms adopted age limits to remove blocks on the road to partnership of the ambitious young. They had the kind of wisdom and influence, born of age and experience, that gave them powers of persuasion to handle forceful clients denied to a wet behind the ears silk. Edward Walker-Arnott, senior partner of Herbert Smith, was another of that august ilk. I greatly admired him for the way in which he manoeuvred Alan Sugar, another powerful tycoon, without risking the latter's favourite catchphrase 'You're fired'. But then Edward was no apprentice.

All's well that ends, but what of the final score card? Until the Supreme Court started streaming its proceedings there was no permanent record of the advocacy skills of barristers: only transcripts which can no more convey the mood of the moment than can a musical score convey the sound of a symphony. So unlike writers they cannot point to any enduring body of work. Their reputations for posterity depend on the bare list of reported cases in which they were involved and on the memory of those who heard them. The verdicts may be various. The beauty of the oratory depends upon the ear of the audience.

Barristers have a natural reluctance to confer bouquets on their peers for fear that it may divert the attention of solicitors from their own qualities. Chat over tea (but in those frenzied days was there ever time for tea?) would more usually focus upon the shortcomings of one's opponent than upon his merits. But now, all passion spent, I can identify more freely those whom I esteem as my great contemporaries.

My list is obviously biased because I barely practised in criminal law where the scope for luminous oratory is greater; and because I have to limit it to those whom I encountered with some frequency. Tom Bingham was, by all accounts, as exceptional at the bar as he was on the bench. But I only heard him once when he secured a verdict for my aunt Nora of whom *Private Eye* had claimed that, in search of a story, she had been to bed with half the Cabinet but that nothing improper had occurred – a two-edged libel if ever there was – and Tom was of a senior generation. Nor can I include many of my outstanding juniors because I never heard them on their feet. My unsophisticated test for inclusion in my list is this – if I passed by a court in which X was making submissions, would I have thought it worthwhile to slip into the back row to listen.

With those qualifications, I name the usual suspects, with all of whom I have drawn swords, David and Jonathan (Pannick and Sumption), Sydney Kentridge and George Carman, Derry Irvine and Gordon Pollock, Stephen Sedley and John Laws – the Castor and Pollux of the Public Law Bar, Charlie Falconer and Peter Goldsmith, the Blairite pair, Ed Fitzgerald, from their left to Bob Alexander from their right, Peter Scott, whom Anthony Lester once deliciously described during the Crown Agents enquiry as 'carrying an air of indefinable menace about him', Tony Grabiner and Christopher Clarke – the rough and the smooth. Tony made full use of his height and rasping voice. He explained to the Court during the Northern

Rock Litigation that he didn't become a surgeon because he disliked blood and didn't become an accountant because he couldn't count (which may explain why he tended to be dismissive when questions were raised in Parliament about the size of his fees). Christopher emphasised each syllable of his melodiously constructed sentences in a kind of aristocratic drawl.

I would add, and not only because they were Blackstone colleagues, James Eadie, for so many years the Government's formidable frontman, displaying stamina and sangfroid in equal proportions, Dinah Rose to whom the adjective feisty was repeatedly attached by critics and admirers alike – the second group by far outnumbering the first, and Shaheed Fatima, the youngest of my selections. If I think of any of the foregoing I can hear them in my mind's ear. Whether their weapon was bludgeon or rapier, whether their chief quality was power or charm, whether their submissions were a seamless web or a patchwork quilt, their distinction is that they were or are distinctive.

I consider myself by contrast to these galacticos an all-round speechifier who could turn his tongue to use on a range of different occasions, from lectures to debates, from memorial addresses to after-dinner speeches, from barmitzvahs to the unveiling of a sculpture[21] or the inauguration of a library lift for the disabled. A jester with a sentimental streak, if I could make others laugh, I could make myself cry. I revelled in the infinite possibilities of language, loving pun and paradox. In private I reordered sentences, fashioned a vocabulary which only my family could interpret and sang nonsense verses in the shower, all of which I extravagantly equated to a pianist practising scales. I have a relish for sounds, words and unusual names – Bouillabaisse, Baluchistan, Borsumato, Kirilenko, Escartefigue, Haronordiquy.[22] My choice of motto for my coat of arms was designedly ambiguous,[23] 'Verbis delectando' (delighting in words – the shy version – or with words – the vain version). It was just my good fortune that I pursued a career in which forensic fluency was at a premium.

I could seek to weigh my professional life quantitatively, with only the slightest massage of the mathematics and a minimum of gaps, in the style of the carol 'The Twelve Days of Christmas' as notionally amended by Bridget Jones. In such offbeat exercise I could enumerate: named lectures I've given (12); Commonwealth jurisdictions I've appeared in (10); Departments of State I've acted for (9); Foreign Governments I've advised[24] (ditto); forewords I've written to other authors' books (6); *festschrifts* I've contributed to (ditto); magic circle firms I've been instructed by[25] (5); honorary degrees conferred

[21] Oscar Nemon's 'Eternity'.

[22] My all-time favourite is the French M 4x100 m sprint team of the mid-1990s: Moriniere; Quenerve; Trouabal; Marie Rose; first reserve Sangouma. Pure motion in poetry.

[23] Vouched for by Peter Brown, a Dragon contemporary and long-serving Fellow in Classics at Trinity.

[24] Australia, Saudi Arabia, Iraq, Iceland, Malaysia, Cayman, Trinidad and Tobago, Hong Kong, Gibraltar. I shall not count the Interim Administration of Afghanistan of the Karzai era.

[25] Adding Clifford Chance to the traditional quartet of Slaughter and May, Allen and Overy, Freshfields and Linklaters.

on me (4); overseas jurisdictions in which I've given expert evidence[26] (ditto); fellowships of learned societies elected to (3); honorary fellowships (2); Directory Awards received (1).

I could list the distinctions attained by my numerous juniors – two judges of the International Court of Justice (ICJ); one judge and two advocates-general of the ECJ; one judge of the EctHR; the Chief Justice of the Bahamas; a judge of the Eastern Caribbean Court of Appeal; the first woman judge of the Trinidad and Tobago Court of Appeal; the Attorneys-General of Hong Kong, Gibraltar, Trinidad and Tobago; the Solicitor-General of Cayman; too many English Appeal Court and High Court judges to count, the President of the Queen's Bench Division; a President of the Supreme Court (who was once my second junior) and two Justices, not to speak of two Oxford and two Cambridge Heads of House.[27] Didn't they do well? Thanks for the memories one and all. It's been a privilege.

He who blows his own trumpet makes a discordant sound. Better to ask someone else which I shall now do for – I promise – the very last time.[28]

Using that frayed camouflage, I could pray in aid generous comments made about me both inside and outside court.[29] (This is, I confess, a not very subtle surrogate for self-praise; but then, what are friends for if not, like the Victorian mediaevalists Stubbs and Freeman, flatteringly to ladle butter on each other?) I could mention other comments in print[30] as well as the hyperbole employed about me by journalists with a Roget's Thesaurus to hand when they thought the unadorned noun lacked punch – distinguished (which hardly counts since it is another epithet all but indissolubly glued to the acronym QC), legendary, iconic, charismatic, great, impossibly grand (but do I detect a note of sarcasm?), highly (sometimes well or very) experienced, remarkable, respected, revered, renowned, formidable, heavyweight, top, high powered etc. 'Leading' is sometimes used but it is tautologous. But I've never been called fashionable, the obsolescent adjective, attached to silks in the 1950s and 1960s of the kind portrayed in black and white B feature movies and have invariably been called scruffy and bearded, even when for my Birkenhead lecture I'd invested in a specially made new suit. I was also somewhat disconcerted when in a Focus on

---

[26] Norway, Ireland, South Africa, and New Zealand. I shall pedantically not count New York under this heading.

[27] One Cambridge Master was previously a judge of the ICJ.

[28] Griffin, the anonymous diarist of Graya, benevolently suggested that a magazine profile description 'emphasized the complete lack of pretentiousness, which those who know Michael Beloff will all confirm' Graya no 111 pp 8–9. Lack ? I wish.....

[29] In named lectures by Lord Justice Moses in referring to me as 'That Pre-Eminent Advocate' in his Ann Ebsworth Lecture (the pre is the key, all silks are by hallowed convention called eminent). Lord Pannick QC – referring to my 'usual verve and wit' in his Francis Mann Lecture. Lord Neuberger MR – 'I was led by none other than Michael Beloff' in his Robert Alexander lecture and best of all, Lord Bingham 'Michael Beloff, ... an accomplished and much sought-after advocate' in his Birkenhead Lecture.

[30] Although for a brief spell a legal magazine compiled a cruel ranking of bad judges, no one has yet embarked on a similar exercise for the bar.

the Public Law Bar[31] an anonymous consultee said 'very good once he's sufficiently interested in something' – and if I wasn't interested, then what ...? In his resuscitated classic[32] Anthony Sampson, anatomist of Britain, wrote 'Certainly the richest QCs contain outstanding minds', linking me with David Pannick and Jonathan S. I cannot claim to have David's brain power or Jonathan's natural feel for the law. I had to work slowly up the slope towards the summit on which they, with one bound, landed so effortlessly.

I value still more the private tributes from those I've worked with, kept in a bulging file called with only just a touch of self-mockery 'Songs of Praise' from solicitors and clients alike.[33] An influencer, in the media sense, I've never been; but if I've had some positive influence on the stars of the bar generation after mine I shall be more than merely satisfied. Once a younger opponent in a case in the House of Lords suddenly exclaimed what an honour it was to appear against me though this may have been a subtle tactic to embarrass me – certainly that was its effect.

I could list the numerous profiles in journals ranging from *The Times* to *Runners World*, my unbroken appearances for more than 30 years in legal directories' rankings, my regular inclusion in lists of top barristers in generalist newspapers and magazines, sometimes under such contrived rubrics as 'Big Wigs', 'Super Silks' or 'Top Brass'; in my position as one of the 10 barristers of the decade in *Legal Business* and (slower off the mark) *The Independent* in 2001, my lifetime achievement award at Chambers Directory annual prize-giving (how many more times am I going to mention this?), my appearances in the two *Times* lists of the 100 most influential lawyers in England in 2009 and 2011.

In his first memoir Simon Brown[34] called me

> another outstanding advocate of the time whom I encountered frequently and with invariable pleasure down many years. Michael is blessed with a fertile mind, great oratorical skills and a rich command of language. Whilst, however, a delight to listen to, I have often found his arguments almost impossible to note: every submission seems to slip seamlessly into the next, parentheses are legion and no sentence ever ends. Michael

---

[31] *The Lawyer* (18 November 1997).

[32] *Who Runs This Place?: The Anatomy of Britain in the 21st Century* (Sampson, 2004) p179.

[33] The newly appointed High Court Judge who wrote 'at your best you were the best advocate I ever heard' leaving open the question of how often I was at my best and less ambiguously the instructing solicitor who wrote that my reply (in the House of Lords) was the best he had heard in 20 years in the law – but for all that, never instructed me again. I was particularly touched when Davinder Singh wrote to me 'I recently did an interview during which I talked about the huge impact you made on me and my career. It is in the link below of the podcast and the relevant part starts from 29:30 mins. I thought you should know what I said from my heart. Thanks again Michael for everything'. https://podcasts.apple.com/sg/podcast/advocates-the-podcast/id1538754665?i=1000511362819 (if you don't believe me) and by a card from Berth Tandy, a disabled teenager, for whom I successfully retained her entitlement to home tuition which the local authority wished to cut on costs grounds ([1998] AC 714). I noted that the file contains one item of abuse from an all but vexatious litigant in person who waged continuous war with the civil service and who wrote that I was a 'dishonorable txrd' and made various threats which, since they arguably amounted to a contempt of court, I had to pass on to Potts J, the judge in charge of the case.

[34] (Brown, 2020) p 136.

has, I know, told against himself of an occasion when, apologising for rudely interrupting him mid-flow, I said: 'Mr Beloff, if ever you reach a semi-colon, do please let me know. There is a question I am anxious to put to you.' That said, there are few advocates at the Bar I would rather have on my side in times of trouble.

I shall not demur from that benign judgment, including the sting in the centre, and I have a ready riposte to those who indict me for further boastfulness in quoting it, provided by none other than Simon Brown himself. He similarly cited, as a tribute to be treasured, what Tom Bingham had once said about him, and anticipating the possibility of similar criticism, wrote robustly 'It is a price worth paying for the chance now to savour, cherish and actually broadcast this accolade'.[35] I cannot improve on that mitigation.

Nonetheless, purportedly for balance, I should add two more nuanced comments from David Pannick in his once regular column in *The Times*, 'Great advocates from Cicero to Michael Beloff have managed to represent clients forcefully without resort to masturbatory gestures'[36] and 'Jonathan Sumption and Michael Beloff have managed to enjoy successful careers without any such soubriquet'.[37] (The soubriquet in question being Mad Dog, the nickname of Charlie Sheen's lawyer.) Truth be told I never thought I was as good as others made out; but if you asked me who of my peer group I thought was obviously better than me at my best, you might not have sufficient time to wait for an answer. Cross-examination has always depended upon putting the right question in the right way.

So, what's it all about, Alfie? Barristers cannot claim the influence on the law enjoyed by judges. At most in an adversarial system their influence is indirect not direct. It is judges who mould the law. The contribution that advocates make is to seek to persuade them to travel in a particular direction (or more usually) to remain immobile. Very occasionally an advocate will create an argument which, if successful, will open up new areas of law – though the advocate is also dependent on being briefed for the right client at the right time. Courts prefer to deal with actual cases not hypothetical ones.

Since my taste was for a rapid turnover of cases rather than for incarceration in long hearings – rather like my attitude to marathons, I did them, but infrequently to prove that I could rather than because of any real enjoyment[38] – I gave myself a better chance of helping in a minor way to shape the law's development. Even so the pickings were thin; I have already mentioned the Marshall decisions in the ECJ. On the home front I would instance two cases in particular: St Germain, one of my last cases as a junior, which established that

---

[35] Simon Brown, *Second Helpings* (Brown, 2021) p140.
[36] 3 January 2019.
[37] 24 March 2011.
[38] In my longest, an arbitration over the fate of the Dorchester, in which Counsel treated themselves to a tie with the embossed numbers of the 139 days spent. The Arbitrator, Sir Edward Eveleigh, found a single technical point dispositive which he dealt with in a 10 page award, much of which was background, so shrewdly saving himself any need to grapple with the main issues.

the decisions of Prison Boards of Visitors were amenable to judicial review,[39] so making a breach in the immunity of the so-called disciplined services from judicial control; and *Stevens v Avery*,[40] which, as the judge Nicolas Browne-Wilkinson[41] himself observed, provided the first glimmerings of a privacy right in English law in protecting from disclosure correspondence between two lesbian lovers. And I was relieved to have won a habeas corpus case for 20,000 or so Vietnamese boat people incarcerated in detention centres in Hong Kong for periods of between four to seven years,[42] even if I could not wholly accept my instructing solicitor's[43] hyperbolic suggestion that it was 'quite possibly the most important of its kind since Liversidge v Anderson'. I persuaded both British Airways and Cathay Pacific to equalize the retiring ages of flight crew so that stewardesses gained in experience what they may have lost in purely physical attractiveness and fought off the first effort to have Viagra made available of the National Health – a classic example, the spiteful might say, of a barrister putting his client's interest above his own.

Because this is a memoir about my quasi-public and not my private life, I have all but wholly avoided writing about family and friends (sometimes coincident), sex and love (ditto), leisure and pleasure, health and wealth, yet these have been, for me, as for most people, the subterranean forces most important to me. I must ruefully acknowledge that my professional life certainly impinged on my personal life; as mentioned already I gave a tutorial on the afternoon of my wedding and Judith has continued to have the patience of Penelope. When my daughter was being born I was immured in the Immigration Appeal Tribunal, instructed by David Gold[44] of Herbert Smith, so that it was several hours before returning to chambers that I knew of the gender of my second child (though everyone else there did). When my father died I was on the verge of departing to Lausanne for a CAS case, which had to be interrupted later the same week so I could fly back for his funeral, before returning to the fray. The balance I struck was too lopsided.

Throughout I have led a classic cloistered existence, metaphorically and even architecturally – Eton, Oxford, Gray's Inn, with a narrow bandwidth only enlarged by the wide range of contacts, home and abroad, that I have made through my several professions. Nonetheless I prefer to think that the privilege I have certainly enjoyed is not entirely the consequence of being white. There was in a competitive world, at least some sweat involved, if few tears, and no blood. Luck certainly

---

[39] [1979] QB 425.

[40] [1988] 1 Ch 457

[41] Senior Law Lord.

[42] [1997] AC 97.

[43] I paid this tribute to her as a Gray's Inn member in my Barnards Inn reading, 'Sisters in Law the Irresistible Rise of Women in Wigs'. 'Pam Barker, called at the age of 49, and rejected for a tenancy from the all male set where she did her pupillage not just – she believed – because she was a woman, but because she was a grandmother, who returned to Hong Kong to become the pre-eminent defender of the Vietnamese boat people'.

[44] Lord Gold.

played its key part, but luck or no luck, it was certainly fun while it lasted. What's left now is at most postscript. My professional race is all but run. One aim of this memoir was to achieve closure.

In her diary for 21 September 1967 my mother wrote, 'Michael moans that he is a complete failure. I simply refuse to believe that he won't pull off something tremendous. It would be so much of a waste'. When I last visited her shortly before she died at the ripe old age of 95, she asked me 'You have done alright, haven't you?' I replied 'Yes mum'. I said it to please her but maybe it had an element of truth. Samuel Johnson wrote of Mansfield (Lord, not Mike) 'He was no mere lawyer; he drank champagne with the wits'. I'd like to have a similar epitaph, but, in the absence of any equivalent to the Great Cham among my co-evals, I would be content with one which said simply, 'He was good at what he did'.

BIBLIOGRAPHY

Aitken, J (2006) *Porridge And Passion* (Continuum)

Ali, T (2005) *Street Fighting Years: An Autobiography of the Sixties* (Verso Books)

Anderson, E and Nicholson, A (2010) *About Eton* (Long Barn Books Ltd)

Anderson, J (2010) *Modern Sports Law: A Textbook* (Hart Publishing)

Anderson, J (ed) (2015) *Leading Cases in Sports Law* (New York, Springer)

Archer, J (1996) *The Fourth Estate* (HarperCollins)

Archer, J (2002) *A Prison Diary: Volume 1* (Macmillan)

Archer, J (2008) *A Prisoner of Birth* (Macmillan)

Ashcroft, M (2009) *Dirty politics Dirty times* (Biteback)

Atherton, M (2011) *Glorious Summers and Discontents: Looking back on the ups and downs from a dramatic decade* (Simon & Schuster)

Banner, C and Deane, A, (2003) *Off with Their Wigs!: Judicial Revolution in Modern Britain* (Societas)

Barling, G and Brearley, M (eds) (1998) *Practitioners Handbook of EC Law* (Trenton Publishing)

Beckett, F and Hencke, D (2005) *The Survivor: Tony Blair in War and Peace* (Aurum Press)

Beloff, M (1992) *An Historian in the Twentieth Century* (Yale University Press)

Beloff, MJ (1966) *A Short Walk on the Campus* (Secker and Warburg)

Beloff, MJ (1968) *The Plateglass Universities* (Secker and Warburg)

Beloff, MJ (1976) *The Sex Discrimination Act 1975* (Butterworths)

Beloff, MJ (2012) *Sports Law* 2nd ed (Hart)

Beloff, MJ, (2009) 'The End of the Twentieth Century' in Louis Blom-Cooper (ed), *The House of Lords 1876–2009* (Oxford University Press)

Beloff, M (2000) 'Neither cloistered nor virtuous? Judges and their Independence in the New Millennium' *Denning Law Journal*

Beloff, N (1973) *Transit of Britain* (HarperCollins)

Beloff, N (1976) *Freedom Under Foot: Battle Over the Closed Shop in British Journalism* (Maurice Temple Smith Ltd)

Bingham, T (2011) *The Business of Judging: Selected Essays and Speeches: 1985–1999* (Oxford University Press)

Blair, C (2009) *Speaking For Myself: The Autobiography* (Sphere)

Blake, C and Drewry, G (ed) (1999) *Law and the Spirit of Inquiry: Essays in Honour of Sir Louis Blom-Cooper, QC* (Brill Nijhoff)

Blom-Cooper, L (ed) (2009) *The Judicial House of Lords: 1876–2009* (Oxford University Press)

Bose, M (2012) *The Spirit of the Game: How Sport Made the Modern World* (Constable)

Bower, T (2001) *The Paymaster: Geoffrey Robinson, Maxwell and New Labour* (Simon & Schuster Ltd)

Brandreth, G (2009) *Something Sensational to Read in the Train: The Diary of a Lifetime* (John Murray)

Brockliss, L (2008) *Magdalen College – A History* (Magdalen College)

Brown, S (2020) *Playing Off The Roof & Other Stories: A patchwork of memories (1) (Memoirs)* (Marble Hill Publishers)

Brown, S (2021) *Second Helpings* (Marble Hill Publishers)

Cameron, D (2019) *For the Record* (William Collins)

Card, T (1994) *Eton Renewed* (John Murray Publishers Ltd)

Carman, D (2002) *No Ordinary Man* (Hodder and Stoughton Ltd)

Cartwright, J (2008) *This Secret Garden: Oxford Revisited* (Bloomsbury Publishing)

Chandra, K and Das, C (2003) *Judges and Judicial Accountability* (Universal Law Publishing)

Crick, M (2005) *Mary Archer: For Richer, for Poorer* (Simon & Schuster)

Curtis, S (2000) *The Journals of Woodrow Wyatt Vol. 3: From Major to Blair* (Macmillan)

Day, R (1999) *Speaking for Myself* (Ebury Press)

Dyson, J (2018) *Justice: Continuity and Change* (Hart Publishing)

Dyson, J (2019) *A Judge's Journey* (Hart Publishing)

Egan, D (1999) *Irvine: Politically Correct?* (Mainstream Publishing)

Fernando, Tyrone (2006) *Through Winds of Fire* (Vijitha Yapa Publications Sri Lanka)

Flintoff, JP (1991) 'A Man for all Sessions' 90 *Legal Business*

Folley, M (2001) *A Time to Jump: Jonathan Edwards: The Authorised Biography of an Olympic Champion* (HarperCollins)

Goodman, A (1993) *Tell Them I'm On My Way: Memoirs* (Chapmans)

Grade, M (2000) *It Seemed Like a Good Idea at the Time* (Pan Macmillan)

Greenslade, N (2020) *The Thin White Line: The Inside Story of Cricket's Greatest Scandal* (Pitch Publishing Ltd)

Hair, D (2012) *In the Best Interest of the Game* (HarperSports)

Hale, B (2021) *Spider Woman: A Life – by the former President of the Supreme Court* (Bodley Head)

Hamilton, C (2005) *For Better for Worse* (Robson Books Ltd)

Hancock, S (2005) *The Two of Us: My Life with John Thaw* (Bloomsbury Publishing)

Hemery, D (1976) *Another Hurdle: The Making of an Olympic Champion* (Taplinger Pub Co)

Hewitt, I (2008) *Sporting Justice: 101 Sporting Encounters with the Law* (Sports Books Ltd)

Hollander, C (2021) *A Hundred Years of Brick Court Chambers* (Wendy French, Wilton Publishing Services)

Hollis, C (1965) *The Oxford Union* (Evans Brothers)

Hooper, D (2000) *Reputations Under Fire: Winners and Losers in the Libel Business* (Sphere)

Hope, D (2018) *House of Lords 1996–2009* (Avizandum Publishing Ltd)

Hope, D (2019) *UK Supreme Court … and Afterwards 2009–2015* (Avizandum Publishing Ltd)

Hopkins, C (2005) *Trinity: 450 Years of an Oxford College Community* (Oxford University Press)

Iyer, V (2004) *Constitutional Perspectives: Essays in Honour and Memory of H.M. Seerval* (Universal Publishing)

Johnson, RW (2015) *Look Back in Laughter: Oxford's Postwar Golden Age* (Threshold Press Ltd)

Kaufmann-Kohler, G (2001) *Arbitration at the Olympics, Issues of Fast-Track Dispute Resolution and Sports Law* (Kluwer Law International)

Keene, D (2019) *Leaving the Arena: A Story of Bar and Bench* (Bloomsbury Publishing)

Lewis, J (2016) *David Astor* (Jonathan Cape)

MacDougall, L (2001) *Cherie – The Perfect Life of Mrs Blair* (Politicos)

Millett, P (2015) *As in Memory Long* (Wildy, Simmonds & Hill)

Paterson, A (2013) *Final Judgment: The Last Law Lords and the Supreme Court* (Hart Publishing)

Patten, C (2017) *First Confession: A Sort of Memoir* (Allen Lane)

Popplewell, O (2009) *Hallmark: A Judge's Life at Oxford* (I B Tauris & Co Ltd)

Pym, H, and Kochan, N (1998) *Gordon Brown: The First Year in Power* (Michael Joseph)

Raphael, A (1993) *Grotesque Libels* (Corgi Books)

Reynold, F (2018) *Chance, Cheek and Some Heroics* (Wildy, Simmonds & Hill Publishing)

Robinson, G (2000) *The Unconventional Minister: My Life Inside New Labour* (Michael Joseph)

Rosenstein, N (1990) *The Unbroken Chain* (CIS Publishers)

Ross, A (2005) *Unfinished Business: The Authorised Biography of Britain's Olympic Skier* (Dewi Lewis Media Ltd)

Rozenberg, J (2020) *Enemies of the People?: How Judges Shape Society* (Bristol University Press)

Sampson, A (2004) *Who Runs This Place?: The Anatomy of Britain in the 21st Century* (John Murray)

Saunders, J (1990) *Nightmare: Ernest Saunders And The Guinness Affair* (Arrow Books)

Scott, P (2007) *Tony and Cherie: Behind the Scenes in Downing Street* (Pan Books)

Sedley, S (2018) *Law and the Whirligig of Time* (Hart Publishing)

Shakespeare, N (2013) *Priscilla: The Hidden Life of an Englishwoman in Wartime France* (Harvill Secker)

Seldon, A (2019) *May at 10* (Biteback Publishing)

Singh, R (2022) *The Unity of the Law* (Hart Publishing)

Speed, M (2012) *A Sticky Wicket: A Decade of Change in World Cricket* (HarperCollins)

Stevens, R (2002) *The English Judges: Their Role in the Changing Constitution* (Hart Publishing)

Stevens, R (2005) *University to Uni: The Politics of Higher Education* (Politico)

Sugar, A (2010) *What You See Is What You Get: My Autobiography* (Macmillan)

Taylforth, G (1996) *Kathy and Me* (Bloomsbury Publishing)

Trelford, D (2017) *Shouting in the Street: Adventures and Misadventures of a Fleet Street Survivor* (Biteback Publishing)

Wade, A (2006) *Wrecking Machine: A Tale of Real Fights and White Collars* (Simon & Schuster)

Walter, D (1984) *The Oxford Union* (The book service LTD)

Warner, E (2018) *Sport Inc.: Why money is the winner in the business of sport* (Yellow Jersey)

Welch, J (2020) *The Fleet Street Girls: The Women who Broke Down the Doors of the Gentlemen's Club* (Hachette)

Zaiwalla, S (2020) *Honour Bound: Adventures of an Indian Lawyer in the English Courts* (Harper Collins)

Ziegler, P (1993) *Wilson* (Weidenfeld & Nicholson)

INDEX

Ingram Content Group UK Ltd.
Milton Keynes UK
UKHW022357060623
422999UK00005B/257